Managing Crises and Disasters with Emerging Technologies:
Advancements

Murray E. Jennex
San Diego State University, USA

Managing Director:	Lindsay Johnston
Senior Editorial Director:	Heather Probst
Book Production Manager:	Sean Woznicki
Development Manager:	Joel Gamon
Development Editor:	Michael Killian
Acquisitions Editor:	Erika Gallagher
Typesetter:	Jennifer Romanchak
Cover Design:	Nick Newcomer, Lisandro Gonzalez

Published in the United States of America by
Information Science Reference (an imprint of IGI Global)
701 E. Chocolate Avenue
Hershey PA 17033
Tel: 717-533-8845
Fax: 717-533-8661
E-mail: cust@igi-global.com
Web site: http://www.igi-global.com

Library of Congress Cataloging-in-Publication Data

Managing crises and disasters with emerging technologies : advancements / Murray E. Jennex, editor.
    p. cm.
  Includes bibliographical references and index.
  Summary: "This book offers the most vital, up-to-date research within the field of disaster management technologies, offering research and updates from authors from around the world, with a variety of perspectives and insights into the most cutting edge technology the field has to offer"--Provided by publisher.
  ISBN 978-1-4666-0167-3 (hardcover) -- ISBN 978-1-4666-0168-0 (ebook) -- ISBN 978-1-4666-0169-7 (print & perpetual access) 1. Emergency management--Technological innovations. 2. Emergency communication systems. 3. Social media. I. Jennex, Murray E., 1956-
  HV551.2.M36 2012
  363.34'8--dc23
                              2011051813

British Cataloguing in Publication Data
A Cataloguing in Publication record for this book is available from the British Library.

All work contributed to this book is new, previously-unpublished material. The views expressed in this book are those of the authors, but not necessarily of the publisher.

Table of Contents

Detailed Table of Contents

Chapter 1

There is a wind of transformation blowing across the world today. It is changing the face of emergency management and every field of human endeavor. It is called "social media". These days, social media is redefining crisis preparedness through the increasing participation of the masses in the creation and distribution of content in ways that surpass the capacity of the mass media and public authorities. Public-generated content has been found to be useful in all phases of preparedness. Unfortunately, most public safety authorities are still suspicious of using social media in engaging and disseminating information. This paper examines this new area of transformation that is having significant consequences on public safety and public life. As the scenario unfolds, emergency managers have a tough time choosing between the mass media and social media. Metaphorically, it is a race between a 'hippo' (mass media) and cheetah (social media).

Chapter 2

Recent disasters highlight the importance of social media supporting critical information gathering and dissemination efforts by members of the public. Given that disasters pose unique challenges and social media are evolving rapidly, how can one compare the effectiveness of social media in different disaster situations? Drawing from prior work on e-participation, this paper proposes a novel framework for social media use based on four key modules: selection, facilitation, deliberation, and aggregation. A comparative analysis of social media use following a man-made disaster (the 2007 Virginia Tech tragedy) and during a natural disaster (the 2009 Britain blizzard) exemplifies the value of the proposed framework. Future research can build on and leverage the present work by analyzing and incorporating additional cases on the use of social media in disaster situations.

Chapter 3

Online Social Networking Sites (SNS) enable collaborative information sharing and help build resilient communities in areas exposed to risk. This paper reviews existing research on community vulnerability and resilience, and explores the role of communication in fostering strong community networks. The paper draws upon examples of SNS used to share information and explores how such technology may be leveraged more effectively to provide communities with robust communication networks, thereby creating more resilient communities in areas at high risk of natural disasters.

Connie White, Jacksonville State University, USA
Linda Plotnick, Jacksonville State University, USA

Social media is used in a variety of domains, including emergency management. However, the question of which technologies are most appropriate for a given emergency remains open. We present a framework of dimensions of emergencies that can assist in selecting appropriate social media for an emergency situation. Social media is not a panacea but can be used effectively given the proper functions available from the particular services provided by each of the Web 2.0 technologies available. The main objective of this paper is to identify the best practices for social media to leverage its ability given the complexities that coincide with events. This is a conceptual paper based on the results of preliminary studies involving group interactions with emergency professionals with various backgrounds. In addition, emergency management students who are professionals in the field followed by another interview soliciting information from information systems scientist were surveyed. We found that each situation called forth various dimensions where only sub phases of the stated dimension may be used given the task type derived from the event characteristics. This lays a foundation upon which a more formal approach can be taken to help tame the social media mania into a manageable set of 'best practices' from which emergencies can be managed more effectively given Web 2.0 technologies and social collaborative online tools.

Murali Raman, Monash University, Sunway Campus, Malaysia
Terry Ryan, Claremont Graduate University, USA
Murray E. Jennex, San Diego State University, USA
Lorne Olfman, Claremont Graduate University, USA

This paper is about the design and implementation of a wiki-based knowledge management system for improving emergency response. Most organizations face difficult challenges in managing knowledge for emergency response, but it is crucial for response effectiveness that such challenges be overcome. Organizational members must share the knowledge needed to plan for emergencies. They also must be able during an emergency to access relevant plans and communicate about their responses to it. This study, which employed action research methods, suggests that wiki technology can be used to manage knowledge for emergency response. It also suggests that effective use of a knowledge management system for emergency response requires thorough training, a knowledge-sharing culture, and a good fit between emergency-response tasks and system capabilities.

Michael J. Marich, Claremont Graduate University, USA
Benjamin L. Schooley, Claremont Graduate University, USA
Thomas A. Horan, Claremont Graduate University, USA

This article examines the underlying architecture guiding the development and use of enterprise decision support systems that maintain the delivery of time critical public services. A normative architecture, developed from comparative cases involving San Mateo County and Mayo Clinic Emergency Medical Services systems, provides a collection of characteristics meant to guide an emergency response system toward a high level of performance and enable optimal decision-making. At a national symposium, academics and practitioners involved in promoting effective emergency response information systems provided validation for the architecture and next steps for enhancing emergency response information systems. Normative architecture characteristics and expert perspectives from the symposium are integrated into a framework that offers an enterprise approach for delivering time-critical emergency response services. This article provides recommendations for navigating toward a more incremental approach in developing enterprise-oriented emergency information services and examines future trends involving the application of normative architectural concepts to real-world emergency medical settings.

Ruben Xing, Montclair State University, USA
Zhongxian Wang, Montclair State University, USA
James Yao, Montclair State University, USA
Yanli Zhang, Montclair State University, USA

Most U.S. universities planned and prepared their disaster recovery (DR) and business continuity strategies for their Information Systems after the September 11th attack on the United States. The devastating hurricanes and the most recent catastrophic earthquakes caused unprecedented damage for many campuses within a decade. Some of their plans worked and some of them failed; however, with these lessons learned, Information Systems Management for U.S. higher education must be reexamined, re-planned and redesigned, including DR strategies and procedures. It is equally important that the curriculum of Management Information Systems be updated along with updated DR concerns for all educators in U.S. universities.

Lila Rao, The University of the West Indies, Jamaica
Maurice McNaughton, The University of the West Indies, Jamaica
Kweku-Muata Osei-Bryson, Virginia Commonwealth University, USA
Manley Haye, Jamaica Public Service Company Limited, Jamaica

Disasters have the potential to cripple a country and those countries that are particularly susceptible to disasters must have effective disaster recovery plans (DRP) in place to ensure that the country can return to normalcy as soon as possible after the devastation. However, for the plan to be effective it must be of high quality, which is often viewed as a multidimensional concept containing essential factors for DRP, such as consistency, completeness, reliability and feasibility. Therefore, any methodology for the development of DRP must take these dimensions into account as their affect on quality is considerable. In this regard, the authors describe a quality based methodology for the development of DRP, including a methodology that makes use of ontologies containing properties that are suited to the development of these high quality plans. The applicability of the proposed methodology will be demonstrated through a case study of an electric utility company in Jamaica.

Chapter 9

Jordan Shropshire, Georgia Southern University, USA

Christopher Kadlec, Georgia Southern University, USA

Information technology plays a pivotal role in defining the success of organizations. Given its importance, one might assume that modern organizations take steps to ensure the recovery of IT services following disasters. Unfortunately, this is rarely the case. To understand the variation in degree of IT disaster recovery planning, this research focused on those responsible for managing IT resources and IT directors. For the study, a survey was mailed to 337 financial service institutions in the southeastern United States. Over 150 IT directors completed self-assessments for measuring the extent to which their organization engages in IT disaster recovery planning. In addition, they responded to a number of questions regarding their work-related values, and over 63% of the variance in degree of IT disaster recovery planning was explained by two predictors: uncertainty avoidance and long-term orientation. Results show that firms with IT professionals who prefer to avoid uncertainty and who have long-term outlooks have more developed IT disaster recovery plans.

Ana Goulart, Texas A&M University, USA

Anna Zacchi, Texas A&M University, USA

Bharath Chintapatla, Texas A&M University, USA

Walt Magnussen, Texas A&M University, USA

The technology used in citizen-to-authority emergency calls is based on traditional telephony, that is, circuit-switched systems. However, new standards and protocols are being developed by the Internet Engineering Task Force (IETF) to allow emergency communications over packet switched networks, such as the Internet. This architecture is known as Next Generation-9-1-1 (NG-911). In this paper, the authors present lessons learned from experiments on the IETF standard called Location to Service Translation protocol (LoST). LoST maps the user's location to the address of the emergency call center that serves that location. After implementing the standards in a test-bed with real-world systems, spatial databases, and communication networks, the authors observed performance issues that users may experience. Based on their observations, the authors propose practical ideas to improve the performance of the NG-911 system and LoST protocol operation for mobile users.

Chapter 11

Connie White, Jacksonville State University, USA

Murray Turoff, New Jersey Institute of Technology, USA

This paper reviews crisis literature, identifying factors that most challenge decision makers during extreme events. The objectives are to understand the environment in which the emergency manager is working; isolate factors that hinder the decision maker's ability to implement optimum solutions; and identify structures that best fit the problem type. These objectives are important because extreme events are not well managed. Extreme events are best characterized as wicked problems. Stress, information overload, bias, and uncertainty create an environment that challenges even the best decision makers. Factors must be better understood so that policies, systems, and technologies can be created to better fit the needs of the decision maker. The authors discuss ongoing research efforts and describe systems being designed and implemented that provide a variety of web based collaborative tools, as well as solutions to these wicked problems.

Teresa Durbin, San Diego Gas and Electric, USA
Murray E. Jennex, San Diego State University, USA
Eric Frost, San Diego State University, USA
Robert Judge, San Diego State University, USA

After the 2007 Southern California wildfire events, event-assessment of the efficacy of spreadsheets and paper forms raised the question of whether alternative tools could have achieved greater efficiencies in the logistical support of command centers, the sites from which the local utility's electric restoration personnel were deployed. In this paper, the authors examine what approach would have enabled personnel working on the logistics of the command center effort to have easier-to-use, faster-to-access, command center data stored in, and provided via, a catastrophe resilient platform other than the traditional company computer network. Additionally, the capability to store basic command center requirements from previous emergency responses, thereby saving time during the next emergency, was examined.

Keith Clement, California State University Fresno, USA

This case study discusses the role of education, curriculum development, research, and service in supporting information systems for crisis response management. The study describes the Council for Emergency Management and Homeland Security (CEMHS) organization that designs and develops academic programs and courses in these specialized areas. CEMHS combines all levels of education in California (from K-12 and postsecondary education) into a "state-wide solution" and network of academicians and professionals in emergency and disaster management, crisis response, and homeland security education and training. The organizational purpose is constructing a "vertical track" of academic programs and specialized programs to benefit and enhance information resource and crisis management. The implications and lessons learned from building collaborative partnerships between the crisis and disaster response academic and professional communities in academic program development and research initiatives are also discussed.

John Lindström, Luleå University of Technology, Sweden
Dan Harnesk, Luleå University of Technology, Sweden
Elina Laaksonen, Luleå University of Technology, Sweden
Marko Niemimaa, Luleå University of Technology, Sweden

This paper extends emergency management literature by developing a methodology for emergency management continuity planning (EmCP). In particular, the methodology focuses on inter-organizational continuous and coordinated planning among emergency management organizations. The authors draw on

Soft Systems Methodology (Checkland & Scholes, 1999; Checkland, 2000), using it as a base for better understanding of EmCP. Barriers that must be overcome before the methodology can be introduced and established, as well as potential benefits, are also discussed.

Chapter 15

Social media is being used by individuals during a crisis to alert rescuers to their location, status others on their condition or on environmental conditions, warn of issues, and so forth. However, organizations have been slower to adopt social media for crisis response. This paper explores issues affecting social media adoption by organizations for crisis response and proposes the use of knowledge management strategy as a process for mitigating these issues and guiding organizations in adopting social media into their crisis response plans.

This paper explores the strategic importance of information systems for managing such crises as the H1N1 outbreak and the Haiti earthquake in the healthcare service chain. The paper synthesizes the literature on crisis management and information systems for emergency response and draws some key lessons for healthcare service chains. The paper illustrates these lessons by using data from an empirical case study in the region of Crete in Greece. The author concludes by discussing some future directions in managing crises in the healthcare service chain, including the importance of distributive, adaptive crisis management through new technologies like mashups.

Chapter 17

Lack of relevant information, particularly geospatial information, is one of the major challenges in emergency management. In the past few years, geospatial information created by volunteers and facilitated by social networks has become a promising data source in time-critical situations. This paper discusses the roles that social networks can play in the crowdsourcing of geospatial information for emergency management, data generation and dissemination through social networks, and investigates the relationships and interactions in social networks. Research issues arise in the areas of data access, data quality, information synthesis, emerging patterns of human behaviors in emergencies, analysis and visualization of nested social networks, implementation of information systems for emergency management, privacy, and equity.

Preface

SOCIAL MEDIA: TRULY VIABLE FOR CRISIS RESPONSE?

Introduction

To mitigate the unpredictability of crises and the complexity of crisis response, affected individuals and first responders are using new technologies, particularly social media, to help themselves. Examples include:

- Concerned citizens used a wiki after Hurricane Katrina to organize, collaborate, and rapidly create the PeopleFinder and ShelterFinder systems (Murphy and Jennex, 2006).
- Citizens affected by the 2007 San Diego Wildfires used a wiki to pool knowledge on which homes burned and which survived when the local media failed to support their needs (Jennex, 2010).
- Mumbai citizens used twitter to report their status, let others know where to find friends, relatives, etc., and to solicit blood donations following the 2008 Mumbai terrorist attacks (Beaumont, 2008).
- Victims trapped by falling debris during the 2010 Haiti earthquake used texting and/or Facebook to alert their friends/family to their location and condition (Boodhoo, 2010).

These anecdotes provide evidence of the value of social media to individuals in responding to crisis. However, the question has to be asked, is social media reliable enough for individuals and organizations to include social media in their crisis response plans? This preface explores this question by looking at perceptions of respondents to a survey administered after the great Southwest Blackout centered on San Diego, California on September 8, 2011.

Social Media

Plotnick and White (2010) describe social media as generally being attributed to the collaborative applications supported by Web 2.0 technologies. These include, but are not limited to, Twitter, Facebook, MySpace, wikis, and blogs. Blogs, wikis, and MySpace were the first applications becoming popular in the early 2000s, while Facebook and Twitter are more recent creations. While cloud computing infrastructure is making social media applications more resilient and reliable, the methods users utilize to interact with social media applications are not. Most users access social media applications using their laptops, home computers, or mobile/smart telephones. Cloud computing infrastructure can be supported by highly reliable server farms with self contained back up power supplies to ensure they remain operational should grid power be lost. Private users don't always have this luxury. Home connections rely on grid power to run their computers. Should that power fail, batteries are usually available for laptops, and some users have uninterruptible power supplies (UPS) for their desktops. In both cases broadband users rely on their routers to connect to their Internet Service Provider (ISP) and these routers may or may not be connected to a UPS. Mobile connections rely on the cell phone infrastructure to connect to the Internet. The cell phone infrastructure relies on a series of cell towers to connect mobile phones to the telephony system. Back up batteries are included in cell phone towers should grid power be lost. Ultimately, social media application reliability is not just reliant on having a reliable platform on which to run. Reliability is also dependent upon having a reliable connection system (cell phone infrastructure, landline infrastructure, cable infrastructure) and interface system (mobile, laptop, desktop). The reliability issue then becomes that of being a complex system of inter-reliabilities between multiple systems owned and operated by different, and sometimes, competing, companies.

This author served as the embedded systems and contingency planning project manager for Southern California Edison in their Year 2000, Y2K, program. A major concern of the program was understanding the risk caused by the complexity of systems used to communicate and operate the power grid. The communication (telephone and cell phone) systems were found to be as described above and it took much cooperation between the various system providers to generate an understanding of the relationships and complexities in the communication system, Backup power systems, including battery backups, were reviewed as part of the overall contingency plan should Y2K issues cause failures in the power grid and communication and control systems. It was observed that battery testing and replacement intervals were often not met prior to Y2K resulting in increased awareness and commitment to perform critical battery testing and maintenance. One of the concerns of this preface and a motivation for this research is a concern that this is still a practice and a risk following a loss of power event that causes social media to be unsuitable for crisis response and management.

The Great Southwest/San Diego Blackout

The Great San Diego/Southwest Blackout began at 3:38 PM on Thursday, September 8 2011 when a maintenance worker in Yuma, Arizona performing maintenance on a 500 kv transmission line caused that line to trip, stopping power flow to San Diego. The line was restored to operational status within several minutes but during that period of inoperability instabilities in the grid caused a power generator in Mexico to trip offline. The loss of the Mexican power generator caused further instabilities in the grid resulting in a low voltage situation that caused the San Onofre transmission substation and nuclear plant to trip offline. The San Onofre nuclear plant trip reduced available power while the trip of the transmission substation isolated the grid between San Diego and Los Angeles. The San Onofre transmission substation trip prevented the spread of the instabilities to Los Angeles and Orange County but also resulted in insufficient power for San Diego with the result that the San Diego/Southwest power grid collapsed and the region went into a blackout condition (CNN, 2011; Lee, 2011).

The blackout lasted approximately 15 hours affecting approximately 5 million people, 1.4 million of them in San Diego (Lee, 2011 and Page and Grieco, 2011). However, while the blackout was of relatively short duration, there were many significant problems. First, the blackout occurred at the start of evening rush hour and caused the failure of the traffic signaling system (virtually all traffic lights defaulted to blinking four way stops). This caused huge traffic congestion throughout San Diego with a dramatic increase in commute times (the author's commute time went from 40 minutes to 2 hours, a fairly common example). Additionally, the trolley system failed with all trolleys stopped where they were at the time of the blackout as well as all train signaling systems causing non-electrical trains to have to reduce speed drastically. Finally, airports were forced to suspend operations due to reduced communication and control systems. Second, elevators, escalators, automatic doors, etc. in all buildings without backup power failed stranding a large number of people between floors or in stalled elevators. Third, water and water treatment equipment failed allowing some backflow and causing many residents to have to boil water before using it for humans. Fourth, refrigerators, freezers, stoves, televisions, and all home appliances without backup power failed. Among these failures were home computers and routers without UPS and laptops without charged batteries. Finally, and an additional motivation for this preface, the cell phone system experienced a great deal of degradation as observed by the author as he attempted to communicate with the local television stations to provide expert opinion on the causes and expected duration of the outage.

An early concern during the outage was that the blackout was the result of terrorist action. The concern was due to the failure of both main transmission lines into San Diego failed at nearly the same time. The author as well as the power company authorities was quick to ally this fear once it was recognized that the San Onofre substation failed on low voltage (this was recognized to be the correct action for the substation given the known failures in the rest of the grid system). However, getting this information to the affected population proved to be difficult as cell phone communications were failing for the author as he moved from cell tower to cell tower, and for the authorities as cell phone circuits were overloaded. These cell tower failures occurring within several minutes to an hour following blackout initiation is another motivator for this preface.

Recovery from the blackout began as soon as the cause of the San Onofre substation trip was understood and the restoration of the Southwest Powerlink (the original failed transmission line). Restoration began with restart of power generators and then the expanding recovery of distribution loops radiating out from the recovered power generators. The power grid was restored within 15 hours of blackout initiation.

Methodology

This is an exploratory study that utilizes an exploratory survey to collect opinions and experiences related to the performance of social media during the Great San Diego/Southwest Blackout on September 8, 2011. The survey instrument was generated based on the research question of how reliable was social media during the Great San Diego/Southwest Blackout; and was distributed within three days of the event. Survey Monkey was used to administer the survey and San Diego State University's Blackboard system was used to distribute a link to the survey to selected students at San Diego State University. Students were selected based on their having been students of the author. Responses were collected for two weeks with one follow up email sent. As this was an exploratory study with no theory or model testing attempted; survey results were analyzed using only descriptive statistics.

College of Business and Homeland Security students were selected as respondents as they are representative of the population expected to use social media, they were available, and they could be contacted rapidly. Rapid access was considered to be the primary requirement as it was important to collect survey responses while the event was still fresh in the memories of those solicited. Approximately 500 students were solicited. The exact number is not known due to the open invitation to pass the link on to acquaintances and family members as well as there being an issue with cross posting due to students taking multiple classes with the author. A total of 370 responses were received. All responses were used although some respondents did not answer all the items. To protect the identity of the respondents no personal identifiable information was collected. This eliminates potential follow up but was considered important for guaranteeing anonymity. The following reflects the demographics of the respondents.

Respondents were nearly evenly split on gender with 184 (49.9%) being male and 185 (50.1%) being female (of those reporting gender; 3 respondents did not report gender). As expected, the majority of respondents were mid twenties (since they were predominately graduate level students) although given the great diversity of the San Diego State University student body and a request to pass the survey link on to family and friends, there was a spread of ages as reflected in Table 1.

The respondents also reflect a diversity of social relationships in the San Diego area (the largest population area affected by the blackout) as reflected in Table 2.

This data was collected as it was felt that the larger the local social network of the respondent the more likely the respondent was to utilize social media to contact/coordinate actions during the blackout. As can be seen in Table 2, over two thirds of the respondents had some family social network in San Diego.

Table 3 shows the numbers of respondents who use various social media tools. This Table shows that large numbers of the respondents routinely use cell phones, text messaging, Facebook, and the Internet. Combined with the family social networks of the respondents it was expected that these respondents would be representative of those affected persons in the San Diego area that would use social media to contact and coordinate during the blackout crisis.

Ultimately it is concluded that the respondents are representative of those that should have knowledge of the performance and availability of social media during the blackout and are thus a representative sample of those possessing that knowledge. Additionally, the sample size of approximately 370 is sufficient to analyze and come to conclusions on the performance and availability of social media during the blackout crisis.

Results

Table 4 shows that respondents primarily used their cell phones (over 90%), text messaging (approximately 90%), and Internet access via their cell phone (approximately 70%) during the blackout crisis. It is somewhat surprising that so few used Facebook (approximately 40%) or Twitter (approximately 11%) given the popularity of both. This could be a reflection of the age of the respondents (primarily in their 20s) and reflects that this age group utilizes other social media.

Table 1. Respondent age distribution

Age	Number (Percent)
Under 20	35 (9.4%)
20-29	223 (60.1%)
30-39	69 (18.6%)
40-49	17 (4.6%)
50-59	22 (5.9%)
60-69	3 (0.8%)
70 and over	2 (0.5%)

Table 2. Family relationships in the blackout area

Situation	Number (Percent)
I live alone or with roommates and have no family in the affected blackout area	112 (30.6%)
I live alone or with roommates but have family in the affected blackout area	54 (14.8%)
I live only with my significant other and we have no family in the blackout area	30 (8.2%)
I live only with my significant other and at least one of us has family in the affected blackout area	41 (11.2%)
I live with multiple family members and no other family members live in the affected blackout area	21 (5.7%)
I live with multiple family members plus have more family in the blackout area	105 (28.7%)
I was a visitor to the area during the blackout (I live outside the blackout area)	3 (0.8%)

Table 3. Social media routinely used

Social Media	Number (Percent) Using
cell phone	343 (98.0%)
Facebook	257 (73.4%)
other social networking site	54 (15.4%)
Twitter	56 (16.0%)
Skype	60 (17.1%)
Internet via my phone	229 (65.4%)
Internet at home	306 (87.4%)
text messaging services	313 (89.4%)

Table 4. Social media activities attempted during the blackout

Activity	Yes (Number/Percent)	No (Number/Percent)
Attempt to update status or comments on Facebook?	141 (39.7%)	214 (60.3%)
Attempt to tweet status or questions?	39 (11.1%)	313 (88.9%)
Attempt to use your cell phone to make a call?	333 (93.5%)	23 (6.5%)
Receive a call?	287 (80.8%)	68 (19.2%)
Attempt to send a text message?	323 (90.2%)	35 (9.8%)
Receive a text message?	313 (87.7%)	44 (12.3%)
Attempt to use your phone for Internet access?	250 (69.8%)	108 (30.2%)
Attempt to use Skype/other VOIP?	13 (3.7%)	334 (96.3%)

Table 5 reflects the observed availability of the social media services used. It should be noted that over 70% of respondents for every social media tool reported loss or degradation of service. This is backed up by Table 6 that shows that approximately 60% of the respondents attempted to use social media at least hourly to every few minutes. This reflects the author's observation of frequent messages of "all circuits are busy" to "service unavailable" messages received during the crisis and possibly reflects an expected saturation of capacity condition as the affected population attempted to contact and coordinate with their social networks. Table 7 is somewhat surprising in that it shows that over 95% of the respondents only attempted to communicate with 10 or fewer individuals. It is postulated that this

Table 5. Observed social media service availability

Observation	Yes (Number/Percent	No (Number/Percent)
My cell phone coverage was normal (I always had bars where I normally have bars)	81 (23.0%)	270 (77.0%)
My Internet availability was normal	55 (15.7%)	296 (84.3%)
I had no trouble making or getting phone calls	75 (21.4%)	276 (78.6%)
I had no trouble sending or receiving tweets	29 (8.7%)	305 (91.3%)
I had no trouble updating my status	58 (17.2%)	278 (82.8%)
I had no trouble staying connected to my family/friends	73 (20.8%)	277 (79.2%)
I had no trouble sending or receiving text messages	97 (27.8%)	252 (72.2%)
I had no trouble getting updates/news using my Internet enabled phone	64 (18.5%)	282 (71.5%)

smaller number of contacts reflects the focus on contacting/communicating with family and/or close personal friends rather than reaching out to all acquaintances. This is not an unexpected observation or result.

Table 8 reflects observed loss of service during the blackout. It is interesting to note that television virtually disappeared and that Internet connectivity and land line based phone service were severely impacted. It is promising that while cell phone service was degraded, over 75% respondents had at least some cell phone service. This reflects that cell phones may be safe to count on in the initial stages of a crisis. However, it is expected that had the blackout lasted more than a couple of days then virtually all local cell phone service would have been lost. Table 9 shows that over 80% of the respondents were less than satisfied with the cell phone and Internet coverage available during the blackout. This is disturbing in that it shows there is an expectation that there would be better service.

Table 6. How often did you attempt to use social media?

Frequency	Number (Percent)
every few minutes	88 (25.3%)
hourly	118 (33.9%)
every other hour	34 (9.8%)
more than once	55 (15.8%)
once	53 (15.2%)

Table 7. How many people did you attempt to reach?

Number Range	Number (Percent)
1 - 10	333 (95.4%)
11 - 25	15 (4.3%)
26 - 50	0 (0.0%)
Over 50	1 (0.3%)

Discussion

The first issue to discuss is if San Diego is representative of modern cities and that if experience with social media performance and availability following a blackout is potentially applicable to other cities. San Diego is the 14th most wired city in the United States (Forbes, 2010) while the United States is ranked 7th (OECD) in wireless users and 15th in broadband users (IT-Hall). This doesn't make San Diego a leading city for being wired, but it is in the top tier of wired cities. This has a couple of implications. The first is that for other wired cities the San Diego experience is applicable and perhaps a harbinger that reliance on social media for crisis response following a major disaster that severely disrupts power distribution will not be successful. The second is that for those cities much less wired than San Diego and thus more reliant on traditional media such as television and land lines the situation following a disaster that severely disrupts power distribution may be even worse given the very poor performance of these media/services in San Diego. However, it is a fair assumption to determine that San Diego is a representative city and that the Great San Diego/Southwest Blackout is representative of what may occur during blackouts in the developed world.

The second issue to discuss is what does this all mean? It is clear that access to Internet sites was severely hampered. Home users virtually had no Internet so any Internet based communication via social media on the web would have failed. Additionally, any Internet based crisis response systems that can be accessed by home users would have been unavailable to those reliant on home based connections. Additionally, over 65% of respondents access the Internet via their cell phones and almost 90% use text messaging. This implies that a large number of respondents would have been able to access the Internet and use social media as well as use texting social media. Given that almost 70% of respondents

Table 8. Communication media lost during the blackout

Communication Media	lost - totally	didn't lose service but it was degraded	no - didn't lose service at all
Internet Connectivity	226 (64.6%)	94 (26.9%)	30 (8.6%)
Television	320 (94.1%)	7 (2.1%)	13 (3.8%)
Radio	118 (35.8%)	88 (26.7%)	124 (37.6%)
Phone Service	163 (52.6%)	91 (29.4%)	56 (18.1%)
Cell Phone Service	75 (21.6%)	215 (61.8%)	58 (16.7%)

Table 9. Satisfaction with cell/Internet coverage during the outage

I am satisfied with the level of service/coverage	Number (Percent)
strongly disagree	76 (21.7%)
disagree	89 (25.4%)
slightly disagree	47 (13.4%)
neither agree nor disagree	24 (6.9%)
slightly agree	46 (13.1%)
agree	48 (13.7%)
strongly agree	20 (5.7%)

attempted to contact someone within a few minutes to an hour of the blackout starting it is fairly safe to say there were many attempts to use social media to update status (about 35% tried Facebook, 11% Twitter, and 90% text messaging). The observation is that users expected to use their social media and mobile during a crisis. It is interesting that users did not expect a blackout to affect their cell phones or social media. Given that cell tower infrastructure uses battery backups it is interesting that there was so much cell phone degradation (77% reported less than usual signal strength, 83% reported lost coverage or degraded service). This wouldn't be expected, although circuits being busy would be expected. It is suspected that batteries failed to perform as expected (although there has been no published accounts verifying this). This is troubling from a crisis response viewpoint as it would be expected that cell phone service should be fully available (as long as the cell phone tower infrastructure is physically intact) for 8 hours (per FCC order and as confirmed by FCC order 07-177 based on a review of communication failures following Hurricane Katrina) (Note that this rule also requires that phone switches and routers have 24 to 48 hour backup power supplies with additional fuel for generators on site with the equipment) (compliance with the FCC orders was to be within 12 months of the date of the orders (approximately October, 2008)). The implication is that perhaps the cell phone system is much more complex than expected and that battery backups are not all that are needed to ensure system operability following loss of grid power. Another possibility is that cell phone tower back up battery maintenance and testing is not sufficient, much like what was found during Y2K approximately 12 years prior. That backup battery maintenance and testing is not sufficient is a very troubling but somewhat expected possibility as these programs tend to suffer during tough economic times as experienced world wide the last few years.

In summary, users expected to be able to use their cell phones for Internet and social media access during the Great San Diego/Southwest blackout. However, most of them were unsuccessful or had limited success. That there was an expectation of available service is a reasonable expectation. Federal Communication Commission rules had specified, based on an analysis of Hurricane Katrina, that all cell phone towers be equipped with an 8 hour battery backup and that other phone system equipment be equipped with 24-48 hour backup power systems with available fuel supply. Crisis response planners also expect cell phones and perhaps social media to be available following a loss of power grid event. However, this did not happen during the Great San Diego/Southwest Blackout.

Conclusion

Ultimately the Great Southwest Blackout can be considered a massive, unplanned, backup battery test. Did cell phones and social media pass the test? This is somewhat debatable. On one hand 83.4% of respondents lost or had their cell phone service degraded, 93.4% had their Internet service lost or degraded, and 60.5% were not satisfied with their level of service or coverage following the blackout. On the other hand 78.5% of respondents had some degree of cell phone service, 35.5% had some degree of Internet service, and 32.5% were satisfied with level of service or coverage. While many may consider it surprising so many respondents had some service during a blackout; if we judge these results from a crisis response lens the blackout test is failed. The duration of the blackout was less than 24 hours. It is proposed that for a service to be considered for crisis response support it should be reliable and rugged enough to survive for a sufficient period of time to allow for utility/maintenance first responders to either preserve the system or implement backup systems. Less than 24 hours is not sufficient to ensure all cell towers, Internet access points, routers, and switches are in service. Backup power supplies should provide the time for this to occur and FCC rules require it. However, it does not appear that backup power supplies worked as anticipated resulting in the widespread system/service outages. This author, as previously mentioned, served as the embedded systems and contingency planning project manager for Southern California Edison in their Year 2000, Y2K, program. Backup power systems, including battery backups were reviewed as part of the overall contingency plan should Y2K issues cause failures in the power and communication and control systems. It was observed that battery testing and replacement intervals were often not met prior to Y2K resulting in increased awareness and commitment to perform critical battery testing and maintenance. A similar review was conducted by the FCC following Hurricane Katrina. It is concluded that much like the observed behavior of many organizations who vow to be prepared for the next crisis just after the current crisis ends but then have their enthusiasm and commitment wane as time passes and the "next" crisis does not occur, the same has occurred with backup battery testing and maintenance. The recommendation is that government and industry experts evaluate cell phone battery backup maintenance and test procedures for improvement. Additionally, once cell phone systems can be reasonably considered reliable, social media source sites should be evaluated for inclusion in crisis response management planning and if found to be useful, propose and publish design guidelines that will make social media systems reliable and rugged enough to qualify as crisis response systems (i.e. propose similar rules for battery/power supply backup, etc. as is currently in force for the cell phone system).

Additionally, social media providers generally did not expect that their services would be used for crisis response. Facebook, Twitter, wikis, et cetera were designed to be used to create communities, communicate with friends, and collaborate. The companies that created them did not design them to be reliable in crisis situations. This creates a problem for crisis response managers. Users will use the systems they are familiar with and use every day during a crisis (as evidenced by this study). It is only natural that users will use their social media first. The United States Emergency Broadcasting System does not include social media nor does most government managed crisis response plans, however, given the widespread unavailability of television and to some degree radio following the loss of the power grid, they should assess the viability of including social media as part of emergency broadcasting. Jennex (2010) noted that individuals have led the way in applying social media to crisis response and proposed that organizations use a knowledge management strategy approach to incorporate social media into their crisis response planning. Howe, Jennex, Bressler, and Frost (2011) discuss how self organizing groups are using social media to plan and prepare for large scale crises. The issue is users using innovative systems to do innovative things that the system designers never intended. The conclusion is that a discussion needs to occur between the crisis response community and the social media companies as to what is being done with social media in the field and what changes/enhancements . etc. are necessary to make social media reliable. Included in this discussion should be infrastructure concerns including how to harden and improve the reliability of social media in a crisis situation.

The title of this preface is "social media: truly viable for crisis response?" The conclusion of previous papers is that functionally the answer is yes, social media provide communication functionality that users want in crisis response (Plotnick and White, 2010; Jennex, 2010; and Howe, Jennex, Bressler, and Frost, 2011). However, the conclusion of this preface is that while the functionality of social media is useful, the maturity of social media from a reliability point of view is not sufficient to warrant including social media as operational crisis response systems at this time. Social media are fine for crisis response planning, but not for operational crisis response and it will take some thoughtful redesign of social media infrastructure before they are acceptable for operational crisis response.

Murray E. Jennex
San Diego State University, USA

REFERENCES

Beaumont, C. (2008, November 27). Mumbai attacks: Twitter and Flickr used to break news. *The Telegraph*. Retrieved on December 2, 2010 from http://www.telegraph.co.uk/news/ worldnews/asia/india/3530640/Mumbai-attacks-Twitter-and-Flickr-used-to-break-news-Bombay-India.html

Boodhoo, N. (2010, January 18). Earthquake confirms value of social media. *Miami Herald*. Retrieved November 28, 2010, from http://www.miamiherald.com/ 2010/01/18/1432022/ earthquake-confirms-value-of-social.html

FCC. (2007). *Order on reconsideration*. Federal Communications Commission. Retrieved on December 9, 2011 from http://www.njslom.org/FCC-07-177A1.pdf

Gustafson, C. (2011). Unprecedented outage left millions in the dark. *San Diego Union Tribune*. Retrieved December 8, 2011, from http://www.signonsandiego.com/ news/2011/sep/08/ widespread-power-outages-across-san-diego-county/

Howe, A. W., Jennex, M. E., Bressler, G. H., & Frost, E. G. (2011). Exercise 24: Using social media for crisis response. *International Journal of Information Systems for Crisis Response and Management*, *3*(4), 36–54. doi:10.4018/jiscrm.2011100103

IT-Hall. (2011). The most wired countries in the world. *IT-hall.com*. Retrieved on December 2, 2011, from http://www.it-hall.com/89/most-wired-countries-in-world/

Jennex, M. E. (2010). Implementing social media in crisis response using knowledge management. *International Journal of Information Systems for Crisis Response and Management*, *2*(4), 20–32. doi:10.4018/jiscrm.2010100102

Lee, M. (2011). Cause of blackout eludes investigations. *San Diego Union Tribune*. Retrieved on December 8, 2011, from http://www.signonsandiego.com/news/2011/oct/26/cause-blackout-eludes-investigators/?page=2#article

Murphy, T., & Jennex, M. E. (2006). Knowledge management, emergency response, and Hurricane Katrina. *International Journal of Intelligent Control and Systems*, *11*(4), 199–208.

OECD. (2011). *Wireless users drive further broadband growth, says OECD*. Organization for Economic Co-operation and Development. Retrieved on December 2, 2011, from http://www.oecd.org/document /4/0,3746,en_2649_34225_42800196_1_1_1_1,00.html

Page, E. S., & Grieco, S. (2011). It's over: Power returns to San Diego. *NBC San Diego*. Retrieved on December 8, 2011, from http://www.nbcsandiego.com/news/local/San-Diego-Communities-Experience-Blackout-129493378.html

Plotnick, C., & White, L. (2010). A social media tsunami: The approaching wave. *International Journal of Information Systems for Crisis Response and Management*, *2*(1), i–iv.

Raman, M., Ryan, T., Jennex, M. E., & Olfman, L. (2010). Wiki technology and emergency response: An action research study. *International Journal of Information Systems for Crisis Response and Management, 2*(1), 49–69. doi:10.4018/jiscrm.2010120405

Wire Staff, C. N. N. (2011). Massive power outage eases as attention turns to cause. *CNN*. Retrieved on December 8, 2011, from http://articles.cnn.com/2011-09-09/us/california.power.outages_1_power-outage-blackout-power-grid?_s=PM:US

Woyke, E. (2010). Americas most wired cities. *Forbes*. Retrieved on December 2, 2011, from http://www.forbes.com/2010/03/02/broadband-wifi-telecom-technology-cio-network-wiredcities.html

Chapter 1
The Transformative Power of Social Media on Emergency and Crisis Management

Gideon F. For-mukwai
University of Nevada, USA

ABSTRACT

There is a wind of transformation blowing across the world today. It is changing the face of emergency management and every field of human endeavor. It is called "social media". These days, social media is redefining crisis preparedness through the increasing participation of the masses in the creation and distribution of content in ways that surpass the capacity of the mass media and public authorities. Public-generated content has been found to be useful in all phases of preparedness. Unfortunately, most public safety authorities are still suspicious of using social media in engaging and disseminating information. This paper examines this new area of transformation that is having significant consequences on public safety and public life. As the scenario unfolds, emergency managers have a tough time choosing between the mass media and social media. Metaphorically, it is a race between a 'hippo' (mass media) and cheetah (social media).

INTRODUCTION

When I watch the stagnation, hesitation and frustration of emergency and public safety authorities in embracing the new wind of change, I am reminded of some battles I once observed growing up in Africa. It was a battle between the forces of transformation and the forces of stagnation.

In the 1970s, everyone in my village used to fetch water in large and rounded gourds, popularly known out there as calabashes. In the 1980s, plastic containers became commonplace. Most villagers resisted changing to the new plastic containers blaming it on the fact that the new containers smelled of lubricants. Notwithstanding the facts that the gourds were easily broken accidentally,

DOI: 10.4018/978-1-4666-0167-3.ch001

the villagers resisted the use of plastic containers. For some reason they were not impressed by the fact that the plastic containers were stronger and sturdier.

In the 1990s, pipe-borne water arrived. More progressive villages invested in pipe-borne water projects to enable everyone to have water in their homes. My beleaguered village and a couple of other conservative-thinking villages once again opposed and resisted the adoption of pipe-borne water in the homes. Their refusal to adopt the pipe-borne water projects reminded me of their hesitation to adopt the plastic containers.

For many years, they lived in denial of the effectiveness of pipe-borne water, totally ignoring the health risk of doing otherwise. They insisted that they did not want to see water pipes running through their homes. They also argued that there was no way tiny pipes could carry more water than the big sturdy plastic containers; which they had managed to adopt after so many years.

Today, when emergency managers and public safety authorities oppose the adoption of the social media, I am reminded of the old water battles in my village. I am also reminded that human beings will resist change, regardless of the facts. Every generation has some "water battles" to confront. Whether public safety authorities will eventually adopt social media, it remains to be seen. One thing is clear, social media battle is akin to the pipe versus plastic battles.

BACKGROUND

Prior to the arrival of the Internet in the early 1990s, the mass media was the main source of information in the public sphere. From its inception, the mass media—print, radio and television (Benkler, 2006), has gone through varying degrees of independence. Historically, it has been controlled by the state in some countries, while in others it has been owned and operated by independent owners who depended heavily on advertising for revenue.

As such, the mass media has never been completely independent of prevailing socio-economic and political forces.

When the Internet arrived, it was a milestone in the public communication arena because it launched a new era of democratization of information. This was possible because its ownership and operation was no longer in the control of state or big media organizations. It was owned and controlled by individual citizens. This constituted a major shift because the emergence of Internet was a reversal in the way information is generated, distributed and consumed in society at large. Since the arrival of the Internet, the mass media's overwhelming influence on communication has thus been waning in numbers, power and following, thanks to the increasing adoption of Internet-based online forms of communication by the general public.

In the area of emergency and crisis communication, the Internet has also been eroding the mass media's clout of influence. Over the years, mass media has been losing a significant part of its audience to social media networks or the Internet's 'de facto twin-brother.' Online social networks often engage in social production of information. It is thanks to the existence of these social networks that social media has emerged as a platform for collaboration amongst individuals that are organized outside of market and managerial hierarchies (Benkler, 2006).

It is the battle between the mass media and social media (i.e., who creates, mediates and arbitrates the public conversation) that is creating transformational issues for emergency management and public safety authorities today. For many decades, public safety authorities relied upon a public conversation that is mediated by the mass media. The origin of mass media can be traced back to the bourgeois era (Habermas, 1992). With the emergence of social production and social media, public safety authorities are torn between the old and the new media.

Thus, the change in the way the society communicates information is at the root of the transformations that are beginning to happen in emergency management today. In this transition era, emergency managers and public safety authorities are victims of a battle that was neither initiated nor promoted by them. They are simply caught in a crossfire that is not of their making and they were totally unprepared to deal with the push from both sides.

When we change the way we communicate, we change society (Shirkey, 2008). Today, we are witnessing the rapid change and growth of new forms of communication that are bending, twisting and shaping the way our society works. The growing popularity of social media is an indication that major changes are still underway in all fields; emergency and crisis management is no exception. Some of the transformations, which are examined in this paper, are centered on the rapid growth of social networking technologies like Facebook, Flickr, Twitter, blogging, wikis, social book marking and so on.

Facebook for instance has over 200 million (Wikipedia, 2008) active users worldwide. For a network that started only in 2004, this appears to be a tectonic shift in the way people create and disseminate information as well as communicate with one another. In March 2009, Nielsen.com ranked Twitter as the fastest growing site in the online social network sites. The micro-blogging site attracted not only over 55 million visits per month but has also made waves in its ability to break news during an emergency.

While social media sites have been penetrating the heartlands of America and making inroads in all major areas, emergency managers and public safety authorities have largely not been active in using or adopting these tools. They have more or less been resisting the adoption of these tools in the dissemination of information during emergencies and disasters. A recent study found that state emergency managers are not making sufficient use of Internet in emergency and crisis

communication (William Allen White School of Journalism, The University of Kansas, 2008). The vast majority of transformations happening in emergency management today either have been initiated by those outside the field or by the impact of a few early adopters that have embraced the tools in their work.

It is the lessons from both the internal, and external influence of social media in emergency and crisis management that are explained in this paper as a way to encourage further research in this unfolding area that clearly highlights the impact of new technologies in transforming the public conversation within an area that can either make or break public life.

SOCIAL MEDIA - TRANSFORMATION VS. STAGNATION

Given the fact that the Internet was born in the early 1990s, it is still a teenager in human growth terms. It turns out that the Internet is also strikingly human in its growth and development. As a teenager, it is both versatile and volatile. It is also full of both vanity and sanity. In these teenage years, it is both destructive and constructive. It is with this depth and breadth of energy that the Internet's Web 2.0 (i.e., social media) is bound to continue to grow before it matures later in life.

Until that happens, it is certain that social media will continue to transform the way our society evolves. This evolution will continue to shape emergency and crisis management. A study found that more teens are creating content for the Internet today than there are teens able to consume it (Pew Center, 2005). This is a sharp contrast from television as a mass medium that has for decades created generations of passive consumers and no producers.

In the area of emergency management and public safety, similar changes have been taking place in varying degrees of transformation both from internal and external dynamics. This process is far from over. As the teenager matures, perhaps we will see more transformation. For now, it is worth examining eight significant transformations in emergency management that are likely to spur other changes and transformations across the board.

WHAT MAKES TRANSFORMATION OF EMERGENCY MANAGEMENT POSSIBLE?

Before examining how social media is transforming emergency management, it is important to ask the question- how is it possible that invincible online networks can possess so much power and clout to shape the emergency readiness? To a large extent, it is not the computers, the software or the people who run them that have the power. Rather, the power of transformation of social media comes from the social capital that the people behind social media possess by coming together to share ideas and information.

Social capital is based on social ties. Such ties can produce private and public good (Putnam, 2000). A society that is rich in social capital thrives on reciprocity and tends to be more successful than a distrustful society that is rife with suspicion and hatred. Putnam says, "Trustworthiness lubricates social life" (2000, p. 21), because social capital breeds mutual obligations and civic engagement. In the field of emergency management, social capital can be the invincible link that inspires trust during a mandatory evacuation, volunteers to participate in an exercise, donors for safety program and support for critical infrastructure improvement.

Without social capital, social media cannot transform or change emergency management because there will be no people that are involved organizing, sorting, sharing information during a disaster. Thus, if social capital continues to grow via online connections, it is highly likely that there will be further transformation of the emergency

management. So far, social media has already been making inroads in many directions.

Secondly, transformation is also happening because when people congregate, whether online or physically, they have power. To a large extent, social media 's invincible power is also born of the fact the one can never doubt what one person or a small group of co-conspirators can do (Senge, Kruschwitz & Schley, 2008).

HOW SOCIAL MEDIA IS TRANSFORMING EMERGENCY/ CRISIS MANAGEMENT

Collective Intelligence

During the mayhem of a disaster, public authorities often struggle in finding answers to questions like the number of people missing or dead. Historically, the authorities use what is often called "dependable sources" in identifying the dead and missing. This process of victim identification as well as others requiring sensitive information, often takes a long time. Very often, ordinary citizens are left out of the process because they are not considered "dependable sources." When authorities depend exclusively on these "dependable sources," they often ignore the first hand accounts and information that is generated by other ordinary citizens who may happen to be observers, passers-by or curious sources. Without doubt, such by-standers as well as ordinary citizens also possess some amount of critical information that is often left uncovered during disasters.

With the advent of social media or Web 2.0, these ordinary citizens have taken their bit and pieces of information to their online networks where they share it informally. In the course of their informal conversations, they have come to figure out ways pool information and crosscheck facts in ways that surpass the capacity of fewer official sources.

As a result of their collective exchange of information based on their proximity, observation and curious conversations, they often develop what is known as 'collective intelligence' (Vieweg, Palen, Liu, Hughes, & Sutton, 2008). Based on a study of post Virginia Tech shootings (Vieweg et al., 2008) found out that ordinary citizens can self-organize, innovate, and adapt social media to share sensitive information in a way that even public safety officials can learn from them. Facebook analyses indicated that the ordinary citizens and students were able to identify the deceased cases ahead of the authorities because they tapped into the collective intelligence of several people with bits and pieces of information.

This is one of the several areas in social media able to transform the way the business of preparedness can be done and emergency management authorities can learn from this example to refine their techniques of information gathering during a disaster.

Homepage Intelligence

During a public emergency like unrest or instability wild land fires, one of the critical resources that public authorities need is information. In the era of Web 2.0, the creation of web pages and blogs is relatively easy. Sometimes victims of a disaster create the web pages to reconnect, reunite and share feeling and frustrations with others in similar situation. In the aftermath of Hurricane Katrina, 3 out of 4 victims joined online groups or conversations as way to re-unite, to share feelings, reach out and connect with their old fellow city dwellers (Pew Study, 2006).

Because of the relative ease of use and common access, the web presents an alternative source of obtaining important information that could provide clues or bits and pieces of information that can enable authorities in finding solutions to a civil emergency issue. Such information can be refined to complement other sources. Also home pages

can give authorities statistical data or ideas regarding the clout behind an issue of public interest. The political clout of a group can be deciphered from a home page based on the number of users, followers, fans that are supporting an issue, organization or event. This is an indispensable gauge of the number of people that have a stake on an issue. Such information provides information about the unseen undercurrents that can make or break, shape or transform an issue of public concern. Every Facebook site, Twitter and many other similar sites provide a county of the number of fans or followers. Failure to mine the data from such home pages and sites can be detrimental.

For possible lack of homepage intelligence, New York Police Department had to rescind their decision and yield to public pressure to arrest the same woman over what became known online as "Stolen Sidekick cell phone" (Shirkey, 2008). The NYPD were forced to reverse their position because of overwhelming public pressure from followers and sympathizers of the victim of the stolen sidekick cell phone.

In so doing, it became apparent that NYPD had underestimated the power of online mobilization and how that changed the course of the stolen sidekick drama. Apparently, NYPD did not pay attention to the fact that the victim of the theft was using extremely critical online tools like bulletin boards, Digg.com and so on to attract and sustain thousands of supporters who served as lay investigators, camera men, spies and so on. Individually, they made little contributions, but collectively, they brought overwhelming organizational ability to outsmart authorities and the family of the 'thief' that was resisting all efforts to return the phone. The authorities could have avoided the public nightmare of going against their own decision if they had checked the bulletin board to realize that ordinary citizens were building up incredible momentum with thousands checking out the story daily. The thousands of yelling online supporters and offline seekers of justice and detectives patched together all evidence that exposed the 'thief' to return the cell phone after a protracted drama. Certainly online intelligence can change the way authorities do business, going forward.

Online Social Activism

After a flawed election process, a student in Moldova sent out a tweet calling for a protest (New York Times, April 2000). That one tweet brought together 10,000 demonstrators, in a short period of time in early 2008. This was a testimony of the fact that new tools are changing the way public authorities have to plan and react to in today's world.

In a similar case, the post election protests in Iran, also garnered significant Twitter participation. The social media tool was used in mobilizing sympathizers; totally bypassing government efforts to block or crack down on demonstrators by derailing information circulation. The microblogging tool sustained activities of the activists and sympathizers for several weeks across continents, not withstanding government efforts to disrupt their protests. Twitter was effectively used as a tool by protesters to evade bureaucratic bottleneck. On June 24, 2009, over 3000/hour tweets were posted from around the world. Iranian government attempts to shut down the site were unsuccessful and to make things worse, the Iranian language "Farsi" was enabled on Twitter to grant greater access to the protesters. Twitter and other forms of social media continue to change the face of emergency management because they are wide rate of adoption across the world.

Number Game

Social media is partly a numbers game. The more fans, followers and friends a cause can generate, the better the outcome. This is so because people are the backbone of all social networks. To a large extent, the number of followers, fans or friends on that network, determine the net worth of an online group. Any cause or organization that has more followers has more social capital, power and influence that can be converted into measurable goals because networks come with connectors. Connectors are people in networks who often create trends, spread fads, often fuel the growth of networks, (Gladwell, 2007)

Connectors are important to a network because they act as hubs for the distribution of information to multiple nodes. Connectors hold together a community or bind a community through their connections. Through such frame of interconnections, citizens can resolve problem (Putnam, 2000). This is what happens in disasters.

In the month of May 2009 the American Red Cross (ARC), put to good use the strength of its fans through regional connectors. The ARC fundraised $812,000 through Target 's Bullseye Competition. ARC relied heavily on online messages on their Facebook pages, which has 76,098 fans. Their constant Facebook reminders to members earned them the giant sum 812,000 of the $3 million allocated in the competition. Within two weeks, they had won a sizable share of the prize money, thanks in part to their mobilization and strength of numbers that few other organizations could challenge. The fact that they came from behind to earn that sum of money, tells a lot about their sophisticated use of online tools building preparedness and resiliency across America.

Crowdsourcing

In the era of social media, some organizations harness the power of the crowd on the Internet to gain a competitive advantage because online communities are at the heart of crowdsourcing or the act of taking a function once performed by employees and outsourcing it to an undefined (and generally large) network of people in the form of an open call by a company or institution (Howe, 2008).

In 2007, Brians Humphreys, Los Angeles Fire Department (LAFD)'s Public Affairs Department, harnessed the power of the crowd to learn fire conditions across an 800 acres long wildfire. Mr. Humphreys tweeted directly to tweeters across other areas of the fire. They responded with concise information regarding the spread of the fire, which enabled LAFD to inform his operations team to strategically reposition its equipment and fight the fire more effectively. Thanks to that Twitter-facilitated discussion, LAFD was able to get real time information to improve decision-making across 4,210 acres at Griffith Park. It is a seminal example that demonstrates the power of these new technologies in reshaping the way the business of preparedness is done.

Also recently, the City of San Francisco has adopted the use of Twitter by citizens in giving feedback to the 311call center (Government Technology, 2009). In launching the program, San Francisco Mayor indicated that citizens should use Twitter to notify public services about issues like garbage collection, road traffic accidents and so on. If citizens buy into this new wide scale use of Twitter, it is likely to continue to speed up responses to issues like road traffic accidents, apartment fires or issue of public safety that may become relevant over time.

Nudge Factor

People need nudges to make decisions (Thaler & Sunstein, 2008). The advent of social media and Web 2.0 has opened up a new window of opportunity for a gentle and subtle nudge that can help people to make decisions. Historically, nudges have been used in areas like sales in department stores, display of food in canteens, advertisement, design of websites and so on. Recently, disaster relief agencies have experimented with social media nudging to raise funds for disaster relief programs.

In recent weeks, Salvation Army has been using Twitter as a quick and easy way to nudge their

donors, followers and supporters to support them in achieving their goal of providing disaster relief.

On June 30, 2009, the Salvation Army tweeted its followers to donate. The tweet read, "Charity takes hit from economic decline. Salvation Army calling for reinforcements." In another tweet, it declared, "Salvation Army Campaign Drops 8.5 percent in 2009, Army calls for new donations to ease economic woes" (Twitter, 2009).

It is not evident how many people responded to this by tweet call by donating. It is however pretty clear that Salvation Army used this new window to make a case for donations as a way to nudge their donor community/followers as means of staying relevant and in business. With Salvation Army's 983 followers on Twitter, perhaps some re-tweeted to other friends. That sort of gentle nudge can be refreshingly effective way or reminding donors.

In a similar online fundraising cum public advocacy effort, the city of Philadelphia has been using Facebook Pages to mobilize thousands to raise funds to sustain a fire department that was severely affected by budget crises. On June 27, 2009, City of Philadelphia had mobilized 5406 fans to donate money to keep afloat 5 engine companies and two ladder companied that were closed down by the Mayor Michael Nutter (Facebook, 2009).

Public Engagement

A number of cities across America are now tapping into the power of informal networks with online fans, friends on social media platforms to connect and engage the public interactively. This is a great feature of a networked information environment that is robust enough to engender comments, debate and feedback from ordinary citizens, thereby enabling citizens to participate in conversations carried out at many levels of political and social structure (Benkler, 200).

The Los Angeles Fire Department uses blogging to engage the public during important events. During July 4th Celebrations, LAFD 's June 30, 2009 blog post read, "Prepare and Protect Your

Pets From Fireworks". The third paragraph of the story engages citizens in a casual and very cordial tone. It read, "While we encourage attendance at a professional fireworks show, it's a good idea to leave your furry friends safe at home, ideally with someone to watch over them" Retrieved June 30, 2009 from Los Angeles Fire Department, http:lafd.blogspot.com.

It goes on to explain that the furry ones have sensitive hearing and thus become disturbed by fires works. In the past, post cautions, there have been accidents and unfortunate bites on passers by because the fireworks terrified the animals in the city of Los Angeles.

Sensitization

Web 2.0 is changing the way information is produced and consumed. More and more businesses are going for metadata, which is searchable and easier to locate (Weinberger, 2007). This means that with metadata, users can sort, organize, tag, bookmark, classify, play list and so on and so forth. In this process, distributors, consumers and users of information can add some value to information generated by another party. Meta data thus, may have additions like charts, comments that add more value to a piece of information. In essence, the information is plucked from its tree of birth and is made available to everyone who can use it.

When the swine flu emerged in early 2009, the Center for Disease Control and Prevention (CDC, 2009) launched a multi-prong with social media sensitization campaign that aimed at the general population with critical information on what can be done. Even though the virus has become less reported in the media, the CDC still continues to upload information on this subject to give the general public relevant information (Staker, 2009). As of June 30, 2009, the Centers for Disease Control and Prevention CDC had 10,793 fans on its Facebook pages. For well over two months, it has dedicated a tab for providing basic information on how the swine flu (H1N1)

virus is devastating the heartlands and what can be done about it. The information comes in videos, photos and basic tips. More importantly, the CDC makes this information non-proprietary allowing users and fans to share it with others.

CONCLUSION

Based on these trends above, it is likely that the Internet and social media will continue to be a motor for social and political change of all kinds (Bimber, 2003). If technology continues to grow, it is likely that more linkages between technological development and political change will continue to evolve and transform our social and cultural landscape. If Bimber's argument is anything to go by, then, it can be concluded that emergency and crisis management is bound to see more social-cultural impact resulting from new technologies.

Although emergency managers and public safety authorities may be hesitant, they will eventually join the bandwagon of using Web 2.0 or social media. The sooner they join, the better because it will save time in learning basic concepts as the technologies are growing. If emergency and public safety authorities fail to embrace these tools, they may be shortchanged during a disaster because they may lose control due to the overwhelming influence of outside social media.

In conclusion, social media is already making significant changes in emergency and crisis management. The biggest stumbling block so far is that emergency managers are have not fully embraced social media as a complementary platform for both pubic engagement and information dissemination during an emergency. Therefore, if public safety authorities choose to take greater advantage social media, there will be phenomenal changes in the way information is gathered, analyzed, monitored and disseminated to the general population. If this happens, there will be a sea of change because current changes highlighted above already indicate that the public has a vast appetite for consumption of information that is produced in collaboration. The unfolding changes and transformations will also continue to redefine and shift the balance of power between the old and new media. In other words, the fast and furious cheetah (social media) will continue to be a defining force in every disaster (race) involving the old and slow hippo (mass media) that is apparently on life support.

ACKNOWLEDGMENT

Many thanks to Connie White of Jacksonville State University and Linda Plotnick, PhD of New Jersey Institute of Technology for organizing a workshop on Online Social Networking Sites and their impact on emergency management at the Communities and Technology Conference (ComTech) 2009 at Penn State University on June 24, 2009. It is thanks to the workshop that the idea for this paper was born. Beyond the workshop, they have also given me tremendous support in working rapidly through dense maze of academic writing.

I am also grateful for the support from the staff of the Reynolds School of Journalism (RSJ) at University of Nevada, Reno. Without RSJ's support from my Dean Jerry Ceppos, Professors Todd Felts, Larry Dailey, Donica Mensing and I would not have been able to participate in ComTech 2009. I also owe appreciation to Barbara Trainor, Assistant to the Dean and her team for working some magic at the last minute.

REFERENCES

Barabesi, A. L. (2003). *Linked: How Everything is Connected to Everything Else and What It Means for Business, Science and Everyday Life*. New York: Penguin Group.

Benkler, Y. (2006). *The Wealth of Networks: How Social Production Transforms Markets and Freedom*. New Haven, CT: Yale University Press.

Bimber, B. (2003). *Information and American Democracy: Technology in the Evolution of Political Power*. Cambridge, UK: Cambridge University Press.

CDC. (2009). *Novel H1N1 Situation Update*. Retrieved July 22, 2009, from http://www.cdc.gov/h1n1flu/update.htm

Christians, G., Ferre, J. P., & Fackler, P. M. (1993). *Good News: Social Ethics and the Press*. New York: Oxford University Press.

Facebook. (2009). *Help Save the Philadelphia Fire Department*. Retrieved July 27, 2009, from http://apps.facebook.com/causes/242755

Gladwell, M. (2002). *Tipping Point: How Little Things Can Make a Big Difference*. New York: Little, Brown and Company.

Guth, D. (2008). *Untapped Potential: Evaluating State Emergency Management Web Sites 2008*. Lawrence, KS: University of Kansas.

Habermas, J. (1992). *The Structural Transformation of the Public Sphere: An Inquiry into a Category of Bourgeis Society*. Cambridge, MA: MIT Press.

Howe, J. (2008). *Crowdsourcing: Why the Power of Crowd is Driving the Future of Business*. New York: Crown Business.

Humphrey, B. (2009). *Prepare and Protect Your Pets from Fireworks*. Retrieved July 25, 2009, from http://lafd.blogspot.com/

Putnam, R. (2000). *Bowling Alone: The Collapse and Revival of American Community*. New York: Simon and Schuster.

Senge, P. M., Smith, B., Schley, S., Laur, J., & Kruschwitz, N. (2008). *The Necessary Revolution: How Individuals and Organizations are Working Together to Create a Sustainable World*. New York: Doubleday.

Shirkey, C. (2008). *Here Comes Everybody: The Power of Organizing with Organizations*. New York: Penguin Press.

Stewardson, K. (2009). *San Francisco Residents Can Tweet 311, Government Technology: Solutions for state and local government for the information age*. Retrieved July 25, 2009, from http://www.sfgov.org/site/mayor_index.asp?id=105288

Thacker, S. (2009). *Working with Partners to Achieve Success*. Retrieved July 25, 2009, from http://www2a.cdc.gov/podcasts/index.asp

Thaler, R. H., & Sunstein, C. R. (2008). *Nudge: Improving Decisions about Health, Wealth and Happiness*. Ann Arbor, MI: Caravan Book.

Twitter. (2009). *Salvation Army*. Retrieved, July 24, 2009, from http://twitter.com/salvationarmy/

Vieweg, S., Palen, L., Liu, S. B., Hughes, A. L., & Sutton, J. (2008). Collective Intelligence in Disaster: Examination of the Phenomenon in the Aftermath of the 2007 Virginia Shooting. In *Proceedings from 5th International ISCRAM Conference,* Washington, DC.

Weinberger, D. (2007). *Everything is Miscellaneous: The Power of New Digital Disorder*. New York: Times Books.

Wikipedia. (2008). *Facebook*. Retrieved July 24, 2009, from http://en.wikipedia.org/wiki/Facebook

This work was previously published in International Journal of Information Systems for Crisis Response Management, Volume 2, Issue 1, edited by Murray E. Jennex, pp. 1-10, copyright 2010 by IGI Publishing (an imprint of IGI Global).

Chapter 2
The Use of Social Media in Disaster Situations:
Framework and Cases

Guido Lang
City University of New York, USA

Raquel Benbunan-Fich
City University of New York, USA

ABSTRACT

Recent disasters highlight the importance of social media supporting critical information gathering and dissemination efforts by members of the public. Given that disasters pose unique challenges and social media are evolving rapidly, how can one compare the effectiveness of social media in different disaster situations? Drawing from prior work on e-participation, this paper proposes a novel framework for social media use based on four key modules: selection, facilitation, deliberation, and aggregation. A comparative analysis of social media use following a man-made disaster (the 2007 Virginia Tech tragedy) and during a natural disaster (the 2009 Britain blizzard) exemplifies the value of the proposed framework. Future research can build on and leverage the present work by analyzing and incorporating additional cases on the use of social media in disaster situations.

1. INTRODUCTION

The emerging use of information and communication technology (ICT) as social media, including blogging, tagging, and content sharing, facilitates critical information generation and dissemination activities by members of the public during the phases of a disaster (Palen & Liu, 2007). Schol-

ars in the field of *crisis informatics* (Palen et al., 2007b) recently investigated the public's elaborate use of social media following various natural and man-made disasters, including the Indian Ocean earthquake and tsunami, London bombings, Avian influenza outbreak, hurricane Katrina, Virginia Tech shootings, Minneapolis bridge collapse, and Southern California wildfires (Hughes et al., 2008;

DOI: 10.4018/978-1-4666-0167-3.ch002

Liu et al., 2008; Palen et al., 2007a; Shklovski et al., 2008; Sutton et al., 2008; Vieweg et al., 2008). In essence, findings suggest that "social media support critical information distribution activity among members of the public that (...) needs to be better integrated with official disaster response activities" (Palen, 2008, p. 78). This call for attention to social media in disaster management is in line with the overall objective of emergency response information systems, which consists of "providing relevant communities collaborative knowledge systems to exchange information" (Turoff, 2002, p. 29, cited in Van de Walle & Turoff, 2007, p. 31).

However, given that disasters pose unique challenges and social media are evolving rapidly, how can one compare the effectiveness of social media in different disaster situations? In addition, the grassroots nature of social media challenges conventional organization processes and structures in typical incident command centers (Turoff et al., 2008), thus further complicating its integration with official disaster response activities. In an effort to overcome these challenges, a combination of policy reform and technology design research has been encouraged (Palen, 2008). Current work seems to focus primarily on technology design, mainly proposing advanced web-based artifacts such as a dynamic voting wiki (White et al., 2007), an emergency domain online social network (Plotnick et al., 2009), and a mega-collaboration tool (Newlon et al., 2009).

In this vein, this paper aims to further the understanding of social media use by members of the public in disaster situations. In the absence of a generally accepted body of knowledge on social media use, we draw from prior work on e-participation to propose a novel framework for social media use based on four key modules: (1) selection, (2) facilitation, (3) deliberation, and (4) aggregation. The applicability and utility of the proposed framework is highlighted in a comparative analysis of social media use in two disaster situations: following the Virginia Tech tragedy in

2007, a man-made disaster, and during the Britain blizzard in 2009, a natural disaster.

The remainder of this paper is structured as follows. We first provide an overview of prior work on e-participation and present our proposed framework. Next, we describe the methodology of comparative case analysis, followed by a discussion of two different case studies. Finally, we conclude with directions for future research.

2. THEORETICAL BACKGROUND

Due to the lack of an established body of knowledge on the use of social media by members of the public, we draw from prior work that addresses a similar issue: e-participation. In the fields of policy and political science, e-participation generally refers to the use of web applications for public participation in policy making (Macintosh, 2006). E-participation can be seen as a subset of the general mechanisms underlying public participation, which denotes the practice of integrating citizens in the political decision-making activities of organizations (Rowe, 2005). Also in this field, scholars seem to focus now on efforts to design more efficient and effective public participation processes that make use of social media (Abelson et al., 2003).

The intent of the following subsections is to highlight the variety and limitations of the existing concepts in e-participation, which have not yet led to the development of a significant theory of "what works best when" (Rowe & Frewer, 2000). In an effort to overcome these limitations, the last subsection proposes a novel framework for social media use in disaster situations.

2.1. Integration of E-Participation

Arnstein (1969) is one of the first researchers to provide what can be seen as probably the most enduring metaphor of variations in public participation. Her so-called ladder of public participation has eight stages, accounting for the increasing levels of integrating the public in the policy-making process. Wiedemann and Femers (1993) further develop Arnstein's work by combining the public's access to information with the public's rights in the decision-making process. Their conceptualization of public participation ranges from non-participation through sequential stages of increasing integration to the final empowerment of the public, with each stage serving as a requirement to reach the following (Table 1, left column).

After recognizing the increasing use and importance of the Internet, Carver (2003) proposes matching each stage of Wiedemann and Femers' integration of public participation with supporting ICT tools, hence presenting a ladder of e-participation (Table 1, right column) (Carver, 2003; Smyth, 2001). The first stage supports the integration of non-participation, i.e. the public right to know, informing the public, and the public right to object, through online service delivery. Online service delivery includes the unidirectional access to information, as well as the provision of public services, such as payment and the filing of forms online. The following stages support bidirectional communication through the sharing of information, ideas, and feedback. Specifically, Carver (2003) suggests that the use of (1) online discussion supports public participation in defining interests, actors, and determining agenda, (2) online opinion surveys support public participation in assessing risks and recommending solutions, and (3) online decision support systems match public participation in the final decision.

However, the aforementioned ICT tools can be combined or even used independently to support different goals within a single public participation integration stage. The mere usage of an online discussion forum, for example, does not dictate the integration of public participation in defining interests, actors, and determining agenda, or vice versa.

Table 1. ICT support by participation integration (Carver, 2003)

Integration of public participation (Wiedemann & Femers, 1993)	Supporting ICT tool
Public participation in final decision	Online decision support system
Public participation in assessing risks and recommending solutions	Online opinion survey
Public participation in defining interests, actors and determining agenda	Online discussion
Public right to object	Online service delivery
Informing the public	
Public right to know	

2.2. Objectives of E-Participation

To address a similar predicament in traditional public participation, Glass (1979) matches participatory techniques with objectives for public participation (Glass, 1979). Particularly, he specifies four main objectives for the integration of public participation in the governmental decision-making process (Table 2, left column). Several traditional participatory techniques are presented and subsequently matched with their most appropriate participation objective.

Building on Glass' (1979) work on participatory techniques and most appropriate participation objectives, Phang and Kankanhalli (2008) propose matching a number of supporting ICT tools to participatory techniques and in turn, to participation objectives (Table 2, right column).

The first objective, *information exchange*, aims to bring participants and planners together for an open sharing of ideas and concerns, which is traditionally best supported by a drop-in center or a public hearing. In the realm of ICT, the authors suggest implementing a website with an online discussion forum or an online chat, due to their ability to support an easy and open two-way communication between planners and participants.

The second objective, *education and support building*, aims to engage participants from a specific target population over a longer period of time to inform them about the how and why of the government's policy plans, as in the case of traditional citizen advisory committees or citizen panels. In this case, Phang and Kankanhalli (2008) suggest that the best supporting ICT tools are those that allow selecting target participants and maintaining contact over time, such as through online chat, discussion forum, conferencing, and e-mail, among others.

The third objective, *supplemental decision-making*, aims to obtain a specific set of information (e.g. preferences) from a relevant group, which is traditionally done through nominal group processes and value analysis. ICT tools that provide control over how the participation process occurs are suggested for implementation. These include group support systems (GSS) with process restrictiveness features (i.e. agenda setting or specifying a sequence of activities), and online pair-wise structured surveys, optionally supported by visualization tools.

The fourth objective, *representational input*, aims to obtain the public's views on relatively unexplored policy issues, as in the case of traditional citizen surveys. Its online counterpart, according to the authors, is an online opinion survey, which can include open-ended questions through online comment forms, followed by a statistical data analysis.

In Phan and Kankanhalli (2008), the matching of ICT tools with participation objectives seems to fall short of effectively differentiating the underlying characteristics of participatory technologies and the possibility of combining them in specific circumstances. For instance, an online discussion forum can be combined with other ICT tools, or used in several different ways to support multiple objectives.

2.3. Forms of E-Participation

Building on the theory of public choice in constitutional economics, which argues for an inherent trade-off between external costs (e.g. adverse effects) and decision-making costs in every decision-making process (Buchanan & Tullock, 1962), Kumar and Vragov (2009) recently conceptualize ICT support by its potential impact on these costs.

Table 2. ICT support by participation objective (Phang & Kankanhalli, 2008)

Objective of public participation (Glass, 1979)	Supporting ICT tool
Information exchange	Website with online discussion forum
	Online chat
Education and support building	Online chat
	Online discussion forum with login
	Tele-/Video-conferencing
	E-mail distribution
Supplemental decision-making	GSS with process restrictiveness
	Online pair-wise structured survey
Representational input	Online opinion survey
	Online comment form

Table 3. ICT support by participation form (Kumar & Vragov, 2009)

Form of public participation (after (Buchanan & Tullock, 1962))	Supporting ICT tool
Communication	Official website
	E-mail distribution
	Recorded audio and video
Deliberation	Online comment form
	Online chat
	Online discussion forum
	Electronic petition
	Blog
Voting	Online electronic voting

They place ICT tools on a participation continuum that includes the forms of (1) communication, (2) deliberation, and (3) voting (see Table 3).

The first form supports one-way information dissemination activities through an official website, e-mail distribution, as well as recorded audio and video, which can potentially reduce decision-making costs. In contrast, the second and third forms support two-way communication through more advanced ICT tools (e.g. online comments, chat, discussion, etc.), which can potentially reduce external costs and decision-making costs.

Although this approach outlines certain key characteristics of supporting ICT tools, such as the form of public participation and the information flow, it mixes content features with technological features. As such, it does not allow for establishing a true typology, in which the ICT tools in each category remain constant on a number of dimensions.

2.4. Modules of E-Participation

In a comprehensive undertaking to investigate the commonalities and differences of public participation mechanisms, Rowe (2005) differentiates the nature and direction of information flows between participants and planners, establishing three archetypes of public engagement: (1) *public communication*, i.e. one-way information flow from planners to participants, (2) *public consultation*, i.e. one-way information flow from participants to planners, and (3) *public participation*, i.e. two-way information exchange between participants and planners.

In this paper, we focus exclusively on the third type of public engagement, i.e. public participation. The justification for this focus stems from recent empirical findings regarding public engagement in disaster management, which highlight the positive outcomes related to a continuous and open two-way information exchange between participants and planners (Ganapati & Ganapati, 2009).

Rowe (2005) analyzes the contingent effectiveness of participatory mechanisms. In this context, effectiveness refers to the fairness and efficiency of a particular participation mechanism. A participation mechanism has no fairness per se, but is judged by the public as fair or unfair based on its application and the underlying intention of its implementation. Efficiency of a mechanism is defined as "maximizing the relevant information from the maximum number of all relevant sources and transferring it (…) to the other parties, with the efficient processing of that information by the receivers (…) and the combining of it into an accurate composite" (Rowe, 2005, p. 263).

In essence, Rowe (2005) argues that contingent effectiveness "will depend on the particular mechanism chosen and the way in which this mechanism is applied in the specific exercise" (Rowe, 2005, p. 264). Hence, differences in effectiveness among participation mechanisms are due to differences between the mechanisms (*between-mechanism variables*) and differences within the application of the mechanisms (*within-mechanism variables*). Between-mechanism variables exhibit variation across different mechanisms in a specific practical application. In contrast, within-mechanism variables exhibit variation across different practical applications in a specific mechanism. While the former can be induced from the existing plethora of empirical investigations on public participation mechanisms in governmental decision-making, the latter requires comparative case studies, or replications, of the same mechanism in different contexts. Hence, within-mechanism variables are not covered by Rowe (2005) and are subsequently excluded from the present analysis.

Based on an analysis of over 100 case studies involving public participation mechanisms, Rowe (2005) proposes several key between-mechanism variables including relevant levels, related to an efficient public participation mechanism. For the purpose of defining a framework for social media use, this paper focuses on the variables and levels applicable and relevant to the use of social media. We define social media as web applications that process, store, and retrieve user-generated content. User-generated content refers to content that is (1) made publicly available over the Internet, (2) reflects a certain amount of creative effort and (3) is created outside of professional routines and practices (OECD, 2007).

We conceptualize the relevant variables as modules, with each module being either present or absent in any given situation. The conceptualization in terms of modules, as opposed to specific social media environments, provides a higher level of abstraction independent of the particular technological artifacts available at any given time. The four modules are (1) *selection*, (2) *facilitation*, (3) *deliberation*, and (4) *aggregation*. Figure 1 presents the resulting framework for the use of social media.

The *selection* module refers to whether or not social media is used to control the number and relevance of participants. Examples of selection include user authentication, location-based access, by invitation only, etc. The *facilitation* module refers to whether or not social media is used to ensure input from all participants. Examples of facilitation include human moderators, automated reminders, mandatory response fields, etc. The *deliberation* module refers to whether or not social media is used to elicit text, audio, video, or image input without a predetermined set or form of specific response choices. Examples of deliberation include free text forms, sharing of media files, etc. The *aggregation* module refers to whether or not social media is used to produce a unified output based on predetermined rules. Examples of aggregation include voting mechanisms, random drawings, decision-making committees, etc.

Taken together, these four modules describe a formal structure, or *Gestalt*, of social media use. Social media can be administered and combined to form different structures—depending on the presence or absence of a particular module. The

Figure 1. The modules of social media

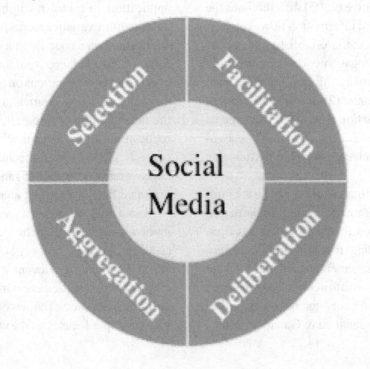

four modules hence allow for a total of 2^4 (=16) variations, as shown in Figure 2.

The 16 variations describe the possible archetypes of social media use (Figure 2, (a)-(p)). Archetype (a) involves social media that supports selection, facilitation, deliberation, and aggregation, as denoted by the four grey quarters. An example of archetype (a) would be a web application that facilitates the moderation of open user responses and structured voting mechanisms within a closed group of users. In contrast, archetype (p) involves social media that supports none of the four modules, as denoted by the four white quarters. An example of archetype (p) would be a simple web form that collects predetermined user responses with no further feedback or functionality. The remaining 14 archetypes involve social media that supports any combination of the four modules.

By formalizing the structure of social media use with four underlying modules, future research can begin to develop a comparative theory of "what works best when" (Rowe & Frewer, 2000). In the natural sciences, the comparative study of formal structure is closely associated with morphological analysis (Ritchey, 2006). Morphological analysis supports problem formulation and scenario building processes by representing variables and their associated levels in a graphical format. Similarly, the present framework presents and allows for the systematic comparative study of social media use. Two particular archetypes of social media use, (d)

and (n), are described in the case analyses section. Moreover, to study the contingent effectiveness of certain social media in context, we propose integrating the present framework with the contextual framework of disaster management. The following section presents the case analysis methodology.

3. METHODOLOGY

To highlight the value of the proposed framework for the use of social media, we use a qualitative comparative case analysis method (QCA) (Ragin, 1987). QCA is an approach that combines qualitative, case-oriented, research with quantitative, variable-oriented, research by reducing in-depth case studies to a series of variables of conditions and outcomes for further analysis and, ultimately, theoretical generalization (Rihoux, 2006). The proposed framework presents one way to adequately model the conditional variables in QCA, thus furthering our main objective to better understand the use of social media by members of the public in disaster situations.

4. CASE ANALYSES

We selected two recent cases of social media use in disaster situations to illustrate the application of the proposed framework. The cases are different in terms of the nature of the disaster (man-made

Figure 2. Archetypes of social media use

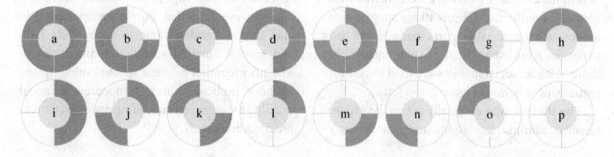

vs. natural) and in the timing of e-participation (1) following a man-made disaster, (2) during a natural disaster. The first case concerns the use of Facebook[1] in the aftermath of the Virginia Tech tragedy, which took place in April 2007 and was investigated by Palen and her colleagues (Palen et al., 2007b, Vieweg et al., 2008). The second case concerns the use of Twitter[2] during the blizzard that hit Britain in February 2009, which to the best of our knowledge has not been investigated yet.

4.1. The Virginia Tech Tragedy

The tragedy at Virginia Tech (VT) occurred on April 16, 2007 in Blacksburg, VA, when an individual killed 32 people on the university campus. An in-depth investigation of the post-disaster citizen-side communication on a Facebook group revealed that citizens were able to construct a list of casualties in a highly distributed and decentralized fashion hours before the names of the victims were officially released (Palen et al., 2007b, Vieweg et al., 2008). The emergence of such socially produced accuracy in a complex problem-solving activity stands in sharp contrast to the typical portrayal of a public in need of policing and control. Moreover, these findings further underscore the importance of social media in disaster situations.

The Facebook group, which was set up by a VT student following this tragic case, supported a group discussion. Although technically possible, access and contribution to this group were not limited to a particular network within Facebook. However, contributions by users who were members of the official VT network were treated with a sense of authority.[3] Observations suggest that absent such membership, participating users had to provide additional evidence to gain equal credibility. Hence, social media were used to control participant *selection* (Figure 3, top left).

The student, who originally set up the group, retained administrator rights and continuously engaged in the discussion through asking questions and verifying information. Although a group administrator has the option to edit and delete other participants' responses, available evidence indicates that such actions did not take place in this case. Nevertheless, the administrator's engagement can be classified as supporting *facilitation* (Figure 3, top right).

The discussion board in a Facebook group supports free-text entry, including links and even the posting of media content, such as photos. Participants were not instructed to act otherwise, thus classifying the response input as *deliberation* (Figure 3, bottom right).

After a few hours, the participants were able to reach agreement on the final list of casualties. However, this information was not aggregated according to pre-specified rules, but rather through public discourse and argumentation. Hence, social media were *not* used to support *aggregation* (Figure 3, bottom left empty).

The archetype resulting from the described configuration of key variables in the VT tragedy is presented in Figure 3. Considering the specific context and the particular outcome of the process, this archetype represents one effective variation of the 16 possible archetypes of social media use (Figure 2, (d)).

4.2. The Britain Blizzard

On February 2, 2009, Britain was hit by an unusually harsh blizzard, bringing the worst snow in two decades. As a result, at least two people died, thousands of traffic-related accidents were reported, all 700 flights at London's Heathrow airport were cancelled, public transportation in and around London came to a complete halt, and several hundred schools remained closed. The prioritization of areas to snow-plough was further complicated, due to the apparent technical inability to gather real-time information on current precipitation levels.[4]

Figure 3. Archetype of social media use in the Virginia Tech tragedy

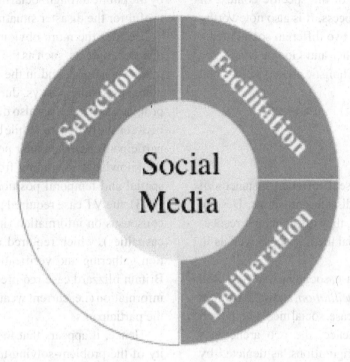

In reply, Ben Marsh, a web developer living in Britain, voluntarily created a Twitter hashtag[5] (#uksnow) and Google Maps mash-up with the specific public request to "Tweet the first half of your postcode, and rate the amount of snow that is falling out of ten (0 for nothing, 5 for steady snow and 10 for arctic blizzard conditions)."[6] Within hours, tens of thousands of users in Britain followed the request and participated via Twitter, allowing everyone interested to gain a better understanding of the current weather situation on the ground.

Basically everyone with a Twitter account was able to equally participate in the Britain blizzard social media use. Although it was technically possible, whether someone was actually located in Britain or not, was not verified. Hence, social media were *not* used to control the *selection* of participants (Figure 3, top left empty).

The users were left on their own and not supported or supervised during the actual process of submitting information. Therefore, social media

were *not* used for information *facilitation* (Figure 3, top right empty).

The public request, which was spelled out in great detail, required a highly formalized response to qualify for the participatory process. Participants' were only allowed to enter their scripted responses in the requested format and were unable to discuss or evaluate this information. Thus, social media were *not* used to support *deliberation* (Figure 3, bottom right empty).

However, in a last step, Ben Harsh developed a Google Maps mash-up[7], which was fed through Twitter's public timeline API that effectively aggregated all individual participation into a common and unified document. Consequently, social media were used for information *aggregation* (Figure 3, bottom left).

Figure 4 presents the archetype resulting from the described configuration of social media during the Britain blizzard. This archetype represents one effective variation within the 16 archetypes of social media use (Figure 2, (n)) requiring further consideration of the specific context of the e-participation process. It is also noteworthy in this example, how two different social media applications (i.e. Twitter and Google Maps) are combined to form one holistic archetype of social media use.

5. DISCUSSION

The two cases represent different instances of social media use in disaster situations. Despite both being successful, they differ in their respective archetype of social media use, as well as in their disaster context.

While in the VT case, social media were used to support *selection*, *facilitation*, and *deliberation*, in the Britain blizzard case, social media supported only *aggregation*. Hence, the two archetypes present opposite configurations, as depicted by variations (d) and (n) in Figure 2. Despite these differences, the resulting information generated

by the public through social media was timely and useful for the disaster situation at hand.

Besides the more obvious differences in the disaster contexts, such as the disaster being man-made vs. natural, and in the timing of the social media use being post vs. during the disaster, the problem-solving tasks also differed considerably between the two cases. While both cases addressed participants based on their positional insight, i.e. the knowledge stemming from the participants' spatial and temporal positioning (Boudourides, 2003), the VT case required participants to reach consensus on information (i.e. the names of the casualties), which required additional information gathering and verification. In contrast, the Britain blizzard case required a mere polling of information (i.e. current weather condition) from the participants.

Hence, it appears that the level of complexity of the problem-solving task is related to the modules in the social media use framework. While we believe that the proposed framework offers

Figure 4. Archetype of social media use in the Britain blizzard

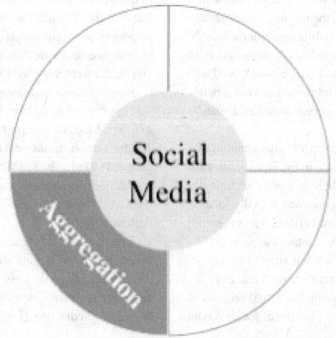

a valuable tool to articulate the differences in social media use, the preliminary insights gained from the two cases must be treated with caution. The cases are meant to showcase the utility of the framework and were chosen in part based on their revelatory potential. Furthermore, the use of social media in disaster situations is not without caveats, including issues of privacy, the potential for conflicts of interest with the operating companies, as well as the threats stemming from social mobs and inequalities of access. Lastly, as with all ICT, social media require certain infrastructure to be available, which might not be guaranteed in situations of power outages, or limited Internet connectivity.

6. CONCLUSION

The use and importance of social media for communication among citizens in disaster situations has been gaining more research attention lately. Recent disasters exhibit the public's use of such ICT tools for critical crisis communication efforts in numerous ways. Given this trend in spontaneous public participation, it is necessary to achieve a better integration of social media with official disaster response activities.

This paper provides a first step to formalize the use of social media by proposing a framework based on four modules: (1) *selection*, (2) *facilitation*, (3) *deliberation*, and (4) *aggregation*. The utility of the proposed framework is exemplified via two case studies on social media use in two disaster situations: one following the Virginia Tech tragedy, a man-made disaster, and the other during the 2009 Britain blizzard, a natural disaster. While the former case is based on a reanalysis of published work, the latter presents new empirical data. The archetypes of social media use represent radically different but highly effective configurations in both situations.

Future research should focus on potentially extending the proposed framework, as well as on formalizing the contexts for the use of social media. Furthermore, empirical studies could investigate the outcomes of the same social media use archetypes in different settings, and vice versa.

ACKNOWLEDGMENT

The authors would like to thank Miriam Belblidia, Gideon F. For-mukwai, Linda Plotnick, Connie White, and the anonymous reviewers for their help in refining the ideas in this article. An earlier version of this paper was presented at the Online Social Networks to Support Community Collaboration Workshop, held June 24, 2009, as part of the 4th International Conference on Communities and Technologies, Penn State University, University Park, PA.

REFERENCES

Abelson, J., Forest, P., Eyles, J., Smith, P., Martin, E., & Gauvin, F. (2003). Deliberations about deliberative methods: issues in the design and evaluation of public participation processes. *Social Science & Medicine*, 57, 239–251. doi:10.1016/S0277-9536(02)00343-X

Arnstein, S. R. (1969). A ladder of citizen participation. *Journal of the American Institute of Planners*, 35(4), 216–224.

Boudourides, M. A. (2003). Participation Under Uncertainty. In *Proceedings of VALDOR 2003: Values in Decisions on Risk*, Stockholm, Sweden.

Buchanan, J. M., & Tullock, G. (1962). *The Calculus of Consent: Logical Foundations of Constitutional Democracy*. Ann Arbor, MI: University of Michigan Press.

Carver, S. (2003). The Future of Participatory Approaches Using Geographic Information: Developing a research agenda for the Ritchey, 2006st century. *URISA Journal, 15*(APA 1), 61-71.

Ganapati, N. E., & Ganapati, S. (2009). Enabling Participatory Planning After Disasters: A Case Study of the World Bank's Housing Reconstruction in Turkey. *Journal of the American Planning Association. American Planning Association, 75*(1), 41–59. doi:10.1080/01944360802546254

Glass, J. (1979). Citizen Participation in Planning: The Relationship Between Objectives and Techniques. *American Planning Association Journal, 99*(2), 180–189. doi:10.1080/01944367908976956

Hughes, A. L., Palen, L., Sutton, J., Liu, S. B., & Vieweg, S. (2008). "Site-Seeing" in Disaster: An Examination of On-Line Social Convergence. In F. Fiedrich & B. Van De Walle (Eds.), *Proceedings of the 5th International ISCRAM Conference*, Washington, DC.

Kumar, N., & Vragov, R. (2009). Active Citizen Participation Using ICT Tools. *Communications of the ACM, 52*(1), 118–121. doi:10.1145/1435417.1435444

Liu, S. B., Palen, L., Sutton, J., Hughes, A. L., & Vieweg, S. (2008). In Search of the Bigger Picture: The Emergent Role of On-Line Photo Sharing in Times of Disaster. In F. Fiedrich & B. Van De Walle (Eds.), *Proceedings of the 5th International ISCRAM Conference,* Washington, DC (pp. 140-149).

Macintosh, A. (2006). eParticipation in Policymaking: The Research and the Challenges. In P. Cunningham & M. Cunninghal (Eds.), *Exploiting the Knowledge Economy: Issues, Applications, Case Studies*. Amsterdam, The Netherlands: IOS Press.

Newlon, C. M., Pfaff, M., Patel, H., de Vreede, G., & MacDorman, K. F. (2009). Mega-Collaboration: The Inspiration and Development of an Interface for Large-Scale Disaster Response. In J. Landgren, U. Nulden, & B. Van De Walle (Eds.), *Proceedings of the 6th International ISCRAM Conference*, Gothenburg, Sweden.

OECD. (2007). *Participative Web: User-Created Content. Report presented to the Working Party on the Information Economy*. Retrieved August 1, 2009, from http://www.oecd.org/dataoecd/57/14/38393115.pdf

Palen, L. (2008). Online Social Media in Crisis Events. *EDUCAUSE Quarterly*, (3): 76–78.

Palen, L., Hiltz, S. R., & Liu, S. B. (2007). Online forums supporting grassroots participation in emergency preparedness and response. *Communications of the ACM, 50*(3), 54–58. doi:10.1145/1226736.1226766

Palen, L., & Liu, S. B. (2007). Citizen Communications in Crisis: Anticipating a Future of ICT-Supported Public Participation. In *Proceedings of CHI 2007,* San Jose, CA (pp. 727-736).

Palen, L., Vieweg, S., Sutton, J., Liu, S. B., & Hughes, A. (2007). Crisis Informatics: Studying Crisis in a Networked World. In *Proceedings of the 3rd International Conference on e-Social Science*, Ann Arbor, MI.

Phang, C. W., & Kankanhalli, A. (2008). A Framework of ICT Exploitation for E-Participation Initiatives. *Communications of the ACM, 51*(12), 128–132. doi:10.1145/1409360.1409385

Plotnick, L., White, C., & Plummer, M. (2009). The Design of an Online Social Network Site for Emergency Management: A One-Stop Shop. In *Proceedings of the 15th Americas Conference on Information Systems*, San Francisco.

Ragin, C. C. (1987). *The Comparative Method: Moving Beyond Qualitative and Quantitative Strategies.* Berkeley, CA: University of California Press.

Rihoux, B. (2006). Qualitative comparative analysis (qca) and related systematic comparative methods: Recent advances and remaining challenges for social science research. *International Sociology, 21*(5), 679–706. doi:10.1177/0268580906067836

Ritchey, T. (2006). Problem structuring using computer-aided morphological analysis. *The Journal of the Operational Research Society, 57,* 792–801. doi:10.1057/palgrave.jors.2602177

Rowe, G. (2005). A Typology of Public Engagement Mechanisms. *Science, Technology & Human Values, 30*(2), 251–290. doi:10.1177/0162243904271724

Rowe, G., & Frewer, L. J. (2000). Public Participation Methods: A Framework for Evaluation. *Science, Technology & Human Values, 25*(1), 3–29. doi:10.1177/016224390002500101

Shklovski, I., Palen, L., & Sutton, J. (2008). Finding Community Through Information and Communication Technology During Disaster Events. In *Proceedings of the Conference on Computer Supported Cooperative Work (CSCW '08),* San Diego, CA (pp. 1-10).

Smyth, E. (2001). *Would the Internet Widen Public Participation?* Unpublished master's thesis, University of Leeds.

Sutton, J., Palen, L., & Shklovski, I. (2008). Backchannels on the Front Lines: Emergent Uses of Social Media in the 2007 Southern California Wildfires. In F. Fiedrich & B. Van De Walle (Eds.), *Proceedings of the 5th International ISCRAM Conference,* Washington, DC.

Turoff, M. (2002). Past and Future of Emergency Response Information Systems. *Communications of the ACM, 45*(4), 29–32. doi:10.1145/505248.505265

Turoff, M., Plotnick, L., White, C., & Hiltz, S. R. (2008). Dynamic Emergency Response Management for Large Scale Decision Making in Extreme Events. In F. Fiedrich & B. Van De Walle (Eds.), *Proceedings of the 5th International ISCRAM Conference,* Washington, DC (pp. 462-470).

Van De Walle, B., & Turoff, M. (2007). Emergency Response Information Systems: Emerging Trends and technologies. *Communications of the ACM, 50*(3), 29–32. doi:10.1145/1226736.1226760

Vieweg, S., Palen, L., Liu, S. B., Hughes, A. L., & Sutton, J. (2008). Collective Intelligence in Disaster: Examination of the Phenomenon in the Aftermath of the 2007 Virginia Tech Shooting. In F. Fiedrich & B. Van De Walle (Eds.), *Proceedings of the 5th International ISCRAM Conference,* Washington, DC (pp. 44-54).

White, C., Plotnick, L., Turoff, M., & Hiltz, S. R. (2007). A Dynamic Voting Wiki Model. In *Proceedings of the 15th Americas Conference on Information Systems*, San Francisco.

Wiedemann, P. M., & Femers, S. (1993). Public participation in waste management decision making: Analysis and management of conflicts. *Journal of Hazardous Materials, 33,* 355–368. doi:10.1016/0304-3894(93)85085-S

ENDNOTES

1. Facebook is a free-access social networking website that is operated and privately owned by Facebook, Inc. It can be accessed at http://www.facebook.com.

2. Twitter is a free micro-blogging service that is operated and privately owned by Twitter, Inc. It can be accessed at http://www.twitter.com

3. Network membership requires verification through an official e-mail account (e.g. name@vt.edu).

4. See http://news.bbc.co.uk/2/hi/uk_news/7864395.stm

5. A hashtag is a keyword, or tag, that is attached to a post on Twitter by prefixing a word with a hash symbol (#).

6. See http://www.benmarsh.co.uk/snow

7. A Google Maps mash-up is a web application that combines data or functionality from one or more sources with Google Maps into a single, integrated user-interface.

This work was previously published in International Journal of Information Systems for Crisis Response Management, Volume 2, Issue 1, edited by Murray E. Jennex, pp. 11-23, copyright 2010 by IGI Publishing (an imprint of IGI Global).

Chapter 3
Building Community Resilience through Social Networking Sites:
Using Online Social Networks for Emergency Management

Miriam S. Belblidia
University of Pittsburgh, USA

ABSTRACT

Online Social Networking Sites (SNS) enable collaborative information sharing and help build resilient communities in areas exposed to risk. This paper reviews existing research on community vulnerability and resilience, and explores the role of communication in fostering strong community networks. The paper draws upon examples of SNS used to share information and explores how such technology may be leveraged more effectively to provide communities with robust communication networks, thereby creating more resilient communities in areas at high risk of natural disasters.

CONTEXT

The use of SNS sites, such as Facebook and Twitter, has grown exponentially in recent years (Golbeck, 2008a; Shneiderman & Preece, 2007), as people build Internet-based networks that reflect their own communication networks (Manjoo, 2009). As the number of users grows and the functionality of these networks expands, SNS have emerged as a

practical tool for use in emergency management (White et al., 2009).

As the nation watched the rising river threatening Fargo on March 28, 2009, President Obama called attention to this utility, "young people have turned social networks into community networks, coordinating with one another online to figure out how best to help" (Obama, 2009). Similarly, citizens have used internet networks

DOI: 10.4018/978-1-4666-0167-3.ch003

in past emergencies. In the 2005 aftermath of Hurricane Katrina, with Gulf Coast evacuees scattered throughout the country, websites like KatrinaPeopleFinder and Katrina Wiki emerged to help locate friends and family (Gertz, 2005). As Hurricane Gustav threatened New Orleans in 2008, a "Hurricane Gustav Digital Support Brigade" group was launched to share information and coordinate volunteers (Carvin, 2008). During the 2008 terrorist attack in Mumbai, residents used Twitter to keep one another informed as the crisis developed (Caulfield & Karmali, 2008).

Such examples of SNS use demonstrate the capacity for use in emergencies. Emergency managers are increasingly turning to online networks in order to communicate with their constituents. The Federal Emergency Management Agency (FEMA) now uses YouTube, Twitter, and Facebook to share information with the public (FEMA, 2009) and the Centers for Disease Control (CDC) is linked to Twitter, Facebook, MySpace, and DailyStrength (CDC, 2009). While these moves represent progress, early warning systems often remain hierarchical in nature, with emergency managers sharing information down to the public (Botterell & Addams-Moring, 2007). An exciting component of SNS is their ability to "flatten" emergency communication by allowing information to be shared not only from the top down, but also from user to user and from the ground up to emergency officials. Such communication, facilitated by SNS, more closely resembles the "flatter, more dynamic, ad-hoc organization that emerges during post-disaster relief efforts" (Manoj & Hubenko Baker, 2007, p.52).

By facilitating resident-to-resident communication, SNS also have the ability to strengthen community networks. Collaborative engagement of local citizens through SNS would serve emergency managers well, as citizens are often informal "first responders" in disasters (Palen, Hiltz, & Liu, 2007). Before technologies such as SNS can be effectively used for emergency management, it is necessary to understand community networks, vulnerability and how to build resilience within these vulnerable communities. If leveraged properly, Social Networking Sites represent a valuable tool to reduce vulnerability and increase resilience within communities.

RESEARCH QUESTION

For the purposes of this paper, Social Networking Sites are defined as any web-based applications that allow individuals to connect, communicate, and collaborate with one another. This is usually done through individual user profiles and allows users to share information and join networks based on geographic location or interests (White et al., 2009). By linking friends, families, co-workers, and acquaintances, SNS are able to reinforce communication networks and transmit critical information.

The utility of Social Networking Sites for emergency management comes from their potential ability to create more resilient communities in areas at high risk of disasters. The central research question of this paper is whether SNS facilitate collaborative action at the community level by strengthening communication networks and enabling communities to self-organize more effectively, thereby reducing their risk. This represents an extension of the use of SNS by emergency managers to communicate critical information and may yield more effective results in producing resilient communities. By using SNS to collaborate and strengthen community networks, these sites have the potential to reduce vulnerability within communities.

This research began with an extensive review of existing literature, using a snowballing technique to cull further sources. While focused primarily on emergency management literature, sociology, computer technology, and psychology literatures were also drawn upon. The research was then organized around significant themes: technology, vulnerability, resilience, social organization, community capacity, hazard mitigation, and community networks. This provided an understanding of how communities build resilience through communication and how SNS may reduce risk.

In gathering further data on the utility of SNS, expert interviews were conducted with researchers whose backgrounds lay in public administration, sociology, and emergency management. A questionnaire was developed to gauge their opinions on the use of technology for emergency management. Interviews were conducted in person with four expert academics from Louisiana universities. These interviews were used to discuss the potential use of SNS in a hazard-prone area such as New Orleans and to further understand crucial considerations in the use of this technology for emergency management.

In exploring how Social Networking Sites may help foster community resilience, this paper examines how such sites facilitate communication and action during the mitigation, preparedness, response, and recovery stages of a disaster. The hypothesis proposed is that social networking sites reinforce social networks by facilitating communication and enabling collaborative action, creating more resilient communities in areas exposed to hazards. The barriers to implementation and use of social networking technology by vulnerable populations are also considered. Finally, the paper examines how such technology may be leveraged to provide communities with a robust tool to increase community resilience.

UNDERSTANDING VULNERABILITY AND BUILDING COMMUNITY RESILIENCE

Framework

In order to effectively use Social Networking Sites for emergency management at the community level, it is first necessary to understand social organization and how community networks

communicate risk. By understanding how a community functions and the networks of individuals, families, and groups that govern behavior within a community, one can begin to search for ways to build social capital and community capacity (Mancini, Bowen, Ware, & Martin, 2007).

The framework used for understanding community networks and resiliency is *Social Organization Theory* (Mancini et al., 2007). This theory focuses on the "collection of values, norms, processes, and behavior patterns within a community that organize, facilitate, and constrain interactions among community members" (Mancini et al., 2007, p. 5). Social Organization Theory provides a framework for improving weaknesses within the system, with networks providing the "context for the development of social capital and for building community capacity" (Mancini et al., 2007, p. 10). Thus, tools that reinforce strong networks increase community capacity, thereby building community resilience.

Community capacity comes from the "shared responsibility, collective competence, and assumptions" that exist within a community (Mancini et al., 2007, p. 14). In times of crisis, how a community builds its capacity depends on the existence of robust networks and social capital, including "information, reciprocity, and trust" that form within community networks (Mancini et al., 2007, p. 13). The need to communicate trusted information is critical during emergencies (Manoj & Hubenko Baker, 2007, p. 52). Increased social capital, in the form of trusted information, helps foster a collective recognition of risk and the impetus to mitigate it. In communities with resilient capacity, networks provide for collective action to mitigate, prepare, respond, and recover from disasters.

In examining community networks, one must distinguish between formal and informal networks. Formal networks include government agencies and established organizations; informal networks, on the other hand, "comprise a web of relationships with friends, neighbors, and work associates"

(Mancini et al., 2007, p. 11), and are therefore more difficult to map. The utility of SNS comes from their ability to facilitate information flow through both formal and informal networks. If a person is connected to friends and neighbors through a website, he or she can easily communicate information horizontally through website postings or messages. Formal networks, such as local emergency preparedness departments, can communicate vertically with greater ease, transmitting information down along their network of constituents. This ability of SNS to communicate critical information through formal and informal channels may help build the capacity of a community and increase its ability to withstand disasters.

COMMUNITY VULNERABILITY AND RESILIENCE

In order to build community resilience, it is first necessary to understand what factors determine community vulnerability. In discussing community vulnerability generally, this paper borrows the *Community and Regional Resilience* report's definition of vulnerability as the "pre-event, inherent characteristics or qualities of systems that create the potential for harm or differential ability to recover following an event" (Cutter et al., 2008, p. 2). Vulnerability is influenced by interaction of the physical environment, built environment, and social characteristics that exist within a community (Mileti, 1999), and varies between communities. Resilience is measured by a community's ability to take necessary steps to mitigate its risk, and to respond to and recover quickly from an event (Cutter et al., 2008).

Limitations exist in our ability to reduce the vulnerability stemming from our physical environments. While coastal restoration projects and environmental conservation may help minimize physical dangers, populations situated along coastal regions, floodplains, or fault lines experience a certain inherent level of vulnerability.

The risk of the physical environment interacts with the built environment of roads, bridges, and buildings (Mileti, 1999). The built environment for populations inhabiting areas prone to risk in the physical environment must increasingly be made to withstand strains. This built environment can be well-constructed and engineered to a high level of sustainability, as the Netherlands demonstrated with its "Deltawerken" system of dams and barriers built to hold back the North Sea. In contrast, the breakdown of the built environment was evident in the levee failures in New Orleans during Hurricane Katrina. As the built system of public utilities, transportation systems, communication networks, and buildings becomes increasingly dense and complex, the potential for catastrophic interactions with physical hazards also increases (Mileti, 1999).

The interaction of the physical and built environments with the social characteristics of individuals determines a community's vulnerability assessment (Mileti, 1999). Individual vulnerability is influenced by a variety of indicators, which can be classified generally as either demographic or socio-economic, with an understanding that the vulnerability indicators often intersect or overlap. Vulnerability indicators, as gathered by the U.S. Census Bureau, include:

- Senior population, 65 years and over, as percentage of total population *(Demographic)*
- Children under 5 years, as percentage of total population *(Demographic)*
- Foreign-born, as percentage of total population *(Demographic)*
- Non-English speaking, as percentage of civilian noninstitutionalized population 5 years and over *(Demographic)*
- Disabled population, as percentage of civilian noninstitutionalized population 5 years and over *(Demographic)*
- Single-headed households with children, as percentage of total family households *(Socio-economic)*

- Renter-occupied housing, as percentage of all occupied housing units *(Socio-economic)*
- Less than ninth-grade education, as percentage of persons 25 years and over *(Socio-economic)*
- Unemployed, as percentage of civilian population in labor force *(Socio-economic)*
- Individuals below poverty level *(Socio-economic)*
- No vehicles available *(Socio-economic)*

The most effective use of SNS for emergency management should be tailored to address the unique demographic and socio-economic vulnerabilities which arise in each community. For example, the outreach techniques that would best serve younger, Hispanic residents in the Mid-City neighborhood of New Orleans will likely not be the same as those targeting older, disabled residents in the Lakeview neighborhood. Vulnerability is complex and efforts to address vulnerability in multiple communities should reflect that complexity.

In order to increase the resilience of local populations deemed more vulnerable to risk, information must be provided in a way that is easily understood by at-risk demographic groups. For example, if a community has a high percentage of elderly residents, steps should be taken to provide greater usability in the face of sensory or cognitive impairments (Wu, Preece, Shneiderman, Jaeger, & Qu, 2007). This may mean tailoring SNS to include information in large print for elderly residents, translated into the native languages of local immigrant groups, and transmitted through appropriate alternative means for the disabled.

Socio-economic vulnerability indicators must be similarly taken into consideration when attempting to increase the resilience of a community using SNS. If a large percentage of the population is without Internet access, attempts should be made to provide access and computer training

through community centers, libraries, and community technology centers (Kiefer et al., 2008). While providing such aid requires resources from local governments or nonprofits, it is preferable to protect and prepare communities in advance, rather than face a community with even higher levels of vulnerability following a disaster.

An individual's connectedness to community networks is a key component of community resilience, along with such factors as economic development, social capital, and community competence (Norris et al., 2007). The following is a proposed list of resilience indicators that would measure the ability of a community to mitigate its risk, respond effectively, and recover quickly (adapted from Goodman et al., 1998):

- Number of active community organizations, such as neighborhood associations or faith-based centers, per capita
- Percentage of the population belonging to community organizations
- Education levels (as an indicator of community resources and skills)
- Rate of home ownership within community
- Percentage of population that is native
- Forums for community dialogue, such as community centers, newsletters, or websites
- Collective recognition of risks to community
- Percentage of households with Internet access (or other forms of social media)
- Percentage of the population with access to health care
- Diversity of local economy

Strong informal and formal networks are crucial to the resilience of a community at all stages of a disaster, as information is shared by community members during preparedness, response, recovery, and mitigation. In their ability to facilitate communication along these networks,

Social Networking Sites represent a promising development in emergency management and may be further leveraged to support resilient communities.

COMMUNICATION OF RISK

Communication of risk remains a critical component in determining how a community chooses to protect itself. If citizens receive unclear and misinformed messages concerning their risk, they are less likely to develop appropriate preparedness, response, recovery, and mitigation plans (Mileti, 1999). In order to use SNS to help individuals make smart decisions at each stage of a disaster, examination of communication networks and behavior is needed to understand how people interpret and internalize warnings, and then choose to act.

Effective communication of risk involves more than simply broadcasting hazard information and assuming citizens will react appropriately (Mileti, 1999; Botterell & Addams-Moring, 2007). In communicating risk, "variations in the source, channel, and receiver of the message and also the impediments to information processing..." must be considered (Mileti, 1999, p. 141). Mileti (1999) outlines the stages individuals go through in deciding to heed a hazard warning:

1. Hearing the warning
2. Believing that the warning is credible
3. Confirming that the threat does exist
4. Personalizing the warning and confirming that others are heeding it
5. Determining whether protective action is needed
6. Determining whether protection is feasible
7. Determining what protective action to take and taking it

At the first stage in communicating risk, many technologies are utilized to spread the warning of an impending hazard. Currently, television and radio are the most widely used technologies capable of transmitting hazard information to a large percentage of the population at risk (Kiefer et al., 2008). However, warning systems have expanded to include websites, blogs, and wikis in recent years (Botterell & Addams-Moring, 2007). As Internet use grows and individuals increasingly rely on online information, the utility of SNS in spreading warnings also increases. With cell phones now capable of Internet access, individuals may receive and communicate warnings even when they are not at home or able to access traditional means of communication (Palen, Hiltz & Liu, 2007).

The second stage of risk communication represents another challenge, in which citizens must believe that the warning is to be trusted. A warning becomes more credible if it is received through multiple sources and channels. Distrust of government officials among vulnerable populations may discourage them from heeding a hazard warning. The utility of SNS at this stage becomes clear, as such sites can create bottom-up, top-down and horizontal communication of warnings. Government officials could use SNS to communicate information from the top down, spreading official warnings to their constituents, while neighbors and churches could also disseminate the warnings to their fellow residents, creating more widespread communication through multiple sources and channels that may be more trusted.

At the third stage, in which residents must confirm that the threat does in fact exist, creating collective risk awareness is key. Again, SNS may help in communicating information regarding a threat to a community. As communication is facilitated through the use of SNS, collective risk awareness could be created more easily within the community as members share information with one another.

In personalizing the warning and confirming that others are heeding it, SNS may be most helpful. Social Networking Sites could allow users to update their personal information to show they have received the warning. As this information becomes visible to other members of the community, it will help confirm that others are heeding warnings and reacting appropriately.

At the fifth, sixth, and seventh stages, in which individuals determine whether protective action is needed, what action is feasible, and then take needed action, SNS could also be useful. SNS could help communicate preparedness and evacuation plans, as individuals post messages to let family, friends, and neighbors know their personal action plans. SNS could also facilitate protective action, such as communication information regarding city-assisted evacuation plans or coordinating ride shares out of the area at risk.

While examining the possible benefits of leveraging SNS, one must also consider the barriers to implementing such technology. Access to web-based networking systems remains a challenge for the most vulnerable members of society, including those with low socio-economic status, the elderly, the disabled, and recent immigrants. As discussed above, ways to provide greater access to technology given demographic and socio-economic vulnerabilities are possible. Additional avenues for expanding access should be explored in further research, keeping in mind that such technology represents just one of many tools to increase resilience and should complement, not replace, existing strategies to increase community capacity (Botterell & Addams-Moring, 2007).

THE USE OF TECHNOLOGY IN EMERGENCY MANAGEMENT

The use of technology has played a significant role in emergency management, with tools designed for information prioritization, decision support, mapping, and the creation of a common operating picture (Carver & Turoff, 2007). While these tools have been utilized by emergency responders (Waugh & Tierney, 2007), technology use has remained largely based on hierarchical communi-

cation of risk (Botterell & Addams-Moring, 2007; Mendonca, Jefferson, & Harrald, 2007) instead of taking on an interactive role that would enable the community to reduce its vulnerability.

The use of collaborative technologies that incorporate community members in the emergency management process requires careful consideration. The willingness to share information in an emergency is critical, and trust must be established between users to ensure credibility (Manoj & Hubenko Baker, 2007; Golbeck, 2008b). Furthermore, such technologies "must be affordable, available, and applicable during day-to-day life in order to ensure that they will be used during a crisis" (Manoj & Hubenko Baker, 2007, p. 52). Tailoring applications so as to encourage collaboration between emergency managers and the public (Kiefer et al., 2008) and providing easy exchange of updates, pictures, and videos (Carver & Turoff, 2007) can further increase the successful use of technology in emergency management. Collaborative communication technologies, such as SNS, are well-suited to the complex and interdependent response systems that emerge in disasters (Comfort et al., 2004; Manoj & Hubenko Baker, 2007).

EXPERT INTERVIEWS

As part of this study of SNS use for emergency management, expert interviews were conducted with relevant academics. Survey participants were asked open-ended questions relating to community resilience, risk, and the utility of social networking technology to build resilience. Participants were also asked to rank in order of importance the sources they believed were currently most used sources from which communities receive and communicate critical information, and what they predicted those sources would be in the next 5-10 years.

The interviews proved to be a valuable tool in evaluating the utility of SNS and critical considerations when implementing such technology. While television and radio were consistently ranked as the most important current sources from which communities at high risk receive critical information, respondents believed that the Internet and phone/text messaging would become prominent in the coming 5-10 years. Respondents overwhelmingly ranked phone/text messaging as the most utilized technology to communicate critical information.

The interviewees also identified the local associations they believed were most important in determining a community's resilience. Churches, community groups, schools, and local businesses were listed as being influential in creating strong communities. One survey participant also cautioned that the importance of these associations "differs based on social class and race."

When asked to evaluate the usefulness of SNS in building resilient communities, respondents pointed to the growing preponderance of mobile phones with Internet capabilities, which allow individuals to easily receive and update personal information. One survey participant said she believed that "social networking technology has huge potential and will come to rival television" in its ability to communicate critical information. In identifying potential barriers to the effectiveness of SNS, respondents pointed to the weakness of the technical infrastructure in large-scale emergencies and financial constraints that limit access to SNS. The consensus from these expert interviews was that SNS may prove to be a valuable tool in emergency management in the coming years; however, further research is needed to fully determine its utility.

SOCIAL NETWORKING SITES

Social Networking Sites provide a valuable addition to existing means of receiving and communicating critical information in an emergency by providing a forum for collaboration that may strengthen community resilience. Part of the strength of SNS is that they allow for easy com-

munication and collaboration even when users are geographically dispersed (Palen, Hiltz, & Liu, 2007). This represents a serious advantage for emergency management, in which residents may be scattered following an evacuation, and can facilitate recovery efforts such as coordinating volunteers or sharing rebuilding information.

Existing models of Social Networking Sites provide valuable lessons for how such tools may be effectively used. One example, the Blacksburg Electronic Village (BEV), was developed in 1993 to serve the community of Blacksburg, Virginia. The BEV sought to "enhance the quality of people's lives by electronically linking residents of a community to each other" (Wiencko, 1993/1994). Utilizing Virginia Tech's expertise to help with training, community outreach, and maintenance, the BEV made itself a test case of community connectivity, with 87% of residents linked through an online community network only five years after its inception (Cohill, 2000).

The BEV was an early example of how websites could be harnessed to enhance community communication and it provided some key lessons to ensure success of similar projects. These lessons included (Cohill, 2000):

- Engage the entire community
- Provide tailored applications
- Focus on people & interactions
- Implement new services on timely basis
- Provide cheap/free Internet service
- Leverage university resources
- Publicize project as source of computer literacy and free computer access
- Make it a source for local information & services
- Work with public schools & library system

Another example of a proposed SNS that would be explicitly used for emergencies has been started through the University of Maryland. Researchers there developed Community Response Grids (CRG) on which "residents could report incidents in seconds, receive emergency information, and request resident-to-resident assistance" (Shneiderman & Preece, 2007). This site increases community capacity while filling gaps in the existing 911 phone systems and information-sharing media like television and radio (Borrell, 2007). CRG's provide a prime example of an SNS that would allow emergency coordinators to gather and disseminate critical information, while also providing a forum for community collaboration.

SOCIAL NETWORKING SITE MODEL

Given examination of existing research on social vulnerability, resilience, and risk communication, a model Social Networking Site for emergency management includes a wide-ranging network of stakeholders and considerations. SNS that could be used to promote community resilience in the face of risk should provide a robust means of reinforcing existing communication networks, create new lines of communication, and facilitate critical information flow (Carver & Turoff, 2007). Contrary to existing use of SNS by emergency managers, such as FEMA's links to Facebook, use of these sites should move beyond top-down dissemination of information to a more collaborative approach.

Online SNS would be primarily used during the mitigation, preparedness, and recovery stages of a disaster. Power outages and overburdened networks may limit the utility of SNS during the response phase for individuals in the disaster area. However, SNS could allow those outside the affected area to receive information concerning the communities at risk and communicate outside information that could be retrieved once power is restored.

The ability to link SNS to mobile phones, text messaging, cameras, and GPS makes it an especially attractive technology for emergency management (Palen, Hiltz, & Liu, 2007). By opening up information sharing to individuals as well as emergency officials, citizens play a larger role in protecting their own communities.

In considering the stakeholders, this model focuses on existing social networks and their interactions. The SNS would begin with the individual, who is then considered part of a local community. This individual would also interact with local stakeholders such as universities, local businesses and employers, libraries and community technology centers, public schools, faith-based communities, nonprofits and community organizations, and local government and emergency response officials. The stakeholder roles are defined as:

- **Individuals:** responsible for becoming active members of the SNS and maintaining personal profiles detailing their emergency plans
- **Community:** responsible for maintaining a neighborhood group with community mitigation, preparedness, response, and recovery plans and communicating risk information. The community group should also be used to communicate basic information concerning neighborhood events, trash collection, etc. so that it becomes a regularly visited community resource. Administration and maintenance could be organized through the existing Community Emergency Response Teams (CERT), which already provide education and support for neighborhoods.
- **Universities:** responsible for providing technical assistance in the creation and maintenance of the SNS. Local universities also could help promote the site and offer training to community residents.
- **Public Schools:** responsible for promoting computer literacy among students and promoting the SNS to students and parents.
- **Libraries and Computer Technology Centers:** responsible for providing computer access and training to those without

home computers; can also be used to help promote the site and offer training to community residents.

- **Faith-based Communities:** responsible for leveraging community support and promoting use of the SNS to ensure the safety of their members.

- **Local Businesses & Employers:** responsible for promoting SNS and providing financial and/or technical assistance.

- **Nonprofits & Community Organizations:** responsible for leveraging community support and promoting use of the SNS to ensure the safety of their members; can also be used to help promote the site and offer training to community residents.

- **Local Government and Emergency Response Personnel:** responsible for maintaining a city group with city mitigation, preparedness, response, and recovery plans and communicating risk information. The city group should also be used to communicate such basic information as city events, service provision, public transit, etc. so that it becomes a regularly visited community resource.

The design of the Social Networking Site would be based on individual profiles, with group profiles for community and interest groups that individuals could join. For example, an individual living in the Mid-City neighborhood of New Orleans would have his / her personal profile, detailing his / her location, emergency plans, emergency contact information, as well as interests and contact information. This individual would belong to the Mid-City neighborhood group and would receive or send any alerts specifically affecting that area of the city. The members of the Mid-City group would also be members of the larger New Orleans group and would receive and communicate alerts affecting the City as a whole. These alerts could come directly from the Office of Emergency Preparedness, the Mayor, or local response officials.

Individuals could also form interest groups, such as virtual representations of their religious congregations, sports teams, or work places.

In considering how to encourage residents to utilize SNS for emergency management, outreach efforts should be made to grow membership (Golbeck, 2008a). This can be continued through a public awareness campaign with local businesses, churches, community organizations, etc. until a tipping point is reached in which SNS membership is widespread. Furthermore, consideration must be given to the SNS design, so that it encourages connections, communication, and collaboration (Golbeck, 2008b).

The SNS would help build stronger communities by enabling information sharing and communication, while also building collective risk awareness. This model allows for bottom-up, horizontal, and top-down communication, thus enabling more effective risk communication. By facilitating communication through multiple users and channels, SNS will enable residents to receive warnings, personalize the warning and their response to risk, confirm that other SNS users are heeding warnings, and take action. These sites should also be linked to email and cell phones, so that emergency alerts could be broadcast through multiple channels.

To be most effective, an emergency management SNS should become a hub of information for residents (Shneiderman & Preece, 2007). In order for such a site to have traction, it needs to include the entire community, provide easy computer and internet access points, and communicate information even in non-emergencies, such as the location of local events, school calendars, how to access government services, and maps of bus routes (Cohill, 2000). By promoting needed services and information, facilitating access, and encouraging user-input, an SNS should become an ingrained community resource, helping to build trust among its users and bolster community resilience (Shneiderman & Preece, 2007).

LIMITATIONS

While Social Networking Sites have remarkable potential to enhance emergency management, limitations exist. An initial concern is how to address issues of privacy and trust in an online context (Golbeck, 2008b). In order for SNS to be successful, users must feel confident that their personal information will not be exploited through the site, and that the information they receive is trustworthy (Golbeck, 2008b). The threat of misinformation spread through the site is of concern when allowing information sharing from unofficial sources (Palen, Hiltz, & Liu, 2007). In order to address these concerns, SNS should not share personal user information with third parties and verification procedures should be utilized to track information sources.

A related problem in using SNS is the threat of information overload, in which an explosion of imprecise information follows a disaster (Manoj & Hubenko Baker, 2007; Mendonca, Jefferson, & Harrald, 2007; Carver & Turoff, 2007). To deal with this potential limitation, technological applications should be implemented to sort data by relevance. Users could potentially search through SNS postings by keywords, for example pulling up information that is only relevant to their neighborhood.

A further concern is the weakness of existing communication infrastructure in the wake of widespread disasters. As with other forms of communication, including mobile phones and television, SNS would not be accessible during widespread disasters like Hurricane Katrina. In the case of infrastructure failure, the hope is that SNS would help reinforce the strong social networks that would increase a community's resilience, while also providing redundancy through multiple internet servers. Luckily, widespread infrastructure breakdowns are rare, meaning SNS remain useful in most emergencies. In addition, technological advances will likely improve the reliability of Internet access (Shneiderman & Preece, 2007).

Lastly, barriers to SNS access must be considered. As discussed previously, the limitations of vulnerable populations must be kept in mind, adapting SNS to better reach these communities. While Internet access may still be limited by socio-economic status, the wide prevalence of mobile phones allows for connectivity via text messaging or phone calls. As mobile phones are increasingly equipped with Internet access, the hope is that the access to SNS will widen (Palen, Hiltz, & Liu, 2007) among those most vulnerable citizens.

CONCLUSION AND FUTURE RESEARCH

This paper has provided an overview of the expanded use of Social Networking Sites for emergency management and proposes that SNS should be explored as a means of building community resilience. Further research is needed to fully gauge the utility of such sites and the means to most effectively develop them for emergency management.

A necessary step in utilizing such technology will be to survey individuals from communities at risk and encourage user input. An in-depth study of citizen technological capacity and receptiveness to SNS for emergency management should be commissioned and additional expert and practitioner interviews should be conducted. Additional consideration should be given to enabling greater access to those members of society currently unable to use SNS technology. Efforts must be made to leverage private, public, and university resources in helping administer and moderate a community-based Social Networking Site.

The use of Social Networking Sites represents an opportunity to expand public participation in emergency management. This expansion from the traditional hierarchical model of emergency management will allow for needed collaboration and encourage citizens to play an active role in ensuring their own community's resilience

REFERENCES

Borrell, B. (2007, February 15). Type 911.gov. *Technology Review*. Retrieved February 1, 2009, from http://www.technologyreview.com/communications/18196/page1/

Botterell, A., & Addams-Moring, R. (2007). Public Warning in the Networked Age: Open Standards to the Rescue? *Communications of the ACM, 50*(3), 59–60. doi:10.1145/1226736.1226767

Carver, L., & Turoff, M. (2007). Human-Computer Interactions: The Human and the computer as a team in emergency management information systems. *Communications of the ACM, 50*(3), 33–38. doi:10.1145/1226736.1226761

Carvin, A. (2008). *Hurricane Gustav Digital Support Brigade*. Retrieved July 27, 2009, from http://www.facebook.com/group.php?gid=25689101658

Caulfield, B., & Karmali, N. (2008). Mumbai: Twitter's Moment. *Forbes Magazine*. Retrieved April 20, 2009, from http://www.forbes.com/2008/11/28/mumbai-twitter-sms-tech-internet-cx_bc_kn_1128mumbai.html

Centers for Disease Control and Prevention. (2009). *Social Media at the CDC*. Retrieved July 27, 2009, from http://www.cdc.gov/socialmedia/

Cohill, A. M. (2000). *Building e-communities: Getting everyone connected*. Address to the Governor's Commission on Information Technology, Richmond, VA.

Comfort, L., Ko, K., & Zagorecki, A. (2004). Coordinating in Rapidly Evolving Disaster Response Systems: The role of information. *The American Behavioral Scientist, 48*, 295–313. doi:10.1177/0002764204268987

Cutter, S., Barnes, L., & Berry, M. Burton, C., Evans, E., Tate, E., et al. (2008). *Community and regional resilience: Perspectives from hazards, disasters, and emergency management* (CARRI Research Rep. No. 1). Oak Ridge, TN: Community and Regional Resilience Initiative, Oak Ridge National Laboratory.

Ehrenberg, L. A., & Hirsch, S. E. (1996). *The war in American culture: Society and consciousness during World War II*. Chicago: University of Chicago Press.

FEMA. (2009, April 8). *Acting Administrator Ward Speaks At The National Hurricane Conference*. Retrieved July 27, 2009, from http://www.fema.gov/news/newsrelease.fema?id=47933

Gertz, E. (2005, September 5). KatrinaWiki, Katrina PeopleFinder: Distributed Technology Responses to Disaster. *World Changing*. Retrieved April 15, 2009, from http://www.worldchanging.com/archives/003437.html

Golbeck, J. (2008a, December). *The Dynamics of Web-based Social Networks: Membership, Relationships, and Change*. Retrieved July 27, 2009, from http://www.cs.umd.edu/localphp/hcil/tech-reports-search.php?number=2008-36

Golbeck, J. (2008b, December). *Trust and Nuanced Profile Similarity in Online Social Networks*. Retrieved July 27, 2009, from http://www.cs.umd.edu/localphp/hcil/tech-reports-search.php?number=2008-39

Goodman, R. M., Speers, M. A., Mcleroy, K., & Fawcett, S. (1998). Identifying and Defining Dimensions of Community Capacity to Provide a Basis for Measurement. *Health Education & Behavior, 25*, 258–277. doi:10.1177/109019819802500303

Kiefer, J. J., Mancini, J. A., Morrow, B. H., Gladwin, H., & Stewart, T. A. (2008). *Providing access to resilience-enhancing technologies for disadvantaged communities and vulnerable populations* (CARRI: PARET Rep.). Oak Ridge, TN: Community & Regional Resilience Initiative, Institute for Advanced Biometrics and Social Systems Studies, Oak Ridge National Laboratory.

Mancini, J. A., Bowen, G. L., Martin, J. A., & Ware, W. B. (2003). *The community connections index*. Paper presented at the Hawaii International Conference on Social Sciences, Honolulu, HI.

Mancini, J. A., Bowen, G. L., Ware, W. B., & Martin, J. A. (2007). *Engagement, participation, and community efficacy: Insights into social organization*. Paper presented at Hawaii International Meeting on Social Sciences, Honolulu HI.

Manjoo, F. (2009, April, 10). The reluctant Twitterer's dilemma. *Slate Magazine*. Retrieved April 10, 2009, from http://www.slate.com/id/2215829/

Manoj, B. S., & Hubenko Baker, A. (2007). Communication Challenges in Emergency Response. *Communications of the ACM, 50*(3), 51–53. doi:10.1145/1226736.1226765

Mendonca, D., Jefferson, T., & Harrald, J. (2007). Collaborative Adhocracies and Mix and Match Technologies in Emergency Management. *Communications of the ACM, 50*(3), 45–49. doi:10.1145/1226736.1226764

Mileti, D. S. (1999). *Disasters by Design*. Washington, DC: Joseph Henry Press.

Norris, F. H., Stevens, S. P., Pfefferbaum, B., Wyche, K. F., & Pfefferbaum, R. L. (2007). Community Resilience as a Metaphor, Theory, Set of Capacities, and Strategy for Disaster Readiness. *American Journal of Community Psychology, 41*, 127–150. doi:10.1007/s10464-007-9156-6

Obama, B. H. (2009, March 28). Weekly Address: Crisis and service. *White House Blog*. Retrieved March 28, 2009, from http://www.whitehouse.gov/blog/09/03/27/Weekly-Address-Crisis-and-Service/

Palen, L., Hiltz, R. S., & Liu, S. B. (2007). ONLINE FORUMS SUPPORTING GRASSROOTS PARTICIPATION in Emergency Preparedness and Response. *Communications of the ACM, 50*(3), 54–58. doi:10.1145/1226736.1226766

Pidgeon, N., Kasperson, R., & Slovick, P. (Eds.). (2003). *The social amplification of risk*. Cambridge, UK: Cambridge University Press.

Shneiderman, B., & Preece, J. (2007, February 16). 911.gov. *Science, 315*, 944. doi:10.1126/science.1139088

Waugh, W. L., & Tierney, K. (Eds.). (2007). *Emergency management: Principles and practice for local government*. Washington, DC: ICMA Press.

White, C., Plotnick, L., Kushma, J., Hiltz, S. R., & Turoff, M. (2009). An Online Social Network for Emergency Management. In J. Landgren, U. Nulden, & B. Van de Walle (Eds.), *Proceedings of the 6th International ISCRAM Conference*.

Wiencko, J. A. (1993/1994). The Blacksburg electronic village. *Bulletin of the American Society for Information Science*.

Wu, P., Preece, J., Shneiderman, B., Jaeger, P., & Qu, Y. (2007). *Community Response Grids for Older Adults: Motivations, Usability, and Sociability*. Retrieved March 28, 2009, from http://www.cs.umd.edu/localphp/hcil/tech-reports-search.php?number=2007-07

This work was previously published in International Journal of Information Systems for Crisis Response Management, Volume 2, Issue 1, edited by Murray E. Jennex, pp. 24-36, copyright 2010 by IGI Publishing (an imprint of IGI Global).

Chapter 4
A Framework to Identify Best Practices:
Social Media and Web 2.0 Technologies in the Emergency Domain

Connie White
Jacksonville State University, USA

Linda Plotnick
Jacksonville State University, USA

ABSTRACT

Social media is used in a variety of domains, including emergency management. However, the question of which technologies are most appropriate for a given emergency remains open. We present a framework of dimensions of emergencies that can assist in selecting appropriate social media for an emergency situation. Social media is not a panacea but can be used effectively given the proper functions available from the particular services provided by each of the Web 2.0 technologies available. The main objective of this paper is to identify the best practices for social media to leverage its ability given the complexities that coincide with events. This is a conceptual paper based on the results of preliminary studies involving group interactions with emergency professionals with various backgrounds. In addition, emergency management students who are professionals in the field followed by another interview soliciting information from information systems scientist were surveyed. We found that each situation called forth various dimensions where only sub phases of the stated dimension may be used given the task type derived from the event characteristics. This lays a foundation upon which a more formal approach can be taken to help tame the social media mania into a manageable set of 'best practices' from which emergencies can be managed more effectively given Web 2.0 technologies and social collaborative online tools.

DOI: 10.4018/978-1-4666-0167-3.ch004

INTRODUCTION

Social media has been used by the public for a number of years to link people together but more recently, has also been identified as playing a role in aiding communications for emergency management (White, Plotnick, Kushma, Hiltz, & Turoff, 2009). Emergency management stakeholders have begun to experiment and explore possible uses that can help support and expedite the diverse needs of various stakeholders (Plotnick, White, & Plummer, 2009). The United States government has acknowledged the potential use of social media for communications as a serious tool to use to help manage day to day operations (Collins, 2009). In mid-2009, the Department of Homeland Security Office for Interoperability and Compatibility, Office of Emergency Communications, FEMA National Preparedness Directorate and the Center for Homeland Defense and Security hosted "The Ogma Workshop: Exploring the Policy and Strategy Implications of Web 2.0 on the Practice of Homeland Security" (Federal News Radio, 2009) which explored these issues. Although this use is catching on and its use confirmed by the workshop participants, after conducting a broad but non-exhaustive literature review, we found no studies conducted testing the effectiveness of attempts to reach various goals sought by these departments. We found little guidance for such efforts in general, either. There are only a handful of lessons learned where others can mimic particular uses of these Web 2.0 technologies and with confidence in their effectiveness. "The learning, in this case, is from those on the front lines already using the technologies, says Essid" (Federal News Radio, 2009).

"Best practice" is a term used by emergency management professions and is defined as "a technique method, process, activity, incentive or reward that is believed to be more effective at delivering a particular outcome than any other technique, method, process, etc. The idea is that with proper processes, checks, and testing, a desired outcome can be delivered with fewer problems and unforeseen complications. Best practices can also be defined as the most efficient (least amount of effort) and effective (best results) way of accomplishing a task, based on repeatable procedures that have proven themselves over time for large numbers of people" (Wikipedia). We identify a set of dimensions that, together, identify the numerous unique states that can exist given an all hazards approach to comprehensive emergency management. From these dimensions, a framework is created that describes the situations which can then be used to identify the appropriate social media to use for that situation.

The dimensions of an emergency situation identified that need to be considered when choosing social media are: the size of the event; the phase of the emergency; the stakeholders and level(s) of government involved; social convergence; time phases; and spatial zone (geographic area impacted). Each of these dimensions needs to be considered both alone and in concert with the other dimensions. For example, it is insufficient to merely identify the stakeholders involved when selecting social media. The phase of the emergency, for example, will also influence what media are feasible to use as infrastructure integrity may vary depending upon the current phase.

This work is important because it gives a foundation upon which social media can be strategically identified for particular uses. The level of security of the data may be an important factor or not, depending upon the situation. This type of information, when analyzed against the needs provided in the dimensions identified, helps guide which technology best fits the present state. But questions remain: what are they really good for, how do you reach your target market, and how do researchers go about considering when these systems will prove effective or possibly destructive? Workshop hosts stated that prior to the Ogma Workshop, "We came across a lot of good examples of, say, YouTube for example, and the Division of Emergency Management in Florida uses that to do staff situational reports. FEMA has established Twitter accounts to send out updates. In Washington DC, they monitored Twitter and Facebook during the Inauguration to see if there was situational information that they weren't obtaining through their more formal sources" (Federal News Radio, 2009). There is such an explosion of growth in social media usage that it's premature to try to predict the future. While social media has been adopted for uses that benefit society, other uses are possible as well. The dark side of social media is raising its ugly head as terrorist groups are finding the same benefits as others in its use (Lamoreaux, 2009) and cyber attacks have proven numerous lately (Government Computer News, 2009).

We describe how the literature and workshop discussions inform the identification of dimensions of an emergency that can guide social media selection. We discuss each dimension describing issues that could be considered during various situations and corresponding task types based on present research. A matrix is offered to help identify each dimension as it relates to the others. We close with some research questions that require further investigation.

BACKGROUND: SOCIAL MEDIA

Social media is defined as "A category of sites that is based on user participation and user-generated content" (searchengine.watch.com/define). Social media include social networking sites, social bookmarking sites, social news sites (e.g., Digg), etc. We also consider that technology is used presently in day-to-day activities and it's this same technology that is the primary basis for input/output of data and information. Social networking sites have been used in a variety of domains including emergency management and have the potential to enrich and expand capabili-

ties for interaction in general, and collaboration in particular, by providing a platform in which social networks can be built and expanded. We adopt a descriptive definition of a social network as "links from people to other people, groups or information objects. Such objects may be messages, photos, videos, wall postings, notifications, current activities, events, widgets, etc. Such links may be created by intelligent agents or by the user" (White et al., 2009).

MOTIVATION

White et al. (2009) and Plotnick et al. (2009) describe the results of surveying emergency professionals to ascertain the functionality they felt is important and the concerns they had for use of social networking sites (SNS) in the emergency domain. Although results were mixed, the chart below (Figure 1, Plotnick et al., 2009) shows the ranking of applicability of a SNS in emergency management.

Which emergency management functions seem to hold the most promise for the use of online social networks? Please put a 1 for the most important application to which such a system might be used. A 2 for the next most important and continue until you don't feel any remaining potential application is suitable for this technology. The scale went from 1 – 10.

Clearly, not all functionality is appropriate for all emergencies, nor for all phases of an emergency. For example, damage assessment and disaster intelligence is not done before the occurrence of the emergency. Therefore, there is a need to provide a framework that describes an emergency in such a way that the appropriate social media (and functionality) can be selected at any given time, in any emergency. In this paper we propose such a framework.

Figure 1. Ranking of applicability of a SNS in emergency management

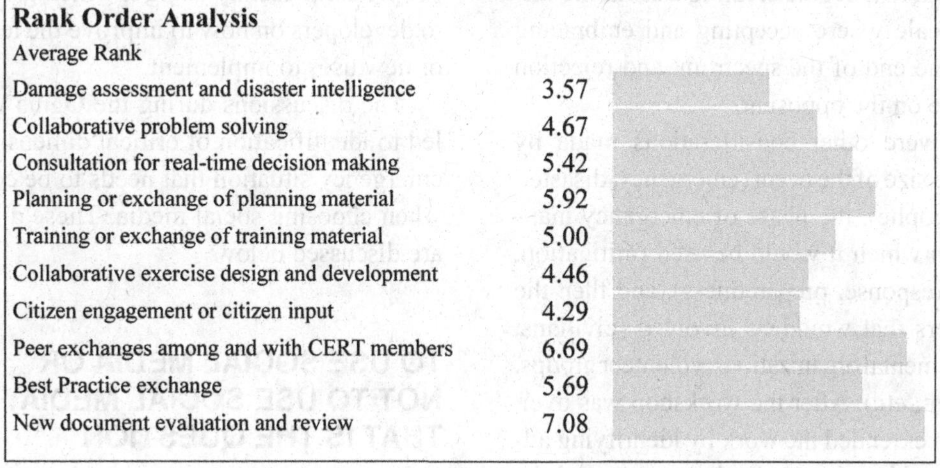

Rank Order Analysis
Average Rank

Damage assessment and disaster intelligence	3.57
Collaborative problem solving	4.67
Consultation for real-time decision making	5.42
Planning or exchange of planning material	5.92
Training or exchange of training material	5.00
Collaborative exercise design and development	4.46
Citizen engagement or citizen input	4.29
Peer exchanges among and with CERT members	6.69
Best Practice exchange	5.69
New document evaluation and review	7.08

METHODOLOGY

The Ogma Workshop was conducted to explore the policy and strategy implications of Web 2.0 technologies on the practice of Homeland Defense and Security. It was held on the campus of the Naval Postgraduate School in Monterey, California from June 30 through July 1, 2009. The goal of the workshop was to "...develop best practices and lessons learned on where this stuff has worked and how it worked" (Federal News Radio), and then to share that information with others. There were 88 participants with a range of backgrounds covering diverse stakeholder perspectives. Participants were divided into four groups in order to give more focus grouping perspectives. The four groups were referred to as: 1) The Behavioral Scientists 2) The Practitioners 3) Network Science/Media and 4) the Technology Sector.

Key workshop questions were:

- What do we know and see in practice now?
- What requires further study, analysis, and exploration?
- What are the requirements to achieve this?
- What partnerships need to be established?

- What collaborative bodies need to be formed?
- What investments (time, personnel, funding) are required?
- What other types of resources are needed to advance our adoption, understanding and the utility of these new forms of communication?

In a round robin style of group interactions, each single group was paired up once with each other group for cross-disciplinary break-out sessions. A moderator was assigned to each group and had leading questions to help give participants focus. These questions evolved each session. At the end of the workshop, each group was asked to answer sets of questions. It's from these interactions initially that the dimensions arose. However, the authors knew from emergency literature, that other dimensions should to be considered as well.

DIMENSIONS FOR SOCIAL MEDIA IDENTIFIED

During the Ogma workshop, observations were made by various groups. On a strategic level, a consideration was to look at the aspects of using social media to a degree creating a semantic differential scale where accepting and embracing were on one end of the spectrum, and rejection and nonuse on the opposing.

There were other considerations made by groups: the size of the event (emergency, disaster, and catastrophe), the phase of emergency management in which it would be used (mitigation, recovery, response, preparedness), and then the stakeholders that would be involved (civilians, nongovernmental organizations, volunteer groups, government, etc). After the workshop was over, the authors extended the work by identifying additional considerations to further understand the ability and capabilities of how social media can be leveraged for emergency management.

Social media can be a powerful communication tool for emergency management if it's used in a strategic manner which is effective. For example, a department of emergency management can create a Facebook account from which information can be distributed, but what type of information is of interest to the user group? Who is the user group? Dimensions to consider when using social media include the size of the event, the stakeholders that who are the users, the levels of government, the phase of emergency management, social convergence, time phases and spatial zones.

Perspectives of this situation are many and each group needs to be considered as to how social media influences their particular interests. Different perspectives consider various aspects. Practitioners, network and media, behavioralist and the developers of such technology are the stakeholders identified. Each group's perspective is different: while the practitioner wants to use this technology, a behaviorist may evaluate how people are presently using it which gives insight to developers on how to improve the technology or new uses to implement.

The discussions during the Ogma workshop led to identification of critical dimensions of an emergency situation that needs to be considered when choosing social media. These dimensions are discussed below:

TO USE SOCIAL MEDIA OR NOT TO USE SOCIAL MEDIA: THAT IS THE QUESTION

One of the major outcomes of the Ogma workshop was considering the implementation of social media along a scale of total acceptance to total restriction of use. The potential benefits were analyzed along with the potential downfalls of implementation (Figure 2).

Size of Event

Events basically occur on three levels, small, medium and large which are defined as emergencies, disasters and catastrophes (Quarantelli, 2002). Each of these has their own decision making problem types (Skertchly & Skertchly, 2001). For example, some emergencies are routine, have been experienced before and are within the resource limitations of local authorities. On the opposing end, catastrophic events are dynamic and volatile, have not been experienced before and far exceed local, tribal and sometimes state or even national resources (Turoff, Chumer, Van de Walle, & Yao, 2004).

Figure 2. To use or not to use social media

←----------------------------------|----------------------------------→

Reject All   **Use Some**   **Accept Fully**

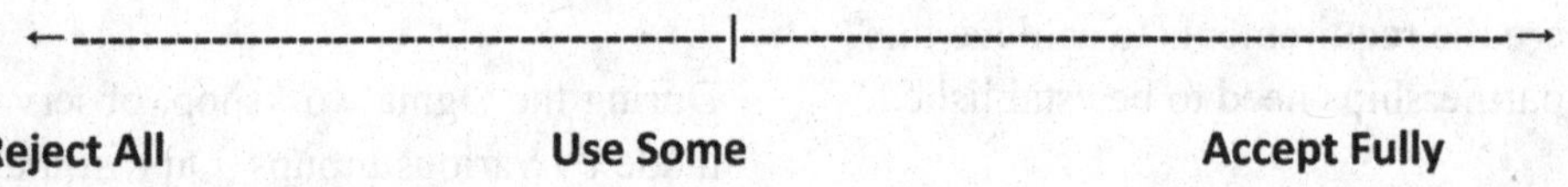

Potential Uses

This shows how social media is used based on the decision making needs of the situation. In the aftermath of a catastrophic event, individuals might be able to send Tweets of information aiding in search and rescue efforts. Civilians could use their cell phones and take pictures of damaged buildings or bridges, uploading this information so that authorities can assess damage more quickly. Each of these sizes of disasters has its own problem types ranging in routine to wicked and hence, has its own set of characteristics which would influence the way people use social media to help emergency management effectively and efficiently.

PHASES OF COMPREHENSIVE EMERGENCY MANAGEMENT

The Washington State Legislature defines comprehensive emergency management as "the preparation for and the carrying out of all emergency functions, other than functions for which the military forces are primarily responsible, to mitigate, prepare for, respond to, and recover from emergencies and disasters, and to aid victims suffering from injury or damage, resulting from disasters caused by all hazards, whether natural, technological, or human caused, and to provide support for search and rescue operations for persons and property in distress" (Washington State Legislature, n.d.). This is the foundation for the definition of the phases of emergency management: mitigation, preparedness, response and recovery. Each phase of emergency management has its own sets of needs (Haddow, Bullock, & Coppola, 2007). Relationships can be built beforehand between people (Plotnick et al., 2009). This can help on a civilian personal preparedness level where neighbors can connect and identify a set of guidelines to help them as a community (White et al., 2009). First responders can meet beforehand

which is a critical step in disaster and catastrophic response (Sutton, Palen, & Shklovski, 2008). Groups can interact and exchange information for policy formations and modifications. These and other such mitigation needs can be fulfilled.

Potential Uses

The Department of Emergency Management in the City of Plano, Texas uses social media with their 'Prepared In Plano' initiative. PreparedInPlano's usage of social media, preparedness is a focus on helping to get survival information and other information that helps identify the needs for the first 72 hours (www.PreparedInPlano.com). They use both Facebook and Twitter to distribute information to fans and followers. This is important as an indicator, a recent study indicated that less than half of all Americans have created a family emergency plan and only half of all Americans have an emergency kit in their homes (Fugate, 2009). This is a strong indication of the need to engage and educate the public as to their responsibilities and needs in preparation for emergencies.

The obvious phase where social media could highly impact is in the response phase. Situational awareness, identification of resources, geographic information sent through smart phones and other mobile devices could expedite response and recovery efforts. However, crucial plans and exercises can be viewed equally important and thus, the uses may be deemed more important for one group versus another.

STAKEHOLDERS INVOLVED

There are many stakeholders involved in emergency management. For example, governmental organizations such as the Department of Homeland Security (DHS), Alabama Department of Emergency Management, and Community Emergency Response Team are beginning to use social media (Collins, 2009). Different countries around the world have different styles of leadership and organizations, but social media use can be tailored to fit the stakeholders involved no matter their geographical origin. Civilians can use social networks to create profiles, meet neighbors, create emergency plans and have them documented for other family members, friends or authorities to use. Volunteer organizations already embrace social media (Plotnick, et al 2009). So much of this technology is free and given it fits the needs of the user, will more likely be used. The Red Cross has local chapters as well as state chapters on Facebook and Twitter. As of the writing of this article, the Center for Disease Control (CDC) has 617,676 followers and is following 76 others. It's this chain of interest that creates a web of information flow between players.

Potential Uses

Social media such as Twitter, when set up strategically, can be used for all kinds of information to be sent between relationship types in the stakeholder environment. For example, 1-to-many or many-to-many, group relationships can be supported by Twitter. These relationships can be supported on various levels:

1. Can be used within a group where members can relate to one another either as individuals or subgroups or any variation of the two.
2. Can be used within group types (subgroups of large organization, local to state)
3. Can be used group to group—groups on any level can interact with other groups

This allows a dynamic aspect to interactivity such that there are no predefined group types and new groups can form, other existing groups can be modified to fit the need of the event.

LEVEL OF GOVERNMENT

Social media can be used differently given the level of government involved be it on the local, tribal, state, national or even international level (Collins, 2009). National groups such as DHS use social media like Twitter and Facebook, RSS feeds, blogs and videos on their website to help distribute information from the heads of government (www.dhs.gov). President Barak Obama has a site www.whitehouse.gov which offers all types of information which users can further drill down on to answer strategic level questions. State level groups such the Alabama Emergency Agency use websites to distribute information. The Alabama Department of Homeland Security www.dhs. alabama.gov has a pilot for other interoperability needs with more secure data for Virtual Alabama. Counties use social media such as Facebook to keep their residents informed. City level officials are critical as they are on the local level. Information can be distributed to anyone who wants to join the county's group page or become a fan of the page so that they receive the information (www.plano.gov).

Potential Uses

Emergency management in Plano, Texas has PreparedInPlano Facebook and Twitter feeds along with a website (www.plano.gov). Facebook is used to send out messages on a daily basis informing their citizens of information that people may or may not find of interest, but is potentially relevant to their needs. Emergency officials post information about local training events, poll citizens for feedback, and offer discussion forums amongst many other functions. Internationally, social media can play a critical role (Herrmann, 2009). Many of the more popular sites support many different languages. Also, given that the Internet is global, the infrastructure already exists upon which people from all the world can collaborate online. Facebook alone supported 63 languages as of the date of this writing, July 28, 2009 (www. google.com).

SOCIAL CONVERGENCE

In designing social media to be used in an emergency, it is not sufficient to just take into account that the public will be active users of the system. How they use the system is critical to understand so that the needs of the various public activities can be met. Hughes et al. (2008), after Fritz and Mathewson (1957), describe seven types of convergent behaviors that the public may engage in on social networks when there is an emergency: helping, being anxious, returning, supporting, mourning, exploiting, and being curious.

We summarize the behaviors and examples of uses of social media described by Hughes et al. (2008) below. Helping behavior is that in which people join together to reach out to help others. For example, Hughes et al. (2008) describe how in the aftermath of the Virginia Tech shootings, Facebook was used by the community to compile a list of fatalities. Being anxious is where people use social media to virtually return to the disaster site in search of information to allay their anxieties. Hughes et al. (2008) tell of how Virginia Tech students monitored their friends IM and Facebook accounts for indicators that the friends were OK. Returning behavior in the physical world is where people return to the site of a disaster to assess losses and salvage property. This is done virtually using social media through such tools as Google maps' images to virtually observe the state of neighborhood and property. People come together in supporting behavior when, for example, in the aftermath of the Virginia Tech shootings tribute pages were created on Facebook Similarly, mourning through social media has been seen as people gather together virtually to mourn the victims.

Exploiting behavior is unfortunately also a fact of life (and not a dimension to be supported by social media). After a disaster merchants have sold commemorative products. Finally, some people converge virtually on social media sites out of curiosity. Yet, Hughes et al. (2008) note that they may then find themselves drawn to engage in other behaviors such as helping.

Each of these behaviors may span phases of an emergency and have different social media needs. For example, helping behavior may be seen in the planning stage of an emergency. People may post on a social media site where resources may be found (e.g., plywood in anticipation of a hurricane). But helping behavior can also be seen during and after the emergency as well. For example, sites on which people can search for the missing and post their own well-being status result in helping behaviors.

TIME PHASES

Time phases are smaller intervals of time that are sub phases of the existing four phases of emergency management: mitigation, preparedness, response, recovery. Killian provides a good description:

1. "**Warning:** the period during which information is available about a probable danger, but before the danger has become immediate, persona, and physically perceivable;
2. **Impact:** the period during which the destructive agent is actually at work;
3. **Emergency:** the post impact period during which rescue, first-aid, emergency medical care, and other emergency tasks are performed;
4. **Recovery:** the period which begins roughly as the emergency crisis passes and during which longer-term activities of reconstruction, rehabilitation, and recovery proceed" (Killian, 2009).

The time phase of the emergency needs to be considered when implementing social media. This is important, for example, immediately after the crisis is when the highest number of responders may be entering the scene. This is also the phase in which the least amount of information is available (Sutton et al., 2008). Damage assessments could be reported more quickly and from a greater number of people, the distribution of resources could be better managed to maximize their scale of operations given the timely and diverse information. It's these particular times of need when information is most needed, but least available, that social media can be play a larger role providing information a new path of communicating where few avenues existed previously. This opens up new opportunities and potential threats which require further exploration.

SPATIAL ZONES

Spatial Zones are the geographic areas defined where there exists a spectrum of total destruction to normalcy. Zones are defined as such: First is the Impact Zone which is defined as the devastated area. This area is further divided into two more zones, the Total and then Fringe Impact Zones. These zones are more clearly divided given the particularly event type such as a hurricane versus a pandemic. Second, a Filter Zone is defined as the fuzzy area "where the flows of persons and goods in and out of the stricken area meet and where first-aid stations, traffic control points and other functions tend to be located" (Killian, 2002). The areas merge as some areas have partial damage and can be used for uses such as a parking lot for the electricity company vehicles. This is very important to consider during the Preparation phase for emergency managers. For example, county emergency managers in the states that line the Gulf of Mexico must forecast and designate sites where the large groups of helpers (Social Convergence Dimension) will be located during the response phase. These can be volunteer organizations or energy companies. After a hurricane hits an area, the first thing that must happen is that the roads must be cleared of debris so that electricity and water and other basic utilities can be restored to the facilities that need it most. Trees must be cut off of lines before power can be restored. Social media would help information get into the worst hit areas quicker as those from the Filter Zone can come and go, recharging and then using text messaging for efficiency purposes. It's in the Filter Zone, in particular, where social media may provide a tool, especially enhancing the citizen's role of participation in information acquisition that these Web 2.0 technologies may offer solutions where none existed before (Palen & Liu, 2007).

THE MATRIX

We provide a matrix as an aid to see how these dimensions interact (see Table 1). Many considerations can be derived by reading from the first row's dimensions and how they relate to the items in the first column. But it only takes one example to show that many of these dimensions should be considered at once. Also, not all of the dimensions have to be taken into account because they may not all pertain to the given situation. Also, only one phase of many in a dimension may be of use. It's these combinations of dimensions that need to be explored further as they can create a template of usage that has a foundation of use, but it flexible enough to fit the volatile nature of events.

To drill down further and analyze one dimension against the others is one approach to find which dimensions should be considered together for particular uses, Table 2.

For example, take the *Size* of event (emergency, disaster, and catastrophe) as it relates to the *Phases of Emergency Management* (preparedness, response, mitigation, and recovery). Next,

Table 1. Matrix of associations and influences between dimensions

	Event Size	Phase of EM	Stakeholders	Levels of Government	Social Convergence	Time Phases	Spatial Zones
Size of Event							
Phase of EM							
Stakeholders							
Levels of Government							
Social Convergence							
Time Phases							
Spatial Zones							

Table 2. Drill down on matrix of dimensions

	Event Size	Phase of EM	Stakeholders	Levels of Government	Social Convergence	Time Phases	Spatial Zones
Size of Event							

consider the *Stakeholders* involved in the various situations posed by the two prior dimensions. To increase community resilience, consider the Preparedness phase, human networking and maintaining relationships between local stakeholders and also those in neighboring districts can be strengthened using sites such as Facebook or LinkedIn (Plotnick et al., 2009). Private groups pooling together, public groups, churches, firefighters, Red Cross, and civilians emergency trained groups like CERT can create, maintain and strengthen relationships amongst members of organizations and organizations with government officials, etc. (White, 2009). Exercises can be better coordinated as communications are increased due to the number of technologies and avenues in which information can be exchanged. Social media and Web 2.0 technologies need further exploration and lessons learned need to be documented with the dimensions identified so that others can begin using these best practices identified in the field.

CONCLUSION

In this social media blitz, dimensions need to be studied further to better understand how they interact with one another and in what way social media can be effectively utilized. Certain 'best practices' for social media need to be developed where the ideas are tested for effectiveness.

Thus, design of social media must take into consideration the ways that the public will use it, not just the fact that they use it. The more that the needs of the public are considered, the more they can be active participants in preparation for, response to, and recovery from emergencies. The public is an untapped source of help in mitigating the deleterious effects of emergency situations.

A concern is that due to the present lack of expectations of emergency management, will officials be able to handle all of the information being uploaded to them? Who will monitor all of this incoming information? There is going to have to be a role developed for a person or a group of people will monitor, filter and redistribute information where social networks are concerned.

Security issues need to be addressed as well: "The mechanisms for social networking were never designed for security and filtering," said an unnamed source at U.S. Strategic Command in the blog entry. "They make it way too easy for people with bad intentions to push malicious code to unsuspecting users. It's just a fact of life" (Shachtman, 2009). Social media was designed for social interactions. But, it has been appropriated by emergency personnel and can be used effectively during all phases of an emergency as long as the special considerations, such as security, of the emergency domain are addressed. Identifying the dimensions of an emergency to consider is a first step in identifying the emergency domain's needs for social media characteristics and functionality. Much is yet to be understood but the potential is clearly there for effective use of social media in emergencies.

REFERENCES

Collins, H. (2009). Emergency Managers and First Responders Use Twitter and Facebook to Update Communities. *Emergency Management Magazine*. Retrieved July 27, 2009, from http://www.emergencymgmt.com/safety/Emergency-Managers-and-First.html

Federal News Radio. (2009). *DHS Listens and Learns from Ogma*. Retrieved July 25, 2009, from www.federalnewsradio.com

Fritz, C. E., & Mathewson, J. H. (1957). Convergence Behavior in Disasters: A Problem in Social Control. Washington, DC: Committee on Disaster Studies, National Academy of Sciences, National Research Council.

Fugate, C. (2009). *Post-Katrina: What it Takes to Cut the Bureaucracy and Assure a More Rapid Response After a Catastrophic Disaster*. Washington, DC: FEMA.

Garton, L., Haythornthwaite, C., & Wellman, B. (1997). Studying Online Social Networks. *Journal of Computer-Mediated Communication, 3*(1).

Government Computer News. (2009). *Security issues may lead DOD to ban use of social media*. Retrieved August 13, 2009, from http://www.gcn.com/Articles/2009/07/31/DOD-ban-social-media-security-issues.aspx

Haddow, G., Bullock, J., & Coppola, D. (2007). *Introduction to Emergency Management* (3rd ed.). Oxford, UK: Butterworth-Heinemann.

Herrmann, S. (2009). Social Media in Iran. *BBC UK News*. Retrieved August 14, 2009, from http://www.bbc.co.uk

Hughes, A., Palen, L., Sutton, J., Liu, S., & Vieweg, S. (2008). *"Site-Seeing" in Disaster: An Examination of On-Line Social Convergence*. Paper presented at ISCRAM08.

Killian, L. (2002). An Introduction to Methodological Problems of Field Studies in Disasters. In R. Stallings (Ed.), *Methods of Disaster Researched*. Newark, DE: International Research Committee on Disasters.

Lamoreaux, L. (2009). Twitter.com and coordinated Mayhem, Counter Terrorism. *Journal of Counterterrorism and Homeland Security International, 15*(2).

Legislature, W. S. (n.d.). *Definitions*. Retrieved August 13, 2009, from http://apps.leg.wa.gov/rcw/default.aspx?cite=38.52.010

Mowshowitz, A. (1997). Virtual organization. *Communications of the ACM, 40*(9), 30–37. doi:10.1145/260750.260759

Palen, L., & Liu, S. (2007). Citizen communications in crisis: Anticipating a future of ICT- supported public participation. In *Proceedings of the SIGCHI Conference on Human Factors in Computing Systems,* San Jose, CA (pp. 727-736).

Plotnick, L., White, C., & Plummer, M. (2009). Design Issues. In *Proceedings of America's Conference on Information Systems (AMCIS),* San Francisco. Retrieved July 28, 2009, from http://www.plano.gov

Shachtman, N. (2009). Marines Ban Twitter, MySpace, Facebook. *Wired.com*. Retrieved August 28, 2009, from http://www.wired.com/dangerroom/2009/08/marines-ban-twitter-myspace-facebook/

Skertchly, A., & Skertchly, K. (2001). Catastrophe management: Coping with totally unexpected extreme disasters. *Australian Journal of Emergency Management, Autumn 2001.*

Sutton, J., Palen, L., & Shklovski, I. (2008). Backchannels on the Front Lines: Emergent Uses of Social Media During in the 2007 Southern California Wildfires. In *Proceedings of the 5th International ISCRAM Conference,* Washington, DC.

Turoff, M., Chumer, M., Van de Walle, B., & Yao, X. (2004). The Design of a Dynamic Emergency Response Management Information System. *Journal of Information Technology Theory and Application.*

Venkatesh, V. (2000). Determinants of Perceived Ease of Use: Integrating Control, Intrinsic Motivation, and Emotion into the Technology Acceptance Model. *Information Systems Research, 11*(4), 342–365. doi:10.1287/isre.11.4.342.11872

Venkatesh, V., Morris, M. G., Davis, G. B., & Davis, F. D. (2003). User acceptance of information technology: Toward a unified view. *MIS Quarterly, 27*(3), 425–478.

Wenger, E., McDermott, R., & Snyder, W. (2002). *Cultivating Communities of Practice*. Boston: Harvard Business School Press.

White, C., Plotnick, L., Kushma, J., Hiltz, S. R., & Turoff, M. (2009). *An Online Social Network for Emergency Management*. Paper presented at the Information Systems for Crisis Response and Management (ISCRAM) Conference, Gothenburg, Sweden.

Zigurs, I., & Buckland, B. (1998). A theory of task/technology fit and group support systems effectiveness. *MIS Quarterly, 22*(3), 313–334. doi:10.2307/249668

This work was previously published in International Journal of Information Systems for Crisis Response Management, Volume 2, Issue 1, edited by Murray E. Jennex, pp. 37-48, copyright 2010 by IGI Publishing (an imprint of IGI Global).

Chapter 5
Wiki Technology and Emergency Response:
An Action Research Study

Murali Raman
Monash University, Sunway Campus, Malaysia

Terry Ryan
Claremont Graduate University, USA

Murray E. Jennex
San Diego State University, USA

Lorne Olfman
Claremont Graduate University, USA

ABSTRACT

This paper is about the design and implementation of a wiki-based knowledge management system for improving emergency response. Most organizations face difficult challenges in managing knowledge for emergency response, but it is crucial for response effectiveness that such challenges be overcome. Organizational members must share the knowledge needed to plan for emergencies. They also must be able during an emergency to access relevant plans and communicate about their responses to it. This study, which employed action research methods, suggests that wiki technology can be used to manage knowledge for emergency response. It also suggests that effective use of a knowledge management system for emergency response requires thorough training, a knowledge-sharing culture, and a good fit between emergency-response tasks and system capabilities.

1. INTRODUCTION

Knowledge management is about making knowledge available to those who need it. Knowledge management systems help organizations make good use of what they know, connecting knowledge sources and knowledge users. Emergency response involves making plans and preparations before an emergency, as well taking action during it and analyzing what happened afterwards.

It might seem natural for knowledge management systems to be used to support emergency

DOI: 10.4018/978-1-4666-0167-3.ch005

response, but a review of the relevant research literature shows that most studies to date have been focused more generally on how knowledge management systems affect organizational performance and competitiveness (Von Krogh, 1998; Hackbarth, 1998; Davenport & Prusak, 1998; Alavi & Leidner, 2001; Jennex & Olfman, 2005, 2006). Yet, recent emergencies (such as the 9/11 terrorist attacks, subsequent anthrax events, the Slammer worm attack on the Internet, the London subway bombings, the 2004 tsunami, and Hurricane Katrina) have spurred interest in research about how to support emergency response in broader terms. A small, but growing, body of research has focused on understanding how knowledge management systems can support emergency response.

How relevant are knowledge management systems to emergency response? Can knowledge management systems be designed specifically to support emergency response in an organizational context? What should a knowledge management system for emergency response include? What do emerging social software technologies, such as wikis, have to offer in the design of knowledge management systems for emergency response?

These questions motivated the study reported here: to create a knowledge management system to support emergency response, specifically the planning and preparation that must occur before an emergency occurs. The study involved using a wiki to develop a knowledge management system for emergency-response activities of the Claremont University Consortium. The Consortium (CUC) is located in Southern California and comprises seven colleges. It exists to help its members, seven co-located private colleges, with common needs, including campus safety, facilities management, library, payroll, textbooks, and emergency response.

The objectives of this research were to understand: (1) what attributes a knowledge management system for emergency response should have; (2) whether a wiki can be used to develop such a

knowledge management system; and (3) if such a system is an effective way to support knowledge management for emergency response.

The paper proceeds as follows. Section 2 provides an overview of knowledge management. Section 3 provides an overview of emergency-response systems. Section 4 briefly examines the relationship between emergency response and knowledge management. Section 5 provides an overview of wikis and their role in supporting knowledge management in organizations. Sections 6 through 9 provide the details of our case study. Sections 10 through 12 present implications for theory and practice, as well as conclusions.

2. KNOWLEDGE MANAGEMENT

Davenport and Prusak (1998) define knowledge as an evolving mix of framed experience, values, contextual information, and expert insight that provides a framework for evaluating and incorporating new experiences and information. Knowledge often becomes embedded in documents or repositories, as well as in organizational routines, processes, practices, and norms. Knowledge is also about meaning, in the sense that it is context-specific (Huber, Davenport, & King 1998). Jennex (2006) extends the concepts of context to also include associated culture that provides frameworks for understanding and using knowledge. A simpler definition of knowledge is that it is the how and why of something. Gaining knowledge is gaining insight into how and why things happen. To be useful, this knowledge must be framed in context and culture, providing the information and data needed to explain how the knowledge was generated, what it means, and how it should be used.

Jennex (2005b) defines knowledge management as "the practice of selectively applying knowledge from previous experiences of decision-making to current and future decision making activities with the express purpose of improving the organization's effectiveness." Knowledge management is an action discipline; knowledge needs to be used and applied for knowledge management to have an impact. Inherent in knowledge management is communication between knowledge creators and/or possessors and knowledge users. A knowledge management system is a system developed to aid knowledge users in identifying, sharing, retrieving, and using knowledge they need.

Alavi and Leidner (2001, p. 114) define a knowledge management system as "Information Technology-based systems developed to support and enhance the organizational processes of knowledge creation, storage/retrieval, transfer, and application." They observe that not all knowledge management initiatives will implement an information technology solution, but they support information technology as an enabler of knowledge management. Additionally, they discuss various perspectives on knowledge that help to determine how a knowledge management system should be designed and used to support knowledge management.

Maier (2002) expands on the information technology concept for the knowledge management system by calling it an Information and Communication Technology system that supports the functions of knowledge creation, construction, identification, capturing, acquisition, selection, valuation, organization, linking, structuring, formalization, visualization, distribution, retention, maintenance, refinement, evolution, accessing, search, and application.

Jennex (2005a) uses a view on systems similar to Churchman's (1979) to expand the concept of knowledge management systems to include users, as well as processes for capturing, storing, searching, retrieving, and re-using knowledge. This expanded view of a knowledge management system is used here.

3. EMERGENCY RESPONSE AND KNOWLEDGE MANAGEMENT

Decisions made during emergencies can be improved by using knowledge from past events to generate current and future response procedures (Turoff, 2002). Analysis of past emergency events for lessons learned and the understanding of what works best in given situations (both examples of knowledge) enables emergency managers to prepare planned responses as a counter to the stress of the emergency.

Integration of knowledge management concepts into an emergency-response system is a recent development (Jennex, 2006; Jennex & Raman, 2009). Specifically, researchers describe that an emergency-response system should support the following features that are also inherent in any knowledge management system:

- Enable individuals and groups to create, share, disseminate, and store knowledge (Turoff & Hiltz, 1995; Turoff, Chumer, & Van de Walle, 2004, Jennex & Raman, 2009).
- Offer the ability to document experiences and lessons that have been learned to the overall organizational memory for dealing with crisis situations (Lee & Bui, 2000; Murphy & Jennex, 2006)
- Support asynchronous and collaborative work (Campbell, DeWalle, Turoff, & Deek, 2004; Murphy & Jennex, 2006, White et al., 2008, Jennex & Raman, 2009).
- Provide emergency-response knowledge that is relevant, accurate, and presented in a timely manner (Turoff, 2002; Turoff et al., 2004; Jennex, 2004).
- Enhance the overall communication process between people involved in emergency response by inserting more structure into the manner in which knowledge is organized and documented (Turoff & Hiltz, 1995; Turoff et al., 2004; Jennex, 2004, Jennex & Raman, 2009).

Wikis are proposed as knowledge management systems to support emergency response by increasing connectivity and collaboration (Jennex, 2006; Raman, Ryan, & Olfman, 2006; White et al., 2008; Jennex & Raman, 2009). A wiki (defined below) allows users to add and edit content collaboratively (Parliament of Victoria, 2005; Wikipedia, 2006). Wikis originated in 1994 (Cunningham, 2005), but only recently come have become popular as content management systems (Mattison, 2003). Recent research has found that wikis are useful for knowledge management; they improve knowledge connectivity by providing content management with knowledge exchange, communication, and collaboration capabilities, including support for leaderless development and collaboration as exampled by Hurricane Katrina response (Murphy & Jennex, 2006; Palen, Hiltz, & Liu, 2007). These and other recent disasters show the value of wikis as a public forum for knowledge sharing and communication (Palen, Hiltz, & Liu, 2007) although there is the issue of building trust in these systems between users who do not know each other (Eryilmaz, Cochran, & Kasemvilas, 2009; Buscher, Mogensen, & Kristensen, 2009). Vazey and Richards (2006) found that wikis can improve decision making and knowledge acquisition. This applies to decision making in an emergency context as well (Jennex, 2006). Finally, White et al. (2008) list several emergency response applications where wikis have been applied. However, these applications are focused on knowledge sharing/exchange and were not used for emergency organization internal planning and training, the focus of this paper.

4. WIKIS

'Wiki' is a Hawaiian word that means 'quick' and is used by the information systems community to refer to an open source, collaborative content management system. Wikis were first implemented by the Portland Pattern Repository group to create a seamless database that enabled their members to create, edit, store, and structure content (text and graphics) in Web format (Wagner, 2004; Leuf & Cunningham, 2001).

Wikis run over the World Wide Web and are browser independent. The hypertext transfer protocol (HTTP) governs the communication process between the client and server within a wiki.

Wiki communities consist of registered members who can edit any page within the wiki website without any additional functional support from the web browser. Members establish topic associations by using hyper-linking capabilities inherent in any wiki.

The value of wikis is greatest when members actively engage in collaborative editing, sharing of knowledge, and creating new pages within a given wiki (Leuf & Cunningham, 2001). The ability of wikis to support the creation, modification, storage, and dissemination of knowledge by many people together has led to wikis being accepted as a collaborative knowledge management technology (Wagner, 2004; Leuf & Cunningham, 2001).

Wiki technology can also address knowledge management goals for emergency response through the capability of wikis to enable:

- Creation and revision of emergency-response Web pages;
- Storage, search, and retrieval of emergency-response-related paperwork, lessons from tabletop sessions, images, and presentations;
- Facilitation of online discussions and collaboration of emergency-response managers, planners, system designers, experts, responders, and other users.

Other conversational technologies can be used to support knowledge management for emergency response (e.g., e-mail, Web pages, discussion forums, chat, streaming media, video/audio conferencing, and group decision support systems [Wagner, 2004, p. 269]). However, we felt that wiki technology is a superior technology for use in supporting emergency response for the following reasons:

- It is available as an open-source technology.
- It is easy to learn and understand.
- It has simple functions for viewing and updating information.
- It supports collaborative authoring and document sharing.
- It allows asynchronous work by its users.
- It can serve as a repository. Wiki pages, once created, are persistent and updateable.

5. METHODOLOGY

This study was conducted as action research. Action research is an accepted methodology within information systems research (Susman & Evered, 1978; Baskerville & Wood-Harper, 1998; Davison et al., 2004; Lindgren et al., 2004).

Lindgren et al. (2004) classify action research as an interventionist method that "allows the researcher to test a working hypothesis about the phenomenon of interest by implementing and assessing change in real-world setting" (p. 441). They further assert that action research is appropriate when researchers emphasize creating a change as an outcome of the research endeavor.

Butler and Murphy (2007) report a participative action research study to design a knowledge management system. They describe the building of the Knowledge Asset Development System (KADS) for a United Nations agency. Some of the features of the system include a knowledge map of the knowledge asset, a set of questions and answers, external resources to supplement these questions and answers, and a list of experts of the knowledge asset network. The action research process was informed by ontological design ("with its emphasis on theory, participation and discussion" [p. 152]) and performed by working with a knowledge asset coordinator from one of

the agency's country offices and users working on a contraceptive logistics systems.

As mentioned, the objective of this study was to design, implement, and evaluate a system that could change the overall preparedness, communication, and knowledge management processes for emergency response within CUC. The lead author was directly involved with them in resolving issues inherent in their emergency-response communication and knowledge management process; that is, between the college consortium and its members. This led to a working hypothesis that the design and implementation of a Web-based knowledge management system could overcome the challenges faced by CUC as they prepare to respond to emergencies.

A formal, five-step canonical action research process (Davidson et al. 2004) was initiated by the lead author and approved by the CUC Board. The researchers, in collaboration with the Chief Executive Officer and the organization's Information Technology department, chose wiki technology as the basis for improvement efforts. The project was implemented over a two-year period (2003-2005), based on the following research tasks: *problem formulation* (December 2003-August 2004); *action planning* (September – November 2004); *intervention* (November 2004 - January 2005); *evaluation* (February-March 2005); and *specification of learning outcomes* (April – July 2005).

5.1 Research Setting

During the study, the lead author worked at CUC as the Emergency Preparedness Assistant, reporting to the Chief Executive Officer (CEO) and Chief Administrative Officer (CAO), starting in December 2002 as a part-time staff member. The researcher spent 3-8 hours per week working on emergency-response issues. His job function included setting meeting agendas for emergency-response meetings, keeping the minutes for the meetings, helping to develop emergency-response policies; answering questions about emergency response from both CUC and its members, and so on.

It quickly became clear to the lead author that existing knowledge about emergency response was poorly organized. The majority of it was stored in paper-based manuals, with some of it outdated.

The previous Emergency Preparedness Assistant had accumulated ten years of information about emergency-response activities and plans on fifteen 3½-inch storage disks. The lead author had to determine what information was on these disks. It included staff-contact information, inventory information, and emergency-response organizational structure, some up-to-date and some not. It was clear that emergency-response knowledge had to be managed better.

In December 2003, the lead author met the CEO and CAO, stating his intention to undertake this study and create—with his newly-formed project team (i.e., his co-authors)—a Web-based emergency-response system for the organization. He introduced the concept of action research to

the CEO, suggesting that the team would use a five-step process, based on the canonical action research methodology (Susman and Evered 1978). The five steps proposed were problem diagnosis, action planning, intervention, evaluation, and specification of learning outcomes. These steps and ideas were approved by the CEO. The researcher was asked to begin a formal problem diagnosis. This meeting marked the formal beginning of the project—called the Emergency Management System [EMS] project—and involved the entities listed in Table 1.

5.2 Problem Diagnosis

The researcher interviewed ten representatives from the MACC and the CCERC to begin to understand the issues in emergency response for CUC and its members. The interviewees were selected based on their regular participation in emergency-response meetings and drills. The interviews were recorded, and then transcribed and analyzed using open coding (Neuman, 2003).

Table 1. Entities involved in the EMS project

Entity	Role in the EMS Project
Claremont University Consortium (CUC)	• Offers central services to its members, including campus safety, facilities management, library, payroll, textbooks, and emergency response. • Employer of the project sponsor (viz., the CEO).
Claremont Colleges (CUC members)	• Members of the consortium. • Each has an emergency-response plan, facilitated by an Emergency Operations Center (EOC). • Each provides a representative from its EOC to the Multi-Agency Coordination Center (MACC). These are the end users of the EMS.
Emergency Operations Center (EOC)	• Plans for emergency response. • Active before, during, and after emergencies. • Separate EOCs exist for the consortium and every member college.
Multi-Agency Coordination Center (MACC)	• Coordinates emergency response activities at CUC. • Activate only during emergencies.
Claremont Colleges Emergency Readiness Committee (CCERC)	• A 'think tank' for the MACC. • Sets the policies and initiatives for the MACC.
Consultant	• Employed by CUC to assist in drills and emergency simulations. • Ensured that the EMS would be aligned with CUC's objectives. • Reviewed system model accuracy and project progress with researchers.
IT Department	• Supports the information and communication processes for emergencies. • Worked with the researchers during system development.

The interview questions specifically sought understanding about the following issues:

1. Understanding of terminology, committees, roles, and responsibilities.
2. Satisfaction with how the MACC and the EOCs respond during emergencies.
3. Concerns about emergency-response information.
4. Sources of knowledge used currently.
5. Satisfaction with the existing knowledge base for emergency response.
6. The role of information technology in emergency response.

Analysis of the initial interviews and follow-on interactions with CUC suggested that the top three concerns about emergency-response knowledge were: (1) information overload; (2) outdated information; and (3) an over-reliance on paper-based documentation.

Overall, respondents were interested in a Web-based system that could better structure emergency-response knowledge. Supporting comments include:

Having information that every service could use would be important. ...(emergency-response information should) be put in such a way that it is easy and simple to use ...the single easiest and powerful way is to use electronic media. ...having something simple for everyone to look at is a start.

We need to devise systems and programs that would enhance our internal and external communication systems. There needs to be joint communication and training efforts. Practice together, sharing of information e.g. Web, audio conferencing and such. There needs to be a combination of hardware and software use. Hardware, e.g. use of ID cards. In terms of software, we have availability of things like wiki, E-log and so on, which can help in some of the issues. Web based information for both staff and outsiders and the public can be enhanced. In

summary, there is significant potential for IT but this would involve resources and training.

To improve to emergency-response initiatives the team recommended designing and implementing a Web-based knowledge management system. Examples of comments received in response to this recommendation include:

We have way too much of information. Everyone works with computers the idea is not technology when something happens, but how it can be used to plan and coordinate efforts in preparing for an emergency situation.

The CEO had the following to say:

There are always flaws and it would be naïve to say that all information sources are accurate; however, over the past several months, the information sources have become much more accurate. Conciseness in emergency-response instructions would eliminate a lot of information overload. This is something over which CUC has little or no control. The binders that we have cannot guide immediate action, as we need information that is quick and relevant when something happens. When an emergency does occur, we are both transmission (from the MACC to colleges) and receiving information (from colleges to the MACC). We don't have time to rely on binders when things happen very quickly.

The result was the decision to proceed with designing and developing the EMS.

5.3 Action Planning: Why Wiki?

The key activities involved during the action planning stage were: (1) determining the user requirements for the proposed system; (2) developing criteria to guide design decisions; and (3) proposing a system given available options and these criteria.

A total of twenty six people were interviewed by the research team to gather their perceptions about creating the EMS and to identify its basic functionality. Detailed requirements, not presented here, were developed.

Action planning involved selecting an approach for designing and developing the EMS. However, the research team did not disregard theory while making design decisions (Davidson et al. 2004). The team used prior work by Alavi and Leidner (2001), Burnell et al. (2004), Jennex and Olfman (2006), Lawrence and Lorsch (1967), Miller (1956), and Turoff et al. (2002, 2004) to guide its decisions. The research team considered a total of seven knowledge management systems technologies as classified by Gupta and Sharma (2004). The technologies considered include document management systems, expert systems, groupware (a wiki being one example), decision support systems, semantic networks, databases, and simulation tools. The team felt that some kind of groupware application might work well to support the emergency-response efforts for CUC.

After considering the various choices within the groupware category, the team opted for a wiki-based approach. Three reasons led to this decision. First, the CEO stressed that the project would not have any budget to spend on technology; this mandated the use of open source tools. Second, wikis have the capabilities needed for the project—ease of use and support for collaborative development of knowledge. Third, the research team had experience working with wikis.

5.4 Intervention: Specific Implementation of Wiki Technology

Once the wiki approach was selected, the team had to select a specific wiki implementation. The software that drives a wiki is the wiki engine (Kille, 2006). A variety of free wiki engines (sometimes called wiki clones) are available from the Web. Examples of the more popular wiki clones are, Wiki (the original wiki [Leuf & Cunningham, 2001]), TikiWiki (www.TikiWiki.org), JOSWiki (a wiki based on Java operating system), and Plone

(a content management system; www.plone.org). Although wikis are easy to use once installed, the installation stage can require experience with databases and server configuration. Individuals and corporations may not have these skills, or the intention of managing a wiki using an internal server. In this context, services from a variety of wiki hosts or wiki farms can be obtained. Wiki hosts or farms, operate wikis for their clients as a for-fee service. Examples of wiki farms are Seedwiki (http://www.seedwiki.com), JotSpot (http://www.jot.com), and Socialtext (http://www.socialtext.com) (Kille, 2006).

TikiWiki was selected as the engine based on the team's experience using it. Tikiwiki 1.7.4 was installed on a test server. The system was migrated to a production server hosted by the IT department. Tikiwiki bundles together the requirements for a Web server (Apache), a database server (mySQL) and front-end Web pages (written in Python). We selected particular components of the wiki that we expected to support user requirements.

The goal in the intervention phase was to implement a system having features needed to manage knowledge about emergency response at CUC. Wiki technology can be customized according to the requirements of the targeted users or wiki community (Leuf and Cunningham 2001). The administrator can create modules related to the different requirements. In this case, the wiki prototype had a total of six modules. The nature of these modules, objectives, and key functions within them are summarized in Table 2. The modules were developed based on feedback from MACC members and the consultant.

Overall, the technology was to be used to support the use by the MACC and the EOCs of knowledge from different sources, including emergency-response plans, weather reports, lessons from drills, training materials, and information about emergency supplies.

The system was functionally tested by two IT department staff members. The main objective of functional testing was to ensure that: (1) the

Table 2. Key system features

Module	Module objectives	Functions
MACC Information	This module offers quick links to information about the status of supplies and resources, such as debris-removal equipment, housing, first aid kits, and food.	Responders in charge of supplies can regularly update this information. This information can also be shared though the MACC, for all phases of emergency-response
Consortium Links	This module provides access to emergency-notification protocols, phone directories, and meeting note summaries.	Allows MACC members to easily update/edit the system, and share this knowledge with all consortium members.
Calendar of Events	Information about meetings, meeting summaries, drills training events and other related activities. Assists EOCs and the MACC to coordinate activities.	Allows the MACC and EOC members to update and share information.
Emergency knowledge base	This module has links to local weather conditions, transcripts from drill sessions, and governmental emergency-response agencies.	MACC and colleges EOC members can update and add relevant links share knowledge with one another via the wiki.
Maps	This module offers links to maps of member colleges and service units within CUC.	The maps can be embedded with building specific information, such as where hazardous material is located and where emergency supplies are maintained.
Situation board	This module permits real-time updating and knowledge sharing between the MACC and EOCs during a crisis.	Wiki pages can be edited by anyone from anywhere and shared instantaneously.

system could support different user groups, i.e., administrators, users, and casual browsers; (2) the identification and password protection feature was functioning well; and (3) all links were operational.

The consultant verified that the links and page formats for the system were realistic and supported basic requirements. An internal planning meeting was held with the consultant, the IT staff members, and the researchers. The purpose of the meeting was to make sure that the IT department staff members were comfortable with TikiWiki, and able to provide support to end users. The role of the consultant was to make sure that the modules created on the system were relevant to emergency response in general. He also provided input about information needed for each module. Adjustments to the design from this meeting were to remove modules for recent updates and calendar, and to replace them with modules for a MACC Situation Board and a Knowledge Base.

5.5 Evaluation

The prototype of the EMS was demonstrated in January 2005. The CEO, two IT Department personnel, representatives from the MACC, the Operations Chief, and the consultant were present in this session. The general response from attendees was that the system could facilitate the emergency-response communication and coordination process by:

- Providing a common platform to document information.
- Maintaining knowledge about what is happening across the colleges.
- Allowing EOCs to shop for resources needed during an emergency.
- Enabling a more effective documentation process for emergency-related policies.
- Making people aware of who was doing what in an emergency.
- Providing users with knowledge that is needed rapidly.

- Offering users an alternative process for sharing knowledge about emergency response.

It was decided, with the support and endorsement of the CEO, that the system be used to facilitate a campus-wide earthquake drill in February that year. The MACC members were to use the system as part of their emergency training during this event.

The demonstration we closed with the following question:

Do you people think that we can sell this to the members involved in emergency preparedness at the All Colleges level?

The Operations Chief remarked:

I think as I mentioned earlier, we are light years ahead with this system. I don't think we need to sell this; I am going to inform the group [MACC] that this is how we are going to proceed in the future. I don't wish to delay in implementing this system, I am telling them this is what we need to do.

Another member said:

I like the system in that it consolidates information in a single space. We also need to give access to our representative to the city [the MACC sends one of its members to represent the consortium at the City emergency operations center]. He needs to know how to use the system as it can be used remotely. Having access to the city would help him get a bigger picture of what is happening here.

A systems training session was conducted on February 14, 2005 for all MACC members, prior to use during the earthquake drill. The training session audience was fourteen people from four different colleges and the consortium. The CEO and the CAO were also present. The lead author led the session, with support from the consultant.

The system was then used during the drill, which presented the scenario of the consortium having been hit by a 6.9 magnitude earthquake. The MACC was activated. The Operations Coordinator posted key information about the situation on the home page of the system. Fifteen drill participants from several colleges reported to the MACC and were asked to use the system to report the situation, campus action, and status of their respective resources, based on a predetermined set of scenarios for each college. The MACC Situation Board module was supposed to guide emergency-response coordination between the MACC and the respective EOCs.

System effectiveness was evaluated through a series of one-on-one interviews with MACC members. An instrument had been developed to facilitate the evaluation process, and this was used to guide the interview sessions. Thirteen individuals were interviewed. These individuals were selected based on the following:

- Regularity of participating in emergency response activities.
- Familiarity with emergency response at the consortium.
- Attendance at both the February 14 training and the February 17 drill.
- Key positions held within the MACC.
- Willingness to participate in the interview process.

The instrument had two parts. In part one, the respondents were asked to indicate their perspectives about the usability of the system based on ten statements. The statements, based on the work of Brooke's Systems Usability Scale (1996), are:

1. I think that I would like to use this system frequently.
2. I found this system unnecessarily complex.
3. I thought the system was easy to use.
4. I think that I would need the support of a technical person to be able to use this system.

5. I found the various functions in this system were well integrated.
6. I thought there was too much inconsistency in this system.
7. I would imagine that most people would learn to use this system very quickly.
8. I found the system very cumbersome to use.
9. I felt very confident using the system.
10. I needed to learn a lot of things before I could get going with this system.

Respondents were asked to provide ratings for this set of statements, as well as to discuss (in an open-ended response) any aspects of the system with which they were uncomfortable. Ratings involve a five-point scale: Strongly Disagree (1), Disagree (2), Neutral (3), Agree (4), and Strongly Agree (5). Ratings were reversed, as appropriate, to adjust for statement direction.

Part two of the instrument had two open-ended questions to ascertain (1) if the system would be useful to capture knowledge about emergency response; and (2) if it would enable people involved in emergency response to share knowledge.

The emergency knowledge management system received an average score of 69.5 points, of a possible 100. Stated differently, in terms of its usability, the system scored approximately 70%. A maximum score of 100% means that the system is very simple to use. A score of 70% means that the system could be improved from the users' perspective. Although the respondents were able to use the system during the drill, they indicated that the system could be improved in terms of overall structure and design. In addition, they mentioned that more training and familiarity with wiki technology were needed. The following statements are quotes from interviewees about aspects of the system they were not comfortable with.

One respondent called for better navigation:

We need to have more links such as link to traffic updates. When we had our drill the other day, I was sitting next to one of the campus safety officers. He had pointed out that the action list where we have the list for All Schools laid out in one page, could end up a list that is simply too long. Every school is on the same page. It might make more sense to break the page down or create new pages by school, but this is subject to further discussion. In the event of a real emergency that list could be very long and might be too hard to manage. I could see why they want everything on one page, but it could become cumbersome or time consuming if all this information was on one page. That would be one aspect that I am not totally comfortable with the system.

Another suggested that an e-mail feature inbuilt within the wiki would be useful:

There needs to be an easier way to send an e-mail message. This feature will make the system less cumbersome. For me to send an e-mail using the system based on the training, I need to open a smaller e-mail window and keep another window for the emergency management system. This was cumbersome. In an ideal world there should be a way for us to send an e-mail message to anyone, and this should be done via the system itself. This can prevent one from needing to shrink a particular window that can be cumbersome. And if one were upset or anxious during an emergency this could become even more cumbersome.

Several respondents stressed on the need for more training:

I have nothing in particular to comment, at this time. But I may need some technical support to show me how to create links both within the system and also how to use and develop external links. Perhaps some example in the form of writing will help.

I think that there must be an easier way of going between screens. If you can somehow lock the navigation bar on the left then this might help us further. Because you do have to go pretty far down the MACC Situation Board pages, we may need tabs on top of the system to smooth out the navigation process. These can be incorporated for future training sessions.

I guess that it's just a matter of getting used to the navigational aspect of the technology and becoming more familiar with it. I guess more training is needed.

The many different screens were a hindrance. It would have been nice to be able to stay on one screen for the most part, and just use a single click to get to another screen. In editing the screens, we had to weed down through everyone else's fields especially the case on the resources page. I think navigation can probably be improved overall in the future.

The majority of the users requested a written step-by-step "cheat sheet" that guides how each module can be used. Particularly, they requested guidelines for creating new pages (links) and also editing information in a given page.

5.5.1 Knowledge Capture

In general, the members felt that system would be useful to capture knowledge about emergency response. Following are examples of the responses that we received.

One respondent described the notion of the system as a knowledge book. Nevertheless, she was quick to point out on the importance of knowledge sharing.

I think that it will help us create an archive of every actual emergency drill, and also any other related activities that we conduct. This tells me that the system might serve as a useful knowledge book, or "book of knowledge" so to speak. People must be willing to contribute to this book though.

In general the respondents agreed that the features in the wiki were useful to capture knowledge about emergency response.

Yes the EMS can support information and knowledge capture about emergencies. The central location to post information and other documentation that is up there, such as all the PDF files that I have given you [referring to one of the researchers], will be a useful information base.

Yes, the system can help us capture information/knowledge about emergency planning and response.

Certainly, the scribe could copy and paste information into any Microsoft program such as Excel or Microsoft Word for later usage.

Yes, it is smart to be on the computers because much of the communication/information with our campuses and the world outside can easily be obtained if the MACC rep is connected to a computer.

There are many links that reflect the capability of this. It does give us more accurate information. Now we have a written record of everything that is done and by whom.

Yes, as long as people are willing to follow the plan and keep to it, we should be on track.

The system provides a common platform/space, structuring of information.

One respondent stressed the fit between the task and the technology:

Yes, the system can support information and knowledge capture, but technology should support the nature of tasks we have in that room, and not hinder it.

5.5.2 Knowledge Sharing

In general, the members felt that the system would enable people involved in emergency response to share knowledge with one another. However, issues such as need for training and the existence of a knowledge-sharing culture must be considered.

One respondent said:

As mentioned, easy access to the system and a fairly direct way to input ideas will allow people to share knowledge about emergency preparedness with each other. It will; it will allow them to populate the database or to fill in the blanks.

Another suggested the importance of having an overall objective of using the system to support knowledge sharing efforts:

Yes the system can support knowledge sharing, but there needs to be a clear "big picture" page that is one click away. We will be so busy entering information that an update page should not be a hurdle to find knowledge that we need.

Other responses were:

Yes the system can support emergency knowledge sharing efforts. Once the system can import and export information via e-mail, and other programs, it is really simple to do that. You can get an idea of what's happening and answers to your questions from the system, when required.

Yes the system supports knowledge sharing efforts. The system has useful refreshing abilities, and allows sharing of information and knowledge with each other instantaneously. It provides timely information and therefore can help better communication between the EOCs and the MACC.

Two respondents stressed the importance of a knowledge-sharing culture:

The system is a useful communication tool, and when and if people share information, we can use this to support reporting functions as well.

Yes, the technology can support this effort. However, frankly, I don't think all the members from the various colleges have a knowledge-sharing culture. Based on my experience here, my guess is that people need to share more information about emergency planning with each other. It seems easier to share with some relative to others. I guess we are comfortable with speaking directly with people, and may not be willing to share information in an open platform. This needs to change though. People must be willing to share information with each other.

The above findings support the viewpoint of Butler and Murphy (2007) who suggest that tools for knowledge management should include features based on 'practical theory' and insights from hermeneutics. One consideration is to foster a knowledge-sharing culture at CUC, maximizing the value of the EMS.

9. CHANGES MADE IN RESPONSE TO USER FEEDBACK

The lead researcher left his position with CUC after completing his doctoral study in 2005. Before leaving the organization, the research team took the following measures and provided several recommendations to CUC. First, the team developed a written document that explains the purpose and use of every module in the emergent management system. The team suggested that this document be used to guide training on emergency response, as well as how the system could be further developed. Second, the led researcher trained his successor in the use of the system and what needs to be done to enhance its usability, particularly in terms of navigational aspects.

It has been almost two years since the original system was implemented. It has been improved significantly, with respect to overall flow, documentation, and navigation. The system, as it is today, inherits many features from the original EMS. These features include codification of expert information on emergency-response issues, blogs, and links to relevant resources.

10. CONTRIBUTIONS TO THEORY

Turoff et al. (2004) provide researchers and systems designers with a framework for designing systems to support emergency response. The authors discuss nine premises:

- The system must be used in training and simulations.
- The system must consolidate information and prevent information overload.
- The system must enable responders to document their learning and experiences, e.g., an organizational crisis management memory should exist.
- The system must integrate information and knowledge from various sources.
- The system should support collaborative work and ensure unrestricted access to responders and planners.
- The system should specify the role and responsibility for people involved in emergency management, and how these roles might evolve during an actual emergency.
- The system must provide valid and timely information.
- The system must support and enable free-flow of exchanging information.
- The system must enable people and entities involved in emergency management to coordinate with each other.

Turoff et al. (2004) does not explicitly mention that the design of emergency-response systems should be based on sound knowledge management principles. However, one could argue that these nine premises, as described above, are closely linked to the goals of knowledge management (Murphy & Jennex, 2006).

This study indicates that an organization's culture and effective utilization of any emergency-response system within the organization may be related. The authors accurately mention that any system designed to support emergency management must support free exchange of knowledge and information. The authors take a systems-design perspective in discussing this premise. The outcome of this project suggests that, although a particular technology can support free sharing of knowledge, the notion of "sharing" will only exist in organizations where a "sharing culture" is nurtured (Davenport & Prusak, 1998; Jennex & Olfman, 2005).

Turoff et al. (2004) does not explicitly discuss the notion of fit between task and technology in the context of emergency response. The project findings propose that successful implementation of an emergency-management system is contingent on the ability of the system to blend with the nature of tasks involved in emergency response. This is consistent with Jennex and Olfman (2001) design recommendations for task and knowledge capture fit in a knowledge management system. During the project-closing meeting with the researcher, the CEO remarked:

The system itself is fine, but the MACC Chair and the Operations Coordinator still have to decide about our response and task of decision making cannot be replaced by the system, albeit can be supported by the system. In addition everyone can have access to a common set of information. This means everyone (with reference to the Emergency Operation Centers) can act prematurely and go talk directly to one another, without going thorough the central body (the MACC) to coordinate efforts. For example during the drill, someone asked, if we need a particular resource and know that someone else has it, why do we need to go through the MACC? This is a valid question. But, the point is, there might be another request for the same resource that is far more urgent that yours, and the MACC has to coordinate this. So, this could be a pitfall of a system. Unless protocols for using the system are established to support the tasks that have been designed, we could face problems in the future.

Figure 1 illustrates how the project findings can further inform theory about systems for emergency response. This study suggests that the environment faced by emergency responders is complex, dynamic, and unstructured. This assertion echoes the work of Burnell et al. (2004). The majority of literature about emergency-response systems does not clearly state that systems designed to support emergency response are associated to knowledge management. This study suggests that the envi-

ronment faced by emergency responders forces them to deal with the following characteristics of knowledge:

- Knowledge for emergency response is used as needed when an emergency occurs; its *use may be ad hoc*. Individuals and groups involved in emergency response can not necessarily plan responses to all particular situations before-hand so need the ability to locate and utilize relevant knowledge.
- The knowledge repositories to respond to a particular crisis tend to be predominantly *decentralized*. In this case, knowledge resides within eight different emergency operations centers, plus the MACC.
- Emergency response requires responders to deal with knowledge that is highly *contextualized*. Every crisis is unique and requires a different set of ideas and response initiatives (Burnell et al. 2004).

Figure 1. Impact on theory

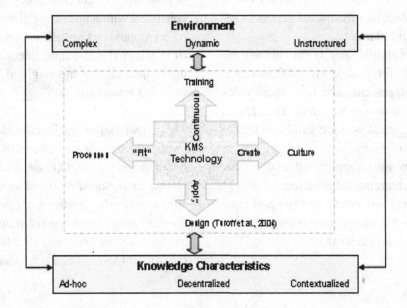

Given the above, the findings of this study suggest that any system designed to support emergency response organizations should be closely linked to ideas inherent within the domain of knowledge management. A particular technology selected to support emergency response should be appropriate for knowledge that is ad hoc, decentralized, and contextualized.

This study suggests that wiki technology is a good option for a system to manage emergency-response knowledge. It is appropriate for knowledge that is dynamic and decentralized (Wagner, 2004). Nevertheless, technology alone is not sufficient to foster effective emergency-response initiatives. The system should be designed to support emergency responders and must be used in every drill and emergency-training activities (Turoff et al., 2004; Jennex, 2008). We add that in addition to effective design and training considerations, two additional factors are required when thinking about emergency-response systems:

- A good "fit" between the knowledge management system and the existing emergency-response policies must be sought. Stated differently, the technology should support, not hinder, emergency-response initiatives.
- There is a need to foster a knowledge-sharing culture between various entities involved in a given emergency-response organization structure. In the case of CUC, this refers to the willingness of different emergency operation centers to share information/knowledge with one another.

11. PRACTICAL IMPLICATIONS

Emergency response is important for every organization (Kostman, 2004; Van Kirk, 2004). This study contributes to organizations that want to use IT to aid in emergency response. Although technology cannot prevent emergency situations from occurring, it can help organizations be ready to handle such situations. The Homeland Security Office recently released a comprehensive document stressing the importance of establishing a comprehensive emergency-response plan for both government and the private sector in the United States. This document is called the National Incident Management Systems (NIMS).

Key NIMS elements, as stated in the FEMA Web site (http://www.fema.gov/nims/), include: (1) Incident Command System (ICS); (2) Preparedness; (3) Communications and Information Management; (4) Joint Information Systems; and (5) NIMS integration center. The focus of this project was to assist CUC in enhancing items (1) and (2). The project can be extended to other entities within the Claremont Colleges. In addition, other organizations with similar emergency-response structure to that of CUC, can model findings and recommendations based on the outcome of this project. Entities that establish a comprehensive emergency response based on NIMS guidelines stand a better chance of receiving federal funding for emergency-related activities and claim for post-emergency reimbursement. Our study suggests that, if designed and implemented properly, wiki technology can support the communication and information management requirements in relation to emergency planning and response.

The nature of wikis promotes several aspects of knowledge management for emergency response. These include the capability of most wiki tools to support multi-author creation and revision of Web pages; storage and retrieval of related documents, images, and presentations; searching of these; management of changes to them; and online discussions during a crisis situation.

The system in this project used an instantiation of wiki technology called Tikiwiki. Tikiwiki is one of hundreds of wiki technology implementations. It was chosen because it is an open source implementation with many additional features to complement the wiki itself. In the two years since this decision was made, the market of wiki products has continued to grow. Some of them are now much easier to install, administer, and use. Their capabilities are greater, as are their interfaces with other software tools. In this study, however, wiki technology appeared to have several drawbacks.

First, the technology was not as intuitive as we expected. Becoming familiar with it took more time than it should have. Not everyone involved in the drill and training in the project was comfortable with the technology. They were more used to "read-only" Web-based systems. The power of wiki technology lies in its ability to capture dynamic changes within its pages based on the edit function. Using and working with this editing capability might require some time and sufficient training, depending on the implementation of wiki chosen.

Second, wiki technology has numerous capabilities and features. Customizing the relevant features so as to support emergency-response activities optimally was not that intuitive, even for the researchers who had reasonable experience with the technology and emergency response. Depending on the 'flavor' of wiki selected, this could be a problem for the design of emergency-response systems.

Third, wiki technology is available open-source. Organizations that intend to develop systems to support emergency response have the option of purchasing off-the-shelf systems that come with vendor support. If financial resources are available, but technical expertise is not, this might be a superior option for some organizations.

12. CONCLUSION

This study uses wiki technology to understand important issues in designing knowledge management systems to support emergency response. Specifically, an action research study was conducted to understand if wikis can be used to implement a knowledge management system and if such a system can support knowledge management for

an emergency response organization. The study suggests that effective implementation and use of a wiki to support knowledge management for emergency response is contingent upon familiarity of both emergency planners and responders with the technology, level of planning involved prior to system implementation and use in an actual emergency, continuous training with the systems, establishing a fit between task and technology, and the willingness of members to share knowledge with one another. Organizations similar in emergency-response structure to the consortium examined should be able to apply the findings and recommendations from this project. Entities that establish a comprehensive emergency-response plan stand a better chance of receiving federal funding for emergency-related activities and claims for post-emergency reimbursement. Wiki technology, based on our experience, if designed and implemented properly, can provide a cost effective technology to support emergency response within a multi-entity organizational environment.

Additionally, it is also concluded that wikis used for knowledge management for an emergency response organization also needs to be able to be integrated into an overall Social Network Site as proposed by Plotnick, White, and Plummer (2009) and White et al. (2009). Knowledge management is also about leveraging what the organization knows and improving connectivity between knowledge sources and knowledge users (Jennex, 2009). While a wiki accomplishes this, it is expected that a Social Network Site integrating several social communication media will do this better.

REFERENCES

Alavi, M., & Leidner, D. E. (2001). Review: Knowledge Management and Knowledge Management Systems: Conceptual Foundations and Research Issues. *MIS Quarterly*, *25*(1), 107–136. doi:10.2307/3250961

Andersen, H. B., Garde, H., & Andersen, V. (1998). MMS: An Electronic Message Management System for Emergency Response. *IEEE Transactions on Engineering Management*, *45*(2), 132–140. doi:10.1109/17.669758

Baskerville, R., & Wood-Harper, A. T. (1998). Diversity in Information Systems Action Research Methods. *European Journal of Information Systems*, *7*(2), 90–107. doi:10.1057/palgrave.ejis.3000298

Bellardo, S., Karwan, K. R., & Wallace, W. A. (1984). Managing the Response to Disasters Using Microcomputers. *Interfaces*, *14*(2), 29–39. doi:10.1287/inte.14.2.29

Brooke, J. (1996). *Systems Usability Scale: A 'quick and dirty' usability scale*. Retrieved March 24, 2004 from http://www.hcirn.com/ref/refb/broo96.php

Burnell, L., Priest, J., & Durrett, J. (2004). Developing and Maintaining Knowledge Management System for Dynamic, Complex Domains. In J. Gupta & S. Sharma (Eds.), *Creating Knowledge Based Organizations*. London: IGP.

Busher, M., Mogensen, P. H., & Kristensen, M. (2009). When and How (Not) to Trust it? Supporting Virtual Emergency Teamwork. *International Journal of Information Systems for Crisis Response Management*, *1*(2), 1–15.

Butler, T., & Murphy, C. (2007). Understanding the Design of Information Technologies for Knowledge Management in Organizations: A Pragmatic Perspective. *Information Systems Journal*, *17*(2), 143–163. doi:10.1111/j.1365-2575.2007.00237.x

Campbell, C. L., DeWalle, B. V., Turoff, M., & Deek, F. P. (2004). *A Research Design for Asynchronous Negotiation of Software Requirements for an Emergency Response Information System*. Paper presented at the Americas Conference on Information Systems, New York.

Churchman, C. W. (1979). The Systems Approach (revised and updated) New York: Dell Publishing.

Cunningham, W. (2005). *Wiki History*. Retrieved October 29, 2005, from http://c2.com/cgi/wiki?WikiHistory

Davenport, T. H., & Prusak, L. (1998). *Working Knowledge*. Cambridge, MA: Harvard Business School Press.

Davison, R. M., & Martinsons, M.vG., & Kock, N. (2004). Principles of canonical action research. *Information Systems Journal*, *14*, 65–86. doi:10.1111/j.1365-2575.2004.00162.x

Eryilmaz, E., Cochran, M., & Kasemvilas, S. (2009). Establishing Trust Management in an Open Source Collaborative Information Repository: An Emergency Response Information System Case Study. In *Proceedings of the 42nd Hawaii International Conference on System Sciences*. Washington, DC: IEEE Computer Society.

Fink, S. (1986). *Crisis Management. Planning for the Inevitable*. New York: American Management Association, AMACOM.

Fischer, H. W. (1998). The Role of the New Information Technologies in Emergency Mitigation, Planning, Response, and Recovery. *Disaster Prevention and Management*, *7*(1), 28–37. doi:10.1108/09653569810206262

Gadomski, A. M., Bologna, S., Costanzo, G. D., Perini, A., & Schaerf, M. (2001). Towards Intelligent Decision Support Systems for Emergency Managers: the IDS Approach. *International Journal of Risk Assessment and Management*, *2*(3/4), 224–242. doi:10.1504/IJRAM.2001.001507

Gheorghe, A. V., & Vamanu, D. V. (2001). Adapting to New Challenges: IDSS for Emergency Preparedness and Management. *International Journal of Risk Assessment and Management*, *2*(3/4), 211–223. doi:10.1504/IJRAM.2001.001506

Gupta, J. D., & Sharma, S. K. (2004). *Creating Knowledge Based Organizations*. Hershey, PA: IDEA Group Publishing.

Hackbarth, G. (1998, August). *The Impact of Organizational Memory on IT Systems*. Paper presented at the Fourth Americas Conference on Information Systems.

Huber, G. P., Davenport, T. H., & King, D. (1998). Some Perspectives on Organizational Memory. In F. Burstein, G. Huber, M. Mandviwalla, J. Morrison, & L. Olfman (Eds.), *Proceedings of the 31st Annual Hawaii International Conference on System Sciences,* Hawaii.

Jennex, M. E. (2004). Emergency Response Systems: The Utility Y2K Experience. [JITTA]. *Journal of IT Theory and Application, 6*(3), 85–102.

Jennex, M. E. (2005a). Knowledge Management Systems. *International Journal of Knowledge Management, 1*(2), i–iv.

Jennex, M. E. (2005b). What is Knowledge Management? *International Journal of Knowledge Management, 1*(4), i–iv.

Jennex, M. E. (2006). Open Source Knowledge Management. *International Journal of Knowledge Management, 2*(4), i–iv.

Jennex, M. E. (2008). A Model For Emergency Response Systems. In L. Janczewski & A. Colarik (Eds.), *Cyber Warfare and Cyber Terrorism* (pp. 383-391). Hershey, PA: Information Science Reference.

Jennex, M. E. (2009). Why Knowledge Management. In M. E. Jennex (Ed.), *Ubiquitous Developments in Knowledge Management: Integrations and Trends*. Hershey, PA: Information Science Reference.

Jennex, M. E., & Olfman, L. (2001). Development Recommendations for Knowledge Management/ Organizational Memory Systems. In M. K. Sein, B. E. Munkvold, T. U. Orvik, W. Wojtkowski, W. G. Wojtkowski, S. Wrycza et al. (Eds.), *Contemporary Trends in IS Development* (pp. 209-222). Norwell, MA: Kluwer Academic.

Jennex, M. E., & Olfman, L. (2005). Assessing Knowledge Management Success. *International Journal of Knowledge Management, 1*(2), 33–49.

Jennex, M. E., & Olfman, L. (2006). A Model of Knowledge Management Success. *International Journal of Knowledge Management, 2*(3), 51–68.

Jennex, M. E., & Raman, M. (2009). Knowledge Management is Support of Crisis Response. *International Journal of Information Systems for Crisis Response Management, 1*(3), 69–82.

Kille, A. (2006). *Wikis in the Workplace: How Wikis Can Help Manage Knowledge in Library Reference Services*. Retrieved April 24, 2006, from http://libres.curtin.edu.au/libres16n1/Kille_essayopinion.htm

Kostman, J. T. (2004). 20 Rules for Effective Communication in a Crisis. *Disaster Recovery Journal, 17*(2), 20.

Lawrence, P., & Lorsch, J. (1967). Differentiation and Integration in Complex Organizations. *Administrative Science Quarterly, 12*, 1–30. doi:10.2307/2391211

Lee, J., & Bui, T. (2000). A Template-based Methodology for Disaster Management Information Systems. In *Proceedings of the 33rd Hawaii International Conference on System Sciences,* Hawaii.

Leuf, B., & Cunningham, W. (2001). *The WIKI WAY. Quick Collaboration of the Web*. Reading, MA: Addison-Wesley.

Lewin, K. (1947a). Frontiers in Group Dynamics. *Human Relations, 1*(1), 5–41. doi:10.1177/001872674700100103

Lewin, K. (1947b). Frontiers in Group Dynamics II. *Human Relations*, *1*(2), 143–153. doi:10.1177/001872674700100201

Lindgren, R., Henfridsson, O., & Schultze, U. (2004). Design principles for competence management systems: A synthesis of an action research study. *MIS Quarterly*, *28*(3), 435–472.

Maier, R. (2002). *Knowledge Management Systems: Information and Communication Technologies for Knowledge Management*. Berlin, Germany: Springer-Verlag.

Mattison, D. (2003). Quickwiki, Swiki, Twiki, Zwiki and the Plone Wars – Wiki as PIM and Collaborative Content Tool. *Searcher: The Magazine for Database Professionals*, *11*(4), 32.

Miller, G. A. (1956). The magical number seven, plus or minus two: Some limits on our capacity for processing information. [Retrieved from http://www.well.com/user/smalin/miller.html]. *Psychological Review*, *63*, 81–97. doi:10.1037/h0043158

Murphy, T., & Jennex, M. E. (2006). Knowledge Management, Emergency Response, and Hurricane Katrina. *International Journal of Intelligent Control and Systems*, *11*(4), 199–208.

Myers, N. (1999). *Manager's guide to contingency planning for disasters: Protecting vital facilities and critical operations*. New York: Wiley.

Neuman, W. L. (2003). *Social research methods* (5th ed.). Boston: Pearson Education.

Nisha de Silva, F. (2001). Providing Spatial Decision Support for Evacuation Planning: A Challenge in Integrating Technologies. *Disaster Prevention and Management*, *10*(1), 11–20. doi:10.1108/09653560110381787

Palen, L., Hiltz, S. R., & Liu, S. B. (2007). Online Forums Supporting Grassroots Participation in Emergency Preparedness and Response. *Communications of the ACM*, *50*(3), 54–58. doi:10.1145/1226736.1226766

Parliament of Victoria. (2005). *Victorian Electronic Democracy - Final Report*. Retrieved October 29, 2005, from http://www.parliament.vic.gov.au/sarc/E-Democracy/Final_Report/Glossary.htm

Patton, D., & Flin, R. (1999). Disaster Stress: An Emergency Management Perspective. *Disaster Prevention and Management*, *8*(4), 261–267. doi:10.1108/09653569910283897

Plotnick, L., White, C., & Plummer, M. (2009). The Design of an Online Social Network Site for Emergency Management: A One-Stop Shop. In *Proceedings of the 15th Americas Conference on Information Systems, Association for Information Systems*.

Raman, M., & Ryan, T. (2004). *Designing Online Discussion Support Systems for Academic Setting-"The Wiki Way"*. Paper presented at the Americas Conferences on Information Systems (AMCIS), New York.

Raman, M., Ryan, T., & Olfman, L. (2006). Knowledge Management Systems for Emergency Preparedness: The Claremont University Consortium Experience. *International Journal of Knowledge Management*, *2*(3), 33–50.

Renaud, R., & Phillips, S. (2003). Developing an Integrated Emergency Response Programme for Facilities: The Experience of Public Works and Government Services Canada. *Journal of Facilities Management*, *1*(4), 347–364. doi:10.1108/14725960310808051

Seeger, M. W., Sellnow, T. L., & Ulmer, R. R. (2003). *Communication and Organizational Crisis*. Westport, CT: Praeger Publishers.

Smith, C. A. P., & Hayne, S. (1991). A Distributed System for Crisis Management. In *Proceedings of the 24th Hawaii International Conference on System Sciences, HICSS* (Vol. 3, pp. 72-81).

Stein, E. W., & Zwass, V. (1995). Actualizing Organizational Memory with Information Systems. *Information Systems Research*, 6(2), 85–117. doi:10.1287/isre.6.2.85

Susman, G. I., & Evered, R. D. (1978). An Assessment of the Scientific Merits of Action Research. *Administrative Science Quarterly*, 23, 582–603. doi:10.2307/2392581

Townsend, F. F. (2006). *The Federal Response to Hurricane Katrina, Lessons Learned*. Washington, DC: U.S. Department of Homeland Security.

Trist, E., & Bamforth, K. (1951). Some social and psychological consequences of the longwall method of coal getting. *Human Relations*, 4, 3–38. doi:10.1177/001872675100400101

Turoff, M. (2002). Past and Future Emergency Response Information Systems. *Communications of the ACM*, 45(4), 29–32. doi:10.1145/505248.505265

Turoff, M., Chumer, M., Van de Walle, B., & Yao, X. (2004). The Design of a Dynamic Emergency Response Management Information System (DERMIS). [JITTA]. *Journal of Information Technology Theory and Application*, 5(4), 1–35.

Turoff, M., & Hiltz, S. R. (1995). Computer Based Delphi Processes. In M. Adler & E. Ziglio (Eds.), *Gazing Into the Oracle: The Delphi Method and its Applications to Social Policy and Public Health* (pp. 56-88). London: Kingsley Publishers

Van Kirk, M. (2004). Collaboration in BCP Skill Development. *Disaster Recovery Journal*, 17(2), 40.

Vazey, M., & Richards, D. (2006). A Case-Classification-Conclusion 3Cs Approach o Knowledge Acquisition: Applying a Classification Logic Wiki to the Problem Solving Process. *International Journal of Knowledge Management*, 2(1), 72-88. Wikipedia. (2006). *Wiki*. Retrieved March 30, 2006, from http://en.wikipedia.org/wiki/Wiki

Von Krogh, G. (1998). Care in Knowledge Creation. *California Management Review*, 40(3), 133–153.

Wagner, C. (2004). WIKI: A Technology for Conversational Knowledge Management and Group Collaboration. *Communications of the Association for Information Systems*, 13, 265–289.

White, C., Plotnick, L., Addams-Moring, R., Turoff, M., & Hiltz, S. R. (2008). Leveraging A Wiki To Enhance Virtual Collaboration In The Emergency Domain. In *Proceedings of the 41st Hawaii International Conference on System Sciences*, Hawaii. Washington, DC: IEEE Computer Society.

White, C., Plotnick, L., Kushma, J., Hiltz, S. R., & Turoff, M. (2009). *An Online Social Network for Emergency Management*. Paper presented at the 6th International ISCRAM Conference.

This work was previously published in International Journal of Information Systems for Crisis Response Management, Volume 2, Issue 1, edited by Murray E. Jennex, pp. 49-69, copyright 2010 by IGI Publishing (an imprint of IGI Global).

Chapter 6
A Normative Enterprise Architecture for Guiding End–to–End Emergency Response Decision Support

Michael J. Marich
Claremont Graduate University, USA

Benjamin L. Schooley
Claremont Graduate University, USA

Thomas A. Horan
Claremont Graduate University, USA

ABSTRACT

This article examines the underlying architecture guiding the development and use of enterprise decision support systems that maintain the delivery of time critical public services. A normative architecture, developed from comparative cases involving San Mateo County and Mayo Clinic Emergency Medical Services systems, provides a collection of characteristics meant to guide an emergency response system toward a high level of performance and enable optimal decision-making. At a national symposium, academics and practitioners involved in promoting effective emergency response information systems provided validation for the architecture and next steps for enhancing emergency response information systems. Normative architecture characteristics and expert perspectives from the symposium are integrated into a framework that offers an enterprise approach for delivering time-critical emergency response services. This article provides recommendations for navigating toward a more incremental approach in developing enterprise-oriented emergency information services and examines future trends involving the application of normative architectural concepts to real-world emergency medical settings.

DOI: 10.4018/978-1-4666-0167-3.ch006

INTRODUCTION

Information systems used by emergency response personnel must provide information and decision support anywhere and anytime it is needed, in a form and format that avoids "overload and miscues" and supports the "coordination of efforts of a great number of organizations and individuals" (Zwass, 2010, p. ix). For example, the perspectives provided by various emergency response organizations that received automobile crash data as part of the Minnesota Mayday System revealed that the new and additional data they received was a good "fit' for them (Schooley, Horan, & Marich, 2010). The importance of receiving the appropriate data in a timely manner is significant since it improved their decision support mechanisms, which led to reduced response times and an increase in the quality of patient care that each organization was able to provide (Schooley, Horan, & Marich, 2010).

Such a need is consistent with findings from the broader Information Systems (IS) business community:, a top management concern is the ability for an enterprise system to make better use of information, while high on the list of supportive applications and technology is business process management (Luftman & Kempaiah, 2008). Making use of information for strategic, tactical, operational, or clinical decision-making has been a focal point for organizations for decades (Berner, 2006; French & Turoff, 2007; Turban et al., 2006). Decision support systems must be designed to "fit" within the context and purpose for which they are intended to support. The contexts in which decision support has proven valuable include a wide range of private and public sector organizations and their respective supply chains.

Recent research has also posited the importance of making better use of information for multi-organizational enterprise systems through information sharing and collaboration to support decision making and, ultimately, the delivery of public services to citizens (Dawes et al., 2004;

Drake et al., 2004; Fountain, 2001; Scholl, 2005). These concepts have been extended to the specific context of public services where time is a critical factor, such as in the case of emergency medical services (EMS), homeland security, law enforcement, crisis response, hazardous material response, fire, search and rescue, and other disaster relief services (Horan & Schooley, 2007; Sawyer et al., 2005; Turoff et al., 2004). While several researchers have presented frameworks and heuristics for conceptualizing, designing, managing, and analyzing emergency information systems (e.g., Drury et al., 2009; Dwarkanath & Daconta, 2006; Horan & Schooley, 2007; Turoff et al., 2004), there is a need to investigate the underlying architectures for guiding the development and use of enterprise decision support systems for time critical contexts (Marich, 2008). Such an investigation would need to be context specific to emergency response, include a multi-dimensional understanding of information use from technological, organizational, and sociological (e.g., governance, management, institutional) perspectives (Manoj & Hubenko-Baker, 2007; Schooley & Horan, 2007), and allow for a prescriptive or normative architectural approach to guiding multi-organizational enterprise wide decision support systems.

This article aims to review findings from a multi-part research project and apply them to enterprise architecture concepts for emergency services, generally, and for the specific domain of emergency medical services (EMS). This article integrates research findings from conceptual framework development, two comparative case studies, and an expert practitioner symposium with an enterprise architecture framework referred to as the Emergency Services Enterprise Framework (ESEF). The ESEF is a framework "that provides an integrated process and technology methodology … [t]o ensure efficiencies and to promote collaborative information-sharing in the complex Emergency Services enterprise" (Dwarkanath & Daconta, 2006, p. 7). This article, then, applies a set of architectural imperatives to the ESEF derived from prior research and defined by EMS practitioners. These imperatives were designed to drive the EMS enterprise "away from inherent business silos and towards greater levels of standardization and integration of information and technology across all stakeholder groups" (Marich, Horan, & Schooley, 2008, p. 452). Recommendations are provided for navigating towards a more incremental approach in developing enterprise-oriented emergency information services and future trends involving the application of normative architectural concepts to real-world emergency medical settings are examined. An overview of the research approach is illustrated in Figure 1.

ENTERPRISE ARCHITECTURE AND NORMATIVE ARCHITECTURE

The Time-Critical Information Services (TCIS) framework suggests that there are several overlapping and simultaneous phenomena that should be understood and analyzed to better understand the nature and performance of a multi-organizational emergency medical services information system (Horan & Schooley, 2008). While the TCIS framework has been determined to be most ap-

propriate for exploring key architectural elements, its usefulness is largely limited to its descriptive, conceptual nature. The research presented here is focused chiefly on the performance aspects of an EMS system and is, therefore, biased toward providing guidance that will inform practice.

An examination of the literature published by the Association of Computing Machinery (ACM) and the Institute of Electrical and Electronics Engineers (IEEE) revealed numerous articles related to the development of high performance architectures for computer hardware involving various processor and memory devices. On the software side, there are numerous articles related to high performance architectures resulting from compiler and programming optimizations. Published research also exists for the development of high performance architectures for communication systems, such as those used in wireless networks. However, there is currently no published research available from the ACM or IEEE related to developing high performance architectures for enterprise-wide, multi-organizational information systems such that support emergency services.

While there is limited published material to work with regarding the development of a high performance architecture, the well-documented

Figure 1. Research approach

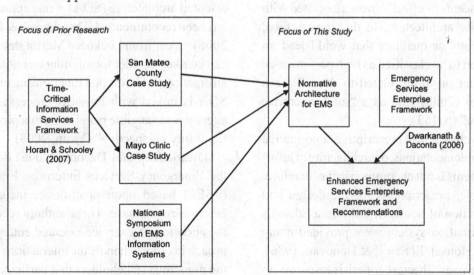

concept of enterprise architecture maturity contains many similarities to which a normative architecture for an EMS system would subscribe. Schekkerman (2004) describes an enterprise architecture as "a master plan which 'acts as a collaboration force' between aspects of business planning such as goals, visions, strategies, and governance principles" (p. 13). Baltzan and Phillips (2008) describe the three components of enterprise architecture as: (1) information architecture – that "identifies where and how important information, like customer records, is maintained and secured"; (2) infrastructure architecture – "the underlying foundation to support the organization's goals" that includes primary characteristics such as performance, availability; and (3) application architecture – that "determines how applications integrate and relate to each other" (p. 154). Ross (2003) indicates that there are four stages that can be used to describe the maturity of an enterprise architecture: business silos, standardized technology, rationalized process, and business modularity. Ross and Beath (2006) state that as firms move through these stages it "incrementally increases the strategic value of IT to the enterprise and enhances enterprise effectiveness" (p. 182).

The operational, organizational, and governance dimensions of the TCIS framework were designed to align with the definition, components, and the concepts of effectiveness associated with an enterprise architecture. In this regard, then, the conditions or qualities that would lead an EMS system to be classified as high performance would center on those related to what Baltzan and Phillips (2008) term as a "solid enterprise architecture" (p. 153).

The development of prescriptive or normative designs, implementations, or architecture of information systems is not uncommon in the literature. For example, prescriptions for the design and implementation of Southern California Edison's crisis information system were provided many years ago (Housel, El Sawy, & Donovan, 1986). A prescriptive architecture for crisis response, an

area of study that is quite similar to emergency response in that it shares many of the same stakeholders, was proposed in the late 1990's (Hale, 1997). Given the prominence associated with the topic of enterprise architecture, and especially the significance of enterprise architecture maturity, we posit the importance of also including a prescriptive or normative architecture within this context to provide guiding principles to aim towards. For the purpose of this research, a normative architecture embodies those high performance qualities that system stakeholders believe are required for the end-to-end provision of emergency medical services information systems across operational, organizational, and governance dimensions. The effectiveness of the normative architecture is a function of its alignment with the high performance architecture, the qualities of which will be discussed further in this article.

OVERVIEW OF THE EMERGENCY SERVICES ENTERPRISE FRAMEWORK

Within the realm of emergency services organizations where there exists a diversity of stakeholders, dissimilar technologies and processes, operational characteristics, and many other factors, a service oriented architecture (SOA) is one approach that has been recommended (Dwarkanath & Daconta, 2006). Greer from Lockheed Martin states, "SOA can be a key enabler for aligning technology with an organization's mission function, but only when SOA is linked with business processes can an agency reap tangible benefits from a process and flexibility perspective" (Yasin, 2008).

Dwarkanath and Daconta (2006) developed the Emergency Services Enterprise Framework (ESEF) based upon practitioner insights into emergency response. These authors recommend the adoption of a service-oriented enterprise approach in order to handle the interactions between the numerous stakeholders that participate in the provisioning of emergency services. The ESEF as described by Dwarkanath and Daconta is depicted in Figure 2 and consists of the following elements:

1. A governance structure composed of an operational component associated with people and processes "to identify the strategic outcomes and objectives for the enterprise" (p. 3) and a technology component that "governs the actual technical, information technology and communication issues, and seeks to ensure the application of policies and re-use of services in the enterprise" (p. 3).

2. Enterprise services composed of line-of-business services that are "domain-specific services offered within a single domain" (p. 4), shared services that are "horizontal services shared across a subset of the enterprise COI [community of interest] and among two or more domains" (p. 3), and core services that are "horizontal services that are shared and used across all domains" (p.3).

3. An enterprise platform that "includes the methods and tools that enable the enterprise services ... [including] the various sets of integration technologies, systems, and standards that are used by the entities" (p. 5) and the enterprise infrastructure that consists of the "access and delivery channels and the various transport modes like terrestrial and satellite communications" (p. 5).

The ESEF provided a context-specific enterprise architecture to apply and integrate research findings from a multi-method, multipart National Science Foundation sponsored research project.

Figure 2. Emergency services enterprise framework (adapted from Dwarkanath & Daconta, 2006)

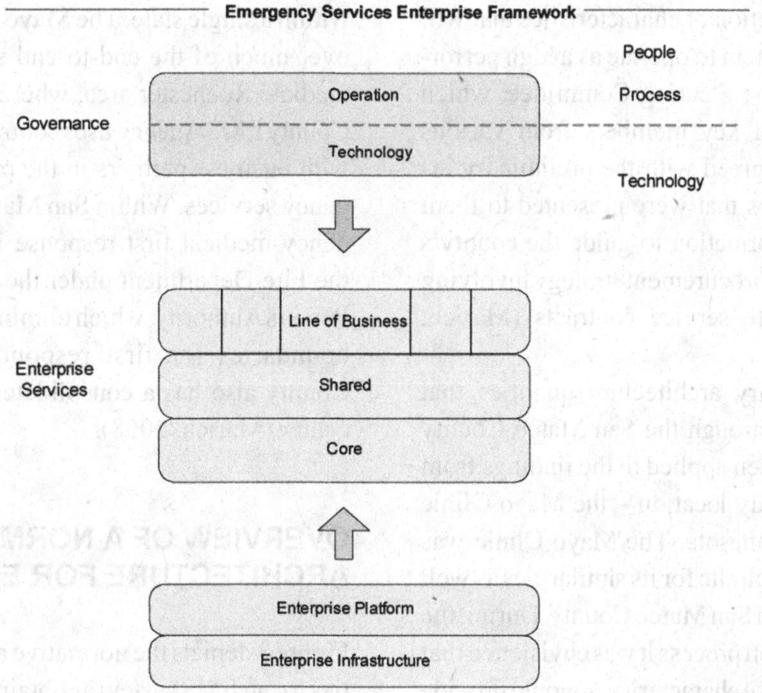

METHODOLOGY

A conceptual framework referred to as the time critical information services (TCIS) framework was previously developed in order to better understand the operational, organizational, and governance structures in which emergency medical services information services are delivered (Schooley & Horan, 2008; Horan & Schooley, 2007). The TCIS framework served as a tool to help define and align the multi-organizational enterprise architecture desired by EMS stakeholder groups. Findings from several focus group sessions, conducted with the San Mateo County EMS Agency in San Mateo, California and with the Mayo Clinic in Rochester, Minnesota, were organized according to this framework. For San Mateo, focus group sessions included participants from across the end-to-end emergency services provisioning chain, as referenced in Table 1 (Marich, Horan, & Schooley, 2008).

A preliminary set of normative architecture qualities, aligned with the TCIS framework, was developed from the focus group sessions. The main purpose of the normative architecture was to provide a collection of characteristics that will allow an EMS system to operate as a high performance system. The Steering Committee, which was comprised of key members from various subcommittees, agreed with the preliminary architecture qualities that were presented to them and used this information to guide the county's long-range, EMS procurement strategy involving public and private service contracts (Marich, 2008).

The preliminary architecture qualities that were explicated through the San Mateo County case study were then applied to the findings from a second case study location – the Mayo Clinic in Rochester, Minnesota. The Mayo Clinic was chosen as a research site for its similarities as well as differences with San Mateo County. During the case study selection process it was envisioned that these like and unlike characteristics would provide opportunities for comparison and contrast. Both

sites are similar in that they serve both urban and rural populations. Excluding the Rochester area, the Mayo Clinic is also similar to other places in the United States, such as San Mateo County, where emergency transport services are used to take patients to a variety of non-associated care facilities for treatment. Both San Mateo County and the Mayo Clinic are also similar for their innovation in applying information technology across their services. San Mateo County, for example, was an early adopter of electronic patient care records and their hospital availability reporting system. The Mayo Clinic continues to be a pioneer in providing quality patient care and is recognized as a world leader in the use of technology in all aspects of the medical field. Focus group sessions conducted at the Mayo Clinic included participants from across the end-to-end process of the emergency services provisioning chain, as referenced in Table 2 (Marich, 2008).

While there were several similarities between both case study locations, there were also several notable differences. The geographical area served by the Mayo Clinic covers a multi-state region, whereas San Mateo is a single county within a single state. The Mayo Clinic has control over much of the end-to-end system in the immediate Rochester area, whereas the San Mateo County EMS Agency uses contractual agreements with business partners in the provision of emergency services. Within San Mateo County, emergency medical first response is provisioned by the Fire Department under the control of a Joint Powers Authority, which eliminates geographical boundaries for first responders. San Mateo County also has a consolidated communication center (Marich, 2008).

OVERVIEW OF A NORMATIVE ARCHITECTURE FOR EMS

Figure 3 depicts the normative architecture qualities for an EMS system as obtained from both case study locations. This figure implies that there exists

Table 1. San Mateo County focus group participants (Marich, 2008)

Organization	Position
San Mateo County EMS Agency	Administrator
	Medical Director
	Emergency Preparedness Specialist
	Clinical Coordinator
	Injury Prevention Coordinator
	Consultant
Ambulance Service Provider	Administration Supervisor
	Operations Manager
	Director of Operations, San Francisco/San Mateo
	Information Technology Director, Western U.S.
	Information Technology Manager
	Information Technologist
County Fire Joint Powers Authority	Coordinator-North Zone, Fire Battalion Chief
	Coordinator-South Zone, Fire Battalion Chief
	Coordinator-Central Zone
	Fire Chief-Millbrae
	Fire Chief-Redwood City
	Fire Chief-San Bruno
	Fire Chief-Belmont
	Fire Chief-Woodside
	Administrator
	EMS Lead, South San Francisco
Care Facilities	Emergency Department Manager-Sequoia
	Emergency Physician-San Mateo Med. Center
	Executive Director-Hospital Consortium
	Information Technology, Kaiser
San Mateo Communications Center	Program Manager, Public Safety Communications
	CAD Manager, Public Safety Communications
	Systems Specialist, Public Safety Communications
Police	Chief-Belmont
County Manager's Office	Assistant County Manager
Consumer Advocate	Emergency Medical Care Committee
Payer	Director of Health Plan of San Mateo
Total Expert Participants: 33	

a performance continuum from low to high; and a set of qualities that comprise the operational, organizational, and governance aspects of service provision. This figure also implies that end-to-end performance is related to the architecture type (low or high).

The following subsections outline the general details of the normative architecture that was derived from interviews and focus group discussions with case study participants. Further details are provided in (Marich, 2008) and (Marich, Horan, & Schooley, 2008).

Table 2. Mayo Clinic focus group participants (Marich, 2008)

Organization	Position
Mayo Clinic Emergency Communications Center	Manager
	Program Coordinator
	Supervisor
Mayo Medical Transport	Administrator
	Chief Financial Officer
	Clinical Nurse Specialist
	Chair of RescueNet Committee
	Director of Air Operations, Mayo MedAir
	Regional Process Coach
Mayo Clinic Corporate Communications	Director
Information Technology	Lead Analyst Programmer
Dept. of Emergency Medicine	Physician, Co-Medical Director—Air
	Physician, Co-Medical Director—Ground
Trauma	Surgeon, Co-Medical Director—Air
Total Expert Participants: 14	

Normative Architecture Details – Operational Level Qualities

The operational level is centered on the performance aspects of the EMS system process, with specific emphasis on the information needs across the inter-organizational service process. The four main architecture qualities that emerged from the practitioner focus groups are outlined below.

Having complete patient information can generally be equated to the availability of a unified, end-to-end patient record. In order to achieve greater overall system performance, EMS practitioners emphasized that an end-to-end patient record would provide critical information pertaining to a patient as they move throughout the EMS system. One of the Pre-hospital/Hospital Technology Committee members remarked that if they could change only one thing to improve an EMS system: "[I would like to see] one electronic health record from dispatch through ED, including critical data points required at each step of the process" (Marich, 2008, p. 46).

Focus group participants also noted that the capability to integrate and share data, especially between pre-hospital system elements (dispatch, ambulance provider, fire, and EMS Agency organizations) and the hospitals that serve a particular geographical area, is essential to measure system performance and determine health outcomes. Removing the gap between the pre-hospital and hospital elements will allow EMS systems to associate patient outcomes with each of the activities that occur within the pre-hospital environment, offering potential enhancements to the quality of service and patient survival. Peter D'Souza, M.D., Medical Director for the San Mateo County EMS Agency, describes the need for EMS practitioners to take a holistic view of EMS systems, declaring that "emergency services should view themselves as an enterprise and become network centric" (Schooley, Horan, & Naomani, 2008, p. 8). However, technology must be carefully chosen so that it does not intrude into the critical responsibilities faced by emergency responders, as evidenced by these comments from a paramedic: "If I have the

Figure 3. Normative architecture for EMS Systems (adapted from Marich, 2008)

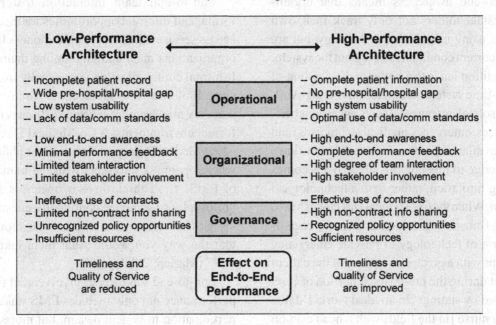

choice between entering data and stopping profuse bleeding, the choice is obvious" (Schooley, Horan, & Marich, 2010, p. 199).

While much has been done in the past to improve information system usability, designing a better user interface to simplify the collection and presentation of information within the emergency context is needed. Lamenting about the overhead involved in using a computer, one Emergency Physician felt that "It takes too much time and effort to go to a computer terminal and log on to get that [emergency medical] information" (Marich, 2008, p. 48). While it is true that many of the calls answered by emergency responders are not time-critical, those that are answered when a person's life is at stake require a special level of system usability that is distinct from information systems used for less time-critical activities.

End-to-end data standards for storing and sharing data, as well as inter-personal communication between system elements, such as the communication that routinely occurs between paramedics and care facilities, are vital for relaying information. For an EMS system to be classified as one that operates at the highest performance, end-to-end data standards must be established so that each of the system elements can trust that the data made available to them will not require extensive and unforeseen modifications in order for it to be useful. However, as Matt D'Ambrosia (President and CEO of Vital Data Technology) pointed out, this is not an easy task since "... the healthcare system is so fragmented under 70+ data standards. Getting some agreement with such a fragmented system has been unproductive" (Schooley, Horan, & Naomani, 2008, p. 11).

Normative Architecture Details – Organizational Level Qualities

The organizational level deals mainly with the organizational and inter-organizational actions that support the collection and use of EMS information, such that information sharing supports timely and high quality end-to-end performance. Focus group participants believed that the following four qualities are essential across the organizational dimension.

End-to-end awareness means that organizational stakeholders not only track their own resources using information technology, but are aware of current conditions throughout the system. This condition leads to a better understanding of near real-time system parameters involving available personnel resources (such as dispatchers, ambulances, emergency medical technicians) and hospital availability status. However, many times the challenge to meeting this objective becomes a funding limitation, rather than a technological limitation. When the Co-Medical Director of Mayo Medical Transport provided a scenario regarding the use of technology to provide emergency physicians with a greater awareness of the patient treatment during the pre-hospital portion of care, he finished by stating: "In an ideal world I'd like to have a nurse [in the field] with a head cam on so I can get real-time information. We can do that technically, but we can't afford it" (Marich, 2008, p. 74).

A system that attains high end-to-end performance feedback not only gathers and reports performance within each of the EMS organizations; it has the capability to draw upon an "Organizational" Performance Feedback System to report various types of performance outcome information to a wider range of system elements. Providing feedback for the events that occurred during a previous quarter would serve to fulfill the human side of the services provided by such system elements as the emergency medical technicians and emergency physicians, to name a few. As noted by the Director of Corporate Communications: "We are working on a few things right now for correspondence back to referring agencies [to let them know] how they did, to give them some feedback, status of the patient, at least current status of the patient. … We are also working on an initiative on the ground side of Gold Cross … to let them know 'good job', 'this went well for you', or 'perhaps we can offer a little bit of training here in this area'"(Marich, 2008, p. 76).

End-to-end team interaction fosters both formal and informal opportunities for discussion across service silos, where practitioners from all organizations meet and talk among themselves. Informal communication is especially important since it allows team members to discuss issues that they may be more reticent to discuss in more formal environments. A Co-Medical Director of Mayo Medical Transport discussed the philosophy where openness intersects with the human side of EMS: "… I think there is openness and the philosophy of someone continually questioning: 'What if this was your wife or your mother? Is that the way you would want them taken care of?'" (Marich, 2008, p. 78)

End-to-end stakeholder involvement for high performance not only includes EMS stakeholder participation in system design, but more importantly, innovative and full participation across all of the stakeholder groups, especially among those groups that are paying for the majority of the services (i.e., the health insurance providers). According to the Administrator of Mayo Medical Transport: "Although Mayo Clinic operations tend to be under one roof in contrast to the majority of EMS providers within communities in the United States, the oversight from the county EMS board is still quite challenging. Our staff believes that outcomes and performance measures are vitally important" (Marich, 2008, p. 79).

Normative Architecture Details – Governance Level Qualities

The governance dimension involves the structures, in terms of policies, regulations, and funding decisions that guide the EMS system. Such things as policy and political factors facilitate the deployment of a timely and high quality EMS system. The following four themes emerged from the focus group sessions.

End-to-end contract relationships can be used to encourage information sharing and include information sharing elements in the contracts that are awarded. A high performing system effectively deals with the issues and challenges resulting from public and private relationships, as well as contractor and subcontractor relationships. When group discussion turned to this subject, it was largely agreed upon that identifying those entities that would benefit from information sharing should contribute to its costs, or as Dr. Zietlow stated: "...if sharing information is going to work for your business plan then you should help pay for it" (Schooley, Horan, & Naomani, 2008, p. 11).

Besides formal contracts, there are considerations that are necessary to facilitate end-to-end non-contractual relationships. One important goal is to achieve consistency in such areas as information sharing. Exploring incentives to handle non-contractual situations may be challenging, but will be necessary in order to keep the system performance at optimal levels. The Chair of Mayo Clinic's RescueNet Committee stated that "[We] provide education to our rural providers. [We] facilitate meetings with the rural Basic Life Support (BLS) providers, telling them: 'this is new', 'this is changing' ... keep[ing] those lines of communication open" (Marich, 2008, p. 83). The Co-Medical Director of Mayo Medical Transport also added that: "Not only are we really integrated [with the BLS providers] we are managing, we are philosophizing, we are directing, and we're training" (Marich, 2008, p. 83).

The realization of policy opportunities (such as concurrent interests in healthcare and homeland security initiatives) that may occur between various system elements, needs to be aggressively pursued. Top performers in this area will find parallel and overlapping policy initiatives to help drive enthusiasm from a range of local, state, and national agencies on the issue of improved information technology for EMS. The Manager of Emergency Communications Center noted: "Refining our processes has helped us control our costs. ... The Balanced Budget Act threatened us greatly. We have come through that absolutely

shining because we have looked at every single thing that we did from buying a needle to sticking that needle in you, what are all the steps that we can do to make that more efficient" (Marich, 2008, p. 84).

The provision of sufficient resources (such as personnel and funding) that are needed to complete the myriad of tasks can be challenging. High performers look for ways to act with agility and continuous improvement of their processes. The Chair of Mayo Clinic's RescueNet offered this example: "... in that perfect world you would be documenting the patient care report and documenting something for the ED all at the same time. So [the patient transport crew members] wouldn't have to touch the patient care report again. The ED will have the report prior to the patient getting there. And from a financial perspective all of our needs would be met" (Marich, 2008, p. 86).

In sum, the performance imperatives described above and organized along operational, organizational, and governance dimensions represent the characteristics of a high-performing EMS system as derived through several phases of research.

EXPERT RECOMMENDATIONS FOR IMPROVING EMS INFORMATION SYSTEMS

The normative architecture was presented and discussed at a national symposium in Washington, D.C. consisting of 33 academics and practitioners involved in promoting more effective emergency response communications. Expert panelists confirmed the importance of the multi-leveled TCIS framework, noting how each level contains critical elements for the overall end-to-end system to perform well. Moreover, representatives from each of the (two) case studies confirmed principle findings of the case studies as well as the overall framework in which they were analyzed. The forum provided additional insight and validation for the normative architecture as a way to address the vision for high-performance EMS information systems.

Dr. Scott Zietlow, M.D., Director of Trauma Surgery at Mayo Clinic, and Dr. Peter D'Souza, M.D., Medical Director of the San Mateo County EMS Agency, shared their practitioner views on the use of information for medical decision support. While both the Mayo Clinic and San Mateo County cases represent the extensive application of IT to EMS systems, both Doctor's Zeitlow and D'Souza noted the challenges to using information for medical decision-making. Dr. Zietlow believes that in addition to the approaching EMS systems analysis from an end-to-end system perspective, the ability of the hospital staff to obtain crash information is enormously significant, citing "crash information remains incredibly important … Knowing a crash occurred and knowing exactly where [the crash occurred] is absolutely crucial, otherwise you're going to make mistakes. For example, in a crash, a velocity greater than 30 increases the death rate by 10% and roll over or ejection drives the chances of a victim dying up by 300%. In addition, the size and weight of the patient is vital for transportation." Dr. D'Souza added that many physicians want the ability to customize the information they receive, and indicated that "too much information isn't always a good thing" (Schooley, Horan, & Naomani, 2008, p. 7). Both practitioners described multi-organizational information sharing environments that have made significant strides towards greater degrees of integration, yet also advocated a need for adaptation and transition in the future.

While both doctors spoke about the use and transfer of information for real-time decision support, Gary Wingrove, Mayo Clinic Program Director of Government Relations and Affairs, pointed out that integrated systems also provide benefits to decision makers at a "system level." Mr. Wingrove emphasized that while careful selection of limited information for real-time decision support may be important for the development of a care provider's user interface; integrated sys-

tems also provide benefits to decision makers at a "system level." He stated, "the more information collected, the better" for policy and management decision making since performance assessment, quality improvement, and research are more robust and far-reaching when a wide range of data can be accessed and used, "…for the first time a solid end-to-end system would finally give the ability to analyze systems, such as small hospitals vs. large hospitals, and as a result improve patient care" (Schooley, Horan, & Naomani, 2008, p. 10).

Organizational representatives came from the case study locales as well as from such emergency response practitioner organizations as the National Emergency Number Association (NENA), the National Highway Transportation Safety Administration (NHTSA), the U.S. Department of Transportation, Intelligent Transportation Systems Program, Health and Human Services (HHS), COMCARE, GM OnStar various other agencies, and representatives from industry and academia. In terms of information sharing for decision support within the EMS systems, Lynne Markus, Professor of Information and Process Management, Bentley College, aptly summed up the groups' thoughts on the subject in the form of a question: "[Why isn't there] a gold standard for the way things are going to be done across the entire nation, as seen in other industries?" Referring to her case study work in the banking industry, she noted that highly significant and sensitive obstacles have been overcome, enabling information sharing across a complex network of financial institutions (Schooley, Horan, & Naomani, 2008, p. 8).

RECOMMENDATIONS FOR THE INTEGRATION OF ENTERPRISE AND NORMATIVE ARCHITECTURES

The Emergency Services Enterprise Framework addresses many aspects of high-performance architecture, for example, with respect to the governance and operational characteristics. Our research has illustrated that the architecture qualities that strongly affect end-to-end system performance may also include a robust inter-organizational dimension. As such, there are several key inter-organizational qualities that we posit should be accounted for in order to increase the performance of multi-organizational emergency response enterprise information systems. The addition of these elements is illustrated in Figure 4 below. The two main recommendations that involve integrating the enterprise architecture with the normative architecture are: (1) the addition of the performance dimension to the emergency services enterprise framework and (2) the gradual evolution of service-oriented EMS systems. These two recommendations are explained below.

Recommendation 1: Adding the Performance Dimension to the Emergency Services Enterprise Framework

For those entities involved in emergency response to achieve a high degree of performance, there are several qualities that they must exhibit. These qualities are shown under the headings labeled organizations, operations, and governance in

Figure 4. This figure highlights the need for inter-organizational linkages, where an exchange of information occurs between the organizations and operations within the emergency services enterprise. Line of business, shared, and core enterprise services are enabled by enterprise and infrastructure platforms. The operational and technology governance components are imposed across each of the elements within the enterprise. Further, the normative aspects of each enterprise layer (organizational, operational, governance) are embedded within the definition and meaning as illustrated on the right hand side of Figure 4. In other words, when developing line of business, shared, and core services, the strategic objective should be to aim towards the high-performance features of the normative architecture.

Recommendation 2: Taking an Evolutionary Stance toward a Service-Oriented EMS System

The day-to-day services that EMS organizations provide to citizens are highly structured and regulated, with each of the organizational entities responsible for performing specific tasks. Hutchinson et al. (2008) argue that a progressive evolution

Figure 4. Revised emergency services enterprise framework

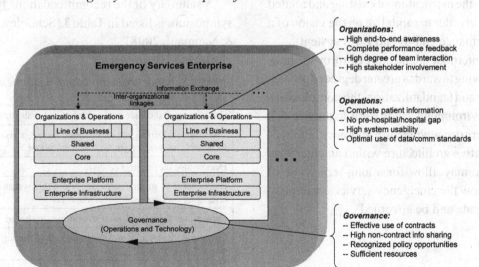

83

approach, whereby a system migrates "through a series of relatively discrete development cycles" (p. 42), would minimize the risk involved in moving an organization to a completely service-based type of system. From our research experience we have observed that EMS organizations have to deal with difficult policy environments (e.g., tight budget constraints) and organizational relationships (e.g., long contractual timelines that span 10 years or more), while attempting to meet public demand to increase the timeliness and quality of services that they provide. This recommendation is also aligned with comments made at the National Symposium, by Dr. Jack Potter (M.D., Director of Emergency Medicine at Valley Health System and COMCARE Vice Chair), when he explained the need to design and build integrated solutions by first understanding and then utilizing the existing health care system. He stated the need to "…drive initiatives that we can ride on that will help get pieces of this in place" using the example of "pay for performance, which is outcome driven, [and] is driving healthcare reimbursements right now. If we can get pieces of this [integrated information system] paid for, once it is in place riding whatever initiative you want, then it is there" (Schooley, Horan, & Naomani, 2008, p. 13). The main thrust, which was confirmed by David Aylward (Director of COMCARE) and others, is to identify, and then utilize, the momentum of existing and related initiatives, in order to capitalize on the vision of a high performance end-to-end EMS system.

While enterprise architecture can provide guidance on moving towards a greater degree of process integration and standardization, the complexities of EMS environments lends itself to a more risk averse enterprise architecture approach. Embedding normative architecture within an enterprise architecture may allow for a long-term view of what and how the emergency services enterprise should operate and be governed.

FUTURE TRENDS

The national symposium, referred to in a previous section of this article, provided a set of next steps and recommendations that included the need to take targeted, incremental steps towards the larger enterprise vision for emergency medical response information systems. Symposium participants believed that the need for an incremental approach is largely due to numerous contextual, organizational, and policy challenges and barriers to implementing enterprise systems, as well as risks associated with making changes to a large-scale, socio-technical system that fundamentally "works", but needs improvement. As such, participants noted the importance of making changes in a manner that does not worsen the existing system for practitioners and ultimately citizens using the service; but rather to aim to achieve the imperatives described in the normative architecture over time. Dr. Zeitlow believes that there is still much work to be done with regards to information sharing and its effect on decision making in EMS, stating "even if information is received in six seconds of the crash, the infrastructure or ER systems to utilize it is not in place yet. Also, the question posed is 'of how much of that info do I want and need, and what is the best information?'" (Schooley, Horan, & Naomani, 2008, p. 10).

A summary of the recommendations from the symposium is listed in Table 3 (Schooley, Horan, & Naomani, 2008).

Table 3. Summary of symposium recommendations

Conduct regional demonstration project and evaluation
Take targeted, incremental steps toward the larger vision for integrated emergency response communications
Demonstrate the business case(s)
Drive change by understanding the health care system and leveraging existing institutional initiatives
Demonstrate the clinical value of information sharing
Conduct more research, including more active sharing of research on the topic

Based upon these expert recommendations, the authors have targeted a portion of the normative architecture and developed a prototype that provides an end-to-end view of the information related to motor vehicle crashes. The prototype addressed feedback acquired during recent focus group sessions with practitioners at the Mayo Clinic.

Ongoing examination by the research team has focused on how the architectural concepts discussed herein might apply to real-world emergency medical settings. From an application level, the team is investigating the role of geographic information systems (GIS) as a platform for visualizing multi-organizational information for both near real-time and retrospective (i.e., historical) analysis. The use of mobile technologies to capture and share information across EMS and trauma/hospital organizations is also being investigated. From an architectural level, researchers are investigating how the use of open, web based, GIS-based, multi-media applications shape the architectural concepts discussed in this article. In other words, how must the architecture adapt as trends continue to push towards distributed cloud computing platforms, data standardization, continued user acceptance of software applications, and continued emphasis on multi-organizational partnership agreements?

CONCLUSION

As we observed in our research, the personnel involved in providing emergency response face numerous obstacles as they provide treatment to injured citizens. Information technology should assist, rather than detract from the job that these personnel perform. A rich set of qualitative and quantitative data was acquired from numerous practitioners during focus group sessions at the San Mateo County EMS Agency and the Mayo Clinic, with a goal of bringing suitable information

technology solutions to bear. The experts in the field of EMS that were involved in these studies cut across all aspects of these services and their insight formed the basis for a set of key normative architecture qualities. These results were then validated at a national symposium comprised of academics and practitioners, whose expertise came from the emergency response field as well as disciplines where similar issues were successfully resolved. The Emergency Services Enterprise Framework, independently developed through practitioner insight, was reviewed based upon the key architecture qualities and presented here. It is envisioned that the resulting framework will be useful in driving requirements development for successful information system deployment in the field of emergency response.

Our research findings indicate that the development of a normative architecture through end-user and stakeholder engagement is a valuable step within the larger scope of enterprise architecture development embedded in the complex, multi-organizational, emergency response context. First, having a well-defined conceptual framework allowed for the expression, classification, and validation of research findings. Second, developing a normative architecture through a close, working relationship with the actual stakeholders of a system provided a significant advantage to the design team assigned to perform architecture analysis and formal requirements definition. The normative architecture, especially in distinguishing between features such as low and high performance characteristics, clearly delineates the goals that system analysts and designers should strive toward. These goals span operational, organizational, and governance dimensions of the end-to-end spectrum of emergency response and are meant to ensure that personnel receive vital feedback in areas that span the range of decision support to policy development.

Similarly, the normative architecture can provide guidance, or act as a measuring stick for architecture maturity migration. As suggested by the participants in the national symposium, future directions for this research should include additional case study work that focuses on the incremental design and migration of emergency response information systems to increased levels of data and process integration and standardization.

ACKNOWLEDGMENT

We sincerely thank the dedicated personnel from the San Mateo County EMS Agency and the Mayo Clinic for their participation in this research. This research has been supported by the National Science Foundation (grant # 0535273). Supplemental support has been provided by the Center for Excellence in Rural Safety (CERS) and ITS Institute, University of Minnesota.

REFERENCES

Baltzan, P., & Philips, A. (2008). *Business driven information systems*. Boston: McGraw-Hill/Irwin.

Berner, E. S. (Ed.). (2006). *Clinical decision support systems: Theory and practice* (2nd ed.). New York: Springer.

Dawes, S., Cresswell, A., & Cahan, B. (2004). Learning from crisis: Lessons in human and information infrastructure from the world trade center response. *Social Science Computer Review*, *22*(1), 52–66. doi:10.1177/0894439303259887

Drake, D., Steckler, N., & Koch, M. (2004). Information sharing in and across government agencies. *Social Science Computer Review*, *22*(1), 67–84. doi:10.1177/0894439303259889

Drury, J., Klein, G. L., More, L., & Pfaff, M. (2009). A principled method of scenario design for testing emergency response decision-making. In J. Landgren & S. Jul, (Eds.), *Proceedings of the 6th International ISCRAM Conference*, Gothenburg, Sweden.

Dwarkanath, S., & Daconta, M. (2006). Emergency services enterprise framework: A service-oriented approach. In B. Van de Walle & M. Turoff (Eds.), *Proceedings of the 3rd International Conference on Information Systems for Crisis Response and Management*.

French, S., & Turoff, M. (2007). Decision support systems. *Communications of the ACM*, *50*(3), 39–40. doi:10.1145/1226736.1226762

Hale, J. (1997). A layered communication architecture for the support of crisis response. *Journal of Management Information Systems*, *14*(1), 235–255.

Horan, T., & Schooley, B. (2007). Time critical information services. *Communications of the ACM*, *50*(3), 73–78. doi:10.1145/1226736.1226738

Housel, T., El Sawy, O., & Donovan, P. (1986). Information systems for crisis management. *Management Information Systems Quarterly*, *10*(4), 389–400. doi:10.2307/249195

Hutchinson, J., Kotonya, G., Walkerdine, J., Sawyer, P., Dobson, G., & Onditi, V. (2008). Migrating to SOAs by way of hybrid systems. *IT Professional*, *10*(1). doi:10.1109/MITP.2008.15

Luftman, J., & Kempaiah, R. (2008). Key issues for IT executives 2007. *Management Information Systems Quarterly Executive*, *7*(2), 99–112.

Marich, M. (2008). *Toward a high performance architecture for time-critical information services: Sequential case studies and action research of regional EMS systems*. Claremont, CA: Claremont Graduate University, School of Information Systems and Technology.

Marich, M., Horan, T., & Schooley, B. (2008). Understanding IT governance within the San Mateo County emergency medical service agency. In F. Fiedrich & B. Van de Walle (Eds.), *Proceedings of the 5th International Conference on Information Systems for Crisis Response and Management (ISCRAM2008)* (pp. 451-461).

Ross, J. W. (2003). Creating a sustainable IT architecture competency: Learning in stages. *Management Information Systems Quarterly Executive, 2*(1), 31–43.

Ross, J. W., & Beath, C. (2006). Sustainable IT outsourcing success: Let enterprise architecture be your guide. *Management Information Systems Quarterly Executive, 5*(4), 181–192.

Sawyer, S., Reagor, S., Tyworth, M., & Thomas, J. (2005, March 17-19). From response to foresight: Managing knowledge and integrated criminal justice. In S. Newell & R. Galliers (Eds.), *Proceedings of the 2005 Organizational Learning and Knowledge Capabilities Conference*. Cambridge, MA: Bentley College.

Schekkerman, J. (2004). *How to survive in the jungle of enterprise architecture frameworks*. Victoria, Canada: Trafford Publishing.

Scholl, J. (2005). Interoperability in e-Government: More than just smart middleware. In *Proceedings of the 38th Hawaii International Conference on System Sciences (HICSS38)*.

Schooley, B., & Horan, T. (2007). End-to-end enterprise performance management in the public sector through inter-organizational information integration. *Government Information Quarterly, 24*(4), 755–784. doi:10.1016/j.giq.2007.04.001

Schooley, B., Horan, T., & Marich, M. (2010). User Perspectives on the Minnesota Interorganizational Mayday Information System. In B. Van de Walle, M. Turoff, & R, Hiltz (Eds.), *Information Systems for Emergency Management* (Vol. 16, pp. 193-225). Armonk, NY: M.E. Sharpe.

Schooley, B., Horan, T., & Naomani, A. (2008). *A report of the symposium: Improving emergency medical response with inter-organizational information systems symposium summary*.

Turban, E., Aronson, J. E., Liang, T., & Sharda, R. (2006). *Decision support and business intelligence systems* (8th ed.). Upper Saddle River, NJ: Prentice Hall.

Turoff, M., Chumer, M., Van de Walle, B., & Yao, X. (2004). The design of a dynamic emergency response management information system (DERMIS). *Journal of Information Theory, Technology, and Applications, 5*(4), 1–36.

Weissenberger, S., Lo, H., & Hickman, M. (1995, July 30-August 2). A methodology for evaluating systems architectures. In *Proceedings of the Vehicle Navigation and Information Systems Conference* (pp. 397-403).

Yasin, R. (2008). Enhanced SOA. *Government Computer News*. Retrieved January 24, 2009, from http://gcn.com/Articles/2008/09/10/Enhanced-SOA.aspx

Zwass, V. (2010). Series Editor Introduction. In B. Van de Walle, M. Turoff, & R. Hiltz (Eds.), *Information Systems for Emergency Management* (Vol. 16, pp. ix-xii). Armonk, NY: M.E. Sharpe.

This work was previously published in International Journal of Information Systems for Crisis Response Management, Volume 2, Issue 2, edited by Murray E. Jennex, pp. 1-18, copyright 2010 by IGI Publishing (an imprint of IGI Global).

Chapter 7
Lessons of Disaster Recovery Learned for Information Systems Management in US Higher Education

Ruben Xing
Montclair State University, USA

Zhongxian Wang
Montclair State University, USA

James Yao
Montclair State University, USA

Yanli Zhang
Montclair State University, USA

ABSTRACT

Most U.S. universities planned and prepared their disaster recovery (DR) and business continuity strategies for their Information Systems after the September 11th attack on the United States. The devastating hurricanes and the most recent catastrophic earthquakes caused unprecedented damage for many campuses within a decade. Some of their plans worked and some of them failed; however, with these lessons learned, Information Systems Management for U.S. higher education must be reexamined, re-planned and redesigned, including DR strategies and procedures. It is equally important that the curriculum of Management Information Systems be updated along with updated DR concerns for all educators in U.S. universities.

INTRODUCTION

Lessons learned from the past decades - the hurricane Katrina in New Orleans, the terror attack on the World Trade Centers, mudslides in the West coast of North America; massive floods in China; and the Boxing Day tsunami in Southeast Asia, and the most recent catastrophe earthquake in Haiti propelled Disaster Recovery Planning (DRP) to the highest status in almost all organizations. Whether commercial, governmental, or educational businesses — rely on some form of

DOI: 10.4018/978-1-4666-0167-3.ch007

technology to manage the various parts of their operations. A disruption to the availability of any of these resources, if even for a few hours, can have serious consequences for their ability to function at normal capacity. These disasters brought about the loss of essential services. More seriously, they may damage the most valuable property of the organizations – their critical information. How quickly and how much the organizations recover their lost properties and resume their operations depends on how well they prepared their recovery technologies and systems. This is where disaster recovery planning comes into play.

Compared with other business organizations, the development of disaster recovery planning for Information Systems Management, in particular in US higher educational institutes has received little attention. The goal of this research is to alert our schools with important facts and practical approaches of their information systems management on how to plan and prepare necessary recovery procedures to prevent from possible terror attacks or natural disasters. Another purpose of this research is to advocate and explain the necessity to integrate the DRP education with other emerging information technologies for the current Management Information Systems (MIS) curriculum.

The integration of enhanced DRP concerns and up-to-date technical solutions in US campuses along with the joint efforts of university IT groups and MIS faculty is emerging as an effective and potentially invaluable resource for answering such questions in regards to disaster recovery planning and management (Toomey, Frost, & Jennex, 2009).

LESSONS LEARNED FROM MAJOR TRAGEDIES

Property Loss

Nine years after the terrorist attacks that brought down the twin towers of the World Trade Center (WTC) on September 11th in 2001, this tragic events was not only deeply remembered by all American people, but also was best learned as a most fundamental lesson for our entire country. Similarly, Hurricane Katrina and Rita devastated entire New Orleans city, ravaged the Southern United States, most Gulf Coast and a large area of Texas five years ago. In addition to several thousands of casualties suffered from both disasters, hundreds of business organizations were wiped out in just few hours. Business giants and tech industry found themselves so vulnerable and paralyzed easily with no offices, telephones, email, or computers. While 250 of a total of 450 WTC tenants declared business disaster, 150 went out of business (IAGS, 2004). Price-Waterhouse- Coopers estimated later that the overall WTC losses were approximately $40.2B. And the losses from business interrupted economic activity caused by Hurricane Katrina exceed $100M per day. This natural disaster is considered the costliest one ever - with the estimated total loss of 125B and insurance industry slice of the clean-up bill reaching as much as US$60B (Foster & Irusta, 2003).

Information Systems Disaster

Disaster recovery planning is one of those management tasks that's easy to overlook (Law Office Management & Administration Report, 2008). Destroyed property losses are comparably recoverable. However, business interruption losses, especially losing critical data, are immeasurable and usually non-recoverable. Above 30% of WTC losses from September 11 attack represent business interruption costs. Of companies that suffer a major loss of computerized records, 43 percent will never reopen, 51 percent will close within two years and only 6 percent will survive long-term (Hoey, 2008). Information is the lifeblood of any organization, and operating without it is a 'non-starter' (Bradbury, 2008). Lighthouse Technology reported that annual data loss to PCs cost US businesses $11.8B in 1998. In 2001, the business downtime caused loss was $1,010,536 per hour for an average of all industries (Peterson,

2003). Meta Group reported this statistic in major financial industries reached $16.6M per hour in 2003 (BusinessWeek, 2003). A study shows, as much as 60% of corporate data resides unprotected on PC desktops and laptops, and more than 109,000 TB of unique enterprise PC data are not being regularly backed up (Please Refer to item 1 in Appendix).

One asset many tenants avoided losing in the September 11th disaster was electronic data. As Morgan Stanley's technology team characterized, the WTC as probably one of the best prepared office facilities from a systems and data recovery perspective (Scheeres, 2001). The road to the disaster recoveries of the WTC tragedy was paved in the wake of 1993 WTC bombing. It led most businesses firms to develop detailed plans that were crisply executed when disaster struck.

After the WTC attack, most people recognize the truth - no business is really secure until its data are recorded on two different sets of media. Nowadays, disaster recovery and crisis management are becoming more challenging, reflecting the rapidly growing complexity of information systems technology and pressures to keep e-commerce systems highly available 24 hours a day. Plus, an effective DRP must be able to protect a business from losing partial or entire physical locations within the shortest time as possible. The Appendix Item 2 shows the average losses from system downtime.

Besides disaster losses, information system vulnerability and site outage caused more losses. The Internet Worm of 1988 is a classic lesson of a security threat that used the Internet as a vehicle to travel around the world within minutes. It infected 6200 computers - 10 percent of the computers on the Internet at the time (Hovav & D'Arcy, 2005).

Industry experts put the total cost of the worm closer to $100M (Harvard Research Group, 2004). Due to web service outage, auction sites lost $2.8M and brokerage sites lost $5.2M within 8 business hours (Harvard Research Group, 2004). Meanwhile, slow performance costs e-commerce site $362M per month, according to The Industry

Standard. EBAY, a major online auction firm, was crippled for nearly 24 hours due to site outage in June 1999. This led to a 26% stock drop in the company's stock price (U.C. Berkeley & Stanford University Press, 2002). In August 1999, a software glitch caused 3,000 MCI WorldCom customers to lose Internet access. The outage lasted for about 10 days. A denial-of-service worm attacked Yahoo in February 2000 (BBC News, 2000). The true cost of downtime takes on a more global perspective, extending well beyond the traditional, immediate user community (Harvard Research Group, 2004). It took the site offline for at least 3 hours and cost millions of dollars in loss (Please Refer to item 2 in Appendix).

METHODOLOGY

To find out the current status and possible approaches regarding the disaster recovery planning for US universities, a methodology for conducting the case study of an information system management (ISM) is presented. Case study research excels at bringing us to an understanding of a complex issue or object and can extend experience or add strength to what is already known through previous research (LIS, 1997). Case study research method as an empirical inquiry investigates a contemporary phenomenon within its real-life context (Yin, 1984). Through the comparisons of the detailed measures, we found out what their DRP plans worked and failed during and after disasters. We focus on the details how universities planned and prepared their information systems before and after the hurricane attack. The cases that we use provide an overview of the methodological problems involved in the study of a specific issue. It describes scientific method in academic environment, presents an elucidation of how a specific ISM case study captures the major features of scientific, academic method. This research also has ramifications that go beyond matters of this DRP related education on Management Information Systems (MIS) case studies alone. For ISM practitioners and MIS educators, the study of the case method might prove interesting for empowering them to identify themselves. The point at which scientific rigor is achieved in an MIS research effort, and beyond which further rigor can be called into question, especially if pursued at the expense of professional relevance (Lee, 1989). With our defined methods, this research followed the six steps based on the case of Hurricane Katrina disaster in Tulane and other US universities:

- Determine and define the research questions
- Select the cases and determine data gathering and analysis techniques
- Prepare to collect the data
- Collect data in the field
- Evaluate and analyze the data
- Prepare the report

GESTURES FROM U.S. HIGHER EDUCATION FACING DISASTERS

DRP Imminence Recognitions

History shows, campus disasters occurred frequently throughout the country. The Table 1 summarizes some typical ones within past 15 years.

Higher education, however, disaster recovery planning is not well prepared at many universities. Enterprise-wide defensive strategies are generally lacking, many organizations have an emergency information systems that may not be adequate (Jennex, 2004). Many of them do not even exist. According to Info-Tech, a surprising 47% of universities and colleges currently have no disaster recovery plan in place (Info-Tech, 2005). Sourced from Campus Technology, these institutions, do, however, acknowledge the importance of having such a plan: 68% of them say they are currently in the process of planning. Unfortunately, it may be some time before many college and university DRPs see implementation: 32% of schools with no current plan concede it may be up to three years before they have one in place, according to the report, and that may be because security and end user support are higher IT priorities than disaster recovery—just a notch above the categories of network/LAN/WAN, Web site and IT governance. But the good news is that, according to Info-Tech, among the 53% of schools currently with a plan in force, a whopping 86% are improving that plan (Schaffhauser, 2005). Figure 1 shows a little progress on IT disaster recovery planning for US higher educations in recent years.

Reluctance for taking DRP actions at campuses is mainly because of traditional cultural and

Table 1. Historical damages for US Universities (LCTTP, Michigan State University)

1989	The earthquake damaged a number of buildings at Stanford University
1992	Hurricane Andrew caused $17M in damage to the University of Miami.
1994	The earthquake damaged three universities in the LA area
1997	The Colorado State University campus was flooded by a local creek; water poured into both the library and the bookstore, damaging hundreds of thousands of books and other valuable documents.
1998	On Labor Day, a severe windstorm damaged many buildings, trees and utilities on the Syracuse University campus, forcing closure of some residence halls and relocation of 600 students
1999	In July, a heat wave resulted in a sustained power outage at Columbia University in New York City, and was not completely restored for two or three days. Damages to the $200M research program were calculated
2001/ 2002	The University of Washington was accidentally caught fire. Many faculty members' research information and student records got lost

Figure 1. Little Progress on IT DRP for US higher educations (Loma Prieta Symposium, 2009)

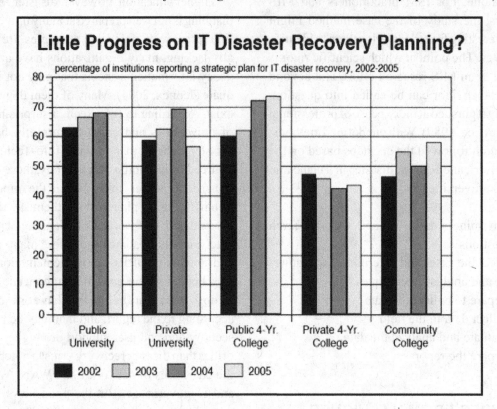

political factors. Also schools create difficult and complex settings to enact change of any kind. Plus, the mission (an emphasis on teaching and learning) at academic institutions is fundamentally different. DRP and information security deficiencies at educational institutions are more pervasive than that at profit driven corporations. New efforts to move to an improved level (of DRP) are not easy and don't happen quickly (Reeder, 2002). Although most universities are doing at least the minimum necessary to protect computer data, few have well-thought-out systems for recovery once a disaster happened (Carnevale, 2003). John W. Toigo, CEO of Toigo Partners International, says, data recovery often isn't a big priority for institutions unless people there have already witnessed some major catastrophe (Forum, 2006).

DRP STRATEGY RECONSIDERATIONS

In the aftermath of Hurricane Katrina, universities in the gulf coast were devastated. State higher-education officials have estimated that the hurricane cost Mississippi's public and private colleges at least $674-million. That includes $495-million to repair and rebuild campus facilities (US EPA, 2009). Table 2 lists rough losses from most of universities.

Non-Recoverable Academic Resources Loss from Hurricanes

Beside huge number of financial losses from these universities, the hurricanes forced full institutional closures longer than any on record (Hart, 2006), and it ravaged a whole region of

Table 2. The cost of Katrina and Rita in 2005 (CRS, 2005)

Institution	Physical Damage
Louisiana	
Delgado Community College*	$132,116,576
Dillard University*	$282,000,000
Louisiana State University Health Sciences Center	$182,800,000
Louisiana Technical College*	$18,188,750
Loyola University New Orleans*	$4,000,000
Nunez Community College*	$32,934,347
Our Lady of Holy Cross College*	$2,750,000
Southern University at New Orleans*	$350,000,000
Sowela Technical Community College*	$20,000,000
Tulane University*	$125,000,000
University of New Orleans*	$103,620,000
Xavier University of Louisiana*	$30,000,000
Mississippi	
Alcorn State University	$3,000,000
Copiah-Lincoln Community College	$100,000
East Central Community College	$665,000
East Mississippi Community College	$74,800
Hinds Community College	$300,000
Jackson State University	$1,200,000
Jones Community College	$2,000,000
Meridian Community College	$232,775
Mississippi Delta Community College	$20,020
Mississippi Gulf Coast Community College	$15,000,000
Pearl River Community College	$50,000,000
Southwest Mississippi Community College	$108,500
Tougaloo College	$2,000,000
William Carey College *	$12,800,000
Alabama	
Spring Hill College	$1,000,000
TOTAL	$1,371,910,768
* Temporarily Closed	

colleges and universities. The wrath of Hurricane Katrina wreaked billions of dollars in damage and claimed hundreds, maybe thousands of lives. In many universities, decades of research, some scientists find, and took the lives of thousands of lab animals were destroyed. For many researchers at universities affected by the storm, it also destroyed or menaced their lives' work.

Many researchers in New Orleans did not know exactly how much they lost. Most of those at Tulane University and at Louisiana State University's Health Sciences Center have not been able to return to their labs to survey the damage or recover specimens. Administrators at both universities have been collecting lists of the most important research materials and working to ferry them out. As many of professors stated that it's tens of millions of dollars of research. It's over 20 years of work. And it's all going to be gone. Cecil D. Burge, vice president for research and economic development, estimates that 25 faculty members lost specimens and collections, some worth millions of dollars (Winstead, 2007). Most of the scientists who lost materials were at the university's Gulf Coast Research Laboratory, in Ocean Springs, close to the beach.

The hurricane's intensity vanquished researchers in other tragic ways. Those who stayed at the Louisiana State University medical school during the storm and subsequent flood ultimately made the difficult decision to euthanize the surviving animals before evacuating. All of the Health Sciences Center's 8,000 experimental animals died or were euthanized -- including the rhesus monkeys belonging to Joseph M. Moerschbaecher, vice chancellor for academic affairs, who was one of the last to evacuate the medical school. There was nothing they could do for the animals, he says (Petfinder, 2005). He estimates that 150 to 175 faculty members lost research materials. That work often involved animals that perished. At Tulane University, the Louisiana State University Health Sciences Center, and the University of

Southern Mississippi, Katrina destroyed thousands of animals -- including fruit flies, mice, rabbits, dogs, and primates -- and materials ranging from tissue samples to cell lines to microorganisms like yeast and bacteria. In some cases, the damage encompassed years, even decades of work. At Tulane, that included invaluable blood samples from the Bogalusa Heart Study, which has been tracing heart disease in thousands of people since 1972, according to Paul K. Whelton, senior vice president for health sciences (Welton, 2006).

In addition to academic losses, information systems and IT resources were damaged badly too. Hurricane Katrina has destroyed tens of thousands of PCs and servers. In New Orleans alone many thousands of computer installations will have been flooded out or damaged. The local IT networking infrastructure will have been severely degraded. It includes the New Orleans mayor's office IT facility. This large scale disaster will bring data protection and IT disaster recovery concerns to the fore. Every business that has an IT data centre in the region, now non-operational because of the hurricane floods, but which has a DR facility will now be thanking their lucky stars (Welton, 2006). They were wise to invest in a DR facility. Those that didn't will either be wishing they had or not be concerned at all - because their entire business has gone.

Worst-Case Scenario

As a typical case, we looked closely at the largest campus in New Orleans - Tulane University which had a disaster plan. Table 3 and Table 4 summarize what of it worked, what of it didn't.

Since many plans could not meet the emergency needs, several prepared measures, and procedures failed to be implemented in expected ways. Compare with the assessment for what Tulane planned and what they prepared:

MISSIONS FOR DISASTER RECOVERY RE-PLANNING

During the Hurricane Katrina attack, there were so many things that both business and schools could not have predicted or prepared for. It is also important to have a disaster recovery team compressed of representatives from all areas of the company (Ecker, 2008). The entire process should include resilience strategies, recovery objectives, business continuity and crisis management plans, and management support for organizing the project within agreed-upon time and budget limits (Hein, 2008). They all had to rethink their plan in the middle of the disaster. With our case methodology, we further collected and studied more lessons learned from Tulane University, summarized some major failures and lessons, reasons and advices for future plans (Table 5).

Critical Campus Resources Redundancy

From what we listed above, it is clear for our colleges and universities that disaster recovery strategies must include maintaining continuity for the scholarly work of faculty and researchers. The importance of the research enterprise calls for paying significant attention to both academic and IT personnel, also preservation of the institution's digital assets, particularly those that are unique to the campus. Campus systems that store these unique digital assets can be found in central IT units and in almost every academic and administrative department. Systems that hold universities' assets including not just those set up specifically to store individual files but also those for campus-wide e-mail, courseware, e-portfolio, and other learning systems (see Table 3).

Since September 11, most companies and campuses recognized the truth - no business is really secure until its data are recorded on two different sets of media. When a primary site gets seriously affected or destroyed, in order to recover essen-

Table 3. Assessment for what Tulane planned (Laura, 2006)

Planning	• Student safety was their first concern. Their disaster plans were based upon time, location, and intensity that is, the hours until a storm's projected landfall, its location in the gulf, and its projected strength. • For information technology, the plan said: "If it's a Category 1 to Category 3 hurricane, we would complete backing up all systems — telephone and network, as well as applications — 24 hours out of landfall." • The university would have a skeleton crew at key locations to keep systems up. • The university would activate their emergency Web site to communicate to students updates on what the university was doing and how close the storm was, with a link on the home page.
True confession	• The university did not have a formal disaster-recovery plan for replacement of machines with any outside vendor or institution. That was a cabinet-level decision, made during times of fiscal stress. • IT Center had just shifted to a decentralized system for fiscal management, so IT was a shared resource. A presented plan for off-site disaster recovery, it was for $300,000 a year or so. • The university decided that they could not ask the deans to pay for that because they were already upset about how much technology was costing them, what they were getting for it, and whether it was giving them value. So it was a conscious decision, knowing there were risks.
Advice to president	• Listen to the chief information officer. • That's the big thing about a disaster — it's a disaster.
Advice to CIO	• Don't take no for an answer. • Somehow they've got to persuade administrators to spend the money on disaster-recovery plans. • Some colleges have done it very well. They have their own backup sites. Other colleges have signed agreements with vendors. Others have made agreements with other institutions.

tial business data, or service availability, either a "cold-site", "warm-site" or "hot-site" is needed. The critical data are backed up at a redundant storage site, and can be restored within different time period. Zero-tolerance requires a "hot-site" (standby-failover-site) mirrored with the primary site. So it is also called "site-mirroring", or "real-time-backup". Some of organizations even started planning their 3rd data center. By doing so, the third data center is able to be technically operational within three hours of a major regional failure affecting both of the primary data centers (Kentouris, 2008). Item 3 in the Appendix shows this strategy designed by Cisco. Each site is configured with Storage Area Network (SAN), Direct Attached Storage (DAS), or Network Attached Storage (NAS) based storage networks and connected through fast link media. Global load balancing, and global replication systems are also needed. When the primary site failed, the hot-site could quickly failover with little interruption break. This feature allows companies to tap into a live system with little or no interruption when disaster strikes. The latest Cloud Computing technology

will provide more reliable and flexible solutions for this practice.

However, the hurricane's aftermath revealed some weaknesses for this most updated model. Some firms had stored backup tapes at their offsite locations, but these sites were also in New Orleans and couldn't be accessed. So many campuses plan to look into doing online backup. For those who had started online backup in advance of the storm, most of their data are safe. This is a lesson learned, and brought a major challenge facing the up-to-date, multi-site-data-recovery-strategy. To deal with worse case in future, how far between each site should be safe enough remains to further study. On the other hand, we should keep in mind that the technology enables disaster response but disaster response is still a human intensive activity. So technology investments should continue, but only to support human actions (Jennex, 2007).

Reliability of Telecommunications

Telecommunications, e-mails and Internet access issues have risen to the top of the priority

Table 4. Assessment for what Tulane prepared (Laura, 2006)

Preparation	• Be prepared to follow the plan and take criticism.
	• Make sure the emergency-operation center is stocked appropriately for the number of people who are going to be in it, for days upon end.
	• Test the communications plan and have a backup;
	• Make sure they're as prepared as possible for the post disaster activity. That means they need to know where people are.
	• The plan needs to know how they can get back, and need to have a place for them to get back to;
	• They also need a business-continuity plan for the institution:
	    o How they are going to function if a disaster happens;
	    o How long can they go without printing transcripts,
	    o How long without sending paychecks out, how long without paying bills?
	    o How long can they tolerate not sending out accounts-receivable statements?
	• They need to make those choices, so they'll know how much money they'll have to spend on disaster recovery.

True confession	• The communications plan was not as robust as they needed. • The telephone switch on their uptown campus lasted longer than anyone expected. They had a generator, they got fuel to it for a while, and it stayed up for a long time. • Their cellular communication went down faster than expected. One now carries a cell phone from one provider on one side of his belt and a phone from another on the other side. • The lines were so clogged they had to keep trying different providers. They even had to get cellular phones with a different area code because the New Orleans code was completely plugged. • They couldn't get hold of people to find out where they were. The CIO had his director of computing evacuating to one city; his director of networking, who was supposed to go with him, ended up in a different city because of traffic. They had people spread out all over. • They had dutifully made backups of all their data, had them all ready, had the pickup scheduled. • When the CIO evacuated, the tapes were sitting in their boxes ready to be picked up. • They had recently moved into a high-rise building downtown. It was leased space. Unknown to them, the building management closed it before the pickup could be made. • The people came to get the tapes, and the building was locked. Their tapes were safe; they were on the 14th floor, in an interior hallway. They just couldn't get to them.
Advice to president	• Finance the backup systems, and provide the funds to evacuate all your key personnel to one place. • You'll have to talk to the lawyers about that because there are some liability issues • You've got to make sure that your key people are in position to help you with determining what your future will be. • Watch out for rumors. Be temperate in your reactions. Verify before you comment.
Advice to CIO	• Don't rely upon cellular and push-to-talk networks. Have an old-fashioned radio system for backup communications on campus. • Educate your key personnel on text messaging. People couldn't make a voice phone call, but they could use text messaging on their phones, because that used so much less bandwidth. • Again, put your key personnel in one location, out of harm's way. • Frankly communicate the information-technology status to the leadership team. • Be realistic about what you can do and when you can do it.

list for most IT managers. New technologies and improved emergency procedures could help avoid prolonged communications outages. Universities should keep a full-time connection with their state government emergency communication systems. However, the system became overloaded as the state moved large numbers of its responders into the affected area. This overload, combined with the loss of public network connectivity failures

caused system degradation and impaired communications. Although there is a common operating system between campuses and state emergency operation center, the statewide system must be expanded to assure collaborative information sharing in a common situational awareness environment among local, state, and federal agencies. Degraded communications among the emergency responder

Table 5. Failures and advices at Tulane (Shepherd, 2009)

Failures & Lessons	Reasons & Advices
Under old accounts receivable system, the controller had set up his own IT shop. When Katrina hit, those machines got flooded, and they were not recoverable.	There are just some things need to have centralized control over – need one point failure or success.
The No. 1 internal complaint was about e-mail systems. After Katrina, only limited subsets of emails were brought up online for administrators and faculty and staff members.	The reason is that Tulane's e-mail system was in New Orleans, and the network was down. IT didn't have those backup tapes for the list of all user names. So e-mail system should be always critical.
The Emergency Web site was failed to be activated right after Katrina attack	• Due to the vendor had made a change for the Web site to virtual servers. The IP address for the site kept changing and IT had to get hold of them to fix. • It's equally important to keep university emergency Web page highly available. The web site provides a major channel for employee registration. University needs to make sure that employees can tell where they are. The web shows employees that the university cares them, and also tells where the resources are. • E-mail and the Web have become our lifeblood. Know their status at all times.
Stuck on short of technical support during the disaster	Should not wait on the technology folks, because they'll have their hands full. Always keep connections with an outside company. So that the call centers, frequent Web updates, the electronic chats can be supported during the emergency,
Vendors' Support	Don't be upset at the use of outside resources — facilitate it. Don't be surprised when old vending partners disappoint you — while other partners support you in unexpected ways.

community severely interfered with their ability to deliver necessary services.

Land-line based telecom systems are being used in most gulf coast area. People were expecting cell phone to help their communications during the disaster. However, only a small portion of cellular call is carried over wireless links. Cellular call is actually carried over cell sites connecting to switching station via T1 and fiber-optic cables. When flooding brought most dramatic effect on land lines, about 1 million land-line phones were knocked out of service in gulf area according to BellSouth. So the wireless communications are not fully wireless. This challenge will be one of major concerns facing telecom companies and all the campuses' future recovery plan.

Several up-to-date technologies are significantly changing the traditional approach to disaster response. For instance, the recent development of broadband wireless communication, called WiMax, the Cloud Computing, and Virtualized computing brought more options for the information systems disaster recovery, also will help

people in real-time wherever tragedies strike (Murphy & Jennex, 2006).

Another key to successful communications during crisis is to train the board on both the process and the key messages they can communicate - and impress upon them the limits of what they can say (Holiday, 2008).

From developer and vendor sites, since most telecom companies are all relaying on backup generators or portable ones carried on panel trucks along with cellular transceivers, the telecommunication services, in particular the cellular and other kinds of wireless services still have difficulties to gain access to most parts of New Orleans. The process to repair, troubleshoot or replace of vendor's networks became rather slow. It made very difficult for the universities in this area to resume their regular communication systems. Universities are working with telecom companies to mount more rooftop cell sites and increase the power. As the latest IT development moves, more companies started considering the use of virtualization to protect critical business applications (Reisinger, 2008).

DRP Drills

No one can tell how well their DR plans will work until the plans get thoroughly tested. The schools fully or partially rely on outsourcing for DRP support, or never drilled their own DR plans, are taking a big risk. They may never know whether their data and IT systems can be correctly backed up/restored on time until an incident strikes. An IBM storage management director says that during those drills, officials will be able to tell whether the stored data are easily accessible and compatible with other equipment. Drills also make people realize that they need spare copies of the software to run the data they've been storing. A survey shows that drills are performed very differently and informally at most schools. Some schools run limited drills when they first set up a new system, and some play drills at backup sites occasionally, testing loaded data from tape, and running production jobs. Several universities never took the drills because of unaffordable costs and disruptive activities.

Usually, many institutions' drills only train people how to evacuate under fire, flood, or earthquake circumstances. Business recovery drills should train people how to protect the safety for both their lives and critical data. Drills make public personnel familiar with DRP processes and procedures. The familiarity facilitates the rapid work speed needed in disaster recovery (Panko, 2003). It is equally important that communications between diverse groups needing to communicate during an emergency drill (Murphy and Jennex, 2006)

Future Approaches for Campus DRP

The message is clear: Campuses must proactively develop, test and implement a comprehensive disaster recovery strategy to ensure business continuity, or be exposed to potentially disastrous losses (Zalud, 2008). Since Katrina's attack, more universities are considering the possibility of extended shutdowns and to look beyond their neighbors for assistance. The University of New Orleans, which kept classes going in Hurricane Katrina's aftermath by using satellite facilities and distance learning, satellite systems and clustered computers, also provided continued e-mail and university web pages access. As a matured technology, Satellite Communications has been utilized for more than 10 years. Its free-geographic limitation, reliable signals. To support with reliable academic operations, universities are planning the following communications services:

- Satellite Broadband Internet
- Satellite Video Broadcasting
- Videoconferencing
- Distance Learning
- Telecom for Academic, Industrial Communications
- Portable and Remote Communications, or VoIP phone systems.

The campus IT personnel and MIS faculty are crucial intelligence resources that should play effective roles during emergency management process. However, these two parties are not working closely and efficiently enough in many US campuses. Their effect function should include having the right set of information that is timely and relevant and that is governed by an effective communication process (Raman, Ryan, & Olfman, 2006).

DRP Lessons Facing MIS Education:

To highly recognize the DRP importance in US campuses, a long term strategy for university development should be considered from now on. Our lessons showed that an efficient information systems management needs close communications and collaborations between school IT personnel and MIS faculty team. Traditionally, MIS instructors have been adequately educated in the fundamental theories and hands-on skills required for their classrooms. Today however, much of the academic curriculum in higher education no longer closely matches the latest DRP concerns. Some curricula may not address the current developmental needs of the DRP technology - others may not provide sufficient teaching and/or research content for students. Typically, the topics of disaster recovery and business continuity are addressed little in MIS education. So far, major MIS curriculums only spent less than one chapter addressing system continuity and recovery issues. Some of them mentioned none of these issues. Moreover, the following core DRP practices and emerging technologies are introduced very lightly or even omitted within current MIS curriculum:

- High Availability Technologies
- Remote Storage Technology & Zero-Tolerance/Site-Mirroring
- Information System Security
- Computing Virtualization,
- Wireless and Cloud Computing Development

So MIS educators should be fully aware of the important concern of the disaster recovery for our students and university staffs. Making the MIS curriculum up to date, redesigning or partially modifying the existing MIS curriculum for students, and preparing appropriate training or short-term courses for school employees are necessary. Meanwhile, developing a dedicated DRP course for business and/or technology majors of US higher education should be an urgent agenda for MIS education as well.

CONCLUSION

After Hurricane Katrina and other disaster attacks, along with many companies, US higher educations are more acutely aware of the vulnerability of campus information systems management. It is mission critical for our universities to review what worked and what went wrong with planned disaster recovery strategies. With the lessons learned from the disaster recovery in universities, we can better re-plan and redesign the procedures to meet future challenges from unforeseen circumstances aiming on new technologies for our campuses. Also, it is the time for educators to update and modify the existing contents of our MIS textbooks with this part of important experiences.

ACKNOWLEDGMENT

We would like to thank Dr. Jennex, the co-editor of IJISCRAM, for his tremendous help and guidance during the period of revising our manuscript. Dr. Jennex suggested several research methodologies and structures, also provided useful resources and other specific suggestions.

REFERENCES

U.C. Berkeley & Stanford University Press. (2002). *Recovery-Orientated Computing Press, 3*.

Bradbury, C. (2008). Disaster! *Manager: British Journal of Administrative Management, 62*, 14–16.

BusinessWeek. (2003). *Finance research forum*. Retrieved January 18, 2010, from http://investing.businessweek.com/research/common/symbol-lookup/symbollookup.asp?textIn=METG

Carnevale, D. (2003). Preparing for computer disasters. *The Chronicle of Higher Education*, 2–28.

Cirillo, A. (2002). *Disaster recovery plans are more important than ever*. AIS News.

CRS. (2005). *Hurricanes Katrina & Rita: Damage and recovery* (CRS Report-3, Order code RS-22241).

Ecker, K. (2008). Data disaster. *Inside Counsel, 18*(202), 42-45.

FEMA. (2008). *Building a disaster-resistant university*. Retrieved June 30, 2010, from http://www.fema.gov/institution/dru.shtm

Forum. (2006). Retrieved December 2, 2009, from http://www.sun.com/events/forum2006/speakers.jsp#jtoigo

Foster, V., & Irusta, O. (2003). Does infrastructure reform work for the poor? *World Bank Policy, 3.*

Glick, M., & Kupiec, J. (2001). Strategic technology. *EDUCAUSE Review*, 11–12.

Hart, R. (2006). *Hurricanes: A primer on formation, structure, intensify change and frequency* (p. 13). Arlington, VA: The George C. Marshall Institute.

Harvard Research Group. (2004). *The total cost of downtime*. Retrieved September 10, 2009, from http://www.hrgresearch.com/pdf/paper4.pdf

Hein, T. (2008). Minimize cost with preparation. *Multi-Housing News, 43*(7), 27–28.

Hoey, S. (2008). How to stop document disasters. *For Buyers of Products. Systems & Services, 45*(7), 68–69.

Holliday, K. (2008). Planning for the worst. *Community Banker, 17*(8), 32–35.

Hovav, A., & D'Arcy, J. (2005). Capital market reaction to defective IT products: the case of computer viruses. *Computers & Security, 24*(5), 409–424. doi:10.1016/j.cose.2005.02.003

IAGS. (2004). *How much did the 9/11 terrorist attack cost America?* Retrieved March 2010, from http://www.iags.org/costof911.html

Info-Tech. (2005). DRP in the education. *Benchmarking Report*. Retrieved November 2009, from http://www.infotech.com/search/?searchterm=Benchmarking+Report&page=6

Jennex, M. E. (2004). Emergency response systems: the utility Y2K experience. *Journal of Information Technology Theory and Application, 6*(3), 85–102.

Jennex, M. E. (2007). Reflections on strong angel III: some lessons learned. In *Proceedings of the Fourth International Conference on Information Systems for Crisis Response and Management* (p.5).

Jennex, M. E. (2007). Modeling emergency response system. In *Proceedings of the 40th Hawaii International Conference on System Sciences* (p.7).

Kentouris, C. (2008). Strengthening data continuity, euro-clear adds backup site. *Securities Industry News, 20*(8), 8–10.

Laura, L. (2006). Lesson learned from Katrina. In *Proceedings of the ACUC Disaster Recovery Planning Conference*. Retrieved February 2, 2010, from http://grants.nih.gov/grants/OLAW/IACUCConf2006_Levy.pdf

Law Office Management & Administration Report. (2008). *Emergence Preparedness Resources, 8*(9), 1-2.

Lee, A. (1989). A scientific methodology for MIS case studies. *Management Information Systems Quarterly, 13*(1), 33–50. doi:10.2307/248698

LIS. (1997). *The case study as a research method*. Retrieved December 2009, from http://www.ischool.utexas.edu/~ssoy/usesusers/l391d1b.htm

Louisiana Office of Homeland Security & Emergency Preparedness. (2005). *Lessons learned.* Retrieved March 10, 2010, from http://emergency.louisiana.gov/

Michigan State University Disaster Recovery Planning. (2003). Retrieved March 5, 2010, from http://www.drp.msu.edu/WhyPlan.htm

Monaco, F. (2001). *IT disaster recovery near the world trade center.* Retrieved March 12, 2010, from http://net.educause.edu/ir/library/pdf/eqm0144.pdf

Murphy, T., & Jennex, M. E. (2006). Knowledge management, emergency response, and hurricane Katrina. *International Journal of Intelligent Control and Systems, 11*(4), 199–208.

Murphy, T., & Jennex, M. E. (2006). Knowledge management systems developed for hurricane Katrina response. In *Proceedings of the 3rd International ISCRAM Conference* (p.622).

News, B. B. C. (2000). *Yahoo attack exposes web weakness.* Retrieved March 3, 2010, from http://news.bbc.co.uk/2/hi/science/nature/635444.stm

Organization, G. B. R. (2003). *The cost of lost data.* Retrieved March 8th, 2009, from http://gbr.pepperdine.edu/033/dataloss.html

Panko, R. (2003). *Corporate computer and network security* (*Vol. 3*, pp. 223–225). Upper Saddle River, NJ: Prentice Hall.

Peterson, R. (2003). Lighting a dark corner of disaster recovery. *Journal of Academy of Business and Economics, 253,* 15–17.

Petfinder. (2005). Retrieved January 23, 2010, from http://www.petfinder.com/forums/viewtopic.php?p=861990&sid=2c51d1d64870febd87acbcb4d22c3c05

Raman, M., Ryan, T., & Olfman, L. (2006). Knowledge management systems for emergency preparedness. *International Journal of Knowledge Management, 2*(3), 33–50. doi:10.4018/jkm.2006070103

Reeder, S. (2002). *Improve higher education information security.* Retrieved July 23, 2009, from http://www.giac.org/certified_professionals/practicals/gsec/1982.php

Reisinger, D. (2008). Disaster recovery goes virtual. *InformationWeek, 11*(88), 23–23.

Repositories, I. (2006). *An opportunity for CIO: Campus impact.* Retrieved January 27, 2010, from http://net.educause.edu/ir/library/pdf/erm0626.pdf

Schaffhauser, D. (2005). Disaster recovery: The time is now. *Campus Technology.* Retrieved February 18, 2010, from http://campustechnology.com/Articles/2005/10/Disaster-Recovery-The-Time-Is-Now.aspx

Scheeres, J. (2001). *Attack can't erase stored data.* Retrieved January 21, 2010, from http://www.wired.com/techbiz/media/news/2001/09/47004

Shepherd, A. (2009). Disaster recovery — lessons from Tulane's response to Katrina. *Record, 21*(3), 10.

Symposium, L. P. (2009). *Past lessons informing future action.* Retrieved February 10, 2010, from http://peer.berkeley.edu/events/pdf/10-2009/Topping_PEER%2010-17-09.pdf

Toomey, T., Frost, E., & Jennex, M. E. (2009). Strategies to prepare emergency management personnel to integrate geospatial tools into emergency management. *International Journal of Information Systems for Crisis Response and Management, 1*(4), 33–49. doi:10.4018/jiscrm.2009071003

US EPA. (2009). Development document for final effluent guidance and standards. *National Service Center for Environmental Publications*, 20-26.

Whelton, P. (2005). *Rebuilding Tulane after hurricane Katrina*. Retrieved December 3, 2009, from http://www.thelancet.com/journals/lancet/article/PIIS0140-6736(06)68248-2/fulltext

Winstead, D., & Legeai, C. (2007). *Lessons learned from Katrina*. Retrieved June 4, 2009, from http://ap.psychiatryonline.org/cgi/content/full/31/3/190

Yin, K. (1984). *Case study research: Design and methods* (p. 12). Newbury Park, CA: Sage.

Zalud, B. (2008). Carrying on after disaster. *For Buyers of Products. Systems & Services*, *45*(7), 12–14.

This work was previously published in International Journal of Information Systems for Crisis Response Management, Volume 2, Issue 2, edited by Murray E. Jennex, pp. 19-34, copyright 2010 by IGI Publishing (an imprint of IGI Global).

APPENDIX

Figure 2. 2003 Downtime average costs of major financial industries

Cost of Downtime	Financial	Retail
14 Days	Incalculable	Incalculable
182 Hours	$3.0 B	$9.57 M
127 Hours	$2.0 B	$6.90 M
73 Hours	$1.2 B	$3.90 M
36 Hours	$567 M	$1.95 M
3.5 Hours	$58 M	$.195 M

Meta Group

Figure 3. In 2002, the average of all industries was $1,010,536 per hour

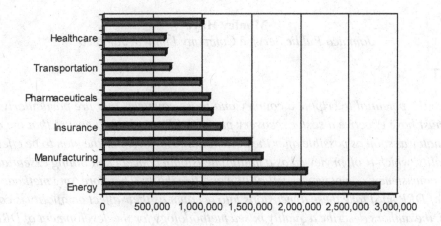

Figure 4. Cisco's zero tolerance

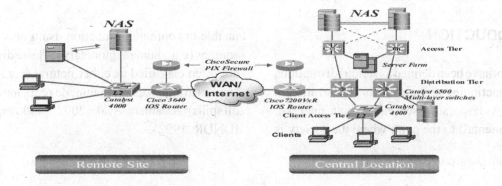

Chapter 8
An Approach to Using Ontologies for the Development of High Quality Disaster Recovery Plans

Lila Rao
The University of the West Indies, Jamaica

Maurice McNaughton
The University of the West Indies, Jamaica

Kweku-Muata Osei-Bryson
Virginia Commonwealth University, USA

Manley Haye
Jamaica Public Service Company Limited, Jamaica

ABSTRACT

Disasters have the potential to cripple a country and those countries that are particularly susceptible to disasters must have effective disaster recovery plans (DRP) in place to ensure that the country can return to normalcy as soon as possible after the devastation. However, for the plan to be effective it must be of high quality, which is often viewed as a multidimensional concept containing essential factors for DRP, such as consistency, completeness, reliability and feasibility. Therefore, any methodology for the development of DRP must take these dimensions into account as their affect on quality is considerable. In this regard, the authors describe a quality based methodology for the development of DRP, including a methodology that makes use of ontologies containing properties that are suited to the development of these high quality plans. The applicability of the proposed methodology will be demonstrated through a case study of an electric utility company in Jamaica.

INTRODUCTION

Disasters have been defined as serious disruptions of the functioning of societies (or organizations), causing widespread losses (e.g., human, material, environmental) to the point where the society is unable to continue to function using only its resources (e.g., human, monetary). These disasters are often classified as either natural (e.g., hurricanes, earthquakes) or manmade (e.g., terrorism, oil spills) (Alcantara-Ayala, 2002; Faulkner, 2001; IDNDR, 1992).

DOI: 10.4018/978-1-4666-0167-3.ch008

Regardless of their classification, disasters are likely to inflict extensive damage on a country's society and infrastructure and the longer it takes to return to normalcy following the disaster, the more costly it will be for the country. The frequency and scale of recent disasters highlights the need for a holistic approach to address and plan for them. The aim of a Disaster Recovery Plan (DRP) is to ensure that entities (e.g., organisations, countries) function effectively during and following a disaster (Bryson et al., 2002). A well thought out DRP can play a major role in an organization's/country's survival/success (Fallara, 2003). However, the plan should be evaluated before it is deployed as this can identify problems in the plan before the consequences are felt.

In order to evaluate the plan, a set of criteria must be defined against which quality is measured. Quality is often viewed as a multi-dimensional concept (Wand & Wang, 1996; Wang et al., 1995). Bryson et al. (2002) identified four properties that could be used to evaluate the DRP: feasibility, consistency, completeness and reliability. Therefore, these quality criteria should be the focus for a methodology that aims to produce high quality DRPs.

Ontologies have been defined as a formal description of a domain that can be shared among different applications and can be expressed in a language that can be used for reasoning (Noy, 2004). Dimensions have been proposed for measuring the quality of these ontologies (Burton-Jones et al., 2005; Rao & Osei-Bryson, 2007), these include completeness (coverage) and consistency and methodologies proposed for the development of ontologies must ensure that the quality dimensions are considered (Rao, Reichgelt et al., 2009).

A comparison of the characteristics of ontologies and the requirements of a disaster recovery plan shows that an ontology can support the development of an effective DRP in a number of ways, for example:

1. It provides a common language for all stakeholders, thus reducing confusion and ambiguity that may arise when different groups of stakeholders come together to make decisions (Altay & Green, 2006; Zhang et al., 2002) as is common in disaster recovery planning.

2. The use of a common language in the development of a DRP, would facilitate the sharing of DRPs among enterprises.

3. If the quality dimensions for DRPs can be addressed through the use of an ontology, it is likely that if the quality of the ontology is high, then the quality of the DRP will be high. Additionally, as the ontology is a formal description, the evaluation can be automated which makes the evaluation process more efficient and is likely to lead to improved quality of the ontology.

Many organizations have realized the importance of these DRPs and do have them in place. However, few have recognized the role that ontologies can play in improving the effectiveness of the plans. This study proposes a methodology for Disaster Recovery Planning that focuses on quality by using ontologies. The applicability of this methodology will be demonstrated by examining the information requirements for recovery management of an electric utility company in Jamaica, a country in the Caribbean that is faced with the annual threat of hurricanes.

The following section reviews the disaster planning and ontology literature and the limited research on applying ontologies to DRP. The methodology for the development of the DRP will be described and its applicability to the electric utility company in Jamaica will be demonstrated. The final section includes some concluding remarks and suggestions for future directions for this research.

LITERATURE REVIEW

Disaster Recovery Planning

A disaster recovery plan (DRP) focuses on ensuring the speedy restoration of services for critical organizational processes in the event that there are operational failures due to natural or man-made disasters. A DRP aims to minimize potential loss by identifying, prioritizing and safeguarding those organizational assets that are most valuable and that need the most protection (Bryson et al., 2002). The plan must be a comprehensive statement of consistent actions to be taken before, during and after a disaster. The contents of the plan should follow a logical sequence and be written in a standard and understandable format (Wold, 2002). Bryson et al. (2002) identified four properties that could be used to evaluate the DRP: feasibility, consistency, completeness and reliability. Feasibility refers to the availability of the resources required for the DRP. Completeness addresses the issue of whether or not the DRP covers all the important organizational resources that need to be protected. The consistency property ensures that the plan *as a whole* is consistent. This is important because the focus is often on subplans and it is possible that even though two subplans of the DRP are individually feasible, taken together they are infeasible (e.g., the two subplans may require the use of the same limited set of solution resources at the same time). Reliability measures the likelihood of the plan achieving its objectives. Developing an ontology for DRP will allow existing techniques for measuring the consistency and completeness of ontologies to be applied to the evaluation of the DRP.

The need for knowledge management to support crisis response has also been addressed (Jennex & Raman, 2009). The organizational and disaster domain ontologies proposed in this paper can become important components of these systems.

Ontologies

Ontologies provide a formal description of a domain that can be shared among different applications and expressed in a language that can be used for reasoning (Noy, 2004). This formal representation facilitates the automation of the process of checking the consistency of the disaster recovery plan. In order to formally describe the domain of discourse and provide some mechanism for reasoning, an appropriate knowledge representation language must be selected. Two such languages first order logic (Fox & Gruninger, 1998) and sorted logic (Kaneiwa & Mizoguchi, 2004) have been proposed. There are also a number of tools that support the construction of domain models and knowledge based applications with ontologies (http://protege.stanford.edu/).

Ontologies have been identified as important components of a number of information systems (Guarino, 1998; Pinto & Martins, 2004) such as knowledge management systems (KMS) (Rao & Osei-Bryson, 2007; Sicilia et al., 2006). As ontologies become more prevalent in information systems, ensuring their quality is an important consideration in the development of the systems of which they are a part. Quality is a multi-dimensional concept, and, in order to assess the quality of the ontology, a set of quality dimensions must be defined. Two quality dimensions are coverage/completeness and consistency (Jarke et al., 1999; Rao & Osei-Bryson, 2007). Consistency has been defined as the consistency of the meaning of concepts, relationships and business rules used in the ontology while coverage has been defined as the extent to which the ontology covers the domain of interest (Rao & Osei-Bryson, 2007). Techniques for ontology development should seek to ensure that the ontology has a high level of coverage and consistency (Rao, Reichgelt et al., 2009).

An enterprise (organizational) model is a computational representation of the structure, activities, processes, information, resources, people, behaviour, goals, and constraints of a business, government, or other enterprise (Fox et al., 1998). These enterprise models are the core of the information infrastructure of the organization. Sharma and Osei-Bryson (2008) extended the organizational ontology proposed by Fox et al. (1998) to include additional concepts and relationships such as business processes and various types of resources (Sharma & Osei-Bryson, 2008).

One of the most commonly used techniques to evaluate ontologies is competency questions (Staab et al., 2001; Sure et al., 2002). Competency questions define the ontology's requirements in the form of questions that the ontology must be able to answer (Gangemi, 2005; Gruninger & Fox, 1994). The idea behind the competency questions is that they are solicited independently of the development of the ontology and then are posed on the ontology. These competency questions can be used for measuring the coverage/ completeness of the ontology as the percentage of the total set of competency questions posed that can be answered by the ontology is indicative of coverage/completeness.

Rao, Reichgelt et al. (2009) described an approach to the development, representation and evaluation of formal ontologies with the explicit aim of developing a set of techniques that will improve the coverage/completeness of the ontology, and thus its overall quality. The initial ontological structure is developed using a hybrid approach that combines the information from existing literature on organizational ontologies with the information obtained by using the laddering knowledge elicitation technique (Rao, Reichgelt et al., 2009). The competency questions are elicited from a different set of end users and are used to evaluate the ontology.

Ontologies for DRP

The use of an ontology could help to address the ambiguity and communication problems that may arise when organizations are required to work together. Developing an ontology to make domain assumptions explicit offers several benefits, these include permitting the sharing of a common understanding of the structure of information among stakeholders in a discipline, facilitating more effective communication and idea-sharing and generally supporting the analysis of domain knowledge (Noy & McGuinness, 2001). These benefits are extremely relevant to DRP as they can help to reduce the possibility of confusion and ambiguity caused when different groups of stakeholders in the disaster recovery domain (e.g., utility companies, government agencies, emergency relief agencies) have to come together and share information to make decisions (Altay & Green, 2006).

Some research has addressed the development of systems for DRP and the application of ontologies to DRP (Joshi et al., 2007; Little, 2003; Mecella et al., 2006; Segev, 2009). Joshi et al. (2007) propose an ontology-based approach for disaster mitigation. They argue that their approach allows for the seamless integration and management of heterogeneous, multi-lateral data from different local, state, as well as federal agencies. They demonstrate the integration of various sub-ontologies using an overly simplified example in which the ontologies are primarily hierarchical. A hierarchical representation for a DRP will be inadequate to detect inconsistencies. Little (2003) proposes a general methodology for ontology construction and demonstrates its applicability using the Disaster-Response Ontology (Dis-ReO) Research Project which is aimed at constructing an ontology for earthquake disaster response. This research speaks to the need for comprehensive and consistent ontologies; however, the work focuses on classifying the terms used in earthquake response not on the development of response plans.

Mecella et al. (2006) describe the main results of a research project (WORKPAD) aimed at building and developing an innovative software infrastructure (software, models, services, etc.) to support the collaborative work of human operators in emergency/disaster scenarios. They stress that in such scenarios different teams, belonging to different organizations, need to collaborate with each other to reach a common goal. The organizational and disaster domain ontology proposed in this paper would facilitate this need.

METHODOLOGY FOR THE DEVELOPMENT OF HIGH QUALITY DRP

Based on the requirements of a DRP and the characteristics of an ontology, a methodology is proposed for the development of high quality disaster recovery plans. The methodology makes extensive use of ontologies and focuses on the consistency and completeness quality dimensions of the DRPs. There are techniques that exist for generating complete and consistent ontologies and, therefore, if these complete and consistent ontologies are used to develop the DRPs, the DRPs will also be complete and consistent. The proposed methodology for the development of high quality DRPs consists of the following steps:

1. The adoption/development of a *complete* and *consistent* organizational ontology
2. The generation of a *complete* disaster domain ontology from the organizational ontology
3. Converting the disaster domain ontology to a formal representation
4. Evaluating the *consistency* of the formal disaster domain ontology

The Adoption/Development of a Complete Organizational Ontology

All organizations have a number of concepts in common and therefore the organizational ontology will be applicable across all organizations (e.g., Goals, Subgoals, Business Processes, Tasks, Resources, Actors and Roles). Rao, Reichgelt et

al. (2009) describe a methodology for the development of a complete organizational ontology that focuses on ensuring its completeness. Their methodology involves an iterative process in which an initial ontological structure is developed using a hybrid approach that combines knowledge elicitation techniques (i.e., laddering) with previously existing organizational ontologies. A set of competency questions, which are used to evaluate the ontology, were also developed. These competency questions were developed using existing knowledge elicitation techniques and the participants in the process were comprised of persons of similar roles as was used for the development of the ontology, however, the same actors were not used as the aim was to make the development of the ontology and the development of the competency independent of each other and then use the questions to evaluate the ontology. Information regarding discrepancies between the ontology and the competency questions can be used to further refine the ontology and/or competency questions. This process is repeated until the competency questions and the ontology are aligned which would indicate that the ontology is adequately covering the domain of interest and therefore is likely to be complete. Based on this methodology, an organizational ontology was proposed (see Figure 1 for adapted version).

The Generation of a Complete Disaster Domain Ontology

As the organizational ontology provides the means to understand the connection between organizational goals and tasks, resources and actors (e.g., domain experts, decision makers) it can be used to support the development of the disaster domain ontology (see Figure 2 for adapted version) and the DRP (Rao, McNaughton et al., 2009). It facilitates the identification of the important concepts that are to be the target of the DRP. For example, from the organizational ontology it is clear that

Figure 1. An organizational ontology

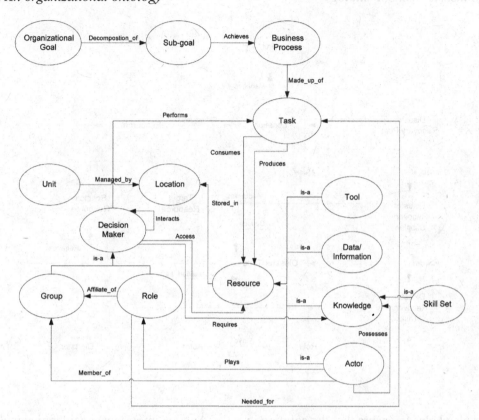

there is a need to identify the actors who should be involved in the plans' development based on their roles, the groups they belong to and the tasks they are carrying out and thus will help to identify those resources and tasks that are critical to the organization and which must be protected at all costs.

The disaster domain ontology will represent the target and solution resources. The target resources are those that need to be protected and must be addressed in the DRP while the solution resources are those that are used to carry out the tasks that must be performed as part of the DRP. It should be noted that it is possible for solution resources to require other solution resources (e.g., the deployment of an emergency vehicle requires the utilization of emergency crews) and this must be represented as it is important to know, at any

time, how many of a given solution resource have been utilized and how many are available.

The disaster domain ontology will also represent the location of the resources which is essential if they are to be protected (in the case of target resources) and located (in the case of solution resources). Information about the location of the resources will also assist in determining where the solution resources need to be deployed. Various disasters are likely to affect different locations and capturing this information before the disaster occurs is essential as it helps to ensure that this is taken into account when generating the DRP. Thus the plan focuses on those areas that are likely to be most affected and helps to ensure that the limited resources are used most effectively. Knowing where the resources are located and which locations are affected by a particular type

Figure 2. A disaster domain ontology

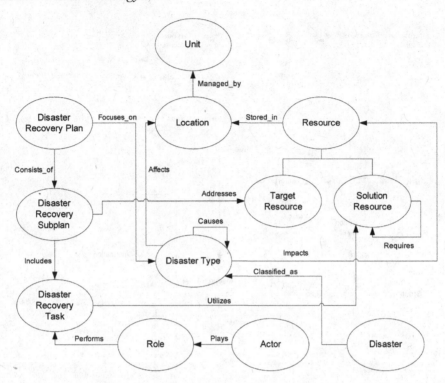

of disaster also helps to ensure that the solution resources are not stored in affected areas. There have been cases where DRPs cannot be put into operation because the solution resources have become inaccessible when the disaster occurs. For example, in New Orleans there was a plan in place to evacuate persons using school buses in the event of a hurricane. However, when Hurricane Katrina struck the location of the buses made them inaccessible because of the amount of flooding in the area. This example also demonstrates the need to ensure that it is well understand beforehand which disasters commonly co-occur as this can also reduce the impact of a disaster. In the case of New Orleans the disaster domain ontology could represent the fact that in the event of a hurricane it is possible that flooding may occur and if it is known where the hurricane is likely to hit, then it could be determined where the flooding is likely to occur.

Another important consideration in the development of DRPs is prioritization. Depending on the type, severity and suddenness of the disaster, it may not always be possible to protect all the resources. In such cases it would be necessary to know which resources are the most important and should be assigned the highest priority in terms of protection, in the DRP. The organizational ontology represents those tasks for which the resources are being used and the business processes, sub-goals and organizational goals achieved by these tasks. Thus, the relative importance of each resource can be ascertained based on the importance of the goals that they are being used to achieve.

Using the complete organizational ontology to develop the disaster domain ontology will help ensure the completeness property of the disaster domain ontology and in turn the DRPs. Completeness speaks to the need for the DRP to cover all the important organizational resources that need to be protected in the event of a disaster. If the organizational ontology is complete then it would represent all the resources of the organization and therefore when the disaster domain ontology is developed from this then it too would represent all the resources that are necessary. When these ontologies are used to formulate the DRP all resources will be addressed and therefore it is likely the DRP is complete.

Similar to the organizational ontology, the concepts covered in the disaster domain ontology in Figure 2 are applicable across organizations and therefore this ontology is reusable. Once the organization acquires the ontology, it will have to identify the instances of each of the concepts, that is, it will have to identify all of its solution and target resources, roles, actors, locations, etc. and include them in the ontology.

Formally Representing the Disaster Domain Ontology

Once this informal representation of the disaster domain ontology has been developed, it will be translated to a formal representation. There are a number of approaches for formally representing ontologies, these include semantic nets, frames, first order logic, sorted logic, (Fox & Gruninger, 1998; Gruber, 1993; Gruber, 1995; Kaneiwa & Mizoguchi, 2004; Noy & Hafner, 1997). The choice of the most suitable representation language should be guided by the requirements of the disaster domain ontology. The language must support the level of reasoning required for the disaster domain.

Additionally, there are a number of suites of tools available for the construction of domain models and knowledge-based applications with ontologies, one of which is Protégé-OWL. OWL is a recent development in standard ontology languages and an OWL ontology may include descriptions of classes (i.e., concepts), properties and their instances. Given an ontology the OWL formal semantics specifies how to derive logi-

cal consequences (i.e., facts not literally present in the ontology, but entailed by the semantics). Therefore, the language supports the formalizing of the domain by defining classes/concepts and properties of the classes/concepts, defining individuals and asserting properties about them and finally reasoning about the classes/concepts and individuals to the degree permitted by the formal semantics of the OWL language (http://protege. stanford.edu/).

Using OWL, the disaster recovery ontology represented in Figure 2 was implemented (see Figure 3). The ontology would include all the concepts (e.g., Resources, Disaster Type, and Disaster Recovery Tasks) and properties (e.g., impacts). In defining the properties, the domain and range of these properties are also defined (e.g., Disaster Type impacts Resource/Resource impacted by Disaster Type).

The OWL representation provides a common formal language for all stakeholders. This reduces the possibility of confusion and ambiguity that might arise when different groups of stakeholders (e.g., government agencies, utility companies, relief agencies) come together to make decisions (Altay & Green, 2006) which commonly happens in disaster recovery planning. All stakeholders would have access to this ontology and therefore all would be searching or querying the same information. The common language would facilitate the sharing of DRPs between enterprises. The sharing of disaster domain ontologies is important especially for smaller organizations that do not have the resources to develop the DRP on their own.

Evaluating the Formal Disaster Domain Ontology

Representing the disaster recovery plan as a formal ontology also allows for the automated evaluation of the ontology and thus helps to ensure that the disaster recovery plans generated are consistent. This is extremely important because evaluating the

Figure 3. OWL disaster domain ontology

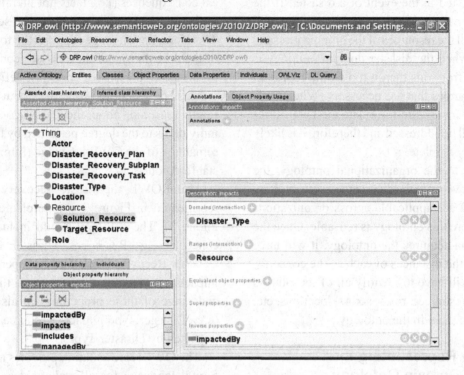

plan before it is deployed can prevent heavy losses, both financial and human, to an organization.

Once the ontology has been developed in OWL it can be checked for consistency by the reasoner. The reasoner automatically computes the classification hierarchy (i.e., the inferred class/concept hierarchy) and checks the logical consistency of the ontology (http://www.w3.org/TR/2004/REC-owl-guide-20040210/). For example, the organization may define some of its resources as Target Resources (i.e., those that need to be protected and therefore must be covered in the DRP) and some as Solution Resources (i.e., those that are used for performing a disaster recovery task). Further, the two may be defined as disjoint, meaning it is not possible for a particular resource to be defined as both a target resource and a solution resource at the same time. If a particular resource (e.g., vehicle) is then classified as a subclass of both a solution resource and a target resource, when the reasoner is invoked this class/concept vehicle will be found to be inconsistent (see Figure 4).

APPLICATION: AN ELECTRIC UTILITY COMPANY IN JAMAICA

Many small island states in the Caribbean, including Jamaica, are faced annually with the threat of extremely dangerous and potentially destructive hurricanes (http://stormcarib.com). A recent National Science Foundation (NSF) press release stated that the number of category 4 and 5 hurricanes has doubled over the past 35 years (NSF, 2005). The damage that a category 3-5 hurricane can cause on a small island is colossal. Therefore, it is imperative that there are DRPs in place at all levels (i.e., organizational and national).

Rao, McNaughton et al. (2009) identified an electric utility company as one of those organizations most integral to the restoration of normalcy after a disaster; the recovery of the country is highly dependent on the ability of these organizations to recover from the disaster as quickly as possible. Additionally, while the power is out there is the potential for an increase in criminal

Figure 4. Inconsistent vehicle class

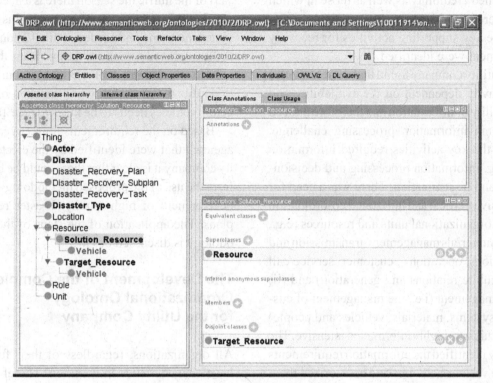

activity which can cause havoc in a country that is already feeling the effects of a natural disaster. Having an effective DRP in place will help the electric utility companies to recover as quickly as possible.

The electric utility company requires a number of user communities to come together to share information (e.g., disaster managers, field engineers, emergency operations centers). Even within the company there is a need for intense vertical and horizontal co-ordination of many organizational units and resources (e.g., finance, materials management, transmission and distributions operations, customer service/call centre, public relations and generation). Additionally, the data for the system are being taken from a number of sources (e.g., external sources, field personnel) and therefore are likely to be heterogeneous. Both the holistic approach and the integration of disparate data require a consistent vocabulary. The ontology will answer this need for a common language

as it provides a formal description of a domain which will permit the sharing of a common understanding of the structure of information among the stakeholders and so facilitate more effective communication and idea-sharing and generally supporting the analysis of domain knowledge. Thus, the ontologies will be used to reduce the communication and ambiguity problems that can arise when multiple groups of stakeholders came together to develop holistic solutions to problems. The organizational and disaster domain ontologies can facilitate the identification of these relevant stakeholders.

In 2004 a deadly category 4 hurricane named Ivan with winds packing 140 mph threatened to hit Jamaica but at the last moment passed just south of it. Nevertheless its effects on the country were still substantial. After the passing of the hurricane, the electric utility company did a damage assessment on the transmission and distribution of power. The company identified the areas in which it performed credibility as well as those in which there were improvement opportunities. From this some key supporting activities for recovery management were identified.

The utility company found that these activities were heavily dependent on the availability and accessibility of information and therefore it faced an extreme information processing challenge. Most of the key activities required information gathering, information processing and decision-making and dissemination. There was a need for (i) intensive vertical and horizontal co-ordination of many organizational units and resources (e.g., finance, materials management, transmission and distributions operations, customer service/call centre, public relations and generation) and (ii) asset management (i.e., the management of customers, systems, materials, vehicles and people) both of which are highly information intensive. The company identified the information requirements for these various activities and categorized them based on when they would need to be performed in the recovery management process (e.g., at the

start of the hurricane season there is a need to test and certify support systems and to do this current system maps may be needed, while 12 hours prior to the estimated passage of the hurricane there is a need to allocate and deploy critical resources and to do this the availability and location of emergency vehicles needs to be known) (see Table 1).

Based on the requirements for recovery management that were identified by the electric utility company it is clear that there could be benefits from the use of the proposed methodology for the development of high quality disaster recovery plans. The application of the steps of the methodology is discussed below:

The Development of the Complete Organizational Ontology for the Utility Company

All organizations, regardless of their function, have characteristics in common. Therefore, the organizational ontology (see Figure 1) is applicable across organizations, including the utility

Table 1. Time period, activity and information requirements for recovery management process

Time Period	Activity	Information Requirements
Start of hurricane season	1. Procure critical materials 2. Train EOC personnel 3. Test/Certify support systems	1. Material inventories and location 2. Current system maps 3. EOC preparedness
12 Hours Prior	1. Activate EOCs 2. Mobilize crews 3. Determine inventory/location of emergency resources 4. Allocate/Deploy critical resources	1. Weather information 2. EOC readiness 3. Material Inventories and Location 4. Emergency vehicle availability and location
During Event	1. Orderly shut-down	1. System status 2. Weather information
48 Hours After	1. Estimate resource requirements 2. Declare disaster areas	1. Damage assessment 2. Material requirements 3. External agency information
Restoration	1. Establish restoration priorities 2. Prepare/Manage/Coordinate work plans 3. Track restoration progress	1. Critical customer locations 2. System Maps 3. Material requirements/utilization 4. Work activities 5. Vehicle location 6. Restoration Progress
Post-Mortem	1. Replenish resources	1. Total Resource Utilization 2. Total Cost of Recovery

company. For example, the utilty company must have a set of organizational goals, subgoals, processes, tasks, resources, roles and actors. Adapting an existing organizational ontology that has been developed using a methodology that focuses on completeness and consistency will reduce the time for the development of the disaster recovery plan without sacrificing on quality and will also improve the dependability of the ontology if it is already tried and tested.

The Generation of a Complete Disaster Domain Ontology for the Utility Company

Once a complete organizational ontology for the utility company has been created, the disaster domain ontology can be generated. The disaster domain ontology proposed in Figure 2 is applicable to the utility company and can be adapted. In the case of the utility company in Jamaica, the types of disasters that would have to be considered include hurricanes, earthquakes and flooding as these commonly occur in the Caribbean region. Flooding may be a disaster on its own, but it may also co-occur with hurricanes. Additionally, the ontology would represent the location of all the resources (e.g., emergency vehicles, technicians, decision makers, information systems) and whether these locations are likely to be impacted by hurricanes, flooding and earthquakes.

The utility company will therefore be required to instantiate the disaster domain ontology (i.e., to identify the instances for the classes and properties). For example, assuming that the focus is on hurricanes the class instances and properties identified in Table 2 would be included in the ontology for the utility company:

The generation of the utility company's disaster domain ontology from the organizational ontology is beneficial as the utility company can use the organizational ontology to identify the important concepts that need to be addressed in

the disaster domain ontology. Developing the disaster recovery plans based on ontologies that are developed using a methodology that focuses on consistency and completeness will help to ensure that the disaster recovery plans will also be consistent and complete (Bryson et al., 2002).

Formally Representing the Utility Company's Disaster Domain Ontology

Once the concepts, classes and instances for the disaster recovery planning domain have been identified (see Figure 2 and Table 2) then the ontology can be formally represented, using Protégé-OWL (see Figure 5). OWL facilitates the formal representation of classes/concepts (e.g., Actor, Disaster and Disaster type), individuals/instances (e.g., Hurricane which is an instance of Disaster type and Hurricane Ivan which is an instance of Disaster), object properties that represent the relationship between individuals

(e.g., Hurricane Impacts Power station, Hurricane Causes Flood, Hurricane Ivan Classified as Hurricane) and data properties that link an individual to a data type value (e.g., Hurricane Ivan has a Category property that has a value of 4). The ontology also represents hierarchical information (e.g., EOC is a Solution resource and Solution resource is a Resource).

Evaluating the Utility Company's Disaster Recovery Plans

When the ontology has been represented in a formal way then it can be checked for consistency (i.e., the reasoner for Protégé-OWL will be invoked). The reasoner of OWL will check the logical consistency of the ontology and compute the classification hierarchy (i.e., the inferred hierarchy). For example, in the case of detecting inconsistency, if two classes are defined as disjoint (e.g., Disaster and Disaster type) then if an indi-

Table 2. Instances of classes and properties

Term	Type	Instances
Disaster Recovery Plan	Concept	Hurricane plan, Earthquake plan, Flooding plan, Information system failure plan, Landslide plan
Disaster Recovery Subplan (see Figure 5)	Concept	Start of season, 12 hours prior, during event, 48 hours after, restoration, post mortem
Disaster Recovery Task (see Figure 5)	Concept	Train Emergency Operations Center (EOC) personnel, Activate EOCs, Cost allocation, Declare disaster areas, Determine location of emergency resources, Establish restoration priorities, Estimate resource requirements, Log calls, Manage work plans, Orderly shutdown, Replenish resources, Test Support Systems
Resource	Concept	Emergency vehicle, EOC, Disaster manager, Field engineer, Electricity infrastructure, Information system
Target Resource	Concept	Electricity infrastructure, Information system
Solution Resource	Concept	Emergency vehicle, EOC, Disaster manager, Field engineer
Disaster	Concept	Hurricane Ivan, Hurricane Gilbert
Disaster Type	Concept	Hurricane, earthquake, flooding, landslide, information system failure
Actor	Concept	Craig Chin, John Brown, Mark Jones, Mary Smith, Sue Green
Role	Concept	Disaster manager, Field engineer, Emergency personnel
Location	Concept	Head office, New Kingston branch, Constant Spring branch
Classified_as	Property	Hurricane Ivan *Classified_as* Hurricane; Hurricane Gilbert *Classified_as* Hurricane
Plays	Property	John Brown *Plays* Disaster manager; Craig Chin *Plays* Field engineer; Sue Green *Plays* Emergency personnel
Performs	Property	Disaster manager *Performs* Train EOC personnel; Emergency personnel *Performs* Estimate resource requirements
Causes	Property	Hurricane *Causes* Flooding; Flooding *Causes* Landslide

vidual (e.g., Hurricane Ivan) is classified as both a Disaster and a Disaster Type the reasoner will identify this as an inconsistency (see Figure 6).

The reasoner will also perform automated classification, which is essential for maintaining large ontologies and keeping them in a logically correct state. For example, it is possible to specify that any individual who is in a Plays relationship must be an actor by converting Plays to a *necessary and sufficient* condition of Actor (see Figure 7).

If a new individual, Veronica Green, is created and assigned a Role (e.g., Disaster Manager), when the reasoner is invoked it will be inferred that Veronica Green must be a member of the Actor class and this would be added in the inferred class hierarchy (see Figure 8, inferred class hierarchy shown in yellow).

If inconsistencies can be identified and resolved and inferences made, it is likely that the consistency and completeness of the disaster domain ontology is high (Rao & Osei-Bryson, 2007) which would mean that it is likely that the consistency and completeness of the DRPs will also be high (Bryson et al., 2002).

CONCLUSION

This paper has demonstrated the applicability of ontologies to the development of *high quality* DRPs. The quality requirements for DRPs are satisfied by the characteristics of ontologies. Developing the disaster domain ontology from a complete organizational ontology will help to ensure that the disaster domain ontology is complete

Figure 5. OWL implementation

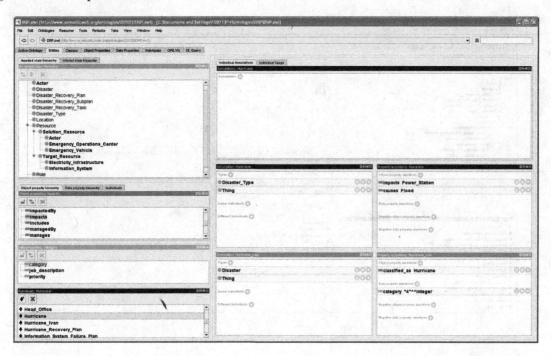

Figure 6. Inconsistency detection

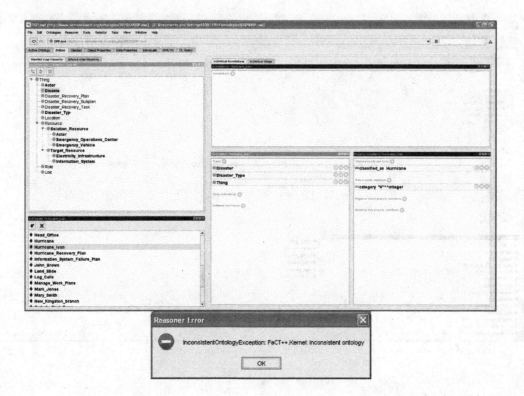

Figure 7. Necessary and sufficient conditions

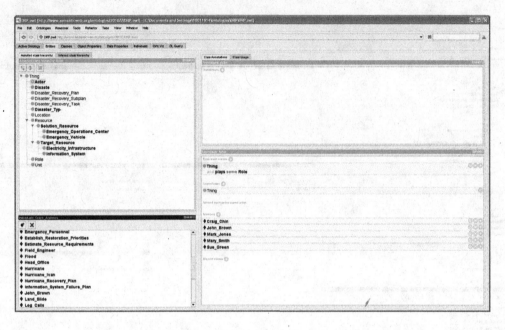

Figure 8. Automated classification

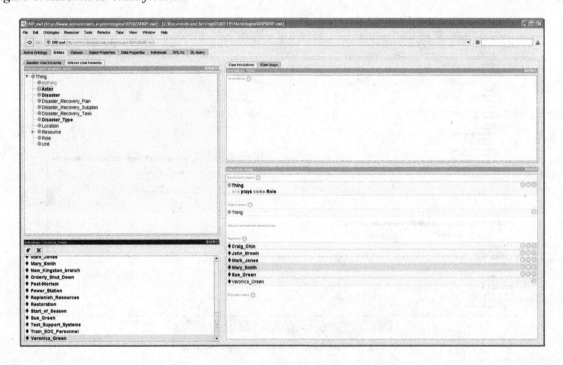

and hence the DRPs are complete. Additionally, having a formal representation of a DRP (using the ontology) allows for its automated evaluation, and thus helps to ensure its consistency before it is deployed. These ontologies can then become components of information and knowledge management systems for disaster response (Jennex & Raman, 2009).

Although, a Jamaican electric utility company was used to demonstrate the applicability of the methodology for developing high quality DRPs proposed in this paper, it would be beneficial to test the applicability of this research to other domains and countries. Disasters require a rapid response as situations arise and therefore it would be beneficial to explore the suitability of an *adaptive* (i.e., modifies the ontology in real time) disaster domain ontology (Segev, 2009).

A more thorough investigation, of the inferencing capability that can be added to Protégé-OWL will be explored. The reasoning mechanism chosen for formally representing the disaster domain ontology must facilitate other types of checks for consistency. The disaster recovery plan could be inconsistent in a number of other ways, these may include:

- In the case of disasters co-occurring, it is likely that if the organization needs a plan for the recovery from hurricanes they would also need a plan for the recovery from flooding. If it is established that flooding co-occurs with hurricanes then both plans may be invoked during the same period. Therefore, the reasoning mechanism must be able to detect whether these plans are utilizing the same set of solution resources and if so must ensure that the same resource is not deployed simultaneously. For example, in the case of flooding, it may be necessary to deploy emergency response vehicles to particular locations to relocate materials in danger of being damaged. However, these emergency vehicles

may also be needed in the plan for hurricanes and therefore, it must be determined if there are being deployed appropriately.

- The location of impact and the location of the response resources could be the same which would mean that the response resources would not be available. If this inconsistency can be detected before deployment the resources could be relocated. For example, emergency vehicles may be parked at the head office and if, in the case of a hurricane, it is likely that it will affect this location then there is a possibility of flooding which could make these vehicles inaccessible. If this is detected as an inconsistency in the plan, the vehicles could be moved to another site before the hurricane hits.

This research shows that ontologies are well suited for the development of disaster recovery plans and further work is required in this area.

REFERENCES

Alcantara-Ayala, I. (2002). Geomorphology, natural hazards, vulnerability and prevention of natural disasters in developing countries. *Geomorphology*, *47*(2-4), 107–124. doi:10.1016/S0169-555X(02)00083-1

Altay, N., & Green, W. G. (2006). OR/MS Research in Disaster Operations Management. *European Journal of Operational Research*, *175*(1), 475–493. doi:10.1016/j.ejor.2005.05.016

Bryson, K.-M., Millar, H., Joseph, A., & Mobolurin, A. (2002). Using Formal MS/OR Modeling to Support Disaster Recovery Planning. *European Journal of Operational Research*, *141*(3), 679–688. doi:10.1016/S0377-2217(01)00275-2

Burton-Jones, A., Storey, V. C., Sugumaran, V., & Ahluwalia, P. (2005). A Semiotic Metrics Suite for Assessing the Quality of Ontologies. *Data & Knowledge Engineering, 55*, 84–102. doi:10.1016/j.datak.2004.11.010

Fallara, P. (2003). Disaster recovery planning. *IEEE Potentials, 22*(5).

Faulkner, B. (2001). Towards a framework for tourism disaster management. *Tourism Management, 22*, 135–147. doi:10.1016/S0261-5177(00)00048-0

Fox, M. S., Barbuceanu, M., Gruninger, M., & Lin, J. (1998). An Organization Ontology for Enterprise Modeling . In Prietula, M., Carley, K., & Gasser, L. (Eds.), *Simulating Organizations: Computational Models of Institutions and Groups* (pp. 131–152). Menlo Park, CA: AAAI/MIT Press.

Fox, M. S., & Gruninger, M. (1998). Enterprise Modeling. *AI Magazine, 19*(3), 109–121.

Gangemi, A. (2005). *Ontology Design Patterns for Semantic Web Content.* Paper presented at the 4th International Semantic Web Conference (ISWC 2005), Galway, Ireland.

Gruber, T. R. (1993). A Translation Approach to Portable Ontology Specifications. *Knowledge Acquisition, 5*, 199–220. doi:10.1006/knac.1993.1008

Gruber, T. R. (1995). Toward Principles for the Design of Ontologies Used for Knowledge Sharing. *International Journal of Human-Computer Studies, 43*(5-6), 907–928. doi:10.1006/ijhc.1995.1081

Gruninger, M., & Fox, M. S. (1994). *The Role of Competency Questions in Enterprise Engineering.* Paper presented at the IFIP WG5.7 Workshop on Benchmarking - Theory and Practice, Trondheim, Norway.

Guarino, N. (1998, June 6-8). *Formal Ontology and Information Systems.* Paper presented at the First International Conference on Formal Ontologies in Information Systems, Trento, Italy.

IDNDR. (1992). *Glossary: Internationally Agreed Glossary of Basic Terms Related to Disaster Management* (p. 83). Geneva, Switzerland: DHA.

Jarke, M., Jeusfeld, M., Quix, C., & Vassiliadis, P. (1999). Architecture and Quality in Data Warehouses: An Extended Repository Approach. *Information Systems, 24*(3), 229–253. doi:10.1016/S0306-4379(99)00017-4

Jennex, M., & Raman, M. (2009). Knowledge Management in Support of Crisis Response. [IJISCRAM]. *International Journal of Information Systems for Crisis Response Management, 1*(3), 69–83.

Joshi, H., Seker, R., Bayrak, C., Ramaswamy, S., & Connelly, J. (2007, July 15-18). *Ontology for Disaster Mitigation and Planning.* Paper presented at the Summer Computer Simulation Conference, San Diego, CA.

Kaneiwa, K., & Mizoguchi, R. (2004, June 2-5). *Ontological Knowledge Base Reasoning with Sort-Hierarchy and Rigidity.* Paper presented at the Ninth International Conference on the Principles of Knowledge Representation and Reasoning (KR2004), Whistler, Canada.

Little, E. (2003, September 16). *A Proposed Methodology for the Development of Application-Based Formal Ontologies.* Paper presented at the KI2003 Workshop on Reference Ontologies and Application Ontologies, Hamburg, Germany.

Mecella, M., Angelaccio, M., Krek, A., Catarci, T., Buttarazzi, B., & Dustdar, S. (2006, May 14-17). *WORKPAD: An Adaptive Peer-to-Peer Software Infrastructure for Supporting Collaborative Work of Human Operators in Emergency/Disaster Scenarios.* Paper presented at the International Symposium on Collaborative Technologies and Systems (CTS'06), Las Vegas, NV.

Noy, N. (2004). Semantic Integration: A Survey of Ontology Based Approaches. *SIGMOD Record, 33*(4), 65–69. doi:10.1145/1041410.1041421

Noy, N., & Hafner, C. (1997). The State of the Art in Ontology Design. *AI Magazine, 18*(3), 53–74.

Noy, N., & McGuinness, D. (2001). *Ontology Development 101: A Guide to Creating Your First Ontology* (No. KSL-01-05 and SMI-2001-0880).

Pinto, H. S., & Martins, J. P. (2004). Ontologies: How Can They Be Built? *Knowledge and Information Systems, 6*(4), 441–464. doi:10.1007/s10115-003-0138-1

Rao, L., McNaughton, M., Osei-Bryson, K.-M., & Haye, M. (2009). *The Role of Ontologies in Disaster Recovery Planning.* Paper presented at the 15th Americas Conference on Information Systems (AMCIS), San Francisco, CA.

Rao, L., & Osei-Bryson, K.-M. (2007). Towards Defining Dimensions of Knowledge Systems Quality. *Expert Systems with Applications, 33*(2), 368–378. doi:10.1016/j.eswa.2006.05.003

Rao, L., Reichgelt, H., & Osei-Bryson, K.-M. (2009). An Approach for Ontology Development and Assessment Using a Quality Framework. *Knowledge Management Research and Practice, 7*, 260–276. doi:10.1057/kmrp.2009.12

Segev, A. (2009). Adaptive Ontology Use for Crisis Knowledge Representation. [IJISCRAM]. *International Journal of Information Systems for Crisis Response Management, 1*(2), 16–30.

Sharma, S., & Osei-Bryson, K.-M. (2008, January 7-10). *Organization-Ontology Based Framework for Implementing the Business Understanding Phase of Data Mining Projects.* Paper presented at the 41st Annual Hawaii International Conference on System Sciences, Big Island, HI.

Sicilia, M.-A., Lytras, M., Rodriguez, E., & Garcia-Barriocanal, E. (2006). Integrating Descriptions of Knowledge Management Learning Activities into Large Ontological Structures: A Case Study. *Data & Knowledge Engineering, 57*(2), 111–121. doi:10.1016/j.datak.2005.04.001

Staab, S., Schnurr, H.-P., Studer, R., & Sure, Y. (2001). Knowledge Processes and Ontologies. *IEEE Intelligent Systems, 16*(1), 26–34. doi:10.1109/5254.912382

Sure, Y., Erdmann, M., Angele, J., Staab, S., Studer, R., & Wenke, D. (2002). *OntoEdit: Collaborative Ontology Development for the Semantic Web.* Paper presented at the First International Semantic Web Conference (ISWC 2002), Sardinia, Italy.

Wand, Y., & Wang, R. Y. (1996). Anchoring Data Quality Dimensions in Ontological Foundations. *Communications of the ACM, 39*(11), 86–95. doi:10.1145/240455.240479

Wang, R. Y., Storey, V. C., & Firth, C. P. (1995). A Framework for Analysis of Data Quality Research. *IEEE Transactions on Knowledge and Data Engineering, 7*(4), 623–640. doi:10.1109/69.404034

Wold, G. H. (2002). Disaster Recover Planning Process. *Disaster Recovery Journal, 5*(1), 29–34.

Zhang, D., Zhou, L. Jr, & Nunamaker, J. F. (2002). A Knowledge Management Framework for the Support of Decision Making in Humanitarian Assistance/Disaster Relief. *Knowledge and Information Systems, 4*, 370–385. doi:10.1007/s101150200012

This work was previously published in International Journal of Information Systems for Crisis Response Management, Volume 2, Issue 2, edited by Murray E. Jennex, pp. 35-53, copyright 2010 by IGI Publishing (an imprint of IGI Global).

Chapter 9
The Relationship between IT Director Values and Extent of IT Disaster Recovery Planning in the Banking Industry

Jordan Shropshire
Georgia Southern University, USA

Christopher Kadlec
Georgia Southern University, USA

ABSTRACT

Information technology plays a pivotal role in defining the success of organizations. Given its importance, one might assume that modern organizations take steps to ensure the recovery of IT services following disasters. Unfortunately, this is rarely the case. To understand the variation in degree of IT disaster recovery planning, this research focused on those responsible for managing IT resources and IT directors. For the study, a survey was mailed to 337 financial service institutions in the southeastern United States. Over 150 IT directors completed self-assessments for measuring the extent to which their organization engages in IT disaster recovery planning. In addition, they responded to a number of questions regarding their work-related values, and over 63% of the variance in degree of IT disaster recovery planning was explained by two predictors: uncertainty avoidance and long-term orientation. Results show that firms with IT professionals who prefer to avoid uncertainty and who have long-term outlooks have more developed IT disaster recovery plans.

INTRODUCTION

Stable, reliable IT services have become the required minimum. Most modern businesses cannot function without information systems for data processing, storage, and communication. Despite their importance, few firms create sufficient IT disaster recovery (ITDR) plans (Gold, 2007; Sheth et al., 2008). ITDR includes more than just data backups (Plotnick, 1999); it involves analyzing IT services, identifying potential threats services, preparing organizational members,

DOI: 10.4018/978-1-4666-0167-3.ch009

creating system recovery procedures, finding offsite storage, and conducting drills (Kadlec & Shropshire, 2010). Although many firms are investing in efforts to improve the security of their data, there is less consistency regarding ITDR planning (Lohrman, 2007; McLaughlin, 2008). The ITDR planning practices of some organizations are not in keeping with the sophistication of their information systems; in contrast, other businesses create and maintain exhaustive plans (Anderson, 2008; Ramsaran, 2005). Even within industries and geographic regions, there is much variation in degree of preparedness (Retelle, 2008). By understanding this phenomenon, it might be possible to improve ITDR capabilities and build more resilient organizations.

This research seeks to explain the differences in degree of ITDR planning by considering those who manage information systems and technology – IT directors. In general, IT directors are responsible for ensuring the continued provision of IT services (Chun & Moody, 2009). They lead efforts to leverage the capabilities of corporate information systems by organizing hardware, software, and human resources (Agarwal & Sambamurthy, 2002). The attributes of IT leaders have previously been linked with firm performance (Sobol & Klein, 2009). In this study, the work-related values of IT directors are analyzed. Values are long-lasting attributes of individuals; they may impact individual attitudes and behavior over time (Fishbein & Ajzen, 1975). Because ITDR planning consists of a series of actions which may take weeks (or even months), attributes more permanent than attitudes or intentions are necessary. Therefore, IT director values are used to explain degree of ITDR planning. Hypotheses concerning these relationships are conveyed and tested.

This paper is of value to IT researchers and professionals. This research represents one of the first efforts to predict organizational outcomes associated with IT disaster recovery planning. It overcomes previous obstacles in model design, testing, measurement, and analysis. It provides

immediate guidance for consultants and managers of information systems by providing actionable recommendations for helping enterprises improve IT disaster recovery planning.

The rest of this manuscript is organized as follows: first, background information on IT disaster recovery planning is supplied. This section focuses on the definition of IT disaster recovery planning and covers the various components included in ITDR plans. Next, the relevant personal values of IT directors are described; these values are used as predictor variables. Next, the methodology, analysis, and results sections are presented. Finally, implications and concluding comments are made.

BACKGROUND

This section provides background information on the elements in the research model. First, the case for planning is made. Next, IT disaster recovery planning is described. Because the variable is relatively new to mainstream IT literature, some background information is provided. In addition, the personal values of the IT director are introduced. For each element, a basic definition, a rationale for inclusion into the present study, and an associated hypothesis are given.

The Case for Planning

Datacenters and systems are quite vulnerable. They rely on a steady stream of resources, such as energy, skilled labor, network connectivity, and cooling systems, to proper function. It is essential to understand that when it comes to IT-related disasters, history repeats itself. Hurricanes flood entire cities, earthquakes flatten buildings, and disgruntled employees destroy server rooms. These threats will occur again, and savvy managers and IT consultants will take these threats into account and prepare for the worst.

Unfortunately, too many enterprises fail to take the risks seriously. Consider, for example, the case of Hurricane Katrina. Immediately following the disaster, media outlets provided 24/7 news coverage. For the next few months, business journals were filled with recommendations and best practices for business continuity planning. IT journals even prescribed methods for IT disaster recovery. Corporate directors, stirred by this coverage, demanded that their firms should create plans for coping with future disasters. There was much activity. However, interest dwindled over the next few months. By the end of 2006, most business publications returned to their normal topics, and enterprises returned to business as usual.

The lesson from Hurricane Katrina is that IT disaster recovery planning is a continual process, not a short-lived trend. IT disaster recovery plans are only useful *before* incidents occur, and because it is impossible to predict the future, plans should be created, updated, and maintained on an ongoing basis.

In general, any IT disaster recovery planning efforts will be of value. Many articles have addressed this topic. A good starting point for most small and medium businesses should be to reference a four-article series written by Mike Pregmon in 2007. It covers risk analysis, internal control, the IT disaster recovery planning process, and IT virtualization. More in depth guidance may be acquired from the SANS institute, which has created an entire reading of white papers devoted to topics ranging from systems prioritization (Lyons, 2007) to security considerations (Velliquette, 2005). Further, recommendations for creating systems for responding to disasters and emergencies may be gleaned from articles such as White and Plotnick (2010) and Gaynor et al. (2009).

IT Disaster Recovery Planning

Despite its relative importance, IT disaster recovery planning has historically been given little attention in the IT community. The topic is generally discussed with fervor following major disasters, but seems to recede in interest once

things are back to normal. When IT disaster recovery planning is mentioned, the discussion is usually limited to backing up data. However, this approach may lead to gaps in ITDR plans. Thus, a more comprehensive definition is used to guide the conceptualization and measurement of ITDR planning (Kadlec & Shropshire, 2010).

With the integration of IT into all business functions and the reliance on technology among organizational members, the complexity of IT disaster recovery planning significantly escalates. There is little guidance in IS/IT literature for the practitioner to develop and maintain an IT disaster recovery plan. Many descriptions of IT disaster recovery planning are incomplete or inconsistent with other aspects of IT management.

The terms "IT disaster recovery" and "business continuity" are often used interchangeably. This is unfortunate, because they should be used to represent two different concepts. Business continuity plans are organization-wide policies for overcoming disasters and remaining a viable entity in the future (Fitzgerald & Dennis, 2005). IT disaster recovery plans are strategies for resuming IT services following disasters. IT disaster recovery plans should be considered subsets of business continuity plans; they should support organizational plans for continuing business operations following disasters.

An often-overlooked aspect of ITDR planning concerns the definition of an IT disaster. IT disasters impact the organization in which the IT service is employed. IT disasters range from the accidental deletion of a file to a hurricane that destroys the building that houses the data center along with the infrastructure (such as electrical power grid) in the area of the data center. Examples of IT services include internet connectivity, telecommunications, and data storage and processing. IT services add value by providing additional capabilities to organizational members. The provision of such services relies on a combination of inputs from multiple resources, including hardware, software, data, human resources, and utilities. The loss of inputs leads to disaster only if it causes a failure in the associated IT services.

It should be noted that IT disaster recovery plans should be aimed at restoring IT services, but not necessarily restoring specific hardware and software architectures. It may not be possible or practical to return to pre-disaster conditions. Thus, disaster recovery for an IT service is complete when the service has been brought back online in a stable condition.

For the purposes of this research, IT disaster recovery planning is herein described as the set of actions (*IT disaster identification and notification, preparing organizational members, IT services analysis, recovery process, backup procedures, offsite storage*, and *maintenance*) which an organization follows in order to improve its ability to resume IT services following a disaster (Kadlec & Shropshire, 2010). Table 1 (next page) summarizes the components of ITDR plans. They are further described in the following paragraphs.

IT Disaster Identification and Notification

The viability of IT services must constantly be monitored (Hayes, 2005). While it may be readily apparent when a service is no longer available, some services appear to be available but may not be yielding useful results. How a service is going to be monitored and what constitutes a working system is therefore a key point to recovering from an IT disaster. In addition to disaster identification, the organization must determine which stakeholders will be notified and how they will be contacted (Davis, 2001; Mearian, 2004).

Organizational Member Preparation

Organizational members must understand their role in when there is an IT-related disaster (Connor, 2005). The decision making structure that will be used during an IT disaster needs to be established (Sliwa, 2005). Once this structure is established,

some members will need to be assigned the task of returning the IT service to a usable state. Others that depend on that service need to know what to do while the service is unavailable (Retelle, 2008). Once the responsibilities and roles of all members are established, everyone needs to be trained to handle an IT disaster (Holliday, 2008).

IT Services Analysis

For an organization to recover from an IT disaster, IT services must be identified within the organization along with the risks to these services (Thibodeau & Mearian, 2005). Since these services may be interrelated and or their criticality to the viability of the organization may be different, prioritization of services being brought "online" must be established (Rolich, 2008).

Recovery Process

The recovery process for each critical IT service needs to be established (Defelice, 2008). This helps to establish the roles that individuals will have in the event of an IT disaster (Cox, 2007; Jepson, 2008). Failure of the facilities that house the IT services must also be taken into account (McLaughlin, 2008). In case of this event, alternative facilities will need to be identified and procedures for establishing IT services in this facility will need to be established (Laliberte, 2007).

Backup Procedures

To ensure the speedy return of IT services, backup procedures for the data, software, hardware, and configurations (and for the disaster recovery plan itself) must be established (Ashton, 2008).

Offsite Storage

Backups should not only be stored where they are easily accessible to quickly recovery from an IT disaster, they should be stored offsite to ensure

Table 1. Summary of IT disaster recovery planning activities

Dimension	Description	Sub-Dimension	Description
IT Disaster Identification and Notification	Procedures which have been developed for detecting IT disasters, for communicating during emergencies, and for warning IT disaster recovery team members and other stakeholders.	Detection	Procedures for detecting IT disasters.
		Warning	Procedures for informing IT disaster recovery team members and stakeholders that an IT disaster has occurred.
		Means of Warning / Communication	Establishment or formalization of communication channels to be used in the event of an emergency.
Preparing Organizational Members	Procedures for IT disaster recovery team training, briefing for key non-team members, and the formalization of a decision-making structure.	ITDR Team Preparations	Team assignments and responsibilities during the disaster.
		Non-ITDR Team Preparations	Training and briefing of non-team members in the event of a disaster.
		Decision Making	Formalization of a decision making structure.
IT Services Analysis	Procedures for cataloging IT services, prioritizing IT services in terms of reactivation, and identifying potential threats.	IT Services Identification	Identification of IT services.
		Prioritizing IT Services	Listing of the order in which services need to be reactivated.
		Risks to IT Services	Identification of risks to IT services and infrastructure.
Recovery Process	Procedures for creating back-up copies of data, software, configuration files, and the IT disaster recovery plan.	Recovery Procedures	Alternative facilities and procedures for switching operations to those facilities.
		Alternative Facilities	Recovery procedures for service inputs such as human resources, facilities, communications technologies, servers, application systems, and data.
Backup Procedures	The degree to which a routine has been developed for creating backups.	Backup copies of data, software, configuration files, and IT disaster recovery plans.	
Offsite Storage	Procedures for ensuring that systems, software and data are made as portable as possible, and those offsite locations have been selected for use as backup storage sites.	Portability	Procedures for ensuring that systems, software, and data are as portable as possible.
		Offsite Backup Locations	Offsite locations to backup data, software, configuration files, the IT disaster recovery plans.
Maintenance	Procedures for testing and updating the IT disaster recovery plan and its associated documentation, and for ensuring that the IT disaster recovery plan fits within the scope of the business continuity plan.	Testing and Updating	Procedures to ensure adequate testing and updating of the disaster recovery plan.
		Documentation	Documentation of configuration and changes to systems, hardware, and software.
		Synchronizing	Procedures to ensure the IT disaster recovery plan is part of the business continuity plan.

that if there is a disaster that makes the IT systems inaccessible, the backups will still be accessible (Fonseca, 2004). Additionally, if there is notice that an IT disaster is eminent, IT systems should be as portable as possible so they could be quickly relocated, offsite (Pabrai, 2004).

Maintenance

Once a disaster recovery plan has been established, it must be tested and updated based on the outcomes of the tests (Vijayan, 2005). Additionally, changes to IT systems must be documented to ensure that when systems are recovered, they are as current as possible (Jaques, 2006). Lastly, the whole ITDR planning process needs be a part of the business continuity plan to ensure that there is not sub-optimization within the organization (Hoge, 2005).

Personal Values

How can differences in personal cultural values give a better understanding of decision making in organizations? Hofstede (1990) found relationships among various organizational outcomes and culture values sets of senior managers. Specifically, the culture values of senior managers directly impact their decisions making, and indirectly shape the actions of their employees, because presumably they shape the culture of their respective departments in activities like goal setting, leadership, motivation, etc.

The personal values of IT directors are therefore assumed to impact the degree to which the organization plans for disaster recovery. Managers of organizational information technology are generally in a position to prioritize work and allocate money, time, and resources to projects accordingly. The decision to conduct IT disaster recovery planning usually rests with IT directors, as they are generally responsible for the continued delivery of IT services. Thus, IT directors have a direct impact on the planning process. Later, they may indirectly impact IT disaster recovery planning via the culture values they share with their respective employees. In this research, it is proposed that the following cultural values, as reported by organizations' IT directors, will be significantly related to IT disaster recovery planning. Of all the personal values constructs, uncertainty avoidance and long term orientation were selected because they were previously found to be the most influential on IT worker behavior (Lee et al., 2007; Straub et al., 1994).

The first value is uncertainty avoidance (UA). This construct refers to intolerance for uncertainty, and is defined as the extent to which an individual feels threatened by uncertain or unknown situations (Hofstede, 1990). The constructs evaluates the ways in which people respond to uncertainties in life. Those with a low tolerance for ambiguity will value options which reduce the risk of unknown outcomes (Yoo, 2002). They will be drawn to activities which increase control of their environment, such as planning. Those who find it easier to accept uncertainty will not place the same degree of value on norms, procedures, and strict plans. It is presumed that IT disaster recovery planning will be considered a means for controlling uncertainties associated with IT service delivery, and thus:

H_1: Higher levels of uncertainty avoidance, as reported by organizations' IT directors, will be correlated with higher levels of IT disaster recovery planning.

The second value is long-term orientation (LTO). This construct is defined as an orientation toward the future and is represented by values such as hard work and persistence (Hofstede, 1990). Long-term orientation fosters virtues oriented toward future rewards or returns on effort. Those with high degrees of long-term orientation are expected to avoid behaviors which can ruin their reputation or bring shame, and take actions to preserve their image over the long run (Yoo, 2002). Because an IT disaster recovery plan is essentially a tool for mitigating the risk of future failures, it is hypothesized that:

H_2: Higher levels of long-term orientation, as reported by organizations' IT directors, will be correlated with higher levels of IT disaster recovery planning.

METHODOLOGY

To test the hypotheses from the previous section, pen and paper surveys, along with web surveys and telephone calls were used for gathering data. To measure the dependent variable, the employee in charge of IT at each participating organization completed a self-assessment of IT disaster recovery planning practices. In addition, IT directors were asked to complete surveys for operationalizing the independent variables. The procedure, sample population, and measures are described in more detail.

Sample

For this research, the sample is comprised of member organizations of the Georgia Bankers Association (GBA). The GBA is over 120 years old; almost every bank in the state of Georgia is a member. To qualify for membership, an organization must be a state or federally charted bank. In total, the association is comprised of 337 member organizations. In terms of relevance, this population is somewhat unique in that banks are required to meet minimum IT disaster recovery planning standards set by the Federal Financial Institutions Examination Council (FFIEC) and the Federal Deposit Insurance Corporation (FDIC). This sample was intentionally selected because the respondents would have an understanding of the concept of ITDR planning due to these regulations.

Measures and Procedures

A survey was mailed to the chief executive officer of each bank. The directions in the cover letter requested that the survey be sent to the organization's IT director or to the individual responsible for managing the firm's information technology. Self-addressed stamped envelopes were included for returning completed surveys. As an alternative to mailing in a paper survey, the directions indicated that the survey could be completed online.

The address of a website containing the survey was provided. To ensure that each organization completed only one web survey, an authentication code was also included; after the code was used once, it could not be used again. The instrument consists of some background and demographic questions, and some 46 scale items (see Appendix A). The measure for the dependent variable, degree of IT disaster recovery planning, was adopted from a previously-validated measure (Kadlec & Shropshire, 2010). The measures for long-term orientation and uncertainty avoidance were all adopted from Yoo and Donthu (2002). The construct measures are operationalized using 5-point Likert scales, in which 1 represented "strongly disagree" and 5 represented "strongly agree."

ANALYSIS

After purging incomplete surveys, there were a total of 153 useable records. This equates to a 45.4% response rate. Because the data were collected using various media, Wilk's Lambda and independent sample t-tests were conducted to ensure homogeneity; no significant differences were found.

Validity and Reliability

Prior to conducting further analysis, steps were taken to classify the constructs as formative or reflective. In contrast to reflective measures, where variation in the items reflects the construct's meaning, items in a formative scale are dimensions which together form the construct. Thus, changes in formative measures affect the meaning of the construct itself (Diamantopoulos & Winklhofer, 2001; Jarvis et al., 2003; Petter et al., 2007). According to the decision rules outlined by Petter et al. (2007), constructs IT disaster recovery planning, uncertainty avoidance, and long-term orientation should be classified as formative. Removal of one item from each measure changes the meaning of each of the constructs. According the classification criteria, this categorizes each as formative. Thus, validity and reliability assessment and path testing followed the procedures specified for formative measures.

Construct validity was assessed by considering the results of a principal components analysis (PCA), and examining item weightings (Chin, 1995). Items were assumed to be valid if their weightings were significant (Diamontopoulos & Winklhofer, 2001). The results of the PCA indicated that all of the item weights were significant at the .10 level of confidence, supporting construct validity (see Table 2).

Because formative indicators need not co-vary, conventional tests of reliability are unjustified (Marakas et al., 2007). In fact, a high degree of reliability may even be undesirable. Indeed, Petter et al. (2007) suggest that if measures are highly correlated, it may suggest that multiple indicators are tapping into the same aspect of the construct. The VIF (variance inflation factor) statistic was used to ensure that items are not overly correlated (Petter et al., 2007; Diamontopoulos & Siguaw, 2006). In this use, the recommended maximum threshold for the VIF statistic is less than or equal to 3.3 (Diamontopoulos & Siguaw, 2006). The calculated VIF statistics were all within the recommended range (see Table 2). As indicated by these tests, the constructs were found to be sufficiently valid for use in this study.

Path Analysis

The relationships were testing using structural equation modeling (SEM). Because the model consisted of formative constructs, bootstrap sampling was used to test the proposed relationships among the constructs (Gefen et al., 2000). Path coefficients and t-values were obtained through this procedure, and are depicted in Table 3. The results indicate that the paths between the predicting variables and ITDRP are significant at the $\rho<.050$ level of confidence. The model's

explanatory power was considered by observing the R^2 of endogenous constructs (Chin, 1998). IT director values, long-term orientation and uncertainty avoidance, collectively explain 63.4% of variance in the dependent variable. Table 4 presents the results of the hypotheses tests; all the proposed relationships were supported. Finally, Figure 1 provides a visual depiction of the structural equation model.

Results

The principal finding is that organizations with IT directors that value uncertainty avoidance and have long-term orientations tend to conduct more thorough IT disaster recovery planning. The number of survey items for the ITDR measure was relatively high (38); this necessitated brevity throughout the rest of the instrument. Out of the field of personal values variables, only the constructs with the most previous support were tested. Fortunately, they proved to be useful predictors.

The exclusion of certain survey items also means that it is not possible to conclusively state that IT directors are the most influential players in ITDR planning exercises. This research did not control for the size of the organization, the amount of time the IT director had been in charge, or his or her indirect impact on recent planning practices. However, because a significant amount of variation in ITDR planning was explained by IT director values, it is reasonable to assume that they exert influence over such activities.

IMPLICATIONS

The chief implication of this study is that if a firm's ITDR plans are lacking, it will be worthwhile to engage the IT director. The improvement of IT disaster recovery plans may start with a simple conversation, guided by principles unearthed in this study. Does the individual believe that he or she has a future with the organization? Individu-

Table 2. Assessment of formative measures

Construct	Item	Weight	t-Value	Significance	VIF
IT Disaster Recovery Planning (ITDRP)	ITDRP1	.177	1.791	ρ=.0507	1.032
	ITDRP2	.173	2.527	ρ=.0125	1.036
	ITDRP3	.189	2.100	P=.0374	1.036
	ITDRP4	.053	2.150	P=.0331	1.003
	ITDRP5	.017	2.868	P=.0047	1.000
	ITDRP6	.417	3.150	P=.0020	1.204
	ITDRP7	.173	2.942	P=.0038	1.030
	ITDRP8	.091	2.090	P=.0393	1.010
	ITDRP9	.201	2.478	ρ=.0143	1.036
	ITDRP10	.449	2.674	ρ=.0083	1.287
	ITDRP11	.243	2.343	ρ=.0204	1.068
	ITDRP12	.066	2.735	ρ=.0070	1.006
	ITDRP13	.155	2.082	ρ=.0390	1.026
	ITDRP14	.175	2.161	ρ=.0323	1.032
	ITDRP15	.086	2.109	ρ=.0366	1.007
	ITDRP16	.051	1.934	ρ=.0550	1.002
	ITDRP17	.006	1.951	ρ=.0529	1.000
	ITDRP18	.044	2.603	ρ=.0102	1.002
	ITDRP19	.264	2.665	ρ=.0085	1.085
	ITDRP20	.323	2.760	ρ=.0065	1.134
	ITDRP21	.135	2.675	ρ=.0083	1.022
	ITDRP22	.248	2.047	ρ=.0424	1.064
	ITDRP23	.279	1.896	ρ=.0599	1.080
	ITDRP24	.344	1.947	ρ=.0534	1.123
	ITDRP25	.010	2.016	ρ=.0456	1.000
	ITDRP26	.159	2.110	ρ=.0365	1.027
	ITDRP27	.310	2.551	ρ=.0117	1.111
	ITDRP28	.085	2.397	ρ=.0177	1.006
	ITDRP29	.007	1.973	ρ=.0503	1.000
	ITDRP30	.043	2.620	ρ=.0097	1.002
	ITDRP31	.160	2.378	ρ=.0186	1.025
	ITDRP32	.537	2.981	ρ=.0033	1.383
	ITDRP33	.316	1.969	ρ=.0508	1.100
	ITDRP34	.066	2.527	ρ=.0125	1.004
Uncertainty Avoidance (UA)	UA1	.148	2.456	ρ=.0152	1.036
	UA2	.136	1.921	ρ=.0566	1.036
	UA3	.479	1.912	ρ=.0578	1.003
	UA4	.219	1.978	ρ=.0497	1.000
	UA5	.780	2.503	ρ=.0134	1.204

conitnued on following page

Table 2. Continued

Construct	Item	Weight	t-Value	Significance	VIF
Long Term Orientation (LTO)	LTO1	.172	2.621	ρ=.0097	1.030
	LTO2	.083	2.510	ρ=.0131	1.010
	LTO3	.096	2.199	ρ=.0294	1.036
	LTO4	.309	2.201	ρ=.0292	1.287
	LTO5	.159	2.192	ρ=.0299	1.068
	LTO6	.632	1.946	ρ=.0535	1.006

als who expect to part ways with the firm are less likely to focus their efforts on long-term work. What is the employee's risk-threshold? Those who do not appreciate the realities of IT disasters are less likely to see ITDR planning as a necessary activity.

As mentioned in the introduction, it was found that the majority of CEOs held misconceptions regarding their firms' level of ITDR preparedness. This was not found to be the case with IT directors. Those who indicated that their firms had strong ITDR plans were generally correct; those who indicated that their ITDR plans were lacking had every reason to be concerned. It is therefore recommended that if the IT director says the plan needs work, then it would be prudent to trust his or her word.

Another point concerns executive education. It is common knowledge that information technology can be a daunting subject; it can intimidate even the most ardent senior manager. However, if the organization fails to recover from an IT-related disaster, ignorance will not be a suitable defense for the CEO. It is therefore suggested that senior managers take steps to acquaint themselves with the basic IT services their organization requires. Technology aside, executives will find that IT disaster recovery planning is largely a matter of organizing resources, formalizing strategies, and delegating authority – activities that they already perform as CEOs.

LIMITATIONS

Some attention must be given to the sample population. Compared with other industries, banking is somewhat unique in that it is highly regulated. Most banks have compliance officers whose job is to ensure adherence to federal and state regulations. However, even with this extra oversight, the results indicate that the industry is not perfect. It is suggested that these findings may be applied to organizations in other regulated industries, such as healthcare, public service, and defense contracting. Because this study did not consider other populations, the focus on just banks may be seen as a shortcoming. This presents a limitation in generalizability. In addition the banks were selected from only on state in the southeastern United States. Thus, while the response rate was almost 50%, the population was limited. From this data, there is no way to tell if the relationship holds for banks in northern states, in more or less populous states, or in more regulated states.

The research model was limited to only two predictors. Although 63.4% of the variance was explained by the current antecedents, it is recognized that other variables should be considered. For instance, other cultural dimensions identified by Hofstede, including power distance, individualism, and masculinity may have an effect on IT director decision making.

Table 3. Path coefficients and their T-values

Hypothesis		Outcome
H₁	Higher levels of uncertainty avoidance, as reported by organizations' IT directors, will be correlated with higher levels of IT disaster recovery planning.	Supported
H₂	Higher levels of long-term orientation, as reported by organizations' IT directors, will be correlated with higher levels of IT disaster recovery planning.	Supported

Table 4. Outcome of hypothesis tests

Hypothesis	Path		Path Coefficient (β)	t-Value	Significance
	From	To			
H₁	UA	ITDRP	.622	2.475	$p<.010$
H₂	LTO	ITDRP	.234	2.090	$p<.050$

FUTURE RESEARCH

In the future, studies should examine more potential factors which may impact the degree of IT disaster recovery planning among organizations. This research focused on attributes of IT directors; other attributes and behavioral variables should be considered. Attributes of firms, such as innovativeness, organizational size, degree of formalization, degree of centralization, reliance on information technology, industry type, growth rate, and agility should also be considered. Further, other populations should be considered. Presently, the authors are conducting IT disaster recovery planning research on firms which are also highly regulated – airlines, healthcare, military/defense, and government. Thus, a definite need exists for IT disaster recovery planning research on firms which are less regulated and occupy different sectors of the economy.

CONCLUSION

ITDR planning is not glamorous. It involves the painstaking creation of plans which may never be used (but must constantly be tested and updated). The value associated with this process is not imme-

Figure 1. Diagram of structural equation model

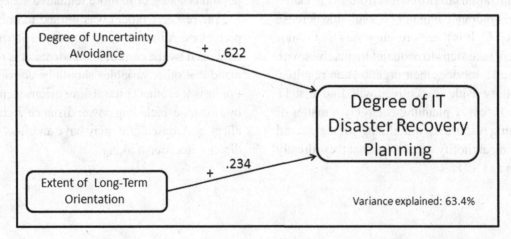

diately salient or easily quantifiable. However, IT disaster recovery planning is absolutely necessary. This work delivers a potential explanation for the variation in degree of IT disaster recovery planning among banks in the southeastern United States by considering the values of IT directors. It was found that uncertainty avoidance and long-term orientation are good predictors of the degree of IT disaster recovery planning. Because this project is one of the first attempts at understanding the IT disaster recovery planning function, this and future research stand to provide significant value to the IT management field.

REFERENCES

Agarwal, R., & Sambamurthy, V. (2002). Principles and models for organizing the IT function. *MIS Quarterly Executive, 1*(1), 1–16.

Anderson, J. (2008). New trends in backup: Is your disaster recovery plan keeping up? *The eSecurity Advisor, 8*(2), 58.

Ashton, H. (2008). How prepared is your business for a calamity? *Japan Inc, 12*(1), 15–17.

Chin, W. (1998). The Partial Least Squares Approach to Structural Equation Modeling . In Marcoulides, G. A. (Ed.), *Modern Methods for Business Research* (pp. 295–336). Mahwah, NJ: Lawrence Erlbaum Associates.

Chin, W., & Todd, P. (1995). One the use, usefulness and ease of use of structural equation modeling in MIS research: A note of caution. *Management Information Systems Quarterly, 19*(2), 237–246. doi:10.2307/249690

Chun, M., & Moody, J. (2009). CIO roles and responsibilities: Twenty-five years of evolution and change. *Information & Management, 46*(6), 323–334. doi:10.1016/j.im.2009.05.005

Cox, J. (2007). The case of the great hot-swap site. *New World (New Orleans, La.), 24*(30), 42–45.

Davis, C. (2001). Planning for the unthinkable: IT contingencies. *International Education Journal, 21*(4), 4–5.

Defelice, A. (2008). Preparing for the worst. *Accounting Technology, 20*(4), 14–19.

Diamantopoulos, A., & Siguaw, L. (n.d.). Formative versus Reflective Indicators in Organizational Measure Development: A Comparison and Empirical Illustration. *British Journal of Management, 17*, 263–282. doi:10.1111/j.1467-8551.2006.00500.x

Diamantopoulos, A., & Winklhofer, H. M. (2001). Index Construction with Formative Indicators: An Alternative to Scale Development. *JMR, Journal of Marketing Research, 38*(2), 269–277. doi:10.1509/jmkr.38.2.269.18845

Fishbein, M., & Ajzen, I. (1975). *Belief, Attitude, Intention, and Behavior: An Introduction to Theory and Research*. Reading, MA: Addison-Wesley.

FitzGerald, J., & Dennis, A. (2005). *Business data communications and networking* (9th ed.). New York: Wiley.

Fonseca, B. (2004). NY IT prepares for IT disaster recovery. *eWeek, 7*(32), 9-10.

Gaynor, M., Brander, S., Pearce, A., & Post, K. (2009). Open infrastructure for a nationwide emergency service network. *International Journal of Information Systems for Crisis Response and Management, 1*(2), 31–46. doi:10.4018/jiscrm.2009040103

Gefen, D., Straub, D., & Boudreau, M. (2000). Structural Equation Modeling Techniques and Regression: Guidelines for Research Practice. *Communications of AIS, 7*(7), 1–78.

Gold, L. (2007). Disaster recovery planning: How do you measure up? *Accounting Today*, *21*(7), 31–35.

Hayes, J. (2005). Reaping the whirlwind. *IEEE Review*, *13*(3), 29. doi:10.1049/ir:20051009

Hoftsede, G. (1991). *Cultures and Organizations: Software of the mind*. Berkshire, UK: McGraw-Hill.

Hoge, J. (2005). Business continuity planning must extend to vendors. *Bank Technology News*, *11*(3), 21.

Holliday, K. (2008). Planning for the worst. *Community Banker*, *22*(8), 32–35.

Jaques, M. (2006). Securing your IT continuity. *Financial Director*, *28*(7), 42.

Jarvis, C., Mackenzie, S., & Podsakoff, P. (2003). A Critical Review of Construct Indicators and Measurement Model Misspecification in Marketing and Consumer Research. *The Journal of Consumer Research*, *30*(2), 199–218. doi:10.1086/376806

Jepson, K. (2008). How 1 small CU perfected its own recipe for disaster recovery. *Credit Union Journal*, *23*(9), 20.

Kadlec, C., & Shropshire, J. (in press). Establishing the IT disaster recovery construct. *Journal of IT Management*.

Laliberte, B. (2007). How disaster-tolerant is your company? *Business Communications Review*, *32*(4), 44–49.

Lee, L., Choi, B., Kim, J., & Hong, S. (2007). Culture-technology: Effects of cultural characteristics on the post-adoption beliefs of mobile internet users. *International Journal of Electronic Commerce*, *11*(4), 1–51. doi:10.2753/JEC1086-4415110401

Lohrman, D. (2007). Disaster Recovery: A process – not a destination. *Public CIO*, *8*(2), 54.

Lyons, B. (2007). *Preparing for a disaster: Determining the essential functions that should be up first. (Tec. Rep. No. 14)*. Bethesda, MD: SANS Institute.

Mackenzie, S., Podsakoff, P., & Jarvis, C. (2005). The problem of Measurement Model Misspecification in Behavioral and Organizational Research and Some Recommended Solutions. *The Journal of Applied Psychology*, *90*(4), 710–730. PubMed doi:10.1037/0021-9010.90.4.710

McLaughlin, L. (2008). Rethinking disaster recovery. *CIO*, *21*(6), 23–26.

Mearian, L. (2004). Key financial firms compare notes on disaster recovery. *Computerworld*, *38*(31), 43.

Pabrai, U. (2004). Contingency planning and disaster recovery. *Certification Magazine*, *5*(8), 38–39.

Petter, S., Straub, D., & Rai, A. (2007). Specifying formative constructs in information systems research. *Management Information Systems Quarterly*, *31*(4), 623–656.

Plotnick, L., & White, C. (2010). A Framework to identify best practices: Social media and web 2.0 technologies in the emergency domain. *International Journal of Information Systems for Crisis Response and Management*, *2*(1), 37–48. doi:10.4018/jiscrm.2010120404

Plotnick, N. (1999). When disaster plans fall short. *PC Week*, *28*(2), 58.

Pregmon, M. (2007). IT disaster recovery: Are you up and ready? Part 1: Analysis. *Journal of the Quality Assurance Institute*, *27*(2), 23–24.

Pregmon, M. (2007). IT disaster recovery: Are you up and ready? Part 2: Internal Control. *Journal of the Quality Assurance Institute*, *27*(3), 25–28.

Pregmon, M. (2007). IT disaster recovery: Are you up and ready? Part 3: The recovery planning process. *Journal of the Quality Assurance Institute*, *27*(4), 10–12.

Pregmon, M. (2008). IT disaster recovery: Are you up and ready? Part 4: IT virtualization. *Journal of the Quality Assurance Institute*, *28*(1), 26–27.

Ramsaran, C. (2005). Running ahead of the pack. *Bank Systems & Technology*, *1*(4), 1–3.

Retelle, M. (2008). Plan for disaster. *Credit Union Magazine*, *21*(9), 80.

Rolich, P. (2008). Setting priorities: Business continuity from an IT perspective – is it better to be right or liked? *Tech Decisions*, *9*(2), 11–14.

Sheth, S., McHugh, J., & Jones, F. (2008). A dashboard for measuring capability when designing, implementing and validating business continuity and disaster recovery projects. *Journal of Business Continuity & Emergency Planning*, *2*(3), 221–239.

Sliwa, C. (2005). Retailers unsure about the status of stores, systems. *Computerworld*, *39*(3), 5.

Sobol, M., & Klein, G. (2009). Relation of CIO background, IT infrastructure, and economic performance. *Information & Management*, *46*(5), 271–278. doi:10.1016/j.im.2009.05.001

Straub, D. (1994). The effect of culture on IT diffusion: E-mail and FAX in Japan and US. *Information Systems Research*, *5*(1), 23–47. doi:10.1287/isre.5.1.23

Thibodeau, P., & Mearian, L. (2005). Users start to weigh long-term IT issues. *Computerworld*, *39*(37), 61–67.

Vellliquette, D. (2005) Computer security considerations in disaster recovery planning (Tech. Rep. No. 11). Bethesda, MD: SANS Institute.

Vijayan, J. (2005). Data security risks missing from disaster recovery plans. *Computerworld*, *39*(41), 16–18.

Yoo, B., & Donthu, N. (2002). The effects of marketing education and cultural values on marketing ethics of students. *Journal of Marketing Education*, *24*(2), 92–103.

This work was previously published in International Journal of Information Systems for Crisis Response Management, Volume 2, Issue 2, edited by Murray E. Jennex, pp. 54-68, copyright 2010 by IGI Publishing (an imprint of IGI Global).

APPENDIX A: SURVEY ITEMS

Construct		Items
Uncertainty Avoidance	UA1 UA2 UA3 UA4 UA5	It is important to have instructions spelled out in detail so that I always know what I'm expected to do. It is important to closely instructions and procedures. Rules/regulations are important because they inform me of what is expected of me. Standardized work procedures are helpful. Instructions for operations are important.
Long Term Orientation	LTO1 LTO2 LTO3 LTO4 LTO5 LTO6	How closely do you associate with each of the following qualities: Careful management of money (thrift). Going on resolutely in spite of opposition (persistence). Personal steady and stability. Long-term planning. Giving up today's fun for success in the future. Working hard for success in the future.
IT Disaster Recovery Planning	ITDRP1 ITDRP2 ITDRP3 ITDRP4 ITDRP5 ITDRP6 ITDRP7 ITDRP8 ITDRP9 ITDRP10 ITDRP11 ITDRP12 ITDRP13 ITDRP14 ITDRP15 ITDRP16 ITDRP17 ITDRP18 ITDRP19 ITDRP20 ITDRP21 ITDRP22 ITDRP23 ITDRP24 ITDRP25 ITDRP26 ITDRP27 ITDRP28 ITDRP29 ITDRP30 ITDRP31 ITDRP32 ITDRP33 ITDRP34	We have procedures for detecting IT disasters We have a means of assessing the magnitude of IT disasters We have procedures for alerting individuals responsible for IT disaster recovery We have procedures for letting stakeholders know that an IT disaster has occurred We have established an alternative means of communications (i.e. cell phones) to use in emergencies We have a an IT disaster recovery team (i.e. a group of employees who are responsible for restoring IT) Those responsible for IT disaster recovery have been assigned specific tasks for restoring IT services Employees and other stakeholders know what to expect during IT disasters We have an explicit chain of command for dealing with IT disasters We have identified all IT services which the IT department offers We have identified all system resources required to provide IT services We have assessed risks to IT services and infrastructure We have ranked the order in which IT services would be repaired, if a disaster occurred Should our primary site go offline, we have a secondary site Should our primary site go offline, we have procedures for relocating IT operations Our plans account for possible losses of human resources (i.e. missing or injured IT workers) We have procedures for restoring physical facilities such as physical buildings, power, and cooling systems We have procedures for recovering communications technologies such cellular phones, email, and VOIP We have procedures for recovering servers We have procedures for recovering applications and software We have procedures for recovering data We have procedures for creating backup copies of data We have procedures for creating backup copies of software We have procedures for creating backup copies of configuration files, change logs, and other documents We have procedures for creating backup copies of the disaster recovery plan itself We have ensured that system resources are as portable as possible (i.e. that they can be transported) We have offsite locations for storing data We have offsite locations for storing software We have offsite locations for storing configuration files, change logs, and other relevant documents We have offsite locations for storing copies of the IT disaster recovery plan We have procedures for testing of the IT disaster recovery plan We have procedures for updating the IT disaster recovery plan We have procedures for ensuring that the IT disaster recovery plan is part of the business continuity plan We have procedures for documenting system configurations, changes, and updates

Chapter 10
Lessons Learned on the Operation of the LoST Protocol for Mobile IP– Based Emergency Calls

Ana Goulart
Texas A&M University, USA

Anna Zacchi
Texas A&M University, USA

Bharath Chintapatla
Texas A&M University, USA

Walt Magnussen
Texas A&M University, USA

ABSTRACT

The technology used in citizen-to-authority emergency calls is based on traditional telephony, that is, circuit-switched systems. However, new standards and protocols are being developed by the Internet Engineering Task Force (IETF) to allow emergency communications over packet switched networks, such as the Internet. This architecture is known as Next Generation-9-1-1 (NG-911). In this paper, the authors present lessons learned from experiments on the IETF standard called Location to Service Translation protocol (LoST). LoST maps the user's location to the address of the emergency call center that serves that location. After implementing the standards in a test-bed with real-world systems, spatial databases, and communication networks, the authors observed performance issues that users may experience. Based on their observations, the authors propose practical ideas to improve the performance of the NG-911 system and LoST protocol operation for mobile users.

DOI: 10.4018/978-1-4666-0167-3.ch010

INTRODUCTION

Every minute, tens of thousands of emergency calls are placed in the United States. Thousands more are probably being made in other countries. Within each country or region, there is usually a common number to reach emergency services (e.g., 9-1-1, 1-1-2, etc). In order to better explain the context of this paper, next we provide a brief history of emergency calls, followed by a description of this paper's motivation.

A Brief History of Emergency Call Systems

It was in 1937, in Great Britain, that the idea of a single emergency number was developed. By dialing 9-9-9, British citizens could contact the police, fire department, or medical services. Only later, in 1958 US legislators began to consider the use of a single emergency number. The number chosen in the US was 9-1-1. It is known that one of the reasons for this choice is that the numbers were located on opposite sides of the key-pad, which reduced the chances of accidental calls.

In 1968, the first 9-1-1 call was made in Alabama. Later that year, the American Telephone and Telegraph Company (AT&T) announced the 9-1-1 service. This first 9-1-1 service is also known as "traditional 9-1-1". It directed all emergency calls to a nearby Public Safety Answering Point (PSAP) which was directly connected, via dedicated trunks, to the telephone company's central office (CO). A typical PSAP consists of a group of call takers who are responsible for answering emergency calls as well as dispatching the appropriate emergency service (such as ambulance, or police, or fire fighters).

Because the plain old telephone system (POTS) network only established and terminated calls, call takers had few resources to determine the caller's location. As a result, traditional 9-1-1 soon gave way to landline Enhanced 9-1-1 (E-911), which greatly increased the ability to locate the caller. E-911 employs an address database called Automatic Location Identification (ALI), which uses the telephone number of the caller to determine his/her identity and location. E-911 was implemented in 1978 and is still being used today (Figure 1).

Landline E-911, however, only temporarily met the new technological need. Cell phones soon made it necessary to again upgrade the system. The Federal Communications Commission (FCC) mandated that all United States wireless carriers provide the location information of the caller (Reed, Krizman, Woerner, & Rappaport, 1998). Implementation of this mandate would enable wireless carriers to "pinpoint" the location of any 9-1-1 caller.

The FCC mandate was divided in two phases: Phase I required the wireless carrier to send the PSAP the location of the antenna or cell site; Phase II required the wireless carrier to send an estimate of the geographic coordinates of the mobile user, typically using some type of network triangulation scheme (Feng & Law, 2002; Sayed,

Figure 1. Evolution of North American 9-1-1 emergency calling system

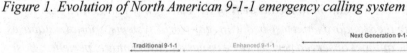

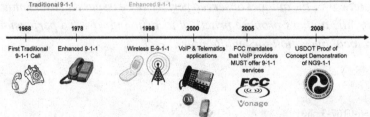

Tarighat, & Khajehnour, 2005). Not all wireless providers have implemented Phase II service as of 2009, based on the National Emergency Number Association (NENA)'s recent 9-1-1 Deployment Reports (NENA, 2010).

In the late 1990s, with the onset of voice over Internet Protocol (VoIP) (Goode, 2002) and other Internet services, researchers and developers have realized that a complete overhaul of the current E-911 system is necessary – proposing a Next Generation 9-1-1 (NG-911) (Hixson, Cobb, & Halley, 2007; NENA, 2007a, 2007b; Schulzrinne & Arabshian, 2002) system that enables both voice and data communications for emergency calls.

Recently, an NG-911 proof-of-concept was developed (Kim, Song, & Schulzrinne, 2006; Song et al., 2008). This development represents a critical step and an important building block to validate IP-based emergency calling. The proof-of-concept allowed the testing of IP-based emergency calls to IP-based PSAPs on five main scenarios: (i) calls from traditional landline phones, (ii) calls from cellular phones, (iii) text messages (SMS), (iv) telematics service messages, and (v) multimedia calls from fixed/enterprise VoIP devices.

In addition, the NG-911 proof-of-concept tested the idea of Emergency Services Router Proxies (ESRPs) for policy-based routing. ESRPs improve the call routing capability of 9-1-1 calls: they can re-route emergency calls to any PSAP (e.g., PSAPs that are not overloaded, or PSAPs with special capabilities such as the ones with sign-language capable call takers). With IP-based emergency calling, a PSAP can now be anywhere, even in a mobile device such as a laptop. The NG-9-1-1 proof-of-concept and all the technology behind it mean that a PSAP does not have to be a centralized call center as before, but can be a much more flexible, portable, and less expensive system.

The NG-911 proof-of-concept concludes our brief history of the 9-1-1 evolution. However, IP-based emergency calling still faces new challenges. Standards are being developed, security vulnerabilities must be addressed, and the transition from PSTN-based PSAPs to IP-based PSAPs is being investigated.

Motivations for This Paper

One important NG-911 research challenge is related to the location of the caller, which can be very dynamic. Enterprise VoIP phones have the flexibility to be connected to any network port. Home VoIP subscribers can be connected to any access network (e.g., an Internet service provider). Also, mobile devices such as dual-mode cell phones (with 802.11 radio), laptops with broadband wireless coverage (using 3G, or 4G cellular data cards) can be constantly changing its location.

Moreover, the architecture for IP-based emergency services will have different entities: the access infrastructure network and the application service provider (such as a voice service provider (VSP)) (Tschofenig, Schulzrinne, Shanmugan, & Newton, 2007). This poses unique challenges to current IP-based emergency systems. For instance, it is the subscriber's responsibility to provide his/her location to the VoIP service provider; however, the subscriber may not update this information when the VoIP device is moved to a different location (i.e., a different access network).

As a result, VoIP service providers may not have the most up to date civic or geographic address of the user.

New Internet Engineering Task Force (IETF) standards have been created to allow the addition of location information (Peterson, 2005; Polk & Rosen, 2009) to the Session Initiation Protocol (SIP) call setup messages (known as SIP Invites) (Rosenberg et al., 2002). In addition, the Location to Service Translation (LoST) protocol (Hardie, Newton, Schulrzrinne, & Tschofenig, 2008; Schulzrinne, Tschofenig, Hardie, & Newton, 2007; Schulzrinne, 2008) has been created to help both end users or SIP proxies to obtain the SIP address of the PSAP where the emergency call must be routed to. This SIP address is known as SIP Uniform Resource Identifier (URI) (e.g., sip:psap1@domain).

Initial experiments using the LoST protocol were performed in (Schulzrinne, Tschofenig, Hardie, & Newton, 2007), which presents the concept of the LoST protocol, introduces the idea of the Emergency Services IP Network (ESInet), and how the protocol queries are performed. The authors conclude the paper with a few performance results, mainly delays of the LoST queries.

Additionally, the use of emergency services by mobile users is described by an IETF standard on best current practices (Rosen & Polk, 2009; Schulzrinne & Marshall, 2008). It provides a set of guidelines on obtaining the location of mobile users, querying LoST servers, and storing the PSAP URI at a cache at the SIP/LoST client (Wu & Schulzrinne, 2004).

In Chintapatla, Goulart, and Magnussen (2010), we presented preliminary results from an initial work with the NG-911 testbed, where preliminary performance results on the LoST queries and processing delay at the mobile client were presented. Now, we present in this paper more detailed experiments, lessons learned, and a complete overview of the operation and performance of the LoST protocol, including description of techniques in computational geometry for processing location information and service boundaries data (both at the LoST client and server).

Contributions

This paper provides a detailed tutorial on the routing of IP-based emergency calls; moreover, it presents experimental results that provide new insights on the operation and performance of the LoST protocol for mobile users. Using real-world service boundaries data, we performed a large set of test-bed experiments; the results helped us identify new algorithms to more efficiently support the caching mechanism (Rosen & Polk, 2009) of the LoST protocol for mobile users (i.e., clients with dynamic location information). This

work is valuable to researchers and practitioners working not only on the transition of traditional emergency communications to IP-based emergency communications but also on applications that use location-based services for mobile users.

This paper is organized as follows. Section 2 provides an overview of the operation of the LoST protocol. Then, Section 3 discusses the issue of detecting service boundary crossings at the mobile LoST client, which can be addressed by algorithms of computational geometry. Section 4 also discusses service boundaries, but from the viewpoint of the LoST server. Section 5 describes our testbed setup, followed by the experimental results which are presented in Section 6. Finally, this paper is concluded in Section 7.

A NEW ARCHITECTURE FOR ROUTING IP-BASED EMERGENCY CALLS

In an emergency call, location information, or a reference to a server that has the location information, must be added to the body of the SIP Invite message. Location information can be obtained by the user or a SIP proxy (Barnes, 2008; NENA, 2006; Polk, Schnizlein, & Linsner, 2004; TIA, 2006). As in traditional E-9-1-1 services, location is needed for routing the call to the appropriate PSAP. In addition, location is needed for dispatching the necessary services.

There are different accuracy needs between routing and dispatching. For routing, typically an approximate location will suffice, unless the mobile user is close to the border of a jurisdictional boundary which could lead to routing the call to the wrong PSAP. However, for dispatching, emergency responders really need an accurate location in order to quickly reach the user.

Concerning the routing of IP-based emergency calls, the LoST protocol is the new protocol specified for call routing in the NG-911 architecture. It maps the caller's location to the PSAP's Uniform

Resource Identifier (URI). In other words, it resolves a user's location to the address of a specific PSAP (in the IP-based architecture, the address is an IP address). Or it could be an IP address of an Emergency Services Routing Proxy (ESRP). In case there is neither location nor mapping information in a SIP Invite, the call is routed to a default PSAP.

Call Flow

Figure 2 illustrates the basic operation of the LoST protocol in our NG-911 test-bed. The Geocoder machine shown in the box includes the SIP proxy, LoST server, and Domain Name System (DNS) server.

As an example, here are the main steps for an emergency call going through the ESINet based on our current test-bed:

1. A caller from College Station in Brazos County makes a LoST lookup on the state-wide LoST server, with the result being that the caller should instead route to Brazos' ESRP.
2. The caller calls his/her local SIP proxy with the "Route" field of the SIP Invite being set to esrp-brazos.tamu.edu.
3. The ESRP makes a LoST lookup on the Brazos County LoST server, with the result that the caller should be connected to College Station's police department at psap-collegestation.tamu.edu.
4. The call is routed to the PSAP server at College Station.
5. The server at College Station's police PSAP distributes the call among its call takers.

Figure 2. NG-911 testbed

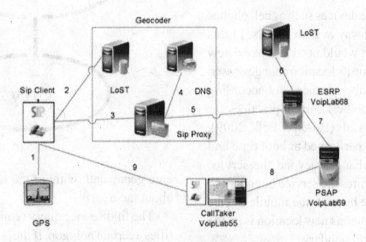

1: Get the location of SIP client using the GPS.
2: Query the LoST server to get the ESRP address.
3: Send the SOS call to ESRP through SIP proxy.
4: DNS query to get the IP of ESRP from the URL.
5: Forward the call to ESRP.
6: ESRP makes LoST query to find out the associated PSAP.
7: Forward the call to PSAP.
8: One of the call takers receives the call.
9: Call taker connects to the SIP client.

Figure 3. Potential hierarchy of LoST databases

It is expected that the end user makes a LoST query when it gets its location information. In this way, the PSAP address is stored in a cache, and updated when the location changes. When the need for an emergency call arises, a new LoST query can be made, or if a new LoST cannot be made or is not successful, the stored results can be used. Then, if an emergency arise, the new (or cached) PSAP URI is added to the header of the SIP message, while the actual location information is added to the body of the SIP message in an XML format known as Presence Information Data Format-Location Object (PIDF-LO) (Peterson, 2005).

A practical hierarchy of LoST servers is illustrated in Figure 3, where different levels of information can be implemented at LoST databases at the city, council of governance (COG), state, country, and even global levels (Schulzrinne, 2008).

Service Boundaries Crossings

Now consider mobile devices such as cell phones moving along a highway at high speeds. In this case, the LoST client would need to make a new LoST query every time its location changes based on its GPS updates, for instance. But according to the IETF's draft on best current practices for IP-based emergency calls (Rosen & Polk, 2009), "mapping should be performed at boot time and whenever location changes beyond the service boundary". This requires the service boundary to be sent to the mobile because the mobile device needs to decide whether its new location is inside or outside the current boundary.

To allow the client to check service boundary crossings, the LoST protocol specifies a getServiceBoundary query. With this query, the client can get the coordinates of the service boundary, which is a polygon. Both findService and getServiceBoundary queries are illustrated in Figure 4. Both transactions can happen between the LoST client and LoST server several times prior to an

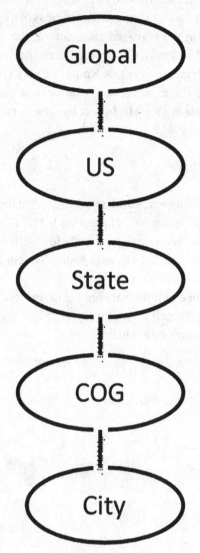

emergency call, without the user even knowing about them.

The findService query returns a key that identifies a certain polygon. If the polygon coordinates are saved in the client's cache, then there is no need to get the coordinates of the polygon. This typically happens when the mobile user returns to a service boundary that he/she has visited before. But if the mobile user has never visited that service boundary, the key will not be in the cache. An additional LoST query needs to be made (getServiceBoundary query) to download the service

Figure 4. LoST queries: findService gives the PSAP USI and getServiceBoundary gives the service boundary

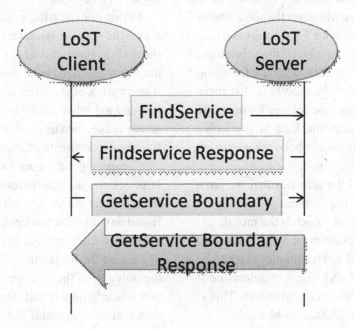

boundary information. Thus, a new boundary will be saved at the mobile user.

To illustrate the findService query, in Figure 5 we show a sample of a LoST findService query sent to our server, using service boundary as reference. The current user location is sent as geographic coordinate (in this example 30.627977 and -96.3344068). The response to this query

provides the PSAP address information (as a URI) and the key to the service boundary for that PSAP. Note that the LoST messages are in Extensible Markup Language (XML) format, carried in HyperText Transfer Protocol (HTTP) and HTTP secure (HTTPS) protocol exchanges.

In summary, each PSAP has a certain area or region it would serve. The area each PSAP serves

Figure 5. A sample of a findService query (XML format)

```
LoST Request to: http://127.0.1.1:8080/lost/LoSTServlet
<?xml version="1.0" encoding="UTF-8"?>
<findService
  xmlns="urn:ietf:params:xml:ns:lost1"
  xmlns:p2="http://www.opengis.net/gml"
  serviceBoundary="reference"
  recursive="true">
  <location id="6020688f1ce1896d"
    profile="geodetic-2d">
    <p2:Point id="point1"
      srsName="urn:ogc:def:crs:EPSG::4326">
      <p2:pos>30.627977 -96.3344068</p2:pos>
    </p2:Point>
  </location>
  <service>urn:service:sos</service>
</findService>
```

is stored as corners of a polygon. Using these points, we can determine which PSAP would serve a particular point. Thus, whenever the client makes a LoST query, along with the PSAP address it also gets the boundary information of the service are that the PSAP is serving. The rationale for doing the boundary checks at the mobile is that there may be thousands of mobile devices for only one LoST server. It reduces the load at the LoST server which otherwise would be overloaded with too many findService queries.

As a drawback of the schemes that we have just described is the requirement for additional calculations at the client, which is the mobile users. This issue is addressed in the Section 3, where we describe in more detail techniques that can be implemented in the LoST client to determine if a location is inside the service boundary. This is usually called *point inclusion* problem.

CLIENT-BASED APPROACHES TO DETECT BOUNDARY CROSSINGS

The calculations done at the client to determine if it has crossed the boundary can be solved using well-established point-inclusion techniques which are based on the Jordan Curve theorem (Preparata & Shamos, 1985; Shimrat, 1962). The main one is known as Ray-tracing algorithm. We also propose a new technique that uses the concept of pre-processing to reduce the calculation time.

Ray-Tracing Method

A simple way to describe the Ray-Tracing method is that a horizontal line (i.e., a "ray") is traced through the point which is our current location. Then we must check if each and every edge of the service boundary intersects this horizontal line. Depending on the number of intersections,

we can determine if the point is inside or outside the service boundary.

Let us consider the point of our location as z and the service boundary as a polygon P, as shown in Figure 6. For checking whether the edge intersects the horizontal line through z, we test if one vertex of the edge is above the horizontal line and the other vertex below it. Once we find such an edge, then using elementary geometry we find the x-coordinate of the point of intersection.

Comparing the x-coordinates of the points of intersection, we can determine the number of intersections which are left of z and right of z. Based on the Jordan theorem, the number of points of intersection is always an even number, except in the case the horizontal line crosses a vertex of the polygon. If the number of points of intersection towards its left and right is an odd number, then that point is inside the polygon. It the number of intersections is even, the point is outside the polygon.

Because the Ray-Tracing method's implementation requires a loop over all the points in the polygon every time the location changes, the processing time whether a point z is internal to a simple N-gon polygon can be determined in O(N) time (Preparata & Shamos, 1985).

Although the Ray-Tracing method is very efficient for checking if the point is inside the polygon for the first time, it is not efficient when we have a dynamic point. In other words, if repetitive calculations are needed, it does not use the information from previous checks to make a decision about the current check. This motivated us to investigate a new method which uses information from previous checks to make a decision. Note that there are other pre-processing calculations that are presented in the literature. For instance, in Preparata and Shamos (1985) a pre-processing approach requires the polygon to be divided into wedges that are then used in the point-inclusion

Figure 6. Point inclusion detection using the Ray-tracing method

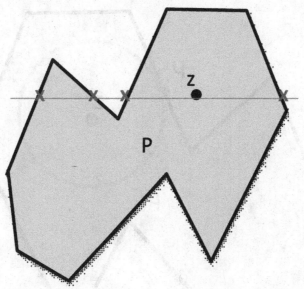

problem. However, when discussing the practical implementation of that approach, we concluded that some of the pre-processing would require calculations at the LoST server. Our approach that uses pre-processing is done at the client side, which is described next.

Minimum Distance Method

In this subsection, a new method is proposed – we call it the Minimum Distance method. It is used with the Ray-Tracing method but it takes advantage of previous Ray-Tracing calculations

The Minimum Distance method aims to determine if a point z is inside a polygon P. The first time there is a location change, the Ray-Tracing method is used to determine if the mobile client crossed the boundary of the current polygon P. Using the points of intersections found using the Ray-Tracing method, we select the closest intersection p. Then using simple trigonometry, we calculate the distance between p and z, which is the minimum distance between the current

location and the boundary of the polygon d_{min}. This can be illustrated as the process of drawing a circle around the current location with a radius equal to the minimum distance, and the point z at the center (Figure 7).

When the mobile changes its location, the algorithm checks if the mobile has moved outside the polygon P by comparing the distance moved d_i with the radius of the circle d_{min}. As long as the total distance moved by the mobile client is less than d_{min}, we do not need to do any other calculation. Once the client moves a distance greater than the radius we need to do a new Ray-Tracing-based check to confirm if the client moved outside of the polygon.

In summary, the advantage of the Minimum Distance method is that once the minimum distance is calculated it takes less processing for future calculations. However, compared to the Ray-Tracing method, the minimum distance method requires additional calculations to find the initial radius (i.e., minimum distance). Also, it may give false positives, when the mobile moves in different

Figure 7. Point inclusion detection using the Minimum Distance method

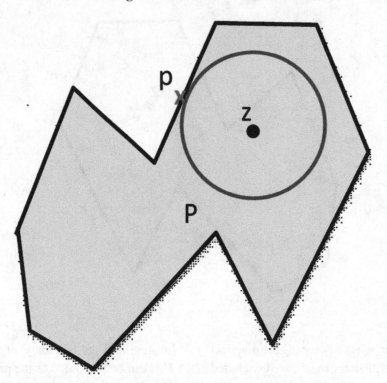

directions within the minimum distance circle, but the total distance moved becomes higher than the minimum distance, the process starts all over again: the minimum distance value will need to be updated.

SERVER-BASED APPROACH TO SIMPLIFY THE SERVICE BOUNDARY

Continuing on the issue of determining service boundary crossing, we also researched potential improvements at the LoST server's side. The new way refers to one sentence of the LoST standard (Hardie, Newton, Schulzrinne & Tschofenig, 2008) that states that a *hint* of the polygon may be sent as a response to getServiceBoundary. Therefore, we investigated changes in the LoST server to allow the use of simplified polygons. This server-based approach was motivated by two

things: (i) to reduce the amount of information sent to the client, and (ii) to make the point-in-polygon calculations faster.

A simplified polygon is an abbreviated version of a polygon. It has less number of corners compared to the original polygon. The example shown in Figure 8 shows two polygons: an external and an internal polygon. (We say that this polygon has a "hole". Surprisingly, in our LoST database we observed several cases of polygons with holes in it, making the point inclusion determination even more complex.) In the simplified version of a polygon in Figure 8, the original corners of the inner and outer polygon are shown in darker color, while the simplified version has corners shown in a lighter color. We can see the reduced number of points in the lighter color.

Using the simplified polygon approach, our LoST server maintained two polygons for every service boundary: the original polygon is used by

Figure 8. Simplified polygon of Brazos County (lighter dots)

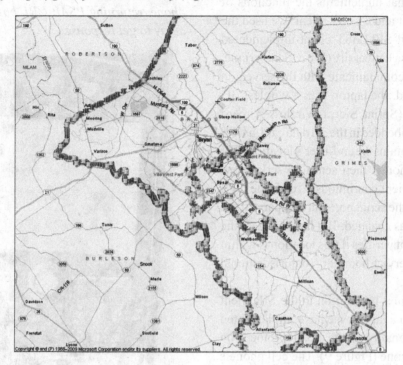

the server to map location to PSAP in findService query; the simplified polygon is sent as a response to getServiceBoundary.

The algorithm we used is the Ramer-Douglas-Peucker algorithm (Douglas & Peucker, 1973). Given two initial points in the polygon, new points are added and a line segment is drawn through them. Then, we measure the distance between all other points and the line segment. The point that is farthest from the line segment is selected first. If the distance from this point to the line is greater than some constant (which is the accuracy required, e.g., 100m) we include the point in the polygon. Then recursively this is done with these two new line segments. In other words, all the points of the simplified polygon are actual points of the service boundary, but in a reduced amount (i.e., points in between are omitted).

Additionally, the calculations of the simplified polygon can be done off-line and installed in the LoST server prior to its operation. Therefore, this method makes changes at the LoST server's side. To ensure compatibility with the LoST protocol, servers that support the simplified polygon should not require major changes in the LoST queries. After presenting our testbed and results in the next sections, we will further discuss this topic of implementation.

TESTBED SETUP – LoST CLIENTS AND SERVER

The NG-911 testbed and call flow has been introduced in Section 2 (Figure 2). We now provide additional details on the types of LoST clients, and the spatial database at the LoST server.

A. LoST Clients

We performed experiments with two different mobile clients:

1. A laptop that implements the functions of a SIP client and a LoST client: we used the multi-agent SIP/LoST client implemented at Columbia University (Wu & Schulzrinne, 2004). To communicate with the servers in the test-bed, the laptop uses a wireless 3G data card (Sprint Sierra Wireless Aircard 597A). Embedded in the 3G data card, a GPS receiver obtains the end-user's location. The GPS location is then sent to a serial port. The SIP client continuously reads the GPS data from the serial port and compares if the location has changed. If it has changed, the LoST client verifies if this location is within the same service boundary (or jurisdictional boundary).

2. A cell-phone: In addition to the SIP client running on a laptop, we have implemented the functionality of the LoST protocol on a smart-phone (Figure 9). The cell phone's LoST client was implemented in JavaME. It runs on the BlackBerry 8820 with the Blackberry 4.5 OS. This LoST client also has a GPS and can use the latitude and longitude readings to perform the LoST queries. To parse the results of the LoST queries we used the kxml parse (http://kxml.sourceforge.net/). The kxml parser is a pull parser: it reads a little bit of a document at each time, while still downloading the data. The application drives the parser through the document by repeatedly requesting the next piece. The LoST client verifies the new GPS reading in the same way as the client on the laptop, by checking for every new location if it is within the current service boundary.

Because the experiments required long trips to physically move the clients to a different service boundary, we have enabled both the LoST client at the laptop and at the smart-phone to read simulated GPS data so that we could test points

Figure 9. LoST client implemented in a smartphone, returning PSAP URI, boundary key, and delay to get response

in several boundaries. We have also tested these points at different cellular networks (e.g., rural and urban areas) (Zhan & Goulart, 2009).

LoST Server/Database

The LoST server was implemented using PostgreSQL with PostGIS for the mapping service. The computer running this service has a dual core processor at 1800 MHz, with 1GByte of memory. Columbia University provided the software implementation of the LoST protocol (Song et al., 2008), and we have populated the database with our local data.

The data contained in our database is at the state level (as in Figure 3) with actual data from the service boundaries in our state (i.e., Texas). There are around 500 service boundaries in Texas.

Out of this large number, we have sampled 198 boundaries to verify their complexity in terms of number of corners. To clarify the concept of "number of corners", the service boundaries consist of data files that contains the geographic coordinates (i.e., latitude and longitude pairs) of each corner. In this way, each data file describes the corners of a polygon.

Figure 10 shows a histogram of our sampled data, in terms of number of corners. The first bar shows that there are 74 service boundaries with less than 1000 corners. Out of 198 samples, this accounts for 37 percent. These low complexity boundaries typically have a regular shape (e.g., rectangular-like shape). However, Figure 10 also shows that there are several boundaries with a few thousands of corners.

It is of our special interest to verify the performance of the LoST protocol for such complex service boundaries, especially boundaries with more than 5000 corners, which accounted for 29 service boundaries in our sample, or 15 percent. We have observed that the complexity of the

boundary depends on geography (borders with neighboring states, rivers, mountains, coastal lines) and population. On the latter, it is significant to mention the size metropolitan areas contribute to the complexity of the service boundary. For example, the four counties with largest population in Texas have service boundaries with more than 5000 corners. Note that the maximum number of corners that we observed in our database was 19278 corners.

EXPERIMENTAL RESULTS

This section presents experimental results that illustrate the operation of the LoST protocol in a NG-911 test-bed (Figure 2) The operation of the SIP and LoST protocol together with the computational geometry algorithms of Section 4 are tested in terms of message sizes, service boundaries' complexity, delays for findService and getServiceBoundary queries, and processing delays for the point inclusion problem.

Figure 10. Distribution of the number of corners from a sample of in 198 service boundaries in the state of Texas

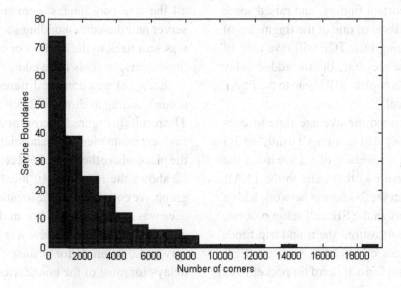

A. SIP Call Flow – Message Size and Delay at the Access Network

The SIP call setup transaction in Figure 11 follows a standard SIP call flow, with mobile's location information added in the initial SIP Invite message. The two intermediate servers are the SIP proxy (geocoder) which is at the side of the SIP client's domain, and the emergency services routing proxy (ESRP) which is at the side of the PSAP, in the Emergency Services IP network (ESInet). Note that all SIP messages in an emergency call are transported over Transport Control Protocol (TCP), which provides reliable transport to IP packets.

From our example (Figure 11), the number of bytes exchanged between the SIP client and SIP proxy to complete the call setup transaction was 4744 bytes. The largest message is the initial SIP Invite message: 2230 bytes. This large size is due to the location information which is in the body of the SIP Invite message, in an Extensible Markup Language (XML) format known as Presence Information Data Format – Location Object (PIDF-LO). In our experiments we are observing that the SIP Invite messages are being fragmented (or divided) in two different packets, whereas regular non-emergency SIP Invites are usually smaller than 1000 bytes and are not fragmented. This was an important finding, and raised some questions on the issue of one of the fragments of the SIP Invite being lost. TCP will take care of retransmitting the message, but the added delay to retransmit the complete SIP Invite to the PSAP can be very critical.

We also measured the average time to connect the emergency call to a PSAP using the 3G data card: it took an average of 1.5 sec using the laptop. There were no other calls to the PSAP. We concluded that the 3G access network adds a considerable delay in the SIP call setup process. For instance, we measured the round trip times (RTT) for wireless connections such as IEEE 802.11g (54 Mbps) and a 3G card for packet sizes from 128 to 1024 bytes (Table 1). From the call flow shown in Figure 4, we can observe that the wireless network we use will affect only those packets which are sent or received by SIP client. However, the wireless access network is the major source of delay in this lightly loaded scenario.

SIP LoST "findService" Query Delays

In this experiment, we measured the delay from the time the LoST client sends a findService query to the time it gets and parses the findService response, which contains the PSAP URI and the key to the service boundary. This is the first two messages shown in Figure 11. We have used as the LoST client the smart-phone, connected to a commercial 3G network. As mentioned in the previous sub-section, the delay at the 3G access network is relevant, and we will see in the next results that this delay depends on the mobile's location.

The data used in the tests correspond to simulated GPS data representing points in five different service boundaries: Stonewall, College Station, Harris, Fort Worth, and Brazos jurisdictional boundaries. These boundaries are of varying complexity, with a minimum number of corners of 322 and a maximum of 10718. For each test, all the five coordinates were sent to the LoST server and the corresponding service PSAP URI was sent back to the client. For each coordinate, three measurements were taken.

Each test was done at different places (rural, urban), adding to a total of 22 different locations. The results in Figure 12 show the average delay of findService queries. The data points are grouped by the place where they were collected, where Figure 12 shows the results in 10 locations. From this graph, we conclude that the location of the mobile user was an important factor in the performance of the LoST client to receive a response from the server. Location 7, for instance. had the worst delays for most of the boundaries.

Figure 11. Emegency call flow (SIP and LoST transations), with message sizes and fragmentation

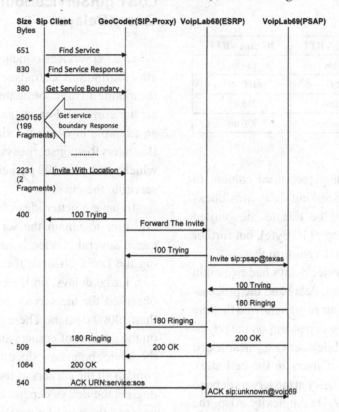

Additionally, Table 2 shows the average delay of all our measurements, in all locations with the correspondent standard deviation. Note that for the service boundary with the smallest number of corners (323 corners) the delays were smaller than all the others, about 200 msec less. This was interesting because we expected that the findService delays by reference were independent of the size of the service boundary. The size in bytes of the queries and responses are about the same (around 600 bytes for the findService query and 800 bytes for the findService response, as shown in Figure 11) no matter which service boundary. Therefore, the network delays are approximately the same, but we suspect that there is an additional processing delay component at the LoST server when it accesses the database.

To verify if there are differences in the processing delays when a server receives a findService query, we have used a packet analyzer (e.g., Wireshark) at the server to to measure the time between the arrival of a findService query and the time the server issues the response. Figure 13 shows the average results for four different service boundaries, ranging from 323 to 13,528 corners. A total of 10 measurements were taken for each boundary. For instance, a 10,700-corner-boundary required approximately 0.5 seconds of processing time at the server. Although the delays at the server had a large variance for a couple of boundary sizes (the ones with 2,045 and 13,528 corners), we conclude that the processing delay increases with the complexity of the boundary, i.e., complexity in terms of number of corners and number

Table 1. Wireless access networks delay comparison

Packet Size	802.11g - RTT	3G card – RTT
128 bytes	6 ms	156 ms
256 bytes	11 ms	160 ms
512 bytes	10 ms	216 ms
1024 bytes	25 ms	270 ms

of holes in the boundary (see third column in Table 2). The high processing delay was unexpected, and this could be due to the limited memory size of our server (1GByte), but further experiments are needed to confirm that.

In short, the findService delays had two main components: the network delay and the processing time at the server. Our results showed that the network delays are very dependent on the physical location of the mobile user (e.g., near a cell tower or the number of users in the cell site), whereas the processing delay at the servers depend on the service boundary's complexity. Also, the difference in processing delays was clearly observed for the polygons with a very small number of corners (such as Stonewall with 323 corners) than the ones with thousands of corners. Next, we will see how the service boundary complexity affects the getServiceBoundary query.

LoST getServiceBoundary Query Delays

When a getServiceBoundary is issued (normally after the findService transaction), the server sends the mobile all the coordinates of the polygon (i.e., all the corners). For instance, Figure 11 shows an example in which the size of the getServiceBoundaryResponse message was 250Kbytes, which resulted in 199 packets sent from the LoST server to the client.

To have a better idea of the delays for a mobile user to obtain the service boundaries, we tested several service boundary downloads using the LoST client at the smart-phone (Figure 13). Large delays, on the order of 1 minute are observed for the service boundaries with more than 10000 corners. There is a clear dependency on the number of corners and the delay to obtain the service boundary, since the response messages contain all the corners of the polygon. In a lesser degree, the delays depend on the location of the user and the type of network access, as discussed previously. The delays also depend on the type of mobile device (e.g., smart-phones had larger delays than laptops). Although boundary downloads occur only when a user changes to a new service boundary, it is clear that such delays are very large. Users can definitely perceive the delay for a LoST client to download complex service boundaries, i.e., with more than 5000 corners (Figure 14).

Table 2. FindServiceResponse Delays

Service boundary name	Number of corners	Number of holes in the boundary	Mean delay for findServiceResponse (ms)	Standard deviation for findservice (ms)
Stonewall	323	0	1946.5	244.0
College Station	2045	0	2151.9	602.7
Harris	5343	17	2291.3	985.1
Fort Worth	10606	7	2160.3	611.4
Brazos	10719	1	2181.0	759.6

Figure 12. FindService query delays for a mobile user at different locations, simulating points from 5 different service boundaries

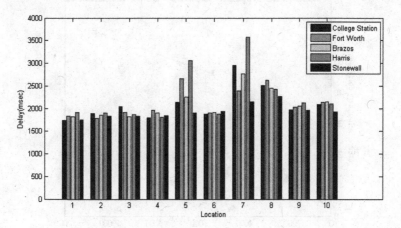

Once the boundary has been downloaded and stored in cache, the mobile will use this data to decide if a new location is within the boundary. This processing delay is discussed next.

Processing Time to Detect Service Boundary Crossings

In this experiment we measured the time the client spends checking whether a given point is inside the polygon. We compare the processing using the Ray-Tracing method and the Minimum Distance method (Section 3). The tests were performed using polygon of different complexities. The simplest polygon has 323 corners, while the most complex has 14,389 corners. To be able to simulate these different service boundaries, we simulated GPS data as inputs to the LoST client, with a new location update every 5 seconds. In this experiment we used the combined SIP/LoST client installed in a laptop.

Figure 13. Processing delay at the LoST server before a findServiceResponse

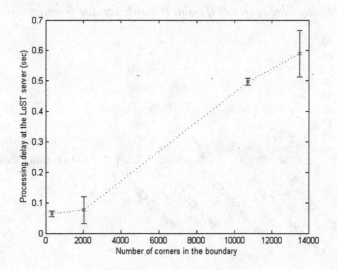

Figure 14. GetserviceBoundary Response delay from server for a mobile LoST client (smart-phone)

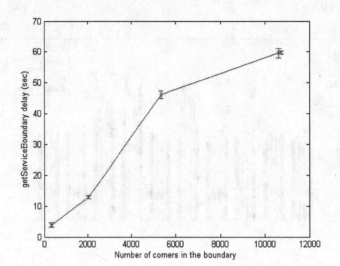

The results are shown in Figure 15. The x-axis represents the different service boundaries and their number of corners. The y-axis shows the processing delay that each method (Ray-Tracing or Minimum Distance) needed to check if the new location is inside or outside the boundary. To measure this processing delay, we used a timer that is triggered every time a program function named "contains" is called. Note that we have two different programs, each with a different version of the "contains" function: one that implements the pure Ray-Tracing method, and one that imple-ments the Minimum Distance Method. At the end of the "contains" function, the timer stops.

The results show that as the number of corners of the polygon increases, the time taken to check whether a given point is inside the polygon in-creases proportionally with the number of corners in the Ray-Tracing method (O(n) where n is the number of corners). This does not happen with the Minimum Distance method, which had small delays that varied independently of the complex-ity of the polygons. The difference in delays be-tween Ray-Tracing and Minimum Distance

Figure 15. Client processing time to detect if point is inside service boundary

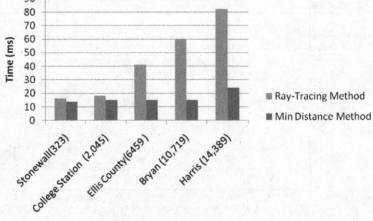

Figure 16. Percentage reduction in the number of points in the boundary polygon using Ramer-Douglas-Peucker Method

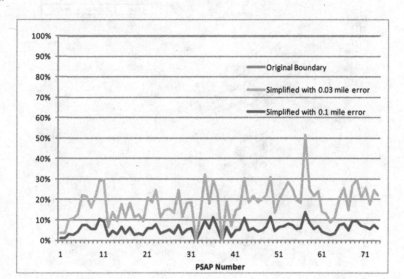

methods is significant for the last three polygons in Figure 15, which have above 5000 corners.

However, with the Minimum Distance method we have an overhead of calculating the minimum distance value for the first time. In the worst case scenario, i.e., for polygons with more than 10000 corners, we measured the overhead as approximately 400ms. Given this overhead, the Minimum Distance method would be advantageous in certain scenarios:

- When the service boundaries has a large number of corners (5000 or more),
- When the mobile is far from the boundary (i.e., the minimum distance will be large).
- When the mobile is stationary or travels at low speed, so the traveled distance would remain smaller than the minimum distance for a long period of time.

Thus, new calculations of the Minimum Distance radius and its implicit overhead would not be needed very often.

Experiments with Simplified Polygons

The previous experiments have shown that small polygons such as the Stonewal service boundary with 323 corners have smaller findService delays, getServiceBoundary delays, and smaller processing delay to verify if a point is inside its boundary than all the other larger polygons. What if all the polygons were as simple as this one? In this section, we show that by using the algorithm described in Section 4 to simplify polygons can considerably reduce the complexity of the polygons.

For instance, using the Ramer-Douglas-Peucker, with two different accuracy values (0.1 miles and 0.03 miles), Figure 16 shows the percentage reduction in the number of corners of the simplified polygon for 75 service boundaries within the state of Texas. All polygons that were simplified had more than 2000 corners in its original version.

Another way to illustrate this dramatic change in the size of the polygons, the average size of all the original polygons was 4998 corners. When we applied the simplification algorithm with accuracy of 0.1 miles, the average size of all polygons became 336 corners. With 0.03 miles, the

Figure 17. The complexity and the simplification of a coastal service boundary

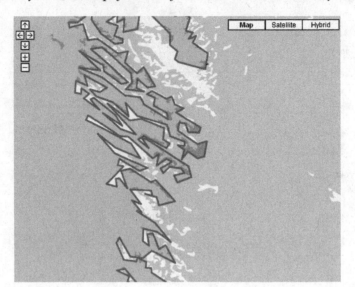

reduction is less but still considerable: the average size of all polygons was 748 corners.

We observed that the number of points in the simplified polygon does not directly depend on the number of points in the original polygon; however, they depend on the shape of the original polygon, as shown in the simplified polygon of Figure 17, which illustrates the boundary at a coastal area. And a polygon with many curves will have more points in its simplified version. But in all the cases the decrease is very significant. For an accuracy of 0.1 mile and for the polygons shown in Table 3, the reduction was in average 92 percent.

Implementing a Database with Simplified Polygons

Once we have the simplified polygons, we updated our LoST database to add a new column named "simplified polygon". This column will have the simplified version of the polygon for each PSAP boundary. Our LoST server uses this polygon to reply to a GetServiceBoundary query. This decreases the GetServiceBoundary response time significantly. For instance, we performed experiments at the border of a service boundary

with 2045 corners. In this case we used the client implemented in the laptop with the 3G data card. As shown in Figure 18 when we queried the LoST server without the simplified polygon (from a location inside the boundary "30.622 -96.34934") it took an average 4.6 seconds to reply, with the worst case being 8.27 seconds. But when we queried a LoST server with Simplified Polygon from the same location it took only 0.4 seconds on an average with worst case being 0.511 seconds.

In our test-bed, we are using the original polygon to respond to the findService query. In other words, the mobile will always get an accurate PSAP URI. But when the client requests the service boundary data, the server sends the simplified polygon along with a warning message. Either the Ray Tracing or the Minimum Distance algorithms may be used to process the point inclusion problem within that simplified boundary. Of course, there will be a loss in the accuracy on the decisions at the mobile.

The approach of using different polygons for findService and getServiceBoundary queries is only for testing purposes. In a real system, we recommend that if a small accuracy loss is acceptable (e.g., 0.03 miles), the same service

Figure 18. GetServiceBoundary query delays using simplified and original polygon

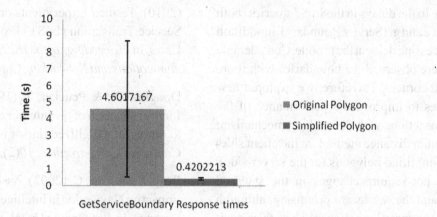

boundary should be used for all queries. The reason is that in very rare situations when our client is near the border of a service boundary, we observed a potential deadlock situation: the mobile's location is inside the original polygon but outside the simplified version, it would lead to a new findService query all the time, which may lead to a performance problem.

CONCLUSION AND FUTURE WORK

In this paper we described the new architecture for routing calls using the Location to Service Translation (LoST) protocol. Since the number of mobile broadband users is expanding rapidly, we focused on mobile LoST clients, such as laptops and smart-phones using cellular access networks.

After implementing and testing the operation of the LoST protocol in a testbed with real-world service boundary information, we observed that the complexity of the service boundaries (i.e.,

Table 3. Reduction in number of points with a 0.1 mile error

Polygon Name	Number of Points in Original	Number of Points in Simplified	% Reduction
Bryan	10717	379	96.46356
College Station	2045	94	95.40342
Harris	14388	2007	86.05088
Stonewall	322	31	90.37267
Anderson	4979	423	91.50432
Houston	9355	1334	85.74025
Fortbend	9680	653	93.25413
Forworth	10620	831	92.17514
Dickens	746	8	98.92761
Eastland	450	10	97.77778
Austin	8070	866	89.2689
Ellis	9337	769	91.76395

number of corners and also number of holes) contribute to the delays in the LoST queries (both findService and getServiceBoundary), in addition to the processing delay at the mobile. Considerable delays were observed for boundaries with more than 5000 corners. Therefore, we explored new approaches to improve the performance of the LoST transactions with the caching mechanism: the minimum distance method (at the client side) and the simplified polygons (at the server side). They do not require changes in the standard protocol and the results are promising, although they do have some limitations such as false positives for the minimum distance method, and the performance issue when the mobile is outside the simplified polygon but inside the original polygon. As one can observe, this is an on-going work and we are still researching further improvements to the operation of the LoST transactions and the approaches here discussed.

Moreover, future work includes tests on IETF's proposed security schemes for the LoST transactions, to assure the confidentiality of both location information and routing information. Also, as fourth generation (4G) cellular technologies are being deployed, we will perform experiments on the performance of the LoST queries and re-evaluate the impact of the complex service boundaries on delays and processing time.

ACKNOWLEDGMENT

This study was supported by a grant from the National Science Foundation (NSF) award no. 0751118.

REFERENCES

Barnes, M. (2008). *HTTP Enabled Location Delivery (HELD) (IETF draft-ietf-geopriv-http-location-delivery-07). Internet Engineering Task Force.* IETF.

Chintapatla, B., Goulart, A., & Magnussen, W. (2010). Testbed Experiments on the Location to Service Translation (LoST) Protocol for Mobile Users. In *Proceedings of the IEEE Consumer Communications and Networking Conference (CCNC)*.

Douglas, D., & Peucker, T. (1973). Algorithms for the reduction of the number of points required to represent a digitized line or its caricature. *The Canadian Cartographer, 10*(2), 112–122.

Feng, S., & Law, C. (2002). Assisted GPS and its Impact on Navigation in Intelligent Transportation Systems. In *Proceedings of the 5th IEEE International Conference on Intelligent Transportation Systems* (pp. 926-993).

Goode, B. (2002). Voice over Internet Protocol (VoIP). *Proceedings of the IEEE, 90*(9), 1495–1517. doi:doi:10.1109/JPROC.2002.802005

Hardie, T., Newton, A., Schulzrinne, H., & Tschofenig, H. (2008). *LoST: A Location-to-Service Translation Protocol (IETF RFC 5222). Internet Engineering Task Force.* IETF.

Hixson, R., Cobb, B., & Halley, P. (2007). 9-1-1: The Next Generation. *9-1-1 Magazine*, 18-21.

Kim, J. Y., Song, W., & Schulzrinne, H. (2006). *An Enhanced VoIP Emergency Services Prototype.* Paper presented at the 3rd International Information Systems for Crisis Response and Management (ISCRAM) Conference.

NENA. (2006). *NENA recommended method(s) for location determination to support IP-based emergency services* (No. 08-505 v1). Retrieved from http://www.nena.org/standards/technical/voip/location-determination-ip-based-emergency-services

NENA. (2007a). *NENA Functional and Interface Standards for Next Generation 9-1-1 Version 1.0 (i3)* (No. 08-002). Retrieved from http://www.nena.org/standards/technical/voip/functional-interface-NG911-i3

NENA. (2007b). *IP-capable PSAP Minimum Operational Requirements Standard* (No. 58-001). Retrieved from http://www.nena.org/standards/operations/IP-PSAP-minimum-requirements

NENA. (2010). *NENA 9-1-1 Deployment Reports & Maps*. Retrieved from http://nena.ddti.net

Peterson, J. (2005). *A Presence-based GEOPRIV Location Object Format (IETF RFC 4119). Internet Engineering Task Force*. IETF.

Polk, J., & Rosen, B. (2009). *Location conveyance for the session initiation protocol (IETF draft-ietf-sip-location-conveyance-13). Internet Engineering Task Force*. IETF.

Polk, J., Schnizlein, J., & Linsner, M. (2004). *Dynamic host configuration protocol option for coordinate-based location configuration information (IETF RFC 3825). Internet Engineering Task Force*. IETF.

Preparata, F., & Shamos, M. (1985). *Computational Geometry – An Introduction*. New York: Springer.

Reed, J., Krizman, K., Woerner, B., & Rappaport, T. (1998). An overview of the challenges and progress in meeting the E-911 requirements for location service. *IEEE Communications Magazine*, 30–37. doi:10.1109/35.667410

Rosen, B., & Polk, J. (2009). *Best current practices for communication services in support of emergency calling (IETF draft-ietf-ecrit-phonebcp-08). Internet Engineering Task Force*. IETF.

Rosenberg, J., Schulzrinne, H., Camarillo, G., Johnston, A., Peterson, J., & Sparks, R. (2002). *SIP: Session Initiation Protocol (IETF RFC 3261). Internet Engineering Task Force*. IETF.

Sayed, A., Tarighat, A., & Khajehnour, N. (2005). Network-based wireless location. *IEEE Signal Processing Magazine*, *22*(4), 24–40. doi:doi:10.1109/MSP.2005.1458275

Schulzrinne, H. (2008). *Synchronizing Location to Service Translation (LoST) Servers (IETF draft-ietf-ecrit-lost-sync-00). Internet Engineering Task Force*. IETF.

Schulzrinne, H., & Arabshian, K. (2002). Providing emergency services in Internet telephony. *IEEE Internet Computing*, *6*(3), 39–47. doi:doi:10.1109/MIC.2002.1003130

Schulzrinne, H., & Marshall, R. (2008). *Requirements for emergency context resolution with Internet technologies (IETF RFC 5012). Internet Engineering Task Force*. IETF.

Schulzrinne, H., Tschofenig, H., Hardie, T., & Newton, A. (2007). LoST: A Protocol for Mapping Geographic Locations to Public Safety Answering Points. In *Proceedings of the IEEE International Performance, Computing, and Communications Conference (IPCCC)* (pp. 606-611).

Shimrat, M. (1962). Algorithm 112: Position of point relative to polygon. *Communications of the ACM Archive*, *5*(8), 434. doi:doi:10.1145/368637.368653

Song, W., et al. (2008). *Next Generation 9-1-1 Proof-of-Concept System*. Paper presented at SIGCOMM '08.

Telecommunications Industry Association. (2006). *Link layer discovery protocol for media endpoint devices (LLDP-MED) (ANSI-TIA-1057)*. Arlington, VA: Author.

Tschofenig, H., Schulzrinne, H., Shanmugan, M., & Newton, A. (2007). Protecting First-Level Responder Resources in an IP-based Emergency Services Architecture. In *Proceedings of the IEEE International Performance, Computing, and Communications Conference (IPCCC)* (pp. 626-631).

Wu, X., & Schulzrinne, H. (2004). SIPc, a multi-function SIP user agent. In *Proceedings of the IFIP/IEEE International Conference, Management of Multimedia Networks and Services (MMNS'04)* (pp. 269-281).

Zhan, W., & Goulart, A. (2009). Statistical Analysis of Broadband Wireless Links in Rural Areas. *The Journal of Communication, 4*(5), 320–328.

This work was previously published in International Journal of Information Systems for Crisis Response Management, Volume 2, Issue 3, edited by Murray E. Jennex, pp. 1-24, copyright 2010 by IGI Publishing (an imprint of IGI Global).

Chapter 11
Factors that Influence Crisis Managers and their Decision–Making Ability during Extreme Events

Connie White
Jacksonville State University, USA

Murray Turoff
New Jersey Institute of Technology, USA

ABSTRACT

This paper reviews crisis literature, identifying factors that most challenge decision makers during extreme events. The objectives are to understand the environment in which the emergency manager is working; isolate factors that hinder the decision maker's ability to implement optimum solutions; and identify structures that best fit the problem type. These objectives are important because extreme events are not well managed. Extreme events are best characterized as wicked problems. Stress, information overload, bias, and uncertainty create an environment that challenges even the best decision makers. Factors must be better understood so that policies, systems, and technologies can be created to better fit the needs of the decision maker. The authors discuss ongoing research efforts and describe systems being designed and implemented that provide a variety of web based collaborative tools, as well as solutions to these wicked problems.

INTRODUCTION

The objective of this article is to examine the emergency and disaster literature in order to identify the factors that challenge crisis managers over the course of a catastrophic event. Characteristics of an extreme event are identified and found to

match the same characteristics that define wicked problems. "An emergency is by definition a unique and unpredictable event, and it is seldom possible, even in retrospect, to assess what the outcome of an emergency response would have been if alternative measures had been followed" (Danielsson & Ohlsson, 1999, p. 92).

DOI: 10.4018/978-1-4666-0167-3.ch011

Responding to the needs of an emergency depends on the severity of the event that has occurred. On one extreme of the scale, there is the routine every day emergency. This includes responding to a car wreck, a heart attack, or to a local flood. These types of problems are structured, occur frequently and protocols exist to mitigate the situation. More severe emergencies, like 100 year floods, earthquakes, and tornadoes, occur less frequently and pose a greater challenge to crisis managers. These are defined as ill-structured problems and can eventually be tamed into a series of structured sub-problems that can be managed (Turoff & Hiltz, 1982). The most severe crisis are catastrophic events like the 1974 Super Outbreak where 148 Tornadoes touched down over a two day period across the United States, the 1980 eruption of Mount St. Helens, the 2004 Asian Tsunami and in 2005, Hurricane Katrina. Extreme events occur rarely, have not been experienced before by crisis management and have no clear solutions to problems. Extreme events are best characterized as wicked structures problems.

The literature reveals that extreme events do have particular characteristics with common themes reappearing throughout scientific literature. Carl Von Clausewitz offers a cohesive observation of the characteristics plaguing extreme events. He wrote:

A commander must continually face situations involving uncertainties, questionable or incomplete data or several possible alternatives. As the primary decision maker, he, with the assistance of his staff, must not only decide what to do and how to do it, but he must also recognize if and when he must make a decision (Clausewitz, 1976, p. 383).

This research is important because the needs of crisis managers must be identified from the literature found within the emergency domain. Too often, systems are designed, policies are created and plans are written that don't consider the ground level decision maker. For disasters to be managed so that the solutions are a good fit to the problem, the systems, policies and plans need to be created by asking:

- Who is the decision maker?
- Under what conditions are these decisions being made?
- What factors pose the greatest threat to making optimal decisions?
- How can a system be designed to overcome the most challenging factors that hinder decision making?

It is important for the results of studies confirming the task type, needs and considerations of the practitioners themselves to be observed so that technology, systems, policy and procedures can be developed to support the needs of decision makers to facilitate a rapid response and recovery given a catastrophic event has occurred. The literature clearly revealed a number of influences that can be managed better if systems are designed to meet those needs.

BACKGROUND

Stressors

Decisions are time critical and can be emotionally stressful when life and death triage type decisions must be made. Crisis managers are confronted with additional stressors that challenge the best decision makers. Simple creature comforts are nonexistent and that affects a human's decision making ability without taking into account, the numerous other stressors that are ongoing. A lack of sleep, personal issues (family, home), proper nutrition, hygiene, and transportation are characteristics of the environment in which the decisions are being made.

After the great Deluge of New Orleans when the levees broke flooding 80% of the city, many first responders' had lost their own homes, their own family members, had no food, no place to sleep and were every bit as much victims as the people they were to help rescue and protect. Responders reacted in a number of ways; most notorious were a small percentage of the police force who abandoned their roles, and a handful who abused their authority (Kushma, 2007). This contradicted the expected roles they represented. These environmental, mental and physical influences were beyond their control and clearly affected their rational decision making ability. In the face of adversity, most these men and women reported for duty. However, reports of police brutality resulting in murder charges and convictions are the end result of those responders who could not handle stress on a personal level (Brinkley, 2006).

Stress is an understandable emotion felt by emergency managers. They must make life and death decisions especially where such tragedies requiring triage may have to be decided in the selection criterion between groups of people (Kowalski-Trakofler, Vaught, & Scharf, 2003). Another source of stress arises when decisions must be made under severe time constraints (Rodriquez, 1997; Kowalski-Trakofler et al., 2003). Decision makers have to forecast and make predictions given the uncertainty in expectations of future events (Rodriguez, 1997). Time is precious, and accurate decisions must be made along a time line at particular points in time over the duration of the event as a disaster evolves (Brehmer, 1987; Danielsson & Ohlsson, 1999), "The operational commander continually faces an uncertain environment" (Rodriguez, 1997, p. 5).

Information: Too Much, Too Little, Too Late

Initially, getting enough accurate and timely data is a challenge, but afterwards information overload can create bias conducive to poor decisions being implemented. This is all confounded by the lack of experience managing similar events of the same magnitude by teams and leadership. If a decision is made one way or the other, no one is sure what the outcome will be so there's a roll of the dice with every alternative.

Critical judgments must be made where large amounts of information are available for consideration creating information overload. To make matters worse, this information can be wrong or incomplete (Kowalski-Trakofler et al., 2003) or sufficient time may be lacking to gain the perfect and complete information needed before the decision is made (Rodriquez, 1997). "In dealing with the uncertainty of a continually changing environment, the decision maker must achieve a trade-off between the cost of action and the risk of non-action" (Kowalski-Trakofler & Vaught, 2003, p. 283). Sometimes these decisions are made on the decision maker's (DM) assumptions and intuition when information is not attainable (Rodriquez, 1997).

One person is in charge of making the final decision for action, but this is a collaborative effort of numerous stakeholders sharing numerous overlapping tasks. "As complexity increases, it becomes impossible for a single individual with the limited information processing capacity to gain control" (Danielsson & Ohlsson, 1999, p. 93). A dynamic decision making approach is a much needed method due to the inherent nature of the chaos characteristic of extreme events (Danielsson & Ohlsson 1999). Extreme events need to be managed using structure with flexibility to improvise or adapt where necessary to achieve agility (Harrald, 2009).

Lack of Experience

Small events occur frequently, and catastrophic events occur rarely (Hyndman and Hyndman, 2006). Protocols or heuristics can be used for the emergencies that are smaller and occur more frequently. However, management is posed with the problem of not having any or little prior experience to larger events where national boundaries are ignored and the demands of the resources needed far exceed the availability of supply. Research reveals that extreme events have different characteristics from smaller disasters (Skertchly & Skertchly, 2001). This calls for a dynamic approach to decision making to fit the task due to the overwhelming nature of these extreme events considered with the limitations of a human's mental capacity and ability to manage a large set of ongoing problems at any one given time. A major problem exists in a decision maker's ability to effectively manage all of the ongoing events simultaneously during an extreme event (Danielsson & Ohlsson, 1999; Kerstholt, 1996).

In the remainder of this chapter, these areas will be explored further probing deeper into the needs of emergency managers. First, how extreme events are different from small emergencies and must be approached as a different task type is covered. Second, extreme events are defined as wicked problems. These characteristics are laid out and mapped against extreme events. Good versus bad characteristics in crisis decision making from the literature are listed in attempts to steer design. Third, types of bias that are specific in emergency situations and decision making are covered. Next, literature findings concerning time, stress and information overload are provided. Methods describing how crisis managers handle information presently are discussed and related to other research concepts already explored in this research effort. Next, research indicating how feedback and expert intuition are used to manage uncertainty is presented. We close by providing some ongoing research endeavors that are being designed to help solve these problems.

Extreme Events

Large scale extreme events are not like small emergencies. Small emergencies occur regularly where most decisions are rule based due to the experience of the event (Rasmussen, 1983). This is referred to as procedural expertise (Adams & Ericsson, 2000). In the event that a small emergency should occur, the EM may not even be notified because firefighters, police and emergency medical attendants already know how to proceed (Danielsson & Ohlsson, 1999). On the other hand, extreme events present a different set of characteristics due to the problem type and task structure (Campbell, 1999; Mitchell, 1999; McLellan et al., 2003).

In large-scale operations, the cognitive demands on the EM are severe (Danielsson & Ohlsson, 1999). Team coordination strategies will evolve from explicit coordination under low workload conditions to implicit coordination as work load increases. Large-scale emergency operations imply distributed decision making in that decisions are disseminated among many stakeholders, of which no single individual has complete knowledge of the current situation (Danielsson & Ohlsson, 1999; Mitchell, 1999; Kowalski-Trakofler & Vaught, 2003).

Wicked Problems

Extreme events possess characteristics, are problem types and have task structures that are categorized as wicked. Wicked problems are volatile and of a very dynamic nature with considerable uncertainty and ambiguity (Horn, 2005). Wicked problems are ongoing and have no stopping rule (Rittel & Webber, 1973, Digh, 2000). They are never resolved and change over time (Conklin, 1998). Wicked problems are solved per se when they no longer are of interest to the stakeholders, when resources are depleted or when the political agenda changes (Horst & Webber, 1973). Many stakeholders with multiple value conflicts redefine what the problem is repeatedly, reconsider what the causal factors are and have multiple views of how to approach and hopefully deal with the problem (Rittel & Webber, 1973; Conklin, 1998; Digh, 2000). Getting and maintaining agreement amongst the stakeholders is most difficult because each has their own perception and, thus, opinion of what is best (Rittel & Webber, 1973).

Extreme events possess the characteristics of those found within the definitions of wicked problems. "Each dysfunctional event has its own unique characteristics, impacts, and legacies" (Skertchly & Skertchly, 2001, p. 23). For example, catastrophic disasters have the following attributes and dimensions many of which are the same as those described in wicked problems:

- *They don't have any rules.
- Often, emergency services are insufficient to cope with the demands given the limited amount of available resources.
- Vital resources are damaged and nonfunctional.
- *Procedures for dealing with the situation are inadequate.
- *No solutions for resolution exist on a short-term basis.
- *Events continue to escalate.
- *Serious differences of opinion arise about how things should be managed.
- The government of the day and the bureaucracy becomes seriously involved.
- The public takes an armchair position and is fed by the media.
- *The number of authorities and officials involved are growing.
- *Sometimes simply trying to identify which of the emergency services and investigative bodies is doing what results in complete chaos.
- The need to know who is in charge is urgent (Campbell, 1999, p. 52).

*are characteristic of wicked problems

Crisis managers' tasks differ from control task types in that, no two events are the same so different decision processes are required to be implemented. Interacting variables are many, and the domain is ill defined and unknown at times (Danielsson & Ohlsson, 1999). An emergency manager cannot project any future decisions with any degree of accuracy due to all of the variables that are involved and all of the different scenarios that can exist due to the great amount of uncertainty involved and lack of experience of the unknown (U.S. Naval War College, 1996).

Decision Making in Emergency Management

Decision tasks are perceived to be difficult by the EM where issues involving life saving operations such as evacuations or triage have the potential to have devastating results if not conducted accurately (Danielsson & Ohlsson, 1999).

Studies show an EMs most difficult aspects of work are:

- Lack of routine and practice–refers to the infrequency of major accidents, making it difficult to get experiences of the command and control proper.
- Communicational shortcomings.
- Information overload is salient during the initial phase of an emergency response and is seen as especially severe if no staff members are available to perform communication duties.
- Technical equipment inadequacy.
- Lack of skills in handling communication equipment.
- Feelings of isolation.
- Lack of peers with whom to discuss common problems (Danielsson & Ohlsson 1999, p. 94).

Other psychological processes are associated with decisions made by crisis decision makers. Effective decision makers must take many factors of the environment into consideration to understand that these are complex, dynamic, time-pressured, high-stakes, multi-person task environments (McLellan et al., 2003).

Some hazard conceptualization and management problems developed from Mitchell (1999) are presented:

- *Lack of agreement about definition and identification of problems

- *Lack of awareness of natural and unnatural (human-made) hazards
- *Lack of future forecasting capabilities
- *Misperception of misjudgment of risks associated with hazards
- Deliberate misrepresentation of hazards and risks
- *Lack of awareness of appropriate responses
- *Lack of expertise to make use of responses
- Lack of money or resources to pay for responses
- *Lack of coordination among institutions and organizations
- Lack of attention to relationship between 'disasters' and 'development'
- Failure to treat hazards as contextual problem whose components require simultaneous attention
- Lack of access by affected populations to decision making
- Lack of public confidence in scientific knowledge
- Lack of capable and enlightened political leadership
- *Conflicting goals among populations at risk
- *Fluctuating salience of hazards
- Public opposition by negatively affected individuals and groups.
  *wicked characteristics

Many of these are also characteristic of the wicked problem types defined earlier and have characteristics in common with those of extreme events (Rittel & Webber, 1973; Campbell, 1999). Other commonalities between wicked problems and extreme events are that the event is continuous; the operation is twenty-four hours a day. The decision maker has to trust others to make his or her decisions when they are not awake. It is unpredictable what the problems will be, who will be involved or who needs to be involved so sharing of the current situation by all involved is critical.

Time

Time lost is always a disadvantage that is bound in some way to weaken he who loses it (Clauswitz, 1976, p. 383).

Time is a critical factor that further complicates the decision making process. In extreme events, an emergency manager must consider an enormous number of factors quickly (Kowalski-Trakofler et al., 2003). Decisions must be made, sometimes forced due to time constraints. "The faster a decision has to be made, the less time the information processing system has to convert or gather enough accurate information to convert assumptions to facts" (Rodriquez, 1997, pp. 7-8). This means that decisions are made under uncertainty and without full consideration. Crisis managers must weigh delaying the decision making against the negative consequences that may occur while waiting for more requested information (Kowalski-Trakofler & Vaught, 2003). Once time has passed, alternative actions are no longer possible and perhaps the best decision has been bypassed leaving only less optimal conditions from which to choose.

Kowalski-Trakofler and Vaught conducted a study of good decision making characteristics under life threatening situations. They found that, during any phase of the decision making process, a set of factors could significantly impact one's ability to deal with complex problems under time critical situations. These factors are:

- Psychomotor skills, knowledge and attitude
- Information quality and completeness
- Stress—generated both by the problem at hand and any existing background problem
- The complexity of elements that must be attended (2003, p. 285).

One research finding indicates that performance can be maintained under time pressure if the communication changes from explicit to implicit (Serfaty & Entin, 1993). They found that

Implicit coordination patterns, anticipatory behavior, and redirection of the team communication strategy are evident under conditions of increased time-pressure. The authors conclude that effective changes in communication patterns may involve updating team members, regularly anticipating the needs of others by offering unrequested information, minimizing interruptions, and articulating plans at a high level in order to allow flexibility in the role of front-line emergency responders (Serfaty & Entin, 1993).

Stress

Stress is defined as "a process by which certain work demands evoke an appraisal process in which perceived demands exceed resources and result in undesirable physiological, emotional, cognitive and social changes" (Salas, Driskell, & Hughs, 1996, p.6).

Studies show that during an emergency, information quality varies on three dimensions: reliability, availability and relevance (Danielsson & Ohlsson, 1999). The decision to use information at any given time and the weight of the usage of the information is based on these dimensions.

Information during an emergency can be the source of stress in many ways (Kowalski-Trakofler, et al., 2003). First, due to technical malfunctions or just poor implementation, the initial warnings can be ambiguous and create a greater need for clarity in a situation. This causes the situation to be interpreted differently and leads to misinterpretations in how people perceive the information and hence, respond. Stressors due to information mismanagement are formed when people do not fully understand what is going on which creates disagreement between stakeholders; the right information is not gathered. This wastes time and causes more stress and frustration.

Poor leadership is a stressor experienced too often. An enormous amount of stress was expressed by the Gulf Coast emergency community during the 2010 British Petroleum Oil crisis. Not being able to protect the wildlife and shorelines were most frustrating to local officials who watched helplessly as the oil decimated the marshlands and white sandy beaches. Poor leadership was exhibited in BP Oil crisis, the President of the United States was weak, the President of BP was weak, both were inexperienced and out of touch. Weak leadership exacerbates a problem, usually delaying resources creating a much worse human disaster due to mismanagement. Last, when technology or other apparatus fails, this leaves people without information and the inability to keep current with response efforts and will add more stress (Kowalski-Trakofler et al., 2003).

Stress is a major factor in decision making especially during life critical situations (Kowalski-Trakofler et al., 2003). One of the primary stressors is the lack of information immediately after the event during the early phase of the emergency response where it concerns determining scale and the characteristics of damage (Danielsson & Ohlsson, 1999).

A major problem occurs when people are making decisions under stress that leads to poor decision making. Research shows all of the feasible choices are not considered, and a decision is likely to be made prematurely (Keinan, Friedland, & Ben-Porath, 1987). This is not good because no matter how experienced an emergency manager may be, he/she will be confronted with situations they have not experienced previously (Harrald, 2009).

Information Overload

Good incident commanders function as if they have a good practical understanding of the limitations of their information processing system, and the corresponding limitations of others (McLellan et al., 2003). In particular, they operated in such a manner that (a) their effective working memory capacity was not exceeded, (b) they monitored and regulated their emotions and their arousal level, and (c) they communicated with subordinates in ways that took into account subordinates' working memory capacity limitations. The foundation of their ability to manage their own information load effectively seems to be prior learning from past experience.

Bias

Many forms of bias exist when it comes to decision making, but emergency management has a set that is associated with disastrous leadership. Research indicates that this is from a lack of self awareness which is a normal reaction concerning information processing. Table 1 lists the bias types along with a brief description derived by Adams and Ericsson (2000).

Muddling Through

A large amount of information must be considered in a very small amount of time. Time to fully explore all alternatives is lacking not to mention, stress has a tendency to make decision makers focus narrowly on the list of available alternatives. Studies found that good crisis managers only focus on the most feasible and reliable solutions and eliminate the nonessential information (Kowalski-Trakofler et al., 2003). This does not compromise the decision making ability to make

good decisions, but rather, simplifies the process allowing them to focus on the critical issues.

This same approach was validated by other research studying decision processes of good decision making (McLellan et al., 2003). The study indicated that all of the information was scanned but focus was only considered on a 'need to know' basis and only on the relevant factors which needed to be considered.

This decision making strategy is described by Charles Lindblom as *Muddling Through* (Lindblom, 1959, 1979). This employs methods that help a decision maker focus on the most relevant subgroup, given a list of alternatives from which to choose for any given task. Muddling through a problem guides decision makers to direct their focus into selecting incremental changes.

The critical aspect of Lindlom is that everyone needs to be involved who is at any level in the organization if there is a problem to be solved which means the open sharing of information from any part of the organization to any other (Turoff, White, & Plotnick, 2009).

Feedback

Timely and reliable feedback is one means to help crisis managers make good judgments. One type of uncertainty is from the lack of feedback or reported information from the initial assess-

Table 1. Bias in emergency management decision making

Bias Type	Description
Sunk-costs	Persisting with a tactic, which to the dispassionate observer is demonstrably ineffectual, simply because time and resources have already been invested in the tactic.
Optimism	Choosing a course of action which necessitates nothing whatsoever going wrong if it is to succeed. For example, positioning a crew on steep sloping terrain with high levels of burnable material above and below them.
Need for Action	Good incident commanders frequently report having to deliberately exercise self-restraint so as not to precipitately commit resources to a course of action before completing a thorough situation assessment
Linear Rate of Change	Associated with disastrous incident command at wildland fires; human beings seem to be incapable of accurately predicting non-linear rates of change.

ment from affected areas. Particularly bothersome to emergency management can be in the lack of feedback where the next decision cannot be made without the present information acquired especially when the damage cannot be visualized (Danielsson & Ohlsson, 1999). This can have detrimental effects on the outcome of the event, because the emergency manager's performance is diminished.

Uncertainty

The demands on emergency management are described by The Catastrophic Annex to the National Response Plan (NRP) (DHS, 2004): "A detailed and credible common operating picture may not be achievable for 24 to 48 hours (or longer)." "As a result, response activities must begin without the benefit of a detailed or complete situation and critical needs assessment" (Harrald, 2006, p. 258). Due to the nature of an extreme event, many judgments must be made with information that is often ambiguous, wrong and incomplete (Kowalski-Trakofler et al., 2003). The operational activities involve "hierarchical teams of trained individuals, using specialized equipment, whose efforts must be coordinated via command, control, and communication processes to achieve specified objectives under conditions of threat, uncertainty, and limited resources, both human and material" (McLellan et al., 2003, p. 2).

Not only are the decisions made presently under questionable information, in addition, forecasting future events poses a challenge due to the uncertainty in the future events as they play out over the duration of the extreme event (Rodriguez, 1997). "To make decisions about an uncertain future, the commander must make many assumptions. Intuitive thinking is an important skill in the ability to make a sound assumption" (Rodriguez, 1997, p. 1). Disconnected bits of data exist where gaps in the logic providing useful information are missing. This is where the experts are using intuition to fill gaps in information needs.

Expert Intuition

Assumptions are used by crisis managers to fill in gaps where uncertainty exists (Rodriguez, 1997). Intuition plays a large role in filling in these gaps and can have good consequences from those with experience. "For experienced commanders, intuition fills in the decision making processes where imperfect information leaves off" (Battle Command, 1994, p. 25).

A study conducted on a large group of top executives supports the concept that intuition was used to guide critical decision making situations. The situations and environments in which intuition was mostly used and helpful were found to be where:

- A high level of uncertainty exists
- The event has little previous precedent
- Variables are often not scientifically predictable
- "Facts are limited"
- Facts do not clearly point the way to go
- Time is limited and the pressure is to be right
- Several plausible alternative solutions are available to choose from, with good arguments for each (Argot, 1986, p 18).

When considering the issue of analytical versus intuition judgment, the National Institute for Occupational Safety and Health (NIOSH) reported:

The point here is that research which focuses on judgment must include scrutiny not only of decisions that are made, but also of real-world variables that influence them. The quality of any decision may have little or no direct relationship to the eventual outcome of its execution in a given situation. This is because a decision-maker is constrained not only by the stress of the situation or personal knowledge and attitudes, but also because he or she can only weigh information that is available (Kowalski-Trakofler et al., 2003, p. 286).

Normal decision making techniques do not suffice in such complex situations as extreme events. Characteristics were identified as:

- Novelty—the officer had never encountered such a situation before,
- Opacity—needed information was not available,
- Resource inadequacy—the resources currently available were not sufficient to permit an optimal response (McLellan et al., 2003, p. 3).

The emergency manager is continually facing an uncertain environment. There is insufficient time for the crisis managers to get the correct information they need and this must be weighed against the need to make a decision at a particular time, so he/she must rely on assumptions and intuition. Intuition fills the gap between disconnected bits of information helping to create a full picture from which problems can be best defined and solution sets available to fit the needs of the emergency manager.

SUMMARY

Ongoing research efforts are addressing ways to solve these problems. It is important to have distributed command and control operations which allow the participation of anyone at any time and any place in both the planning and ongoing operations (Turoff, Chumar, de Walle, & Yao, 2003). Current research explores highly efficient ways for emergent problems to be supported by concerned subgroups addressing complex problems by proposing solution components and comparing via voting their agreement where participating have the ability to supply comments on disagreements (White, Turoff, & Hiltz, 2010). Collaborative systems are being designed to support all phases of emergency management where participants distributed can collaborate on evolving scenarios to support planning (Yao, Turoff, & Chumar, 2009).

Clearly, the literature demonstrates that there is a common theme identifying characteristics that influence a crisis manager's ability to make optimal decisions during and after an extreme event has occurred. The decision maker should be the core focus upon which policies, protocols and systems are designed.

REFERENCES

Adams, R. J., & Ericsson, A. E. (2000). Introduction to the cognitive processes of expert pilots. *Journal of Human Performance in Extreme Environments, 5*(1), 44–62.

Agor, W. H. (1986). *The Logic of Intuitive Decision Making*. New York: Quorom Books.

Battle Command. (1994). *Leadership and Decision Making for War and Operations Other than War*. Fort Leavenworth, KS: Battle Command Battle Laboratory.

Baumgart, L., Bass, E., Philips, B., & Kloesel, K. (2008). Emergency Management Decision-Making During Severe Weather. *Weather and Forecasting, 23*(6), 1268–1279. doi:doi:10.1175/2008WAF2007092.1

Campbell, R. (1999). Controlling Crisis Chaos. *Journal of Emergency Management Australia, 14*(3), 51–54.

Clausewitz, C. V. (1984). *On War*. Princeton, NJ: Princeton University Press.

Danielsson, M., & Ohlsson, K. (1999). Decision Making in Emergency Management: A Survey Study. *International Journal of Cognitive Ergonomics, 3*(2), 91–99. doi:doi:10.1207/s15327566ijce0302_2

Harrald, J. (2006). Agilitly and Discipline: Critical Success Factors for Disaster Response. *AAPSS Annals, 604*(1), 256–272.

Harrald, J. (2009). Achieving Agility in Disaster Management. *International Journal of Information Systems and Crisis Management, 1*(1).

Keinan, G., Friedland, N., & Ben-Porath, Y. (1987). Decision-making under stress: Scanning of alternatives under physical threat. *Acta Psychologica, 64*, 219–228. doi:doi:10.1016/0001-6918(87)90008-4

Kerstholt, J. (1996). *Dynamic Decision Making*. Soesterberg, The Netherlands: TNO Human Factors.

Kontogiannis, T., & Kossiavelou, Z. (1999). *Stress and team performance: principles and challenges for intelligent decision aids*, Safety Science, December, Vol.33, Issue 3, pp. 103 -128,.

Kowalski-Trakofler, K., & Vaught, T. (2003). Judgment and decision making under stress: an overview for emergency managers. *International Journal of Emergency Management, 1*(3), 278–289. doi:doi:10.1504/IJEM.2003.003297

Kushma, J. (2007). Role Abandonment: Should we leave this myth behind. *Natural Hazards Observer, XXXI*(5).

McLennan, J., Holgate, A., & Wearing, A. (2003, September). *Human Information Processing aspects of Effective Emergency Incident Management Decision Making*. Paper presented at the Human Factors of Decision Making in Complex Systems Conference, Dunblane, Scotland.

Mitchell, J. K. (1999). *Crucibles of Hazard: Mega-Cities and Disasters in Transition*. Tokyo: United Nations University Press.

Rodriguez, D. M. (1997). *Dominating Time in the Operational Decision Making Process*. Newport, RI: U.S. Naval War College.

Salas, E., Driskell, E., & Hughs, S. (1996). The study of stress and human performance . In Driskell, J. E., & Salas, E. (Eds.), *Stress and Human Performance* (pp. 1–45). Mahwah, NJ: Lawrence Erlbaum Associates.

Skertchly, A., & Skertcly, K. (2001). Catastrophe management: coping with totally unexpected extreme disasters. *The Australian Journal of Emergency Management, 16*(1).

Turoff, M., Chumer, M., Van de Walle, B., & Yao, X. (2003). The Design of a Dynamic Emergency Response Management Information System (DERMIS). *Journal of Information Technology Theory and Application, 5*(4).

Turoff, M., & Hiltz, S. R. (1982). Computer Support for Group versus Individual Decision Support. *IEEE Transactions on Communications, 30*(1), 82–91. doi:doi:10.1109/TCOM.1982.1095370

Turoff, M., White, C., & Plotnick, L. (2009). *Dynamic Emergency Response Management For Large Scale Extreme Events*. International Journal for Information Systems and Crisis Response Management.

U.S. Naval War College. (1996). *Operational Decision Making. Instructional P Per NWC 4108*. Newport, RI: Joint Military Operations Department, U.S. Naval War College.

White, C., Hiltz, S. R., & Turoff, M. (2008). *United We Respond: One Community, One Voice*. Paper presented at the Information Systems for Crisis Response and Management Conference 2008, Washington, DC.

White, C., Turoff, M., & de Walle, B. V. (2007). *A Dynamic Delphi Process Utilizing a Modified Thurstone Scaling Method: Collaborative Judgment in Emergency Response.* Paper presented at the 4th Annual Information Systems on Crisis and Response Management, Delft, The Netherlands.

Yao, X., Turoff, M., & Chumar, M. (2009). *Designing a Group Support System to Review and Practice Emergency Plans in Virtual Teams.* Paper presented at the 6th Annual Information Systems on Crisis and Response Management, Washington, DC.

Chapter 12
Achieving Electric Restoration Logistical Efficiencies during Critical Infrastructure Crisis Response:
A Knowledge Management Analysis

Teresa Durbin
San Diego Gas and Electric, USA

Murray E. Jennex
San Diego State University, USA

Eric Frost
San Diego State University, USA

Robert Judge
San Diego State University, USA

ABSTRACT

After the 2007 Southern California wildfire events, event-assessment of the efficacy of spreadsheets and paper forms raised the question of whether alternative tools could have achieved greater efficiencies in the logistical support of command centers, the sites from which the local utility's electric restoration personnel were deployed. In this paper, the authors examine what approach would have enabled personnel working on the logistics of the command center effort to have easier-to-use, faster-to-access, command center data stored in, and provided via, a catastrophe resilient platform other than the traditional company computer network. Additionally, the capability to store basic command center requirements from previous emergency responses, thereby saving time during the next emergency, was examined.

DOI: 10.4018/978-1-4666-0167-3.ch012

INTRODUCTION

Gas and electric services in the County of San Diego are provided by San Diego Gas & Electric Company (SDG&E), an investor-owned public utility. Many useful issues can be analyzed from the wildfires that damaged SDG&E's electric system in 2003 and 2007 and certain activities that supported efficient service restoration can be examined and used for comparative analysis for a terrorist attack scenario, earthquakes, wildfires, or any other event that might impact service delivery.

This paper analyzes the logistics support provided during the wild fires to determine what could be improved. This is an important topic as there is little research literature addressing crisis response logistics. Whybark et al. (2010) discuss disaster relief supply chains but only propose a research agenda. We agree there needs to be research in this area and start with this case study. Logistics/supply chains ensure that responders are able to sustain disaster relief. Their importance is illustrated by the response to the 2009 Haiti earthquake where ships and supplies stood empty or unused off the coast because of an inability to deliver supplies and evacuate injured. Keeping responders in the field is critical for long term disaster relief. Providing relief is critical for affected persons and societies to recover. This paper hopes to start this important research area by exploring alternatives to the spreadsheet approach used in the 2007 wild fires.

Finally, the research question for this paper was what alternatives could be used in lieu of paper forms and spreadsheets to achieve more accurate, timely logistics data and solutions?

METHODOLOGY

This paper is a case study using action research to assess whether future activities by the command center support teams can be influenced to convert from paper forms and spreadsheets to something more real-time, as a new solution for crisis response.

The working definition of action research (Zuber-Skerrit & Fletcher, 2007, p. 413) incorporated situations where people reflect and improve (or develop) their own work and their own situations by tightly interlinking their reflection and action; and also making their experience public not only to other participants but also to other persons interested in and concerned about the work and the situation, i.e. their public theories and practices of the work and the situation, and in which the situation is increasingly: data-gathering by participants themselves (or with the help of others) in relation to their own questions; participation (in problem-posing and in answering questions) in decision-making, self-reflection, self-evaluation and self-management by autonomous and responsible persons and groups. This study is action research as the lead author is a team lead of the SDG&E supply chain systems team tasked with assessing logistics performance.

Reflection for this study was done using knowledge management, KM as the reflective lens. Jennex (2005) summarized KM definitions to conclude that KM is about capturing knowledge created in an organization and making it available to those who need it to make decisions and improve organizational performance. Jennex (2007) discussed the role of KM in crisis response and included the role of post event evaluation of lessons learned as a way of capturing knowledge generated during an event and ensuring that knowledge is shared and incorporated into crisis response activities. This implies that KM is a good reflective lens for crisis response research.

The ability to apply KM to the 2007 command center logistical effort and how it can benefit future emergency responders corresponds to KM in support of crisis response as expanded upon by Jennex and Raman (2009). The underlying KM principle upon which this study is constructed are that experience gained from one emergency can be applied as knowledge when shared with others to improve performance during a subsequent emergency. Additionally, improved performance will help an organization meet its goals or mandated objectives acceptably.

Comparing how the basic computer tools used in the 2007 command center set-ups performed against how an alternative process would perform should demonstrate the need to move towards tools that are multi-user, require no consolidation of data, and which can be used with little to no training in the fast-paced environment of an emergency.

Improving an existing business process draws justification from the theory of action research as discussed in the Technology Acceptance Model (TAM) of perceived usefulness (Venkatesh et al., 2003). TAM addresses the realm of computer technology and validation of the usefulness of employees' outputs. Davis (1989) verifies the usefulness of the employees' outputs based on their belief of how they performed in that activity. Additionally, Bandura (1982) reiterated the general concept with his self-efficacy model of people's response and reaction being based on their perception of their competency in face of new technologies resulting from the computer and internet evolution. Bandura (1982, p. 122) stated, "A capability is only as good as its execution." Based on this, converting the paper forms and spreadsheets used for the command center logistical effort in 2007 to an alternative tool might be indicated. The action research of this paper is using lessons learned to convert the information tracked in the spreadsheets to a more technological format for easier and faster access in emergency response. This serves as the impetus for improving the existing emergency response process via a technology tool (Bandura, 1982; Davis, 1989; Venkatesh et al., 2003).

The data used in this paper is from the 2007 Firestorm responses of San Diego Gas & Electric's command center support. Their spreadsheets, emails, phone calls, including the personal ob-servations of the lead author, who participated in the effort, provided the data for this study. The action research format is appropriate for this paper because the research process involved manipulating outputs containing the command center logistical details and their role in the activities in the organization's response to emergency situations. The data that were analyzed related solely to the support of the command center camps and what it took to sustain their mission as bases from which to deploy the electric restoration personnel during the power outages. The details surrounding the ordering, receiving, inventorying, handling, staging, and deployment of construction materials, such as poles and wires, were not the purview of BSLs' work in support of the command centers. Material handling was the responsibility of the Logistics and Warehousing groups.

The spreadsheet listed 25 categories of information that included the following column headings: Region, Need for Site: Yes/Pending, Site Name, Command Center/Staging Area, Site Coordinator & Phone #, Thomas Brothers page, Address, Start Date, Estimated End Date, Total # of People, Food Counts, #B, #L, #D, water buffalo Y/N or 5 gal H2o, # of Porta Potties, Trash bin type: trash/cable/metal/treated wood/recyclables, # of hand-wash stands, Portable Office Trailer, Copier, Lights, Generator(s), Parking Space Reqmnts (Requirements), Material Laydown Space Reqmnts (Requirements), Security, # of Vehicles, Phone /Data/Radio/Printer, BMP Materials, Notes/Comments.

The data that were examined were three versions of the spreadsheet, Firestorm 2007 - Command Centers and Staging Areas, during the time frame of October 24, 2007 through November 10, 2007, to demonstrate the progression of the command centers' expansion and contraction over time. The spreadsheet also displayed the types of items being tracked at a consolidated level.

WILD FIRE LOGISTICS

During the week of October 21, 2007, wind-driven wildfires raged across San Diego County burning more than 360,000 acres and destroying at least 1,700 homes. As soon as the fires had moved through an area, SDG&E crews were on-site to assess damage to the utility's assets. As a result, 750 SDG&E employees, along with 203 neighbor-state mutual-aid personnel and, at peak periods, 78 contract electric crews and 129 digging crews, were deployed to perform the service restoration efforts. Service was restored for approximately 83,000 customers affected by the fire and SDG&E eventually replaced more than 2,170 utility poles, 338 transformers, and at least 35 miles of overhead electrical wire (Geier, 2009).

Four years earlier, after San Diego County's 2003 wildfires, SDG&E had refined a model for supporting the logistical components of establishing and supporting command centers. This model was ready for implementation during the October 21, 2007. SDG&E's electric restoration response to the 2007 fires was supported by teams of employees from the Fleet, Facilities, Environmental, Supply Management, Logistics & Warehousing, Fleet Services, Facilities, Real Estate/Land, Environmental, and Safety departments (Dulgeroff, 2009). These teams were tasked with supporting the logistical needs for electric construction crews allowing the construction foremen and supervisors to be available to perform their core competency of repairing or rebuilding the electric system.

Working in teams of approximately three people per shift, the support team employees were consumed for 10-15 hours a day for the first 10 days of the emergency. They had to respond to central points near the fire-damaged areas where they set-up command center camps to serve three meals a day. The command center sites included restrooms, shaded rest areas, water, ice, and snacks to all the crews who were working 16-hour shifts (Dulgeroff, 2009). In addition, the command center sites needed mobile offices with internet connectivity (often via satellite due to the remote locations and/or damage to on-site power and telecommunications connections). Also required were helicopter landing areas for hard-to-access, power pole replacements, water trucks for dust mitigation in the rural settings, mobile radio repeaters, and dedicated space for all the materials to be staged for the crews' use.

Preventative environmental checklists had to be followed at the rural sites. Straw wattle to prevent run-off, steel shaker plates to keep the vehicles from tracking loose dirt out onto the streets, and traffic control where the extra traffic related to the command center made an impact to normal traffic flow at the entrance were all required. Sites that were designated just as material lay-down locations, still needed restrooms and trash containers (Dulgeroff, 2009).

The region's basic communications infrastructure was not impacted by the fires, therefore alternate communications systems were not needed in the 2007 firestorm. It is timely to note however that emerging technologies leveraging communications devices already being used are being tested for response to emergencies impacting infrastructure. This new type of infrastructure-less wireless network, such as Georgia Tech's LifeNet model (Wilson, 2005), which is formed out of consumer electronic devices such as laptops or smart phones could have great utility in disaster scenarios impacting the traditional means of communications.

Using consumer devices such as smart phones and laptops to remove dependence on a company's local network infrastructure and data center could also be addressed by cloud computing.

In SDG&E's 2007 response, the team members used cell phones and laptops with air cards to track all the support activities and items for command centers, on spreadsheets that were emailed back and forth to the manager leading the command center efforts. This enabled them to track the logistics of all command center sites in a consolidated manner. Each day the team members participated in two conference calls with their counterparts, during which they were given updates from other SDG&E departments supporting the logistical efforts.

OBSERVED ISSUES

The SDG&E team members who were serving as business solutions liaisons (BSLs) between the construction supervisors leading the restoration and rebuilding efforts of the crews, and the departments that procure and oversee delivery of the material and services used to set-up the command centers, reported occasions when their requests for items needed for the command centers were not conveyed exactly, or delivery was late. Other times requests were duplicated, or second and third calls were received from the providers to confirm if materials or meals were still needed, when the items had already been received. The BSLs' daily submittal of the tracking spreadsheet to the manager's administrative support required a significant consolidation chore and lacked real-time status. For example, an impact of the spreadsheet's lack of timeliness was that if the BSLs needed to track something more timely than information from the afternoon before, they would have to participate in both conference calls each day, despite other tasks they might have been performing. Additionally, the BSLs needed to take their own notes as to what each command center team was reporting during the calls. Then, the spreadsheet combined with their handwritten notes provided them with more detailed information, but resulted in an abundance of paper. Further, the daily consolidation of spreadsheets from 17 different command centers contributed to the chance of errors being made. The possibility of achieving efficiencies through a more real-time method, rather than paper forms, repeated consolidation of emailed spreadsheets,

and email requests first arose during the type of miscommunication reported above. This suggested an opportunity for investigation of a more real-time approach to handling the logistics related to the emergency response.

The rush to procure water, meals, tents, lights, portable bathrooms, and mobile offices is all performed in competition with other responding agencies in the region, public and private-sector. Any lag in response time could present the loss of the opportunity to obtain what is essential. Because of that competition for scarce resources, the first five days of a response are the most time-sensitive. Consequently, the potential for errors in the spreadsheets could have represented a loss of needed resources.

Research discusses the range of spreadsheet errors from calculation errors, to one that is more germane to this study, errors in data quality. Caulkins et al. (2005) cite these errors in data quality as one of three typical reasons that contribute to undetected errors in an alarming "91 percent of spreadsheets" (p. 22). These authors contend that a simple task such as a "bad sort can destroy the integrity of a row, or a mismatch of units" (p. 23). This is supported by Panko's research in which he estimated 94 percent of spreadsheets contain errors (Panko, 2007). Therefore, it is clear that any solution must need no manual manipulation of the data such as is needed when using spreadsheets for database functions. An alternate solution must also have virtually no training-time requirements, since the employees assigned to the task in subsequent emergencies will likely have no experience with the solution, nor would they have the luxury of time to learn it. The possibility of SDG&E changing its approach to command center logistics tracking as Commonwealth Edison and Duke Energy were able to do, merits further study.

After the 2007 fires, event-assessment and debrief of the command center support personnel included the subject being raised of the efficacy of spreadsheets and paper forms and the question of whether an alternate approach could have achieved greater efficiencies, especially in the areas where duplications and problems were encountered was posed. This study addresses the following research questions:

- What alternative approach would have enabled the teams working on the command center effort of emergency response to have easier-to-use, faster-to-access data?
- What solution would include the capability to store basic command center requirements from previous emergency responses to save time in addressing the first or most crucial items needed during the next emergency?
- What resiliency could be built into command center logistics tracking in case the company's network was rendered inaccessible at the same time as command centers were needed for service restoration activities?

Therefore, if SDG&E's electric or gas system was damaged by terrorist activity or another natural disaster with equal or greater severity than the firestorms of 2003 and 2007, tracking the command center logistics could become exponentially more difficult proportionate to the severity of the disaster. An alternative solution designed for easy access by users in multiple areas could enhance the support of the logistical efforts to bring the region's critical infrastructure back to normalcy in the most effective manner possible.

This study is designed to investigate the possibility of an alternate, multi-user approach, in order to improve accessibility or timeliness of information in a further refinement of disaster response tools. Results could aid decision-makers in their planning for subsequent emergencies. The present body of knowledge will be expanded by the study of converting from spreadsheets and paper forms currently used for some emergency management activities to more effective tools of response.

POST WILD FIRE ANALYSIS

After the Southern California fires of 2003, the Sempra Energy utilities' vice president of Business Solutions, and Directors leading the support-type departments of Supply Management/Logistics, Fleet Services, Facilities, Real Estate/Land, Environmental, and Safety, formulated a program to further enhance their support to field operations areas in their response to emergencies. That new program was enacted for the first time during the 2007 Southern California fires. Under a dotted line reporting relationship to a manager responsible for all command center and staging area sites, "Business Solutions Liaisons" (BSLs) fulfilled a strategy that was designed to provide them as central points of contact. They were to interface between the operating centers' field operations and SDG&E's high-level central coordination and communications Emergency Operations Center (EOC), during emergencies that necessitated the set-up of staging areas and/or crew deployment areas. The BSLs were selected from a qualified pool of employees from the support departments, and based on their availability to respond to remote locations for ten-hour shifts. The BSLs were to be a visible presence in the field to facilitate proper two-way communications between field operations groups, the support departments, and the EOC, where requests would be received and dispatched to the proper responding support departments. The BSLs were intended to be the "one-stop-shop" for all requests instead of field supervisors having to make requests of many areas for their needs (Dulgeroff, 2009). The BSLs are not examined in this paper as a population. Their data output, however, is the sample examined.

The BSL program would be activated under certain conditions including:

- The utility experiences a major event
- The EOC is activated
- One or more off-property staging areas are needed
- It is requested by EOC staff

The BSLs had to be ready to mobilize at the beginning of an event through response and recovery. They were to engage with operating groups and coordinate with existing emergency response systems. In addition, the BSLs were to be familiar with field operations activities, be prepared for inclement weather, and be field-ready.

Teams of two BSLs were assigned to each location to cover two shifts per day. Sites were determined by identifying areas where the utility's system had sustained significant damage, for economies of adjacency in location decisions. If there was suitable land, and the area met strategic placement guidelines, a command center was located there (Dulgeroff, 2009).

In the first three days of the emergency, the Facilities department was activating its baseline set of plans, to achieve the earliest response to the expected need for some type of field command centers or staging areas. Therefore, they already had contingency plans in place for rapid procurement of several large tents to house the resting and dining functions for the emergency response, generators, lighting, drinking water, catering, and portable sanitation services. As soon as they reported to their assigned command center locations with their laptops and air cards, cell phones, and personal protective equipment, BSLs checked-in with the construction supervisors to receive any logistical requests and support them in their core mission of directing system repair for service restoration of the utility system.

As the emergency unfolded, appropriate numbers of utility personnel, mutual assistance crews, and contract construction company crews were deployed to repair damaged segments of the system (Dulgeroff, 2009) The BSLs were apprised by the construction supervisors, of the crew size increases or decreases, as work progressed across the damaged areas, and as mutual assistance crews arrived. The command center needs were adjusted depending on that crew movement (Dulgeroff, 2009).

In order of priority, meals, water, ice, and sanitation facilities were the most important of the many things needed at the command centers. Shelter (tents), electricity, portable offices, internet connectivity, and garbage containers and garbage collection were next in order of priority. Following in priority were a fuel tanker to refuel the crew trucks and a pad for a helicopter to land, including a water truck to mitigate dust from the helicopter and the vehicle traffic.

As soon as the BSLs reported to their assignments, they were to review the template documents in their binders, time permitting. There were often requests and/or people waiting for the BSLs as soon as they got to their locations, and the BSLs provided rapid response and follow-up on all requests. The One-Stop-Shop was an exceptionally successful response model because the construction supervisors' needs were continuous and the BSLs execution of the ordering and tracking was a better use of company resources.

It quickly became apparent that the paper request forms in the binder were unworkable, for two main reasons. The forms were meant to be handwritten, then faxed to the EOC representative for that request category, however, there were no fax machines available, at least in the first several days of the emergency. Further, the forms required name, date, and time information. The natural inclination of the BSLs was to call the EOC representative and initiate the request via cell phone call, then complete an email note with the same information as a written confirmation, and for ease of follow-up. The email notes automatically recorded name, date, and time information, and the BSL added the other shift's BSL in the carbon copy line. Early in the process, the paper request forms served as helpful visual cues for the details that needed to be included in the phone and email requests, but beyond that were hardly used.

Similarly, the paper BSL Service Request Log was viewed as inconvenient given the Sent Items feature which saves sent-email in a folder in the sender's Outlook program. Not all of the

BSLs used this paper Log knowing their Outlook Sent Items function captured and archived them automatically and more permanently in case the information was needed at a later time. Given that the other shift's BSL had been copied on any emails that alternate shift BSL did not need to review the paper Service Request Log to ensure smooth transition of information.

FINDINGS AND DATA ANALYSIS

What alternative approach would have enabled the teams working on the command center effort for emergency response to have easier-to-use, faster-to-access data? What solution would include the capability to store basic command center requirements from previous emergency responses to save time in addressing the first or most crucial items needed during the next emergency? What resiliency could be built into command center logistics tracking in case the company's network was rendered inaccessible at the same time as command centers were needed for service restoration activities?

The 2007 Southern California fires damaged a large amount of San Diego County's territory including, in some areas, SDG&E's means of delivery of electric service, its poles, wires, cable, and transformers (Dulgeroff, 2009). SDG&E coordinated a full-scale effort to restore service for its customers as soon as possible. "To provide forward support closer to the actual field locations where the bulk of the repair and restoration work was occurring, SDG&E established 'command centers' and 'staging areas' in strategic locations" (Geier, 2009, p. 14). Establishing and maintaining the command centers and staging areas to support the crews in their restoration efforts, and ultimately closing them down, involved approximately 56 employees from supporting departments, for approximately three weeks in a significant logistical exercise (Dulgeroff, 2009).

The process began with: (1) baseline requirements needed for a command center or staging area, (2) personnel assigned to the location to be the points of contact, called BSLs, and (3) the BSLs' laptop computers with air cards for internet connectivity, the BSLs' cell phones, a master spreadsheet to track all the details of all the command centers and consolidate them into one view, and paper forms on which BSLs could make requests for items needed at the sites. The spreadsheets did not look at the causes of the emergency, but helped manage the responses.

The lead author, a team lead of the SDG&E supply chain systems team, served in the BSL capacity. The people who received the requests and information from the BSLs and fulfilled them were support department representatives manning their specific EOC positions. Each EOC position was staffed around the clock at the beginning of the emergency, and as appropriate later in the response, was reduced to 16 hours per day of coverage.

The BSLs received all the requests associated with taking the command centers from their baseline configuration to fully-functioning field operations support, by working as the interface between the construction supervisors, the EOC representatives, and on occasion, directly with the vendors. The defined method for initiating a request for materials or services was in the library of paper forms.

In practice however, instead of using the paper forms to initiate requests, there were two preferred methods by which BSLs sent requests to the EOC representatives. The first method was via cell phone call. The second method was via company email which was available via air card internet connectivity and VPN computer network access. These emails were often written follow-up to the initiating phone call. Also, since they were accessing the network via VPN, all internal drives and intranet pages and systems normally available to BSLs were accessible. The EOC representatives were on-site at SDG&E's company headquarters location, and had the full company network available to them and received BSL email communications in that manner.

The main tool used to handle the command center logistics effort was a spreadsheet. The spreadsheets used for this study are three samples of the daily iterations of the 2007 Firestorm command center and staging area consolidated information. All of the categories represented essential items needed to support response to the emergency. Many of the BSLs' actual practices did not include filling-in the paper forms, which meant the paper forms provided in the binder went unused. The service request log in the binder was also not used by the BSLs as they preferred the daily-updated spreadsheets that conveyed the entire command center landscape. The spreadsheet in its consolidated form was the most significant tracking output of that effort. The main benefit of the spreadsheet was the ability to track, albeit a day later, the logistical details of the command center, which included upward reporting to and by the manager. This information was kept current by the BSLs completing and emailing the spreadsheets back to the manager after the afternoon conference call, for his administrative support's updating. The inherent inefficiency of its manual consolidation prompted the research questions.

A consideration of efficiencies to be gained and opportunities to track more categories of information, if needed, might reveal a new structure for the process, using an alternative approach to the paper forms and the spreadsheet. Consequently, the analysis of efficiency of the spreadsheets compared to real-time access to data, might include a new technology or a combination of several. An examination of the details of forms on smart phones, dashboards, blogs and wikis, and cloud computing would be timely, as SDG&E continuously strives for improvement of its crisis response.

DISCUSSION

Based on the data resulting from SDG&E's 2007 Firestorm command center support response analysis, two hours a day of conference call attendance, paper form requirements, and editing of the spreadsheet by each BSL team, indicates opportunities to improve efficiency exist. Several possibilities for alternative approaches to command center logistics tracking are growing in use and popularity. To address the first research question on what alternative approach to emergency response logistics tracking would be easier-to-use and provide faster access to data, rendering forms on smart phones in replacement of paper forms, blogs for BSLs to convey new situations or information they encounter, via a posting on a webpage, making it readily searchable for the next crisis, wikis, which can capture blog information of a more formal or permanent nature to document processes or procedures, and dashboards as a means to display the real-time, consolidated, command center information, links, and metrics are suggested.

The use of a database as the backend data repository supporting what is displayed in dashboards related to the second question, and the concept of cloud computing related to the third research question will be discussed later. This combination of alternatives incorporates the concept of building resiliency into a company's activities supporting critical infrastructure response work, as well as reducing duplicative or outdated methods. It also can be viewed through the lens of the expanded crisis response system model (Jennex, 2004). The expanded system encompasses more than the basic components of database, data analysis, normative models, and interface. Enhancing the model includes the addition of trained users (where users are personnel using the system to respond to or communicate about the emergency and consist of first responders, long term responders, the emergency response team, and experts), dynamic, integrated, and collaborative (yet possibly physically distributed) methods to communicate between users and data sources, protocols to facilitate communication, and processes and procedures used to guide the response to and improve decision making during the crisis.

This expanded crisis response system model is applicable to the discussion of combining alternatives in order to better respond to the logistics tracking activities of SDG&E's emergency response. Specifically, the dashboards fulfill the model's condition for a dynamic method of communication, based on the real-time nature of the information received and displayed. The potentially constantly updated information supports the optimum display to users of what is residing in the underlying data sources and, further, to non-users such as executive teams, and decision-makers. The dashboards also fulfill the model's component of integrated and collaborative protocols by their attribute of displaying multiple types of information from multiple sources or contributors that would not normally be displayed together in a single view, or viewable by so many different parties. Additionally, the nature of the field operations and the EOC functions being physically separated conforms to the model's almost-certain distributed teams, sites, and means of communications.

The sometimes duplicative activities associated with the BSLs' use of paper forms and follow-up phone calls, and the time-consuming consolidation of that information in a spreadsheet with limited visual display characteristics, implied one or all of these alternatives may have efficacy in improving BSL-related data output in subsequent emergency efforts, as supported by the Jennex expanded crisis response system model. The result of analyzing enhanced concepts to the command center tracking needs, suggests further study of forms on smart phones, and dashboards connected to a robust back-end database already populated with baseline data as a starting template to save time, residing on remote servers in a private cloud. A site linked to the dashboard on which any participant in the command center effort could

blog about any special experience for sharing with the other team members would be timely as well as easy to access. Problems or issues discussed in the blogs and successfully addressed, could be elaborated upon or documented in a more formal and thoroughly developed way and posted as a wiki, as a more permanent and searchable archive. The need for resiliency in case of unforeseen inaccessibility, suggests the use of private cloud computing, which would result in a virtual, secure, remote location for SDG&E-related command center activities to be developed, housed, and delivered. That need for secure software and data is important because of the proprietary nature of the information. Therefore, a practical solution to help the utility in case of a catastrophic loss of its computer network might include private cloud computing. Possibilities of technological alternatives other than these may be suited for transforming the spreadsheets and the paper forms, and displaying command center logistics however, the intricacies of the related technology need to be addressed as further suggestions.

The viability of these technologies in support of alternative systems for crisis response is derived from Jennex and Raman (2009). The forms on smart phones, blogs and wikis, cloud computing, and the dashboards similar to those developed by SDSU's Visualization Center for flu tracking in San Diego County when implemented together, can all be considered components in the fusion of KM systems (Jennex & Raman, 2009).

Filling out paper forms and completing the spreadsheets was actually just the manual assembling of a list of data in columns and rows. It was not a meaningful transfer of ideas, needs, and information. When ideas, needs, and information are assembled without further requirement for consolidation or user adaption, and then easily rendered visually, it results in expedient crisis response through impactful visual cues and a more efficient transfer of knowledge.

The implication is the tacit knowledge from BSLs' previous experiences can not be appropriately conveyed in a single file when the information is simply housed in a spreadsheet's columns and rows format. However, the multi-dimensional, graphical layering, and photographic images displayed in a dashboard format heralds the emergence of knowledge transfer that would benefit the evolution of SDG&E's emergency response model. Blogs to capture BSLs special experiences or issues, and wikis to more permanently archive the blog posts that lend themselves to formal processes and procedures, provide a searchable, easy to access forum for command center participants' specific information, and should be included as links in the dashboard. Handling the knowledge in support of crisis response in this manner substantiates the Jennex and Raman (2009) assertion that, decision makers, when under stress, need systems that do more than just provide data, they need systems that can quickly find and display knowledge relevant to the situation in a format that facilitates the decision maker in making decisions.

IMPLICATIONS AND RECOMMENDATIONS

The research related to the spreadsheets revealed that they performed in an adequate manner based on the fact that the command center logistics tracking was generally accurate and the consensus among the interfacing groups was that the command center model performed very well. However, the lag time in displaying updated information on the distribution of the crews across the command center landscape during a day, and how that impacted meal counts which, potentially dramatically affected the crews' perception of well being, can be surmised due to the manual consolidation effort necessary to keep spreadsheet data current. The literature validates the significance of the crews' perceived well being as having substantial importance.

Relative to the discussion of the crews' well being, a tangent factor of the BSLs' efforts in the command center support was their stated feelings of satisfaction related to their accomplishments, as discussed in a BSL debrief meeting in November 2007. The perceived usefulness of their efforts and their feelings of self-efficacy gave an indication of how likely BSLs would be to embrace alternative approaches to the work if it meant further improvement in their response to a crisis. While this relates to implementing knowledge management systems in support of crisis response (Jennex & Raman, 2009) it must be acknowledged that the responsibility for efficient and timely restoration of essential services is still a mandate from the federal government as codified in HSPD7. Despite SDG&E's culture of dedicated restoration activities, the BSLs' satisfaction in support of the company mission, or the opportunity to leverage computer technology and knowledge management systems to enhance the logistical support, the restoration activities would still be required by the federal government even in the absence of those company requirements and employee satisfaction drivers.

It also should be recognized that there could be a scenario when the normal network systems for achieving compliance with HSPD 7's requirements would be completely interrupted. In the event of a loss of SDG&E's computer network infrastructure, an alternative to the company network would be needed to handle the on-going restoration tracking efforts. One alternative to the traditional and local company network would be via cloud computing.

In the event SDG&E's computer network was rendered unusable, whatever applications were needed for the command center response could be housed on virtual servers in the cloud, and accessed via the internet, likely through wireless connectivity such as the BSLs' air cards. The implication is SDG&E could continuously access its disaster response support tools if they were housed and delivered outside the company network. The security aspect would be addressed by using the cloud computing model known as the private cloud, in which processing, storage, networking, and the application, are via an intranet, allowing for user authentication, and encryption of the company's proprietary data.

Computing via the cloud also allows for applications to be used on a pay-as-you-go pricing schedule (Vanmechelen et al., 2006). This would allow the cost of an important emergency response tool, after its initial development costs, to be borne only at the time the company is experiencing an emergency. Responding to emergencies often carries great costs, some of which can be recovered in rates if SDG&E's governing regulatory agency grants such a request. Matching the costs of a pay-when-used type of emergency response support tool to the infrequent occasions of emergencies impacting SDG&E's critical infrastructure, supports a position of careful stewardship of costs the company will eventually request to recover. Further, using cloud-based tools to house an emergency response logistics tracking application securely outside SDG&E's territory and having it be accessible via any internet-based connection along with VPN, provides a resilience to catastrophic wildfire- or earthquake-caused network destruction that would interfere with tracking of, although not halt, SDG&E's restoration activities in the field.

Analysis of the manual, and not-well-used paper forms for BSLs to send requests to the EOC, demonstrated the need for an alternate request method. As was demonstrated by actual practice, phone calls and follow-up emails were preferred to the paper forms. However, the email was duplicative to the phone call, which suggests a less-than-optimal use of the BSLs' time. The rendering of a paper form for display and user input on a smart phone has potential utility as the technology to replace the paper forms for command center logistics requests.

Data initiated by the request is needed to execute the activity and provides the EOC recipient with record of the exact details needed for accurate fulfillment, almost always better than a phone call request, but usually not faster. Yet the BSLs all had cell phones and continuously made requests initiated by phone calls then followed-up with emails for solid confirmation. An alternative is using a smart phone with a form accessed from the phone's embedded memory. The efficiency of using the hand-held portability and instant communications of a cell phone, while having the accuracy and full detail inherent in a form, can both be achieved with this technology. The electronic forms housed in the smart phones' memory could also be available in a library of request forms linked on the dashboard, as a secondary and back-up location to the smart phones. The practices of the BSLs in the field imply this alternative merits further investigation and possible piloting during future SDG&E emergency drills.

Another implication for future research addresses the need to experiment with the dashboard as a more informative alternative for the current spreadsheet data and to house links to other BSL-needed information. A test model would include a dashboard being provided to the BSLs, their decision-makers, and related support departments for further determination of the efficacy of the technology. The user requirements of both dashboard and cloud computing would be structured by the technical staff at SDG&E to determine whether cloud computing and dashboards are viable alternatives to replace the current emailed spreadsheet.

The spreadsheet as the most significant tracking output of the BSLs' 2007 efforts is important when considering how such a single, relatively simple file was the source for tracking a great deal of valuable SDG&E-owned or rented assets, providing the manager with the ability to report to the EOC and the Executive team, the extent of the command center support of field operations and his decision-making related to consolidations of sites, or needed geographical changes, particularly while the fires were still burning. Considering those substantive uses of the spreadsheet, the lag time in the data's accuracy due to the need for consolidation, indicates the audiences could be better served as more real-time technologies become achievable for this specific purpose. Furthermore, the recognition of the potential need of other categories and/or sources of information implies the spreadsheet format was already at the limit of its utility. The need for a tool with the ability to display data in a visual, real-time format, with links to additional helpful or related sources of information such as BSL-related blogs and wikis, seems a likely area for future study, since dashboards provides internet-browser display of many categories of data from potentially many sources.

Dashboards also provide for understanding of performance indicators of importance to a specific audience, by summarizing them and often displaying them by graphical icon. The summarized data displayed in a dashboard can be the starting point to drill down to their detail. Conveying the data in a summarized, graphical way represents a significant, behind-the-scenes effort of collection, consolidation, and presentation of the data that starts to transfer tacit knowledge when the consolidation allows for decision-making based on the whole picture that is drawn by the dashboard. Dashboards support two important points made by Turoff, supplying the best possible up-to-date information is critical to those whose action may risk lives and resources and that an emergency response information system must be an integrated electronic library of external data and information sources (Turoff, 2002). The data in SDG&E's command center tracking spreadsheet has the potential to become enhanced decision-making information and therefore knowledge that can be applied by its users through the use of baseline data from past command center experiences to respond to a present emergency.

Using a dashboard displaying data taken from the spreadsheet categories in a more actionable manner could enhance decision-making or at the least, readability and timeliness. The summarization and display of all of these types of information sources in a single dashboard enables viewers to drill down to access other websites, company intranet pages, participant blogs, related wikis, detailed data from maps and databases, and have it all accessible real-time. It would be a significant enhancement to the ways this information was available to SDG&E's emergency response support teams in previous emergencies. This practice of selectively applying knowledge from previous experiences during turbulent moments of decision making, to current and future decision making activities with the express purpose of improving the organization's effectiveness, would be possible via a KM system (Jennex & Raman, 2009) such as a dashboard along with its underlying means of delivery.

CONCLUSION

This paper proposes using knowledge to drive an alternative to SDG&E's paper request forms for command center needs, and suggests the use of request forms rendered on smart phones assigned to the BSLs for the duration of the effort. In addition, the development of dashboards, including links to command center participant blogs and wikis, is suggested as an effective alternative to spreadsheets to track the command center logistics, and provide easy to access information by means of links. Finally, the use of cloud computing as the development platform and host of an SDG&E dashboard application is recommended as a timely evolution to a KM system approach to achieve logistical tracking efficiencies.

REFERENCES

Bandura, A. (1982). Self-efficacy mechanism in human agency. *The American Psychologist, 37*(2), 122–147. doi:10.1037/0003-066X.37.2.122

Caulkins, J. P., Morrison, E. L., & Weidemann, T. (2005). Spreadsheet errors: Are they undermining decision making in your organization? *Public Management, 34*(1), 22–27.

Davis, F. (1989). Perceived usefulness, perceived ease of use, and user acceptance of information technology. *Management Information Systems Quarterly, 13*(3), 319–340. doi:10.2307/249008

Dulgeroff, A. (2009). *Application of San Diego Gas & Electric Company (U 902 M) for authorization to recover costs related to the 2007 Southern California wildfires recorded in the Catastrophic Event Memorandum Account (CEMA)*. Retrieved from http://www.sdge.com/regulatory/documents/a-09-03-011/testimony-dulgeroff.pdf

Geier, D. L. (2009). Investigation on the Commission's own motion into the operations and practices of Cox Communications and San Diego Gas & Electric Company regarding the utility facilities linked to the Guejito Fire of October 2007.

Jennex, M. E. (2004). Emergency Response Systems: The Utility Y2K Experience. *Journal of Information Technology Theory and Application, 6*(3), 85–102.

Jennex, M. E. (2005). What is knowledge management? *International Journal of Knowledge Management, 1*(4), i–iv.

Jennex, M. E. (2007, August 25). *Knowledge Management in Support of Crisis Response*. Paper presented at the ISCRAM China Workshop.

Jennex, M. E., & Raman, M. (2009). Knowledge Management is Support of Crisis Response. *International Journal of Information Systems for Crisis Response and Management, 1*(3), 69–82.

Panko, R. P. (2007). Two experiments in reducing overconfidence in spreadsheet development. *Journal of Organizational and End User Computing, 19*(1), 1–23.

Turoff, M. (2002). Past and future emergency response information systems. *Communications of the ACM, 45*(4), 29–32. doi:10.1145/505248.505265

Vanmechelen, K., Stuer, G., & Broeckhove, J. (2006). *Pricing substitutable grid resources using commodity market models*. Retrieved from http://www.coms.ua.ac.be/publications/files/KVM_GECON_2006.pdf

Venkatesh, V., Morris, M., Davis, G., & Davis, F. (2003). User acceptance of information technology: Toward a unified view. *Management Information Systems Quarterly, 27*(3), 425–478.

Whybark, D. C., Melnyk, S. A., Day, J., & Davis, E. (2010). Disaster Relief Supply Chain Management: New Realities, Management Challenges, Emerging Opportunities. *Decision Line*, 4-7.

Wilson, S. (2010). *Next generation disaster communications technology now a reality with LifeNet*. Retrieved September 25, 2010, from http://www.scs.gatech.edu/news/next-generation-disaster-communications-technology-now-reality-lifenet

Zuber-Skerrit, O., & Fletcher, M. (2007). The quality of an action research thesis in the social sciences. *Quality Assurance in Education, 15*(4), 413.

This work was previously published in International Journal of Information Systems for Crisis Response Management, Volume 2, Issue 3, edited by Murray E. Jennex, pp. 36-50, copyright 2010 by IGI Publishing (an imprint of IGI Global).

Chapter 13
Curriculum Design and Development at the Nexus of International Crisis Management and Information Systems

Keith Clement
California State University Fresno, USA

ABSTRACT

This case study discusses the role of education, curriculum development, research, and service in supporting information systems for crisis response management. The study describes the Council for Emergency Management and Homeland Security (CEMHS) organization that designs and develops academic programs and courses in these specialized areas. CEMHS combines all levels of education in California (from K-12 and postsecondary education) into a "state-wide solution" and network of academicians and professionals in emergency and disaster management, crisis response, and homeland security education and training. The organizational purpose is constructing a "vertical track" of academic programs and specialized programs to benefit and enhance information resource and crisis management. The implications and lessons learned from building collaborative partnerships between the crisis and disaster response academic and professional communities in academic program development and research initiatives are also discussed.

INTRODUCTION

There has been an increasing expectation for active and vigorous government and Non-Government Organization (NGO) in responding to natural and man-made disasters. This expectation has translated into greater responsibility, higher vis-

ibility, and more media attention in the preparation, response, and management of meteorological, environmental, political violence, and other exigencies. In light of several significant and recent international disasters, including the Thailand tsunami, Haiti and Chile Earthquakes, floods in China and Pakistan, forest fires in Russia, and

DOI: 10.4018/978-1-4666-0167-3.ch013

Hurricane Katrina, have dramatically raised global consciousness and salience for a need to enhance crisis and disaster response and management. Due to the critical need to enhance preparedness, prevention, recovery, and mitigation in dealing with catastrophic or emergency incidents, crisp and efficient action is required to accomplish the "all-hazards" crisis response mission. The tremendous loss of life and human misery coupled with huge costs for disaster relief and crisis response has evolved into a critical necessity to develop policies, social institutions, technology, and a culture of preparedness to protect lives, society, critical infrastructure, various sectors of the economy, and property.

It is with little surprise that there are many changes to the topographical maps and two-way radio of yesteryear's disaster and crisis planners, managers, and responders. Today, Geographic Information Systems (GIS), web-based applications, Google Earth, readily available satellite data, communications technologies, voice and data fusion on mobile devices and handsets are all common tools of the trade for emergency and crisis managers and responders. In an increasing technological world and social milieu, the role and value of information has grown exponentially. This is particularly true when designing and managing "real time" information resources, remote sensing assets, and additional knowledge systems in response to the data intensive demands of crisis response in the modern digital age. Developing and deploying information systems are critical tools in the response, preparedness, decision-making, and communication of emergencies. Crisis response personnel must have access to actionable information in order to make informed, effective, and speedy decisions as dynamic incident events unfold on the ground.

Technology and information management are crucial components of crisis and disaster response. Public safety and emergency response personnel must be intimately familiar with current technological tools to assist in effective crisis response, improved preparedness, and enhanced humanitarian disaster management capability. This is due in part because of the critical "need for speed" in efficient crisis response: establishing situational command and control, restoring basic public health care services and business continuity, restoring transportation, critical infrastructure and additional logistical matters, utilizing geovisual analytics, managing information resources, and communicating information reliably (for those in need and for those responding) and any additional steps necessary towards crisis mitigation and recovery. Several "core principles" in Emergency Management include "comprehensive, progressive, risk-driven, integrated, collaborative, coordinated, flexible, and professional" (IAEM, 2007). These are substantial demands that are placed on our crisis responders and managers and we must work to build additional tools to increase our performance and utilization of information in crisis management.

Given the totality of life and death decisions and hazard to property and security, a substantial need exists for quality and accessible education and training programs at the nexus of academic and professional interests in areas related to information systems, crisis response, and international disaster management. The need for academic programs and courses to support and prepare the current (and next) generation of information systems and crisis response management professionals has grown significantly as technology advances near daily. Thus, developing and enhancing education programs in this subject area is an important objective for several reasons. Education programs provide an avenue for faculty research, opportunity for students, enhances pedagogy and teaching practices, and further develops our knowledge base. Education and research programs can contribute to greater levels of community and university service for faculty, staff, and students as well as improves community engagement (as well as communities assisted through better trained, educated, and prepared crisis response teams).

However, questions exist about emergency management and crisis response education and training programs. What is the current state of these programs? How are quality and accessible programs and courses designed, developed, and implemented? Are there comprehensive and co-ordinated academic programs that fully prepare specialized crisis response and managers in the utilization of information systems (and other important contributing fields) when coping with disasters? If this is not currently the case, how can academicians and practitioners work together to develop education standards and programs to further support and enhance academic areas like information management, remote sensing systems, and knowledge systems dedicated to enhanced crisis management and response? These are some of the primary questions, issues, and themes addressed over the course of this case study.

In terms of organizing this paper, we first discuss the role of education, curriculum development, research, and service in supporting a variety of academic disciplines and fields that contribute to effective crisis response. It is important to discuss the role and value of education, curriculum development, and implications in the field of information systems and crisis response. Next, and the primary purpose of this case study, is the description and discussion of an organization, the Council for Emergency Management and Homeland Security (CEMHS) that designs and develops academic programs and courses in these specialized areas. CEMHS is an interesting case study because it draws together all levels of education in California (from K-12 and Postsecondary Education) into a "state-wide" solution that links a network of academicians and professionals together in the fields of emergency and disaster management, crisis response, and homeland security education and training. Finally, we discuss the implications and lessons learned from collaborative partnerships between the emergency management and homeland security academic and professional communities in academic program development and research initiatives.

THE ROLE OF EDUCATION AND CURRICULUM DEVELOPMENT FOR INFORMATION SYSTEMS AND CRISIS RESPONSE MANAGEMENT

What are the implications for academic programs implementation in advanced scientific fields such as information systems management as related to crisis response? These questions quickly become complicated when talking about dynamic, technical, and scientific disciplines and specializations like information resource management. In addition, the past few years have seen an increased need and demand for a specialization in crisis management and disaster response education and training programs. "In most societies education is constantly being asked to do more and more things, to higher and higher standards, with greater accountability and finite (if not diminishing) resources." (Davies, 1999, p. 108). Due to the relatively new entry of crisis response and management related subjects into academics, colleges, and universities, there is much planning, design, development necessary for implementation and adoption at higher education institutions. This is particularly true for more focused scientific disciplines like information resource management. Any absence in quality education and training opportunities reduces our capability to prepare, respond, mitigate and recover from natural and manmade catastrophes. Thus, any potential challenges and rewards for developing quality disaster management and academic programs justify the creation of partnerships among key stakeholders and partners to achieve long-term program sustainability and development.

Scholars and practitioners should develop and communicate best practices" to improve the management and utilization of information as a resource to enhance international disaster response capabilities and performance. Technology and information resources and needs indicate that scientific, technical, and professional workforce and skill demand must be readily prepared and skilled to support the many diverse fields that participate in disaster and crisis response. We must find ways to support development (and subsequent response capability) by designing and implementing education and training programs to support global information needs by enhancing knowledge systems management through education and training strategies. It is important that educators contribute their expertise to crisis response and disaster management academic program organization and structure. Educators contribute to the solution through the development, codification, and transmission of important expertise, knowledge, skills, and experience relevant to emergency and disaster management. "The demands being made upon teachers and others who provide education call out for educational practices to be based on the best available evidence as well as the professional skills, experience, and competence of teachers" (Davies, 1999, p. 117).

To increase supply and capacity of quality education and training in this area, we must understand the current state of these academic programs, discover potential gaps in content and curriculum, adopt quality control and evaluation measures, and support enhanced academic standards. If education program and course supply and demand needs can be met, we can enhance the availability and quality of crisis response and management through standardization of programs, government incentives and funding for program development, and the benefit of employment of students graduating from these reputable academic programs. One solution may be the creation of a template or blueprint to guide the design, development and implementation of academic programs at various levels of education. This would assist in the furtherance of education, training, and research collaboration, global partnerships, and an enhanced network of experts to deploy in the field, data visualization centers, command and control, joint incident command posts, and on incident response teams. It is also critical to seek educational and training solution to further integrate the areas of crisis response and information systems.

CEMHS ORGANIZATION

The Council for Emergency Management and Homeland Security (CEMHS) was formed in 2008 to enhance and strengthen Emergency Management (EM) and Homeland Security (HS) education and training programs and research partnerships within the State of California. CEMHS is a multi-campus faculty affinity group within the California State University and promotes quality and accessible EM-HS academics, research initiatives, and university/community service connections. The purpose of CEMHS is to link comprehensive programs, courses, and curriculum through the promulgation of "model programs" as developed by faculty and professional subject matter experts teams and carefully linked with effective pedagogical practice. The organizational purpose is accomplished through the utilization of a curriculum design development framework and blueprint that guides the construction and development of different types of emergency management and homeland security degree and certificate programs (Associate through Doctoral programs). CEMHS promulgates the development of a "state-wide education and training solution" in the form of comprehensive "vertical track" education and training programs to improve disaster and crisis response and, for example, the efficient utilization of information resources and technology.

In the program design and curriculum development phase, it is important to ensure that programs contain all requisite skills and knowledge competency areas necessary to master and perform within a given field or discipline. The "templates" and "best practices" framework are intended for replication as a model curriculum by additional educational institutions interested in offering these programs and courses. Thus, there is the development of a clear road-map in academic programs from professional training to advanced terminal degree program in disaster and crisis response and information systems management. CEMHS provides facilitated coordination to help develop academic programs to enhance crisis response and information systems management and greatly benefit the international disaster response community.

The Importance of Partnerships and Collaboration

The primary means of achieving organization education and research objectives is through collaboration and partnering between state educational institutions and major stakeholders and the development of participation within the emergency management and crisis response community. As an organization, CEMHS fosters a shared vision in designing and promoting EM-HS curriculum and programs with the active participation and critical input of key partners and stakeholders. Particular emphasis is placed on building facilitative and stronger relations in a growing network of academicians and professionals within the field. It is important to foster partnerships and collaboration and develop a strategic plan to implement education and training programs at various levels of government: international, national, state, and local, educational partners, additional public organizations, and the private sector.

The discussion of EM-HS curriculum and initiatives should be conducted within the framework of delivering standardized, portable courses and programs that fulfill the needs of key partnering agencies, faculty, students, and respective campuses. It is vital to coordinate streamlined crisis response and emergency management academic programs. This is particularly true for specialized

academic disciplines like information systems and management. In order to handle disasters efficiently, crises responders should have achieved specific competencies and mastery to perform their respective tasks and duties. All involved in crisis response should be properly prepared and experienced in handling incidents. All crisis responders and information resource team members should be on the same page to accomplish tasks as necessary. This is accomplished through education, training, and practical experience.

To help sate a demand for information and knowledge, key partnerships within the academic and professional communities have formed and coalesced with the purpose of enhancing disaster preparedness, crisis response, through education and training programs. The objectives of CEMHS include building of strategic partnerships among key stakeholders in collaborative partnerships to support the programmatic and curriculum development needs. There is a need to develop education programs to provide a firm foundation for the many specialized areas of crisis response like information management, public health, nursing, civil engineering, victim services, and many other contributing fields and disciplines. This activity is achieved through increased "predictable collaborative action" and through building multi-campus consortiums and university-agency partnerships. Since many of the courses utilized in these programs already exist, it is primarily an issue of getting involved stakeholders together and deciding the critical questions of what these programs look like and making it happen.

In this way, the needs of major partners are reflected in the types of academic and training programs developed, curriculum and content designed, and necessary skill and knowledge areas emphasized.

Education, research, and service initiatives are supported and represented by a variety of key stakeholders (agencies, universities and colleges, the private sector, public organizations). In terms of educational partners, members are found on campuses from the University of California, California State University, California Community Colleges, County School Boards, and Private Universities. In terms of professional partners, the California Emergency Management Agency (Cal EMA) has provided grant and funding support for CEMHS. As of August 2010, CEMHS has over 525 participants drawn from academic and professional partners. IN ADDITION, presentations have been made to the United States Department of Homeland Security (DHS) and the Federal Emergency Management Agency (FEMA) Emergency Management Institute (EMI). CEMHS has worked closely with the Disaster Resistant California Community Colleges (DRCCC) group and the City of Los Angeles Emergency Management Department's EM University Consortium (LAEMUC). In addition, the International Association of Emergency Managers (IAEM) has an official liaison with CEMHS workgroups. These partnerships have been mutually beneficial and supportive and results in much feedback from colleagues in the many diverse fields contributing to crisis response management.

The California Emergency Management and Homeland Security Education and Training Strategic Initiative

Current CEMHS activity consists of preparing a strategic vision and framework to design, develop, and implement EM-HS education and training programs for K-12 and Postsecondary Education state-wide. This framework, the *California Emergency Management and Homeland Security Education and Training Strategic Initiative*, sketches an outline and blueprint to guide and develop a "vertical track" of seamless, standardized, and portable Emergency/Disaster Management and Homeland Security education and training programs at various levels of education from Training Academy through Associate, Bachelor, Master and Doctoral degrees. The benefit of the vertical

track is that students would have the opportunity for academic programs through terminal degrees. The Cal EMA has funded the development and writing of the EM-HS Strategic Initiative for 2009-10. Details of the Strategic Initiative, including mission, vision, and objectives are discussed in the following sections.

Strategic Initiative Mission and Vision

The primary mission of the *Strategic Initiative* is to design, develop, and implement a comprehensive, seamless, standardized, and coordinated 'vertical track' of emergency/disaster/crisis management education and training programs and curriculum at all stages of educational attainment (K-12 and Post-Secondary Education) to support the critical needs of key stakeholders and partners in this important subject area. The vision of the Strategic Initiative is to facilitate a collaborative partnership between public and private educational institutions to develop "standardized, seamless, and portable" education and training programs with the consultation and guidance of key partners, critical stakeholders, and Subject Matter Experts (SMEs).

Strategic Initiative Objectives

There are a variety of objectives to foster collaborative relationships and partnerships within the academic and professional community in the disaster and crisis management and help reinforce a culture of preparedness, awareness, and safety on-campus and within our communities. The primary objective of the Strategic Initiative is to provide a comprehensive and linked series of academic programs designed to meet the complexity and rigor of needs and skills to fully support the academic and professional communities for safer, more resilient, and better prepared communities.

The first objective is to develop a common understanding of crisis and disaster management education and training programs (i.e. core principles and goals found in these program; types of important knowledge, skills, and courses to include within programs and courses; and how programs are linked together to support the development of an academic culture and student support means) required to provide this important area of education and training, workforce development, and enhance operational capability. The second objective is to seek to determine current capacity (and gaps) within the EM-HS education and training programs and fill these capability gaps. This includes a discussion of the mission and vision of EM-HS education and training programs, foundational goals and types of courses/materials to teach and related values like civic engagement, development of a public service ethos, program/ course delivery methods, internships, service learning, and other auxiliary functions to support core campus academic programs throughout K-12 and Postsecondary Education.

Third, it is important to design, develop, and implement a linked network and portfolio of EM-HS programs (through various levels of educational attainment). Also to assist in matriculation and transfer opportunities among these linked programs to develop a coordinated "vertical and horizontal track" of EM-HS (and related programs) through terminal degree programs. The ultimate objective is to design a model curriculum and series of program/course templates replicable across schools, universities, and colleges to further support emergency management and homeland security education and training. This is accomplished through the development of "templates" and "best practices" for a model curriculum that details courses, content, and student learning objectives for programs and courses in this critical subject area. EM-HS program templates should be structured and designed with respect to the academic and curriculum review process of a particular campus (i.e. covering student learning outcomes, course descriptions, and relevant institutional policies).

Towards this end, a tremendous amount of courses and materials already exist within the public domain to coordinate into a workable set of organized programs easily structured and modified by respective campuses based on their program specifications and curriculum review process. In other cases where little program and course material currently exists, new programs courses, and specializations to "fill in the gaps" will be designed and built to round out EM-HS education and training programs. We need to frame the discussion of key components of the Strategic Initiative in the context of a "minimum baseline" and guidelines to enhance EM-HS academic programs.

At the end of the day, campuses should be able to utilize a template for minimum baseline requirements for whatever degree or certificate program they are interested in; add respective institutional strengths and faculty specializations, geographical location considerations, community interests; any additional requirements (a capstone or internship class) and call the program their own. Some have kindly referred to this as the "CEMHS Menu Approach" to education/training program development. The "menu approach" reference signifies that there are many different factors that educational institutions keep in mind when making the decision to build and offer various programs and courses. Some of these factors —types of program, intended student audience, anticipated demand, available resources, faculty and institutional strengths, etc. are instrumental in the decision to offer (or not) respective academic programs. Programs should be planned and designed with these factors in mind.

IMPLICATIONS AND LESSONS LEARNED

In order to "assist the development of an educated and well trained scientific and technical workforce to respond to information demands and crisis response," we link vast resources, programs, and faculty expertise together and provide education and research solutions to designing comprehensive EM-HS core and specialization programs and courses in a multiple campus consortium. Due to the many factors and components involved in academic program development (and regardless of discipline or specialization), there are four linked elements of education, teaching, research and service/humanitarian outreach implications and lessons learned in the development of information systems and crisis response academic programs. These are examples of the implications and lessons discussed in this case study.

- Primary Education Strategies
- Auxiliary and Education/Training Support
- Faculty/Student Research Opportunities
- Service/Community/Humanitarian Outreach

Primary Education Strategies

Primary education strategies involve matters of core and specialization curriculum design and development. CEMHS is developing a core curriculum and templates corresponding to various EM-HS degree and certificate programs based on "model practices" content and pedagogy and deliverable through various delivery modes (traditional, online, hybridized) and through collaborating campuses. Based on institutional and faculty interests, specializations, strategic needs; program coordination is facilitated with program coordination and key partners to develop programs to serve STEM fields (Science, Technology, Engineering, and Mathematics) needs (at the international, regional, and national levels). In addition to core curriculum, a full slate of programs that correspond with special areas of "strategic interest" or addressing specific gaps in "high needs" technology gaps should be designed and developed soon.

These specific areas of education and training are "specializations." Different specializations are found on all campuses as each campus individually develops a respective culture relating to teaching, research, and faculty/staff expertise. Campuses often collaborate and link together within the context of networks or "multi-campus" consortiums to provide these programs. Each campus in the consortium contributes to the offering of general programs as well as specializations based on important considerations like geographic location, institutional strengths, faculty/staff expertise, additional funding sources/research centers, etc. In other words, programs are blended into various levels of education, and tailored to the needs of students pursuing different educational goals, with the types of programs that institutions chose to develop and implement them.

In program areas of exceptionally high academic need, external funding sources would be utilized to support the development of critical topic areas that meet the technical and scientific needs of partners and stakeholders, like in the areas of data visualization, cryptology, communications interoperability, remote sensing and many others. There is a particular need for some types of programs to be designed and develop and guided by the needs and specifications of key stakeholders and their view of current (and future) needs of the EM-HS workforce. In addition to the development of primary education programs, there is an additional need for auxiliary support and the development of faculty and student opportunities in the areas of crisis response and management.

Auxiliary Education/Training Support and Faculty/Student Research Opportunities

Supporting the implementation of a comprehensive and coordinated education and training programs in a vertical track of academics is an initial first step. However, we must also develop educational infrastructure to assist in student and faculty success during the nascent EM-HS program development process. Without too much detail, one important factor that partially differentiates crisis/disaster management education and training from more "traditional academic pursuits" is in the operational and experiential needs and information systems management connection with international and national government agencies, NGOs, private sector, and others involved in crisis response.

It follows intuitively there must be additional linkages between agencies and academics so experiential learning environments should be developed. Linkages and partnerships include internships, field placements, career and job skill development fairs, drills, exercises, tabletops, etc. In addition to providing linkages and connections between academics and professionals in terms of experiential learning and research opportunities, there is also interest in deepening the network between professional and educational partners in the development of EM-HS academic programs at various levels of education.

Service/Community/ Humanitarian Outreach

It is important to support international disaster response and information systems through engagement of Service Learning and Civic Engagement within our communities and internationally. Commitment to community engagement should reflect in the curricula and programs designed as well as in building experiential learning networks between professionals and academicians. This could be accomplished by developing international information, academic technology, communications, and interoperability groups to coordinate disaster response with current technologies, data-analysis, and visualization capabilities to support additional student and faculty education and research opportunities. Finally, support additional collaborative efforts for education, training, research, and community outreach programs and initiatives.

Build linkages with additional public and private organizations, and tribal governments to support community outreach in EM-HS fields and promote community and campus preparedness, mental health and victim services, and enhance resiliency.

CONCLUSION

As relating to the area of information systems and crisis response, it takes many working together as a team to design, develop, and deploy technical solutions to disaster and emergency management. These experts in-training require education and training programs to reach their professional goals. We need geography and geology researchers to understand the dynamics of earthquakes and wildfires as well as utilize remote sensors and enhance GIS technology and delivery. Victim services personnel for crisis response, future educators, and squaring away educational needs for groups making valuable contributions to more resilient communities are important as well. Thus, there are a wide variety of knowledge and skill areas to deliver efficiently and effectively. Many of these key curriculum decisions relate to the educational learning objectives promulgated by the specific program under design and development.

Workable and feasible "real-life" programs are needed to improve access, availability, and quality education programs in information systems crisis response. One important case study theme is an interest to develop and enhance education, training, and research programs. These programs, courses, and curriculum should be designed with the input and feedback of agencies and professionals (state, federal, local) and private-sector partners regarding necessary skills and knowledge areas required for mastery in these critical subject areas. In addition, these academically rigorous programs and courses must be fitted seamlessly so that students can sequence from training/vocational academy through community college and bachelors and masters degree programs. Various modes of effective program and course delivery are also explored (traditional courses, asynchronous delivery, hybrid/blended models, etc.) There are many necessary details to discuss in the process of designing and developing EM-HS academic programs.

There has generally been a low level of coordination and integration of educational resources and programs towards the development of a comprehensive national or state-wide solution for education and training programs. The boundaries of the field, programs, and courses require additional development and specification related to curriculum, content, and program delivery methods. Academicians and professionals should collaborate to develop a "common understanding" of important principles and subject area content to design quality EM-HS education and training programs that meet the needs of both communities. In closing, one purpose of this case study is to provide guidance and information on designing

and developing education programs that promote preparedness and response and reflect sound crisis and disaster management principles and "best practices." This gives us pause to consider themes like how information systems and crisis management should be reflected in post-secondary education programs and course content. It is important to build programs that speak to the critical relationship between information, technology, and how to apply these to crisis response situations that occur across the globe.

REFERENCES

Davies, P.(199). What is Evidence-Based Education? *British Journal of Educational Studies*, *47*(2), 108–121. doi:10.1111/1467-8527.00106

IAEM. (2007). *Principles of Emergency Management*. Retrieved August 10, 2010, from http://www.iaem.com/EMPrinciples/documents/PrinciplesofEmergencyManagement.pdf

This work was previously published in International Journal of Information Systems for Crisis Response Management, Volume 2, Issue 3, edited by Murray E. Jennex, pp. 51-60, copyright 2010 by IGI Publishing (an imprint of IGI Global).

Chapter 14
A Methodology for Inter-Organizational Emergency Management Continuity Planning

John Lindström
Luleå University of Technology, Sweden

Dan Harnesk
Luleå University of Technology, Sweden

Elina Laaksonen
Luleå University of Technology, Sweden

Marko Niemimaa
Luleå University of Technology, Sweden

ABSTRACT

This paper extends emergency management literature by developing a methodology for emergency management continuity planning (EmCP). In particular, the methodology focuses on inter-organizational continuous and coordinated planning among emergency management organizations. The authors draw on Soft Systems Methodology (Checkland & Scholes, 1999; Checkland, 2000), using it as a base for better understanding of EmCP. Barriers that must be overcome before the methodology can be introduced and established, as well as potential benefits, are also discussed.

INTRODUCTION

This paper introduces a methodology for achieving continuous and coordinated inter-organizational planning among emergency management organizations. How such planning arrangements can work in inter-organizational settings is far from clear, since networked organizations often lack a single authority coordinating common activities (Capaldo, 2007). Comfort (2005) concludes that there is a need to change the standard practice of today towards building networks of emergency

DOI: 10.4018/978-1-4666-0167-3.ch014

management organizations committed to a continuous process of improvement and learning, and Dynes (2000) further proposes that in the future there should be a concern for all types of hazards and that this concern needs to be built into organizations. Harrald (2006) adds that critical success factors are pre-planned inter-organizational planning and organizational learning. As observed by Harrald (2006), what is not addressed in emergency management literature is how planning in between organizations involved in emergency management can be accomplished. In addition, the planning in between organizations involved in emergency management is often kept on too low a level of intensity and is also most likely to occur after an emergency to evaluate the past event, instead of being proactive and continuous. The key issue addressed in the paper is how to achieve a continuous and coordinated planning among emergency management organizations working together at the regional and local level. As a possible way to address this, the paper introduces a methodology for inter-organizational emergency management planning on a strategic level, also taking into account the continuity aspect.

The Soft Systems Methodology developed by Peter Checkland and his colleagues is used in the paper to conceptualize EmCP and bridge business continuity planning and emergency management adapting the methodology to the emergency management context. In addition, the potential use of the proposed methodology is discussed in the light of research on Hurricane Katrina by Comfort (2007) and Comfort *et al.* (2010).

The rest of this conceptual paper is structured according to, firstly, a literature review of selected contributions within business continuity planning, soft systems methodology and emergency management (including a synthesis of ideas into a concept where the methodology is needed). This is followed by a section on the methodology for inter-organizational emergency management continuity planning and, finally, a discussion and conclusions.

BUSINESS CONTINUITY PLANNING CHALLENGES

Butler and Gray (2006) state that the theoretical aspects of business continuity planning are underdeveloped in IS literature and influenced by professionals articulating how and why organizations should prepare for unexpected events. Further, Tierney (2006) adds that businesses have only recently begun to be studied as units of analysis in disaster research, and systematic research on different business continuity matters is lacking, despite the importance of businesses for society. Influenced by related research from, for instance, disruption risk management, supply chain management and disruptive events like 9/11, a more networked focus is emerging involving parts of the network (or eco-system) around the organization and its processes (Verstraete, 2004; Hiles, 2007; Bajgoric, 2008). Having both an organizational and inter-organizational focus is for many organizations important, as their processes often are not just dependent on what the own organization does but also on what the other organizations, i.e. business partners, part of the processes, do or do not do. Thus, an organization's business continuity planning activities are commonly also to a varying degree involved in their business partners' ditto activities.

Efforts with business continuity planning in dynamic environments commonly need to have both an organizational and networked focus. Business continuity planning seeks to reduce or eliminate impacts of serious events or disaster conditions before they occur (Cerullo & Cerullo, 2004). As stipulated by regulatory or legal requirements, many organizations must develop a business continuity plan based on their unique situation. A business continuity plan should be dynamic and evolve as the business environment changes and as dependencies on technology, suppliers/business partners, etc. change (Cerullo & Cerullo, 2004). This allows an organization to cope with events or conditions that are inflicted by internal or external causes. Further, Lam (2002) prescribes that during the design of a business continuity plan, an organization needs to identify and engage potential business continuity partners. Verstraete (2004) adds that if one supplier or business partner is unable to deliver what is required, planning should have prepared alternatives that can be quickly established and used. In addition, Bajgoric (2008) underlines that partners or service providers, etc. should be investigated and assessed regarding capabilities, financial power, reputation, methods of risk management, and also that any influence of outsourcing needs to be examined. Verstraete (2004) remarks that organizations with their own processes under control, but operating in an ad hoc manner with their partners, will have a larger latency compared to if they have joint agreements with their partners to address change. A lack of a predefined approach for addressing change is a strong barrier to agility. Within business continuity planning, different types of inter-organizational agreements are used to coordinate and maintain a level of continuity. The agreements cover how to manage any changes that can affect important aspects of the business continuity level in the business network (Doughty, 2001; Hiles, 2007; Roberts, 2006).

Wylder (2004) suggests that the top management and the CEO need to be involved in the business continuity planning efforts, and that such planning should be regarded as a strategic matter. Further, Wylder (2004) adds that a CEO reports to an organization's board on preparations for risk management and how to react to events that are outside of the normal course of business. Verstraete (2004) states that responsible organizations not only have their business processes well established across their eco-systems, but further also proactively look at how to react in case of disruptive events. To reduce the latency, scenario planning methodologies are recommended. According to Verstraete (2004), one way to reduce the time it takes for planning and implementing change is to proactively establish an office that is responsible for planning, tracking the implementations of change, and developing the necessary strong communication channels.

Business continuity planning is often questioned by top management, since many managers believe they are already able to cope with serious events or conditions affecting the organization, and that the probability of events occurring is low to impossible (Smith, 2004). This is one of the main barriers, as a lack of top management support makes business continuity planning less important, and its results less likely to be taken up and used by the organization. Further, business continuity planning is placed in a tough spot by the minimization of testing and maintenance efforts (Cerullo & Cerullo, 2004). This is evident in a survey conducted by Ernst & Young (2002), which reveals that critical business systems were increasingly interrupted and that some 75 percent of organizations world-wide had experienced partial or full unplanned availability problems.

Thus, there are a number of challenges regarding business continuity planning. As mentioned above, one is to keep up with dynamics or changes in the eco-systems surrounding the own organization and its critical business processes, and another is to actually keep the maintenance process of the business continuity framework going to respond to changes and dynamics in the business environments as well as to new risks (Lindström, 2009).

SOFT SYSTEMS METHODOLOGY

Soft Systems Methodology (SSM), developed by Peter Checkland and his colleagues, has been widely used to make sense of problematic management situations and to manage change (Checkland, 2000). However, within research in business continuity planning, emergency management and other closely related areas, SSM has been applied to only a limited degree. Despite the volume, prior research has identified that SSM holds a great deal of promise to manage non-structured problems in strategic work (Wang & Wu, 2008) and to support multi-agency planning (Gregory & Midgley, 2000), as well as showing the usefulness of SSM in crisis management planning (Srijaj & Khisty, 1999). Additionally, the possible value of systems ideas has been noted in the emergency (crisis) management literature (Borodzicz, 2005; Sriraj & Khisty, 1999; Wang & Wu, 2008). Furthermore, Lang and Allen (2008) argue that ideas from SSM can inform scenario practice of long-term, strategic future direction of an organization. We think that a systemic approach provides an efficient way to coordinate inter-organizational emergency management planning. The planning can be continuously improved when an inter-organizational emergency management network is seen as a system sharing a common goal. The network benefits from having a holistic view over the system and from the emergent properties of the system, where the whole is greater than the sum of its individual parts (Wilson, 2001).

SSM is a mature and well-established methodology (Checkland & Winter, 2006; Mingers & White, in press) reflecting upon systems ideas (Checkland, 2000). SSM encourages a holistic and rigorous approach to make sense of and to continuously manage (social) situations perceived as problematical (Checkland & Poulter, 2006). It is a set of methods and principles (Checkland, 2000; Checkland *et al.*, 2000; Checkland & Winter, 2006) and an organized way (Wilson, 2001) of tackling messy, ill-structured real-world situations (Checkland, 2000; Checkland & Poulter, 2006). Although SSM has been criticized (Bergvall-Kåreborn, 2002; Basden & Wood-Harper, 2006), it is widely used (Mingers & White, in press).

Central to SSM is to view real-world problem situations involving human actors as complex and messy (Checkland, 2000), whilst the process of thinking about the real world can be simple, precise and defensible (Wilson, 2001). In the 'classic' form, the methodology includes seven stages (Checkland, 1999), but has evolved into a more flexible 'inquiring/learning cycle' where

relevant models of purposeful activity are used to structure the debate about situations perceived as problematical (Checkland, 2000). The desired outcome is to improve the situation (Checkland, 2000). A cyclic learning process enriches thinking about the situation and brings new perspectives to the situation, opening up room for innovation and improvement (Checkland *et al.*, 2000). The foundation for the innovation and improvement is to "lift the thinking in the situation out of its normal, unnoticed, comfortable grooves" (Checkland, 2000, p. 21), a shift from defining something that exists in the real world to making models of what might be (Checkland *et al.*, 2000). Through different analyses, the ambiguities of cultural and political aspects regarding the problem situation are considered holistically (Checkland, 2000), aiming to find systematically desirable and culturally feasible change (Checkland, 2000).

To define purposeful activity (Checkland, 2000) and to ensure a systemic nature of the modeling process (Srijaj & Khisty, 1999), the method's root definition (RD) and mnemonic CATWOE will be used in our conceptual ideas in the following section. The root definition defines what the system is by answering to the questions "what to do", "how to do it" and "why to do it", while CATWOE aims at capturing the essence of a particular purposeful activity system (Checkland, 2000) by defining C (Customers), A (Actors), T (Transformation process), W (Weltanschauung), O (Owner(s)) and E (Environmental constrains) of the system The environmental constraints are "*elements outside the system which it takes as given*" (Checkland & Scholes, 1999, p. 35) and should be constraints that seldom change (Basden & Wood-Harper, 2006). However, Mingers (1992) has noted that important constraints are overlooked, as there is a tendency to focus on very general constraints. He suggested the Environmental constraints to detail the surrounding wider system in which the system under inspection exists. Bergvall-Kåreborn *et al.* (2004) have instead suggested the Environmental constraints to include "constraints that the system needs to take as given, determinative and normative, external and internal." (p. 69). We will in our paper follow Minger's and Bergvall-Kåreborn's insights regarding the Environmental constraints.

In summary, SSM offers a methodological approach and a set of methods to deal with human activity in ill-structured problem situations that can be applied both flexibly and adjusted to the given area of interest (Checkland & Scholes, 1999; Checkland *et al.*, 2000).

TOWARDS EMERGENCY MANAGEMENT CONTINUITY PLANNING (EMCP)

Drabek (2006) points out five areas within emergency management for future research that are more critical than the others: "(1) development of a theory of disaster response effectiveness; (2) development of a theory of emergency management; (3) cross-national studies of complex catastrophes; (4) impacts and limitations of information technologies; (5) assessments of alternative managerial models" (p230). Drabek's fifth area is emphasized by Comfort (2007), who argues based on the experiences from Hurricane Katarina that the standard model of emergency management collapsed. Further, Comfort (2005) concludes that building networks of organizations committed to a process of continuous inquiry, informed action, and adaptive learning help to build a more flexible and robust strategy compared to standard practice. Standard practice commonly tries to establish control over possible threats through administrative structures. We think that a committed inter-organizational administrative structure, of which the objective is to achieve a continuous and coordinated planning on strategic level, is a way to address the issue. However, the level of commitment and ability to adapt and change are, as in most cases, a maker or breaker.

Our conventional thinking regarding crisis management policy and capabilities has, according to Kouzmin *et al.* (1995) and Kaufmann (1991), been made obsolete by the process of change. Kouzmin *et al.* (1995) further note the importance of improving inter-organizational relationships with respect to, for instance, coordination, organizational structures used and bureaucracy during uncertainty. Centralization of decision-making during a crisis has serious drawbacks, meaning that alternative ways are needed to later avoid ad hoc problem-solving and decision-making (Kouzmin *et al.*, 1995). Canton (2007, p. 190) states that "a plan is never more than a snapshot of an organization's intent at a specific point in time. Many plans are out of date almost as soon as published" and argues that it is better to focus on coordination. In addition, Ritchie (2004) notes that it is important in an organization to prepare for controlling and managing complex crisis situations in a more effective manner by using proactive planning to reduce risk, time waste, poor resource management and impacts from crises that arise. We think that many of these ideas could be used in an inter-organizational setting to improve coordinated planning and add proactive ways of thinking.

Enhanced efforts on integration and coordination are required to complement existing emergency management capabilities (Bhimaraya, 2006). Improvisation, adaptability and creativity are further nonstructural factors critical to coordination, collaboration, communication, and problem-solving in disaster response (Harrald, 2006). Harrald (2006) posits that discipline (structures, doctrine and process) and agility (creativity, improvisation and adaptability) form orthogonal dimensions that must be achieved during the design of organizational systems for emergency response. Further, Hocevar *et al.* (2006) suggest using Galbraith's framework for organizational design to build inter-organizational collaborative capacity to find and deal with inter-organizational barriers. Wilson and Oyola-Yemaiel (2001) and Canton (2007) argue that this requires a professionalization of emergency management regarding roles, definitions, structures and processes of certification/accreditation of programs. We agree that an increased level of professionalism is required, even among the (professional) emergency management organizations, to be able to design for successful inter-organizational planning.

Methods of network analysis, computational simulations, information structure, long-term policy goals and network strategies offer important alternatives to hierarchical structures that prove vulnerable in certain environments (Comfort, 2005). Further, Comfort (2005) points out that in the USA after 2000, FEMA and a number of federal agencies started to coordinate consequence management and plan for emergency support functions in an inter-organizational coordination effort. Later, developments were also initiated by the US Department of Homeland Security. Parts of this effort included looking at the logic of uncertainty regarding after-action reviews, improvement of decision-making under stress, understanding of order versus chaos and action models. Additionally, Turoff et al. (2004) suggest a status measure, Emergency Preparedness (EP), which can be used by any organization. We consider EP as important and possible to augment to also include inter-organizational coordination aspects for emergency management organizations. Using something like EP would highlight the need for preparedness and give it the status necessary for its fulfillment.

Other identified ways to address planning issues include planning models, integrated approaches, scenario methodology, games and strategic forecasting. Dynes (1990) supports planning models for disaster management that also incorporate conceptual efforts towards anticipating situations where planners have little or no experience, using only conventional wisdom from experiences. Dynes (2000) adds that more adequate models of disaster management emphasize the capacity of communities to maintain a considerable continuity in their pre-disaster activities, whereas today a lot of the models focus, instead, on response. In addition to Dynes' view of maintaining a consid-

erable continuity in pre-disaster activities, Moe and Pathranarakul (2006) propose an integrated approach to disaster management using a combination of proactive and reactive strategies for successful and effective management of disasters. We consider this combination crucial for developing the management of emergency.

Alexander (2000) concludes that using scenario methodology is useful in developing skills regarding time management, cognitive mapping, team management and decision-making under stress. Additionally, Ringland (1998) stresses that perhaps the greatest use of scenario methodology has been to facilitate planning, and Turoff et al. (2005) suggest crisis planning via scenario development using gaming. Using gaming increases the ability to cope with the unfamiliar and unexpected in the planning process, to find new insights and reflections. Foster (1980) states that within emergency management a scenario is a postdictive reconstruction of past events or hypothetical future ones, looking for answers to "what happened" or "what if". The use of future scenarios and gaming can both be seen as acting proactively, but gaming can also be used to enhance learning from past events and, i.e. enhance reactive acting. In addition, Foster (1980) affirms that it is necessary to investigate outcomes of hazard impacts, or reactions to these, that can lead to probable consequences. Even though Foster's insights are a bit dated, they are still most valid and useful. Kash and Darling (1998) favor strategic forecasting of events using trends. The scenario analysis involves consideration of favorable and unfavorable situations that can arise and alternatives for preventing or thwarting what is causing the situations.

An Emergency Management Continuity Planning Concept

Although the literature points to the need to achieve a continuous and coordinated planning on a strategic level among emergency management organizations that need to work together, it offers little guidance on how to address this need. To move towards an emergency management with continuity and coordination in the inter-organizational planning, informed by the SSM (Checkland & Scholes, 1999; Checkland, 2000), the following EmCP concept (see Figure 1) synthesizes ideas from emergency management (mainly Dynes, (1990, 2000) on usage of conceptual efforts without experience and continuity in pre-disaster activities, Comfort (2005) on building networks committed to a continuous process of improvement, and Harrald (2006) on preplanned inter-organizational coordination) and business continuity planning (using inter-organizational agreements coordinating changes in relationships within the business network (Verstraete, 2004; Baijgoric, 2008). Thus, Emergency Management and Business Continuity Planning becomes Emergency Management Continuity Planning (or EmCP).

To form and maintain inter-organizational relationships (or networks) in between organizations is an important task for emergency management organizations (Comfort, 2005). Working in an ad hoc manner with others does not necessarily lead to a bad result in terms of planning, but it is more likely that a well-considered and joint way to plan will produce better results over time, making it non-dependent on specific personal relationships, etc. Figure 1 describes a common

emergency management process with the "real-world" phases: 'Before', 'During' and 'After'. There is a feedback loop from the 'After' phase leading to the "systems thinking about the real world" where there is an 'Evaluate' phase with a following 'Update' phase of the existing emergency management framework also generating input for training and practicing. In the 'Evaluate' phase, the collected feedback on the emergency management framework and summary of acting and actions during the emergency are evaluated. Without the suggested additional EmCP concept in between the 'Evaluate' and 'Update' phases, the after-action review would mainly cover actual events that have occurred leading to improvement in the 'Update' phase. Two problems related to an emergency management process are that it is hard to maintain a continuous and proactive updating of the emergency management framework, and further that most input to the updating only comes from real emergencies in past time (i.e. the after-action reviews). After-action review is a commonly used method to improve the existing emergency management framework. We suggest that, to anticipate and cover more risks than experienced, both real emergency scenarios and hypothetical scenarios should be used to develop the emergency management framework. In addition, to be able to maintain the continuity of the inter-organizational

Figure 1. Emergency management process with feedback loop

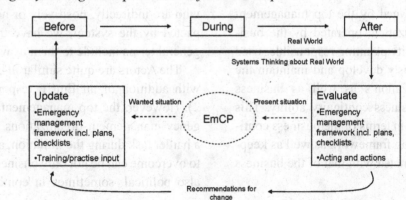

planning in between organizations, the proposed EmCP concept can be used to extend or integrate the 'Evaluate' and 'Update' phases (or, i.e. "the systems thinking about the real world") with other organizations. To support the EmCP concept, emergency management information systems used can be enhanced by incorporating knowledge management tools and concepts to get better coordination and decision-making during the response as well as for training and inclusion of knowledge from other sources (Murhpy & Jennex, 2006).

SSM Contribution to the EmCP Concept

We use the CATWOE elements to identify similarities between two contexts, thus extending the use of CATWOE analysis. In the analysis, root definitions can be used to express the core purpose of a purposeful activity system (Checkland & Scholes, 1990). Below, we state root definitions later used to derive the CATWOE elements for each respective context. In this way, we use the SSM methods to connect the ideas from business continuity planning to the EmCP concept.

Business continuity planning, which can be considered as informed or influenced by theories like 'disruption risk management', 'supply chain management', 'operations management', 'organizational routines' and 'narrative networks', etc., can have a root definition formulated as:

- A system owned by the top management in an organization, operated by the business continuity planning responsible, used to continuously develop and maintain the own organization's as well as business partners' business continuity ability. This is embodied in terms of the business continuity planning framework as well as keeping it coordinated with that of the business partners.

A root definition for the EmCP concept can be formulated from the problem and concept description as:

- A system owned by emergency management organizations, operated by emergency management responsible roles, used to continuously develop and evaluate past and hypothetical emergency scenarios in order to maintain the coordination of emergency management frameworks in between these organizations on a strategic level.

To view how the SSM has informed the EmCP concept and its methodology, Tables 1 through 6 show how the SSM CATWOE elements from Checkland and Scholes (1990) are derived from the above and formulated for a business continuity planning as well as an EmCP context.

The difference between the business continuity planning and EmCP contexts is that, in the latter, emergency management organizations care for Customers with or without an already existing relation, whereas in the former organizations care only when there is an existing relation. This difference makes it harder for emergency management organizations, as they need to operate with often unknown and unprepared Customers. The organizations themselves in the respective context both need to prepare for the expected as well as the unexpected. Since Bergvall-Kåreborn *et al.* (2004) state that the Customers should not be too narrowly defined, but should also include those who are indirectly, positively or negatively impacted by the system, we have tried in rather general terms include to them as well.

The Actors are quite similar in both contexts, with addition of an EmCP responsible (Table 2). However, the top management in the emergency management organizations probably has a harder task during the initiation, as the barriers to overcome can be not only business-logical but also political, sometimes in combination with

Table 1. SSM CATWOE elements used and mapped onto the EmCP concept (C – Customers)

CATWOE (definitions from Checkland & Scholes,]1990, p. 35)	CATWOE elements formulated for a business continuity planning context	CATWOE elements formulated for an EmCP context
C – customers: the victims or beneficiaries of Transformation process	An organization together with its business partners (customers, suppliers or other partners).	The emergency management organizations as well as those that in the end are helped by these organizations like the public or other organizations are those affected and beneficial of the methodology.

unfamiliarity with other organizations, inadequate communication and information sharing (Hocevar *et al.*, 2006). Important to take into consideration, according to Bergvall-Kåreborn *et al.* (2004), is to not only look at 'who would do Transformation process' but also that those persons have adequate competencies to carry out the actions needed "especially when working together in cross-disciplinary teams" (Basden & Wood-Harper, 2006, p. 63).

The Transformation process for the EmCP context is augmented using ideas from the business continuity planning context (and the SSM) (Table 3). Here the contribution is large from the business continuity planning context. Like Mathiassen and Nielsen (2000) and Bergvall-Kåreborn *et al.* (2004), we consider the Transformation process, to be an ongoing complex process instead of a discrete goal-directed transformation with defined input and output, since the output can be in many forms, leading to change or im-

provements in the emergency management framework, or as input to training/practice.

The Weltanschauungs making the Transformation process meaningful are not as different as they look in the same direction, although different words are used (Table 4). For instance, Checkland and Scholes (1999) and Wilson (2001) suggest that more than one Weltanschauung can be used if multiple CATWOEs are used to define the purposeful system. However, here, we view each system using a single Weltanschauung and use two CATWOEs, i.e. one for the business continuity planning and one for the EmCP context.

Similarly, the cases for the respective Owners are not very different (Table 5). A problem with ownership in public organizations is that the ownership resides in several places (Basden & Wood-Harper, 2006), and is not always crystal clear. This is also evident in our derivations of the Owner, or i.e. that there is not just one 'owner' but many, where we also focus more on author-

Table 2. SSM CATWOE elements used and mapped onto the EmCP concept (A – Actors)

CATWOE	...bus. cont. planning context	...EmCP context
A – actors: those who would do Transformation process	There are plenty of roles and competences that must be involved, for instance: top management, business continuity planners and responsible roles, IT/IS, critical process owners, departments involved in the critical processes etc. Further, some liaison officers or business continuity planning responsible roles at the business partners also need to be involved as the business continuity planning spans beyond the own organization's boundaries. If additional measures or competences are needed at the partner organizations, more roles need to be involved.	In the emergency management organizations there are plenty of roles and competences that need to be involved, but in the actual work after the initial set up the EmCP responsible roles and evaluators/planners have key roles in the "transformation process". The top managements of the respective organizations also have key roles in the inception phase, policy making as well as to give the necessary support over time.

Table 3. SSM CATWOE elements used and mapped onto the EmCP concept (T – Transformation process)

CATWOE	...bus. cont. planning context	...EmCP context
T – transformation process: the conversion of input to output	The transformation process is commonly described in a business continuity planning framework, using first an initial process to build it up and then continuing with a maintenance process. These processes can use the methodology described in Lindström *et al.* (2010).	The transformation process, the Evaluate and Update phases, is augmented by the proposed EmCP concept including the methodology found in following section. See Figure 1 for specific input and output parameters.

ity and responsibility than actual ownership of the system (Bergvall-Kåreborn *et al.*, 2004).

The Environmental constraints for the respective contexts have a lot in common but have different influencing elements, factors and barriers (Table 6). The EmCP context also borrows the idea of having a common policy (or some sort of agreement) for the emergency management organizations involved. Basden and Wood-Harper (2006) mean that it is hard to differentiate between which constraints to accept or which can be changed, in dynamic situations or environments. We have tried to cover the most influential constraints both within and surrounding the system, as using only the outside ones may overlook important constraints (Wilson, 2001).

Regarding the question 'when is the CATWOE final?', we have used the CATWOE as an intellectual device to enrich our structured thinking,

reaching a level where we think it is saturated. We do not find any immediate use for another CATWOE using a different Weltanschauung, which could have been different if the research team had had members with a more diverse background and experiences.

Thus, we find a number of implications for the EmCP concept from business continuity planning resulting from using parts of the SSM methodology. Selected implications are as follows:

- SSM gives a holistic view of the system as well as assuring that both CATWOEs are on the same system level (Lang & Allen, 2008). Lang and Allen (2008) discuss scenario planning and how elements in scenarios can be leveled, achieved by using the CATWOE, which contributes to consistency among scenarios.

Table 4. SSM CATWOE elements used and mapped onto the EmCP concept (W – Weltanscha-uung)

CATWOE	...bus. cont. planning context	...EmCP context
W – Weltanscha-uung: the world view which makes this Transformation process meaningful in context	The world view that makes the transformation process meaningful/useful in a business continuity planning context is first of all legal and regulatory requirements on due diligence/care for many organizations, as well as their ability to continue their business operations (critical processes) at almost any situation or event. This might require cooperation and coordination with business partners under stress (or in distress). Thus, the world view is strongly colored by top management interests. Positive side effects from the planning are less complexity and increased transparency regarding processes, business partner network confidence and preparedness for managing problems or crises, etc.	The world view that makes the transformation process meaningful/useful in an emergency management context is a view of that better inter-organizational coordination and continuity among emergency management organizations renders higher proactivity, as well as efficacy, efficiency and effectiveness over time. The public also requires a good and coordinated emergency management service/process, independent of which emergency management organizations needed to be involved in a specific accident, etc. It is in the interest of the top management to develop and maintain relations and an ability to work with other emergency management organizations. Working in an "EmCP manner" can increase the trust/confidence from the public.

Table 5. SSM CATWOE elements used and mapped onto the EmCP concept (O – Owners)

CATWOE	...bus. cont. planning context	...EmCP context
O – owner(s): those who could stop Transformation process	Able to stop (or limit) the transformation process are primarily the owners, board and top management of the respective organization, but the other roles involved within the organization as well as at business partners can also stop or hinder the transformation process.	Able to stop (or limit) the transformation process are primarily the governing body, board and top managements of the respective organization, but the EmCP responsible or evaluators/planners in an organization can also stop or hinder the transformation process.

- SSM provides a structured way of analyzing stakeholders and their roles/impact, requirements, conversion/transformation process, constraints and impacting factors, etc.
- Pertaining to the CATWOE, the most significant contributions to the EmCP concept from the business continuity planning are from the Actors/Transformation process/Environmental constraints elements.

The tables show that SSM is useful to structure the thinking on system level and its elements, and how the elements impact or are affected – as well as to learn if the ideas are relevant for the context or not. Further use of the SSM in the EmCP concept is the "real-world/systems thinking about real world".

A METHODOLOGY FOR INTER-ORGANIZATIONAL EMCP

In the previous section on SSM, where the root definitions are formulated and CATWOEs are analyzed, we use the SSM and CATWOE to bridge the business continuity planning and EmCP contexts by showing that they have a lot of elements in common.

The proposed EmCP concept ensures that all involved organizations are on the same level and know each others' frameworks to such an extent that efficient collaboration is facilitated during emergencies. New or hypothetical scenarios on a strategic level can in the concept be used on a continuous basis (not just after events) to find weaknesses in the existing emergency management frameworks and come up with input to training/practice for emergency management personnel. Further, the actual evaluation and up-

Table 6. SSM CATWOE elements used and mapped onto the EmCP concept (E – Environmental constraints)

CATWOE	...bus. cont. planning context	...EmCP context
E – environmental constraints: elements outside the system which it takes as given. Internal and external ones (Bergvall-Kåreborn, 2002). The surrounding wider system (Mingers, 1992) (where there are elements of importance that are possible / not possible to affect or control) is also considered here	Internal elements taken as given are top management and board expectations on progression. External elements are business partners and in particular customers expecting both progression but also an adequate level of preparedness at all times. That other business partner organizations keep their business continuity planning frameworks up to date. This requires finding a common (mutual) interest to overcome personal, organizational, contractual etc. barriers. A business continuity agreement, or making that as a formal part of business agreements, among the business partners ensures the engagement and dedication.	Internal elements taken as given in the EmCP concept are top management and board expectations on progression. Elements given outside of the concept that can be seen as given are the public, organizations and politicians that require top performance from a tight budget as well as continuous progression. In the environment outside the concept, there are also plenty of elements, factors or barriers that can impact. In the text above, for instance Comfort (2007), Hocevar *et al.* (2006), Cummings (1984) and Harrald (2006) have brought up a number of those. To manage some of these, the EmCP concept proposes to have a common policy stating how it all should be initiated, operated and maintained.

date phases can be seen as training on planning for the personnel involved.

Comfort (2007) defines coordination, as "aligning one's actions with those of other relevant actors and organizations to achieve a shared goal" (p. 194). She states further that coordination requires the participating actors to align their activities voluntarily, to avoid coercion and "free riders". A facilitating factor to get the inter-organizational collaboration working in the EmCP concept is to have a common policy stating that the emergency planning frameworks shall be continuously maintained, that necessary information will be shared, and that parties responsible for this on a strategic level in all involved organizations will be designated. Thus, there is a need for an "emergency management responsible" or an "EmCP responsible" role (Hocevar *et al.* (2006) suggest having a coordination committee or liaison officer) in all organizations involved working together. This challenge should be elevated to a strategic level above the individual organizations working inter-organizationally.

Hocevar *et al.* (2006) have identified barriers for inter-organizational collaboration such as: lack of familiarity with other organizations, inadequate communication and information sharing, etc. that need to be managed to build collaborative capacity. Earlier, Cummings (1984) lists these as indicators of problems in "under-designed" systems, and in these systems institutional mechanisms for coor-

dination in inter-organizational relationships are unlikely to exist or are underdeveloped (Hocevar *et al.*, 2006). Thus, the EmCP concept will not work unless there is a vision for cooperation, leadership, budget, responsibility and accountability.

A methodology for the work in the EmCP concept is needed to support and ensure a proper continuous and long-term maintenance of all the different emergency management frameworks that potentially are involved in the management of emergencies. If no common methodology is used, instead relying on varying methods, ad hoc engagements or measures, the value added from the relationships is likely to be smaller compared to using a common methodology. This methodology can/should be used both within the individual organizations and for the work on inter-organizational level. A methodology for such purposes in Business Continuity Planning has been developed by Lindström *et al.* (2010) and is below adapted for an emergency management context.

Figure 2 shows a staircase or capability maturity model regarding EmCP capabilities. The advantage of using a staircase or capability maturity model is that it is a commonly known methodology concept and can be adapted to most organizations. An organization starts at the bottom of the staircase and climbs upwards using the proposed methodology according to the dashed arrow. The dotted arrows are "situations" which are events that can develop into a crisis. The length of

Figure 2. High level staircase or capability maturity methodology

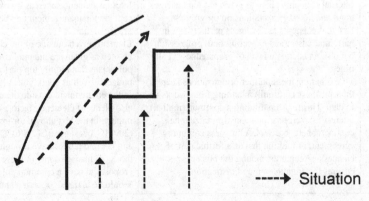

-----▶ Situation

the situations symbolizes increased severity, and thus the higher up in the staircase an organization resides, the more severe situations can be managed without going into a crisis. As it addresses certain measures, an organization climbs upwards a step at a time, gradually improving its ability to manage situations. Having climbed one step, an organization will be able to manage a situation that could have developed into a crisis, had the measures not been taken. The more steps that are climbed, the better an organization will be able to handle increasingly severe situations without ending up with an unmanageable crisis. Conversely, if the EmCP measures are not maintained and kept updated, the organization will start to roll down the staircase and not have the same ability to manage situations anymore.

Figure 3 is a more detailed version of Figure 2. Using the methodology can help increase an organization's maturity level regarding emergency management, both internally and inter-organizationally. The inter-organizational aspect is of great concern according to Comfort (2005), who argues for networked strategies and long-term policy goals as alternatives to hierarchical structures proven vulnerable in uncertain environments. The methodology, which can be seen as part of a networked strategy using a coordinative policy,

can be summarized briefly in an emergency management context as:

1. Set objectives and limitations
2. Process analysis, pinpoint critical parts and deadlines, etc.
3. Resource analysis – what is needed in the process(es), are all resources available when needed (or how long before available)
4. Risk analysis and assessment, impact analysis, risk mitigation planning
5. Development of emergency management plan and a maintenance plan
6. Implementation, tests and training
7. EmCP maintenance process start up (continuous)

where step 7 intends to keep all results achieved during the previous steps 1-6 up-to-date, as well as to further, on a continuous basis, develop the overall emergency management framework. In steps 4 and 5, gaming, scenario methodology or other ways to look at both past and hypothetical events are recommended to be used to get a mix of acting proactively and reactively. If needed, the methodology can be extended with more steps or measures needed. The methodology is

Figure 3. Staircase methodology applied on inter-organizational level

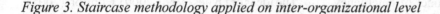
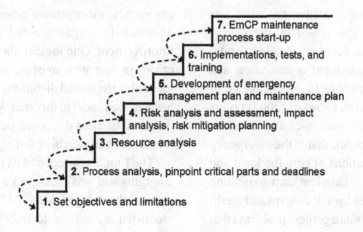

in agreement with Carley and Harrald's (1997, p. 310) statement "by changing, by adapting, organizations should be able to better respond to future disasters".

If emergency management organizations use the methodology internally as well as on an inter-organizational strategic level continually, both the intensity of the work and the inter-organizational maturity level will likely rise considerably.

The methodology is based on improving and maintaining the processes involved in the actual management of emergencies as well as the emergency management framework itself. To do both, requires effort, resources, and management involvement and support. Harrald (2006) brings up critical success factors such as pre-planned inter-organizational coordination and identified stakeholders for the preparation and prevention phase, and notes that organizational learning is achieved in the transition/demobilization phase. The EmCP concept addresses these factors on a strategic level. Further, Weick (1998) uses the term "mindfulness" describing organizations' culture and ability to detect, respond to and manage the unexpected earlier and swiftly. We think that the EmCP concept embraces "mindfulness" starting on a strategic level and, hopefully, also spilling over on tactical and operative levels.

As earlier mentioned, Comfort (2007) argues, based on the experiences from Hurricane Katrina, that the standard model of emergency management collapsed. "The failure was not a lack of communication.... Rather the issue was the cognition of the risk posed by the storm" (p. 190) and a gap in between detailed formal plans used by a hierarchical organization and actual practice. To improve the performance of emergency management, Comfort (2007) favors cognition in addition to communication, coordination and control. We think that if the emergency management organizations at both the local and regional levels in Louisiana had used something similar to the proposed EmCP concept and methodology, many of the management problems that

occurred could have been avoided. What could have been improved, for instance, is encouragement of proactive thinking (addressing cognition and communication i.e. to recognize the degree of emerging risk a community is exposed to and to communicate and act on that information) and coordinated and continuous inter-organizational planning among the involved emergency management organizations (addressing coordination and control). Comfort *et al.* (2010) contend that the recovery process in New Orleans is struggling from a lack of a clear policy and administrative processes supported by professional administrative practice. The recovery planning is part of step 5 in our proposed methodology, and thus it is applicable for this purpose too.

To summarize, the EmCP concept and its methodology can be used to augment an existing emergency management process to extend and integrate the Evaluate and Update phases with other organizations. The outcome from doing this can be that risks in addition to those experienced are analyzed/mitigated and that the continuity of inter-organizational planning is maintained, increasing the maturity level of the emergency management organizations.

DISCUSSION

The ideas of Dynes (1990, 2000), Comfort (2005), Harrald (2006) and other mentioned work within emergency management research points out a direction for organizational development and improvement. One logical question is why more effort, in line with existing sound and feasible ideas plus suggested directions of needed change, has not been spent in this area. We suspect that the potential barriers discussed below have affected this, at least in practical settings.

The EmCP concept and its methodology have strengths and weaknesses like any other concept and methodology. Many of the weaknesses identified are related to the barriers to initially implementing them, and these barriers are further discussed below. However, we believe that the strengths (or benefits) of using the same methodology in inter-organizational settings, which allows all organizations to work together and support continuous update of the emergency management frameworks, are factors that outweigh the weaknesses. Accompanied with a new methodology, which will change how things are conducted as well as the behavior of people or organizations, there are barriers that need to be overcome for a successful uptake and implementation. Below are a number of barriers that can be expected and needed to be managed within and among the organizations planning to use the methodology:

- Initiative. Someone has to initiate use of the EmCP concept and its methodology. Capaldo (2007) brings up the problem that networked organizations often lack a single authority for coordination of common activities, and that the strategic management of the network requires a distinct set of relational capabilities to sustain innovativeness. Thus, a leading authority comprising the EmCP responsible from each organization is needed to get started and lead the continuous improvement efforts.
- Political initiative. Will an EmCP initiative work as well as if the involved organizations do this on their own as it would if the initiative were to originate from political structures? Comfort (2007) considers that the participating actors (i.e. organizations) should align their activities voluntarily, and we favor the "own initiative", since it is almost always more interesting to realize one's own ideas compared to others'.
- Top management commitment and support. Without management's support there is no point in doing it at all. Hocevar *et al.* (2006) note that a strong leadership expressing commitment to a vision of collaboration with other organizations provides an incentive to organizational members to

be part of the activities. Adequate funding is also needed as part of the top management support.

- Mindset. People need to change the mindset that we live in a world free of error, and learn to change their organizations to be able to minimize the impact of "failures" as well as move towards "failure-free response" (Carley & Harrald, 1997).
- Human and organizational resistance to changes. A certain resistance is always to be expected in a change situation (Carley & Harrald, 1997), but the level of resistance is commonly lower if the top management openly gives support and points this out as a strategically important area for improvement.
- Coordination among partner organizations. Comfort (2007) brings up issues on coordination among partners, i.e. if it should be voluntary or policy-based. We think that a voluntary approach could be used when getting started, but then there is a need to formalize it using a policy or similar to get the continuity aspect to stick. Another aspect is if there are voluntary organizations, i.e. non-profit organizations, that have less means and are potentially less inclined to work according to a policy or agenda that is not their own. Using a policy for the coordination requires that the inter-organizational problems brought up by, for instance, Hocevar *et al.* (2006) are addressed.

The SSM has been deemed as useful in many research fields, and its use seems to be gaining momentum again by looking at the number of papers published. The SSM with additions from a number of researchers has been useful in our research giving a modeling structure to the EmCP concept. We consider that the SSM has potential for further research within the emergency management field. The CATWOE method facilitated analyzing and finding the aspects of the system, which we would not as easily have found otherwise.

The EmCP concept and its methodology can help emergency management organizations to move from being reactive to instead acting proactively. A move towards acting proactively requires engagement, support and organizational change (Carley & Harrald, 1997), but will be rewarding for both the Actors and Customers in making it worth while.

CONCLUSION

Increasingly, the literature in emergency management addresses the problem of managing emergencies with a mixture of rescue organizations (Comfort, 2005, 2007). However, the focus is on how different organizations manage the actual emergency through effective coordination of available resources. The result is often excellent emergency relief operations from which emergency organizations gain increased knowledge (Jennex, 2007). However, such an approach is not integrated with emergency organizations' long-term planning perspectives and also impairs the collaborative nature of emergency response. This problem is addressed by Comfort (2005) who argues for networked strategies and long-term policy goals as alternatives to hierarchical structures proven vulnerable in uncertain environments. A methodology for emergency management continuity planning provides a way to maintain a long-term planning perspective together with other designated emergency organizations.

In conclusion, the proposed EmCP concept and its methodology provide a simple and straightforward addition to a general emergency management process. They use ideas from business continuity planning and SSM, also adding an aspect of inter-organizational continuous coordination for planning in line with Comfort (2005, 2007, p. 194) and her statement to "achieve a common goal". This enables emergency management organizations to move towards acting proactively instead of being reactive.

FUTURE WORK

Comfort (1999) has shown that a notable factor during relief operations for response organizations is the creative ability to form adaptive networks. We intend to investigate this issue further in future research.

REFERENCES

Alexander, D. (2000). Scenario methodology for teaching principles of emergency management. *Disaster Prevention and Management, 9*(2), 89–97. doi:10.1108/09653560010326969

Bajgoric, N. (2008). *Continuous computing technologies for enhancing business continuity*. Hershey, PA: Information Science Reference.

Basden, A., & Wood-Harper, A. T. (2006). A Philosophical Discussion of the Root Definition in Soft Systems Thinking: An Enrichment of CATWOE. *Systems Research and Behavioral Science, 23*, 61–87. doi:10.1002/sres.689

Bergvall-Kåreborn, B. (2002). Qualifying Function in SSM Modeling – A Case Study. *Systemic Practice and Action Research, 15*(4), 309–330. doi:10.1023/A:1016396304746

Bergvall-Kåreborn, B., Mirijamdotter, A., & Basden, A. (2004). Basic Principles of SSM Modeling: An Examination of CATWOE from a Soft Perspective. *Systemic Practice and Action Research, 17*(2), 55–73. doi:10.1023/B:SPAA.0000018903.18767.18

Bhimaraya, A. M. (2006). Disaster mitigation framework for India using quality circle approach. *Disaster Prevention and Management, 15*(4), 621–635. doi:10.1108/09653560610686577

Borodzicz, E. P. (2005). *Risks, Crisis & Security Management*. Chichester, UK: John Wiley & Sons.

Butler, B. S., & Gray, P. H. (2006). Reliability, Mindfulness, and Information Systems. *Management Information Systems Quarterly, 30*(2), 211–224.

Canton, L. G. (2007). *Emergency Management: Concepts and strategies for effective programs.* Hoboken, NJ: John Wiley & Sons.

Capaldo, A. (2007). Network structure and innovation: The leveraging of a dual network as a distinctive relational capability. *Strategic Management Journal, 28*(6), 585–608. doi:10.1002/smj.621

Carley, K. M., & Harrald, J. R. (1997). Organizational Learning under Fire: Theory and Practice. *The American Behavioral Scientist, 40*(3), 310–332. doi:10.1177/0002764297040003007

Cerullo, V., & Cerullo, M. J. (2004). Business Continuity Planning: A Comprehensive Approach. *Information Systems Management, 21*(3), 70–78. doi:10.1201/1078/44432.21.3.20040601/82480.11

Checkland, P. (1999). *Systems Thinking, Systems Practice. Includes a 30-year retrospective.* Chichester, UK: John Wiley & Sons.

Checkland, P. (2000). Soft Systems Methodology: A Thirty Year Retrospective. *Systems Research and Behavioral Science, 17,* 11–58. doi:10.1002/1099-1743(200011)17:1+<::AID-SRES374>3.0.CO;2-O

Checkland, P., Challender, S., Clarke, S., Haynes, M., Hoebeke, L., & Leemhuis, J. (2000). The Emergent Properties of SSM in Use: A Symposium by Reflective Practitioners. *Systemic Practice and Action Research, 13*(6), 799–823. doi:10.1023/A:1026431613200

Checkland, P., & Poulter, J. (2006). *Learning for action: a short definitive account of soft systems methodology and its use, for practitioners, teachers and students.* Chichester, UK: John Wiley & Sons.

Checkland, P., & Scholes, J. (1990). *Soft Systems Methodology in Action.* Chichester, UK: John Wiley & Sons.

Checkland, P., & Scholes, J. (1999). *Soft Systems Methodology in Action. Includes a 30 year retrospective.* Chichester, UK: John Wiley & Sons.

Checkland, P., & Winter, M. (2006). Process and content: two ways of using SSM. *The Journal of the Operational Research Society, 57,* 1435–1441. doi:10.1057/palgrave.jors.2602118

Comfort, L. K. (1999). *Shared risk: Complex systems in seismic response.* Pittsburg, PA: Pergamon.

Comfort, L. K. (2005). Risk, Security, and Disaster management. *Annual Review of Political Science, 8,* 335–356. doi:10.1146/annurev.polisci.8.081404.075608

Comfort, L. K. (2007). Crisis Management in Hindsight: Cognition, Communication, Coordination, and Control. *Public Administration Review,* 189–197. doi:10.1111/j.1540-6210.2007.00827.x

Comfort, L. K., Birkland, T. A., Cigler, B. A., & Nance, E. (2010). Retrospectives and Prospectives on Hurricane Katrina: Five Years and Counting. *Public Administration Review,* 669–678. doi:10.1111/j.1540-6210.2010.02194.x

Cummings, T. G. (1984). Transorganizational development . In Staw, B. M., & Cummings, L. L. (Eds.), *Research in organizational behavior* (*Vol. 6*, pp. 367–422). Greenwich, CT: JAI Press.

Doughty, K. (2001). *Business Continuity Planning.* Boca Raton, FL: Auerbach/CRC Press.

Drabek, T. E. (2006). Community Processes: Coordination. In H. Rodriguez, E. L. Quarantelli, & R. R. Dynes (Eds.), *Handbook of Disaster Research.* New York, NY: Springer Science + Business Media.

Dynes, R. R. (1990). *Community emergency planning: False assumptions and inappropriate analogies.* Newark, DE: University of Delaware Disaster Research Center.

Dynes, R. R. (2000). *Governmental systems for disaster management*. Newark, DE: University of Delaware Disaster Research Center.

Ernst & Young. (2002). *Global Information Security Survey 2002*. New York, NY: Author.

Foster, H. D. (1980). *Disaster Planning: The Preservation of Life and Property*. New York, NY: Springer-Verlag.

Gregory, W. J., & Midgley, G. (2000). Planning for disaster: developing a multi-agency counseling service. *The Journal of the Operational Research Society, 51*, 278–290.

Harrald, J. R. (2006). Agility and Discipline: Critical Success Factors for Disaster Response. *The Annals of the American Academy of Political and Social Science, 604*(1), 256–272. doi:10.1177/0002716205285404

Hiles, A. (Ed.). (2007). *The definitive handbook of business continuity management* (2nd ed.). Chichester, UK: John Wiley & Sons.

Hocevar, S. P., Thomas, G. F., & Jansen, E. (2006). Building collaborative capacity: an innovative strategy for homeland security preparedness . In Beyerlien, M. M., Beyerlien, S. T., & Kennedy, F. A. (Eds.), *Innovation through collaboration: Advances in Interdisciplinary Studies of Work Teams* (*Vol. 12*, pp. 255–274). Oxford, UK: JAI Press.

Jennex, M. E. (2007, January). Modeling Emergency Response Systems. In *Proceedings of the 40th Hawaii International Conference on System Sciences, HICSS40*. Washington, DC: IEEE Computer Society.

Kash, T. J., & Darling, J. R. (1998). Crisis management: prevention, diagnosis and intervention. *Leadership and Organization Development Journal, 19*(4), 179–186. doi:10.1108/01437739810217151

Kaufmann, F. X. (1991). Introduction: issues and context . In Kaufmann, F. X. (Ed.), *The public Sector: Challenge for coordination and learning* (pp. 3–28). Berlin, Germany: Walter de Gruyter.

Kouzmin, A., Jarman, A. M. G., & Rosenthal, U. (1995). Inter-organizational policy processes in disaster management. *Disaster Prevention and Management, 4*(2), 20–37. doi:10.1108/09653569510082669

Lam, W. (2002). Ensuring Business Continuity. *IT Professional, 4*(3), 19–25. doi:10.1109/MITP.2002.1008533

Lang, T., & Allen, L. (2008). Reflecting on Scenario Practice: The Contribution of a Soft Systems Perspective . In Ramírz, R., Selsky, J. W., & van der Heijden, K. (Eds.), *Business Planning for Turbulent Times, New Methods for Applying Scenarios* (pp. 47–63). London, UK: Earthscan.

Lindström, J. (2009). *Models, methodology and challenges within strategic information security for senior managements. Unpublished doctoral disseration*. Sweden: Luleå University of Technology.

Lindström, J., Samuelsson, S., & Hägerfors, A. (2010). Business Continuity Planning Methodology. *Disaster Prevention and Management, 19*(2), 243–255. doi:10.1108/09653561011038039

Mathiassen, L., & Nielsen, P. A. (2000). Interaction and Transformation in SSM. *Systems Research and Behavioral Science, 17*, 243–253. doi:10.1002/(SICI)1099-1743(200005/06)17:3<243::AID-SRES316>3.0.CO;2-9

Mingers, J. (1992). Questions and suggestions in using soft systems methodology. *Systemist, 14*, 54–61.

Mingers, J., & White, L. (in press). A review of the recent contribution of systems thinking to operational research and management science. *European Journal of Operational Research*.

Moe, T. L., & Pathranarakul, P. (2006). An integrated approach to natural disaster management. *Disaster Prevention and Management, 15*(3), 396–413. doi:10.1108/09653560610669882

Murphy, T., & Jennex, M. E. (2006). Knowledge management, emergency response, and hurricane Katarina. *International Journal of Intelligent Control and Systems, 11*(4), 199–208.

Ringland, G. (1998). *Scenario Planning: Managing for the Future.* New York, NY: John Wiley & Sons.

Ritchie, B. W. (2004). Chaos, crises and disasters: a strategic approach to crisis management in the tourism industry. *Tourism Management, 25,* 669–683. doi:10.1016/j.tourman.2003.09.004

Roberts, W. (2006, October). Business Continuity Planning for disasters is just good planning. In *Proceedings of the Military Communications Conference (MILCOM 2006),* Washington DC.

Smith, D. (2004). For whom the bell tolls: Imagining accidents and the development of crisis simulation in organizations. *Simulation & Gaming, 35*(3), 347–362. doi:10.1177/1046878104266295

Sriraj, P. S., & Khisty, C. J. (1999). Crisis Management and Planning Using Systems Methodologies. *Journal of Urban Planning and Development, 125*(3), 121–133. doi:10.1061/(ASCE)0733-9488(1999)125:3(121)

Tierney, K. J. (2006). Businesses and Disasters: Vulnerability, Impacts, and Recovery. In H. Rodriguez, E. L. Quarantelli, & R. R. Dynes (Eds.), *Handbook of Disaster Research,* New York, NY: Springer Science + Business Media.

Turoff, M., Chumer, M., Hiltz, S. R., Klashner, R., Alles, M., Vasarhelyi, M., & Kogan, A. (2004). Assuring Homeland Security: Continuous monitoring, control & assurance of emergency preparedness. *Journal of Information Technology Theory and Application, 6*(3), 1–24.

Turoff, M., Chumer, M., Yao, X., Konopka, J., & Van de Walle, B. (2005, April). Crisis Planning via Scenario Development Gaming. In *Proceedings of the 2nd International ISCRAM Conference,* Brussels, Belgium.

Verstraete, C. (2004). Planning for the unexpected. *IEE Manufacturing Engineer, 83*(3), 18–21. doi:10.1049/me:20040304

Wang, Z.-N., & Wu, Y.-Y. (2008, September). Coping Strategy on Non-structured Problems of Enterprise Crisis Management: Based on Seamless Integration of CMP and Checkland SSM. In *Proceedings of the 2008 International Conference on Wireless Communications, Networking and Mobile Computing (WiCOM'08),* Dalian, China.

Weick, K. E. (1998). Improvisation as a mindset for organizational analysis. *Organization Science, 9*(5), 543–555. doi:10.1287/orsc.9.5.543

Wilson, B. (2001). *Soft Systems Methodology. Conceptual Model Building and Its Contribution.* Chichester, UK: John Wiley & Sons.

Wilson, J., & Oyola-Yemaiel, A. (2001). The evolution of emergency management and the advancement towards a profession in the United States and Florida. *Safety Science, 39,* 117–131. doi:10.1016/S0925-7535(01)00031-5

Wylder, J. (2004). *Strategic Information Security.* Boca Raton, FL: Auerbach/CRC Press.

This work was previously published in International Journal of Information Systems for Crisis Response Management, Volume 2, Issue 4, edited by Murray E. Jennex, pp. 1-19, copyright 2010 by IGI Publishing (an imprint of IGI Global).

Chapter 15
Implementing Social Media in Crisis Response Using Knowledge Management

Murray E. Jennex
San Diego State University, USA

ABSTRACT

Social media is being used by individuals during a crisis to alert rescuers to their location, status others on their condition or on environmental conditions, warn of issues, and so forth. However, organizations have been slower to adopt social media for crisis response. This paper explores issues affecting social media adoption by organizations for crisis response and proposes the use of knowledge management strategy as a process for mitigating these issues and guiding organizations in adopting social media into their crisis response plans.

INTRODUCTION

Organizations need to be prepared to respond to crises. Traditionally organizations prepare themselves for crisis response through planning, preparing response procedures and a crisis response system, and performing at least basic overview training to expected crisis responders. Crisis planning involves identifying potential crisis scenarios and determining what resources and actions will be needed to mitigate them (Raman et al., 2010). Crisis response procedures provide direction to responders on how to recognize the crisis, what

immediate actions to take, what communications to make, what long term actions are to be taken, and how to end the crisis (Jennex, 2004a, 2008). Crisis response systems support communications, data gathering and analysis, and decision-making.

To aid in preparing for crises individuals and organizations use available knowledge and technologies. A set of technologies of rising significance is social media. Social media can be described as web supported technologies used to connect users. Individuals are using social media to meet and share data, information, and knowledge with people usually outside their immediate

DOI: 10.4018/978-1-4666-0167-3.ch015

geographical area. Organizations are using social media to connect with customers and employees for sharing data, information, and knowledge.

Social media are also being used in crisis response. Most of this usage is by individuals with many organizations struggling to implement social media in ways that clearly demonstrate value to the organization. This paper discusses organizational issues associated with using social media and proposes using knowledge management, KM, and specifically KM strategy, to ensure that organizational use of social media for crisis response will either generate value or prevent value from being lost.

To do this the paper will provide an overview of crisis response system, discuss KM and social media, issues associated with social media, and finally, an approach for implementing social media by organizations to support crisis response using KM strategy.

CRISIS RESPONSE SYSTEMS

Crisis response systems are rarely used but when needed, must function well and without fail. Designing and building these systems requires designers to anticipate what will be needed, what resources will be available, and how conditions will differ from normal. A standard model for a crisis response system is from Bellardo, Karwan, and Wallace (1984) and identifies the components as including:

- Database
- Data analysis capability
- Normative models
- User interface.

This model has been modified by Jennex (2004a, 2008) using experience with the Year 2000, Y2K, response, Hurricane Katrina, the Strong Angel III and Golden Phoenix exercises, and the 2007 San Diego Wildfires to add:

- Trained users (where users are personnel using the crisis response system to respond to or communicate about the emergency)
- Dynamic and integrated (yet possibly physically distributed) methods to communicate between users (responders, concerned citizens, and victims) and between users and data, information, and knowledge sources
- Protocols/ontology to facilitate communication
- Geographical information systems or other mapping tools
- Processes and procedures used to guide the response to and improve decision making during the crisis.

The goals of the expanded crisis response system model are to:

- Facilitate clear communications
- Improve data, information, and knowledge transfer and use
- Improve the efficiency and effectiveness of decision-making
- Manage data, information, and knowledge to prevent or at least mitigate information overload.

Crisis response training prepares expected responders to use the crisis response system and respond effectively to the crisis. Training can take several forms, from table top exercises to full blown dress rehearsals. Also, it can be done once, annually, or at some other interval as determined by the organization (Patton & Flin, 1999; Turoff, 2002; Andersen, Garde, & Andersen, 1998; Lee & Bui, 2000; Fischer, 1998; Renaud & Phillips, 2003).

Unfortunately, crises can happen at any time making it difficult for organizations to have appropriate resources (responders, expertise, and material) where and when they are needed. Additionally, most organizations have little to no experience with real emergencies. The crisis response system needs to assist these organizations in taking advantage of all available experience and technologies to support the decision making needed in fast paced and high stress/tension circumstances. A final concern for the crisis response system is that the complexity of communicating, collaborating, and decision making processes in the context of crisis response efforts should not be underestimated or trivialized.

To mitigate the unpredictability of crises and the complexity of crisis response, affected individuals and first responders are using new technologies, particularly social media. Examples include:

- Concerned and/or affected citizens used a wiki after Hurricane Katrina to organize, collaborate, and rapidly create the PeopleFinder and ShelterFinder systems (Murphy & Jennex, 2006).
- Citizens affected by the 2007 San Diego Wildfires used a wiki to pool knowledge on which homes burned and which survived when the local media failed to support their needs (this has not been previously reported in the literature but was an activity performed by my students during the event).
- Mumbai citizens used twitter to report their status, let others know where to find friends, relatives, etc., and to solicit blood donations following the 2008 Mumbai terrorist attacks (Beaumont, 2008).
- Victims trapped by falling debris during the 2010 Haiti earthquake used texting and/or Facebook to alert their friends/family to their location and condition (Boodhoo, 2010).

These anecdotes provide evidence of the value of social media to individuals in responding to crisis. However they do not indicate that organizations can benefit from the use of social media during crisis response. This paper provides a process and reason for incorporating social media into organizational crisis response planning and systems. The process is based on using knowledge management, KM, as the guiding approach to implementing social media as a technology for improving connectivity and knowledge transfer among crisis response teams.

The inspiration for this paper comes from the disputed 2009 Iranian elections. Plotnick and White (2010), Gheidary (2010), and the Wikipedia summaries on this election include several references discussing how protesters used social media such as Twitter and Facebook to organize and manage the protests (Wikipedia, 2010b, 2010c). This is interesting but not the inspiration for the paper. The inspiration comes from the possible use of KM by the protest organizers to create a coordinated protest. The author knows of this from his role as editor-in-chief of the *International Journal of Knowledge Management*. Approximately nine months prior to the election protests the author received a request for a copy of his knowledge management success model paper from an Iranian academic colleague. The colleague was queried on why they wanted the paper and the response was that they were researching how to create autonomous, self-organizing youth teams. The author found this an odd application at the time but sent them the paper. It wasn't till the election protests nine months later that it became apparent what the possible use of the autonomous, self-organizing youth teams was. While the supposed use cannot be verified, it did cause reflection on the problem of finding crisis response applications for social media and initiated research into using KM as the process for creating the strategy and process for incorporating social media into organizations for their crisis response.

SOCIAL MEDIA AND KNOWLEDGE MANAGEMENT

Plotnick and White (2010) describe social media as generally being attributed to the collaborative applications supported by Web 2.0 technologies. These include, but are not limited to, Twitter, Facebook, My Space, wikis, and blogs. Blogs, wikis, and My Space were the first applications becoming popular in the early 2000s while Facebook and Twitter are more recent creations. While popular with the public, organizations have struggled to find business uses for social media. Wikis have been the first social media adapted by organizations as they have been found to be very useful in supporting collaboration within teams and work groups and has been incorporated into popular enterprise systems such as Share Point. Facebook, Twitter, and blogs are not always looked at favorably by organizations. Many consider them information leaks and venues for dissatisfied employees and/or customers to vent their complaints without any control by the organization.

Jennex (2010) summarized KM as being about using knowledge and experience gained from past events and activities as an aid in making current and future decision making. Knowledge management systems, KMS, provide tools and repositories for acquiring, storing, searching, manipulating, displaying, and transferring knowledge. KM/KMS focuses on two issues:

- Leveraging what the organization "knows" so that it can better utilize its knowledge assets, and
- Connecting knowledge generators, holders, and users to facilitate the flow of knowledge through the organization

Jennex and Raman (2009) discussed how KM can be used to support crisis response. They consider a crisis response system as a form of a KMS. This paper expands on Jennex and Raman (2009) by applying KM to the specific issue of how organizations can incorporate social media into their crisis response plans. This is done using Jennex and Olfman's (2006) investigation of what was necessary for KM/KMS success and the identification of twelve critical success factors, CSFs. Among these are having a knowledge strategy and an integrated technical infrastructure. These two CSFs can be used to align social media with organizational based crisis response.

An integrated KM technical infrastructure includes networks, databases/repositories, computers, software, and KMS experts (Alavi & Leidner, 1999; Cross & Baird, 2000; Davenport et al., 1998; Ginsberg & Kambil, 1999; Jennex & Olfman, 1998, 2000; Sage & Rouse, 1999; Yu et al., 2004). Social media assists in several ways. As it is Web 2.0 based, social media operates over a global integrated network. Wikis, blogs, You Tube, social networking sites all provide repositories that can be harnessed for crisis response. Additionally, these same applications provide methods of connecting to experts. Overall, social media provides a good solution to the need for an integrated technical infrastructure.

KM strategy identifies users, user experience level needs, sources, where knowledge needs to flow, knowledge processes, storage strategy, knowledge and links to knowledge for the KMS and goals for the KM initiative (Ginsberg & Kambil, 1999; Holsapple & Joshi, 2000; Jennex, Olfman, & Addo, 2003; Koskinen, 2001; Sage & Rouse, 1999; Yu et al., 2004). This CSF is critical for assessing how to use social media in the organizational setting. KM strategy drives the organization to plan the use of social media. KM strategy guides the organization in finding/identifying crisis response knowledge sources as well as those needing this knowledge to assist in their crisis response. KM strategy also drives the organization to plan the storage of knowledge by driving the organization to taxonomy and ontology as well as storage formats. Social media provides methods for storing and organizing unstructured knowledge such as video, audio, victim stories, lessons learned, etc. Social networking applications such as Facebook provide methods for creating and communicating networks of links to expertise, as well as methods for connecting experts. Overall, preparing a crisis response KM strategy guides the organization into planning the adoption and implementation of social media into their crisis response plans.

To summarize, these two CSFs (KM Strategy and Integrated Technical Infrastructure) and the focus on connecting knowledge generators, holders, and users drive the adoption of social media as a KM technology. Social media provides technology that links KM participants and KM strategy is what helps the organization determine how to use social media.

ORGANIZATIONAL ISSUES WITH SOCIAL MEDIA

Social media suffer from three significant weaknesses. The first is managerial control. Organizations find it very difficult to control how members used social media and what they post online. This lack of control has resulted in reluctance in implementing social media applications. Second, social media also has had reliability issues. This relates to the control issue as organizations found that since they did not control the social media infrastructure they could not control version releases, reliability of accessibility, overall access to the application, and security of data, information, and knowledge placed in social media repositories. Thirdly, social media has a trust issue with respect to postings and content. Due to the aforementioned lack of control, postings and content could be posted by anyone with no quality or truthfulness control being applied. This was an initial concern with Wikipedia as the initial thought that the power of crowds would monitor content and postings did not work as well or as quickly as expected. The issue has been mitigated by the use of expert editorial review boards reviewing and approving content updates prior to their posting.

The advent of cloud computing is mitigating some of the reliability concerns. Wikipedia describes Cloud computing as Internet-based computing, whereby shared resources, software and information are provided to computers and other devices on-demand, like the electricity grid (Wikipedia, 2010a). Highly reliable server farms hosted by companies providing cloud services provide reliable data, information, and knowledge storage as well as reliable web and web application hosting. Other benefits include the abundance of open source software. Crisis response software is available to organizations at little to no charge. Of course the issue of control is not mitigated by the cloud or open source software.

Can and should organizations be concerned with control and truthfulness/accuracy of data, information, and knowledge? Of course they should be concerned. Data, information, and knowledge are critical resources that need to be protected. Access and/or misinformation by unauthorized persons during a crisis can cause confusion and intentional interference affecting the organization's ability to respond. Can KM assist organizations in addressing these issues? Again, of course, Jennex and Zygier (2007) addressed incorporating security into KM. Jennex and Zyngier (2007) utilized the National Security Telecommunications and Information System Security Committee model (NSTISSC 1994), commonly known as the CIA (Confidentiality, Integrity, Availability) model, to incorporate security into KM. Security in KM involves incorporating security processes into KM strategy. KM strategy should incorporate the use of risk management to identify threats with corresponding risks (consequence and probability) to crisis response data, information, and knowledge and includes the identification of security policies for mitigating these threats and risks. These security policies should address access control, technologies for storing, transmitting, and processing data, information, and knowledge, and processes regulating the update, use, and ultimate archiving of crisis response data, information, and knowledge.

To summarize, social media provides a rapid response and collaboration tool set that can be utilized by organizations for crisis response.

APPLYING KM STRATEGY

It is proposed that a KM strategy for crisis response can be used to guide the adoption of social media for crisis response in organizations. It was previously discussed that Jennex (2004b) outlines the critical issues that an organization faces in creating a KM strategy. These are summarized and applied to crisis response as follows:

- **Identifying Users of the KMS:** Without knowing who is expected to use the KMS and for what purpose, designers do not know what knowledge or level of context needs to be captured. The organization needs to identify who will be using social media for crisis response. This allows the organization to create access control for twitter feeds, wikis, Facebook, etc. Also, analyzing the roles these users perform aids the organization in identifying what functions social media needs to support.
- **Having an overall organizational KM Strategy:** Without an overall organizational KM strategy many organizations tend to fail in implementing a crisis response specific KM initiative. This issue focuses organizational leadership on supporting crisis response KM and aids in getting leadership support for the use of social media in crisis response.
- **Identifying a Representation Strategy:** Crisis responders tend to be a transient workforce with a regular rate of turnover, this generally drives the organization to

codify into computerized knowledge repositories as much data, information, and knowledge as possible. Also, new workers tend to need to talk to knowledge holders providing a driver to capturing as many links to knowledge as possible. Additionally, given the variety of formats that knowledge is created and used in organizations must specify how they will manage long term storage of data, information, and knowledge. Social media tends to be in the moment, connecting users but not readily capturing the content of the connections. A representation strategy will also aid the organization in formulating methods for capturing crisis response communications, data, information, and knowledge from social media such as twitter and Facebook.

- **Flooding the KMS with content:** Information overload is a real issue in crisis response (Jennex & Raman, 2009). Knowledge strategy has to identify that data, information, and knowledge necessary to support crisis response decision making and focus on capturing, storing, and displaying this data, information, and knowledge. Social media is especially susceptible to information overload unless the organization places controls on crisis response postings via twitter and Facebook and utilizes the content management capabilities of wikis, blogs, and Facebook to control the amount of information sent to crisis responders. A KM strategy for crisis response guides the organization in identifying and implementing these controls.
- **Inadequate search capabilities for the KMS:** Crisis responders need data, information, and knowledge when they need it and cannot be expected to spend much time searching. Knowledge needs to be stored and organized in a format and with labels/tags that facilitates search and retrieval. Social media does not automatically have

good search and retrieval functions. A KM strategy guides the organization in creating ontology and taxonomy for crisis response and identifying methods for search and retrieval. Social media can be organized for search and retrieval by using the ontology for a tagging system and using the taxonomy to organize wikis and YouTube technology based repositories.

- **Senior Management Support:** Crisis response needs sensitive data, information, and knowledge that without top management support for encouraging knowledge sharing and for allocating resources, will not be available. A KM strategy guides senior management identifying and controlling this sensitive data, information, and knowledge as well as specifying policies for conduct and disclosure when using social media. This is critical given the open nature of social media and the propensity of individuals to disclose data, information, and knowledge through social media.

- **Security:** KM processes need to ensure critical crisis response data, information, and knowledge is secure. KM strategy provides the KM processes used to identify data, information, and knowledge security requirements including the controls needing to be implemented.

- **Maintaining currency of knowledge:** Crisis response data, information, and knowledge must be accurate and relevant temporally for users to use the KMS. KM strategy provides the process for reviewing and evaluating data, information, and knowledge life cycles and retention periods.

- **KM Goals and Purpose:** Crisis response KM initiatives need a clearly identified and communicated set of goals and purpose so that the impact of the initiative can be measured. KM strategy generates these goals and specifies the measures to be used.

- **An Organizational Learning Culture:** Organizations, and specifically the crisis response organization, need a strategy that fosters a learning organization including incentives to share and use knowledge. KM strategy provides the structure for identifying incentives and personnel assessment processes.

While addressing the above crisis response KM strategy issues, special consideration should be given to the following set of issues before the organization adopts social media for crisis response:

- What technologies should be used?
- Who should use the technologies? (an expanded discussion on users)
- What data, information, and knowledge should be made available for response?
- What security policies should be implemented?
- What is the value proposition for social media in crisis response?

The following section discusses how to resolve these issues.

IMPLEMENTING SOCIAL MEDIA FOR CRISIS RESPONSE

What Technologies should be Used?

Technologies should be adapted based on their ability to integrate/interface with the organization's existing technical infrastructure. Additionally, the organization should conduct a crisis response needs analysis and select technologies that meet that analyzed need and assessed capability of the technology to meet that need. Some general guidelines for social media.

Wikis are excellent for collaborative authoring and storage, organization, and dissemination of documents, processes, and solutions. Wikis are appropriate for crisis planning, training, response, and recovery (Raman et al., 2010; Jennex & Raman, 2009). The key advantage is support for distributed expertise to collaborate synchronously or asynchronously. Additionally, secure wiki technology is being made available in organizational applications such as Sharepoint which are useful for internal collaboration between organizational experts. Non-secure wikis available via open source or as a service are useful for collaboration with external experts, victims, and the general public as well as for dissemination of data, information, and knowledge to the public. External wikis from partner organizations should be identified and vetted before use. Knowledge management should also be used to identify data, information, and knowledge to be collected and made available. Finally, KM should be used to determine the format for storing the collected data, information, and knowledge.

Blogs are an excellent communication tool. As illustrated by the 2010 Gulf oil spill, blogs can be used to get an organization's message out to the public, to affected persons, and to internal members. It should also be noted that blogs are easy to set up and be used by external participants, some of whom may not be sympathetic to the organization's response.

Twitter and instant messaging applications are excellent for keeping responders statused or calling for specific needs or responses. Implementations should have specific users subscribed and the organization should monitor and manage the subscriber list.

Facebook and other social networking sites can be used much like blogs to post public information, updates for internal responders, as an instant messaging system, and to build a sustainable community (Belblidia, 2010). Users should be screened to those on the response team or in the organization for organizational sites. Public sites can be open to all subscribers.

Google map mashups can be used to create custom crisis response maps for responders, crisis management, and victims. Examples include:

- British Blizzard of 2009 where twitter was used to allow users to post snow conditions that were then published on the mashup map (Lang & Benbunan-Fich, 2010)
- The 2007 San Diego wild fires where map mashups were generated to help direct fire response and to alert victims and the public where the fire was, what houses were destroyed, what areas were still under evacuation (Toomey et al., 2009).
- Haiti earthquake of 2010 where a map was generated fusing aerial photography with street maps so that refugee camps could be identified to relief workers so they could deliver emergency food and water supplies (unpublished research from work done in the San Diego State University Visualization Laboratory, article currently under review).

Open source software and software as a service are good choices if from established crisis response support organizations. Two such organizations are Sahana (http://sahanafoundation.org/) and InRelief (www.inrelief.org). Sahana is an open source initiative that provides a full service crisis response system free to users. Users are allowed to tailor the software as needed and can provide changes back to Sahana. InRelief is a data, information, and knowledge service based on Google technology, provided by a registered non-government organization, NGO, and managed by San Diego State University. Both recognize the need for security and access control and provide those features while also allowing for open collaboration between organizations. Both also have a track record of success. Sahana has been used in major crises since 2005 and InRelief has been used to support earthquake response in Haiti and Mexico, the 2010 Gulf oil spill, and was tested by the United States military and other civilian organizations during Exercise 24 conducted at San Diego State University in September, 2010. Finally, both are KM repositories as both provide lessons learned and history from previous crises.

A concluding consideration is what computer/communication technology to utilize. Experience is showing that dedicated crisis response equipment becomes obsolete very quickly (Jennex, 2004a, 2008). It is better to utilize the computer/communication tools used by responders and other crisis response personnel on a daily basis. While wireless enabled laptop computers have been the technology of choice for the last few years, the trend is towards the use of internet enabled cell phones with large built in memories and using data services and away from wireless laptops. This suggests that organizations should move towards hand held mobile computer/communication as it is what the responders will be accustomed to using.

Who should use the Technologies?

Knowledge management processes should be used to identify knowledge sources and users. Social network analysis tools can be used with KM to identify data, information, and knowledge flows. It should be noted that KM analysis usually finds that data, information, and knowledge flows usually do not follow organizational hierarchies. While crisis leadership can be appointed as the organization requires, data, information, and knowledge flows work best if they are designed to fit the actual organizational social networks, including the identified knowledge gate keepers.

What Data, Information, and Knowledge should be Made Available for Response?

Knowledge management success is defined as capturing the right knowledge, getting the right knowledge to the right user, and using this knowledge to improve organizational and/or individual

performance. KM success is measured by using the dimensions: impact on business processes, impact on strategy, leadership, and knowledge content (Jennex, Smolnik, & Croasdell, 2009). As previously discussed, KM strategy is the process for determining the right data, information, and knowledge to capture and store, where this data, information, and knowledge is located, who needs it, and how to get it to them. Organizations need to appoint a KM leader for this strategic effort. Jennex and Olfman (2006) caution that not all data, information, and knowledge can be captured in a computer based repository. Linkages to data, information, and knowledge also need to be identified and captured for that which cannot be extracted from a source and captured in a repository. Typical data, information, and knowledge needed to be capture includes:

- Resource data and information (type, amount, location of resources)
- Expertise needed for response such as process, equipment, risk, and personnel knowledge as well as specialized skills and capabilities knowledge
- Response procedures and processes
- Lessons learned from previous events
- Environmental, geographical, and demographic data and information
- Industry data and information
- Regulatory data and information

Useful tools for identifying critical data, information, and knowledge includes table top exercises and scenario walk throughs, analysis of previous events, and participation in and analysis of large scale crisis response exercises.

What Security Policies should be Implemented?

The previous discussions provide the analysis for this activity. The organization needs to identify the response team and expert sources as well as organization sensitive data, information, and knowledge. Access control is applied by selecting the appropriate technology, secure wikis for collaboration and social networking tools/sites that allow the tool/site owner to manage access control lists. Organizations then need to implement a process for vetting and authorizing membership to the social media source. This is fairly simple prior to a crisis but organizations need to include this process during the crisis to manage adding membership under crisis pressure and where it may need to be done very quickly. A short list of recommended security policies for crisis response follows:

- Access Control (internal and external personnel)
- Initial Hiring including Background Investigation
- Termination
- Communication/Encryption
- Acceptable Use
- Data, Information, and Knowledge Storage and Maintenance
- Software Vendor Qualification
- Application Development and Maintenance
- Data, Information, and Knowledge Validation (internal and external sources)

WHAT IS THE VALUE PROPOSITION FOR SOCIAL MEDIA IN CRISIS RESPONSE?

Ultimately organizations need to show value for their investments. This is especially true for crisis response as many organizations consider crisis response preparation a cost of doing business and have difficulty in showing and measuring value in crisis response. Adopting social media needs to be based on a value statement that states the goal for social media and then contrasts costs to benefits of using social media. The goals for social media

in crisis response are organizational specific but include the following:

- Improving knowledge transfer among crisis responders
- Improving communication/knowledge transfer with customers and/or victims
- Reducing technology infrastructure costs
- Improved crisis response times
- Improved decision making
- Reduced technology purchase/maintenance costs

The costs of social media include traditional costs such as training, maintenance and support, initial purchase and tailoring, and any switching costs (from previous technology to social media). Additionally, as previously mentioned there are issues, i.e. costs, associated with social media of loss of control, reliability, and trust. Tangible benefits of social media include possibly smaller initial purchase costs, lower infrastructure costs, lower training costs, lower maintenance and support costs. The value statement needs to include these costs and benefits plus intangible benefits such as scalability, improved connectivity (within the organization and with its customers/responders), improved knowledge transfer and command and control of crisis situations, faster crisis response times, and improved satisfaction with the crisis response. Intangible benefits are hard to quantify and vary with each organization. Using KM strategy to guide social media application to crisis response guides the organization to identifying the goals and measures that can assist the organization in identifying and quantifying these tangible benefits and constructing the value statement for social media in crisis response.

CONCLUSION

Social media are being implemented by individuals during a crisis. Usually this is a self organizing activity without any organizational control or management. However, organizations can also take advantage of social media for their crisis response as long as they take precautions to maintain the integrity of their proprietary data, information, and knowledge and manage access to these resources to those vetted appropriate. This paper proposes the use of knowledge management strategy incorporating security to assist in this analysis and specifically warns against just adopting social media for crisis response without first considering its impact on and risk to the organization and its members. Knowledge management strategy provides the keypoints for organizations to focus on when considering social media:

- Users
- Data/Information/Knowledge needed for crisis response
- Data/Information/Knowledge representation
- Sources of Data/Information/Knowledge
- Connectivity
- Goals, measurement, and value
- Leadership and support
- Taxonomy and ontology for guiding search, retrieval, and storage
- Security issues and resolution

These keypoints need to be addressed by organizations prior to implementing social media, but if addressed, it is expected that the organization will be successful in implementing social media for crisis response.

REFERENCES

Alavi, M., & Leidner, D. E. (1999). Knowledge Management Systems: Emerging Views and Practices from the Field. In *Proceedings of the 32nd Hawaii International Conference on System Sciences.* Washington, DC: IEEE Computer Society.

Andersen, H. B., Garde, H., & Andersen, V. (1998). MMS: An Electronic Message Management System for Emergency Response. *IEEE Transactions on Engineering Management, 45*(2), 132–140. doi:10.1109/17.669758

Beaumont, C. (2008, November 27). Mumbai attacks: Twitter and Flickr used to break news. *The Telegraph.* Retrieved December 2, 2010, from http://www.telegraph.co.uk/news/worldnews/asia/india/3530640/Mumbai-attacks-Twitter-and-Flickr-used-to-break-news-Bombay-India.html

Belblidia, M. S. (2010). Building Community Resilience through Social Networking Sites: Using Online Social Networks for Emergency Management. *International Journal of Information Systems for Crisis Response and Management, 2*(1), 24–36. doi:10.4018/jiscrm.2010120403

Bellardo, S., Karwan, K. R., & Wallace, W. A. (1984). Managing the Response to Disasters Using Microcomputers. *Interfaces, 14*(2), 29–39. doi:10.1287/inte.14.2.29

Boodhoo, N. (2010, January 18). Earthquake confirms value of social media. *Miami Herald.* Retrieved November 28, 2010, from http://www.miamiherald.com/2010/01/18/1432022/earthquake-confirms-value-of-social.html

Cross, R., & Baird, L. (2000). Technology Is Not Enough: Improving Performance by Building Organizational Memory. *Sloan Management Review, 41*(3), 41–54.

Davenport, T. H., DeLong, D. W., & Beers, M. C. (1998). Successful Knowledge Management Projects. *Sloan Management Review, 39*(2), 43–57.

Fischer, H. W. (1998). The Role of the New Information Technologies in Emergency Mitigation, Planning, Response, and Recovery. *Disaster Prevention and Management, 7*(1), 28–37. doi:10.1108/09653569810206262

Gheidary, L. K. (2010, May). Social media and Iran's post-election crisis. In *Proceedings of the 7th International ISCRAM Conference,* Seattle, WA.

Ginsberg, M., & Kambil, A. (1999). Annotate: A Web-based Knowledge Management Support System for Document Collections. In *Proceedings of the 32nd Hawaii International Conference on System Sciences.* Washington, DC: IEEE Computer Society.

Holsapple, C. W., & Joshi, K. D. (2000). An Investigation of Factors that Influence the Management of Knowledge in Organizations. *The Journal of Strategic Information Systems, 9,* 235–261. doi:10.1016/S0963-8687(00)00046-9

Jennex, M. E. (2004a). Emergency Response Systems: The Utility Y2K Experience. *Journal of Information Technology Theory and Application, 6*(3), 85–102.

Jennex, M. E. (2004b). Knowledge Management Strategy: Critical Issues. *Global Journal of E-Business and Knowledge Management, 1*(1), 35–44.

Jennex, M. E. (2008). A Model for Emergency Response Systems. In Janczewski, L., & Colarik, A. (Eds.), *Cyber Warfare and Cyber Terrorism* (pp. 383–391). Hershey, PA: Information Science Reference.

Jennex, M. E. (2010). Preface: Why Knowledge Management? In Jennex, M. E. (Ed.), *Ubiquitous Developments in Knowledge Management: Integrations and Trends* (pp. xviii–xxix). Hershey, PA: Information Science Reference.

Jennex, M. E., & Olfman, L. (2000). *Development Recommendations for Knowledge Management/Organizational Memory Systems.* Paper presented at the Information Systems Development Conference.

Jennex, M. E., & Olfman, L. (2006). A Model of Knowledge Management Success. *International Journal of Knowledge Management, 2*(3), 51–68. doi:10.4018/jkm.2006070104

Jennex, M. E., Olfman, L., & Addo, T. B. A. (2003). The Need for an Organizational Knowledge Management Strategy. In *Proceedings of the 36th Hawaii International Conference on System Sciences (HICSS36).* Washington, DC: IEEE Computer Society.

Jennex, M. E., & Raman, M. (2009). Knowledge Management is Support of Crisis Response. *International Journal of Information Systems for Crisis Response and Management, 1*(3), 69–82. doi:10.4018/jiscrm.2009070104

Jennex, M. E., Smolnik, S., & Croasdell, D. T. (2009). Towards a Consensus Knowledge Management Success Definition. *VINE: The Journal of Information and Knowledge Management Systems, 39*(2), 174–188.

Jennex, M.E., & Zyngier, S. (2007). Security as a Contributor to Knowledge Management Success. *Information Systems Frontiers: A Journal of Research and Innovation, 9*(5), 493-504.

Koskinen, K. U. (2001). Tacit Knowledge as a Promoter of Success in Technology Firms. In *Proceedings of the 34th Hawaii International Conference on System Sciences.* Washington, DC: IEEE Computer Society.

Lang, G., & Benbunan-Fich, R. (2010). The Use of Social Media in Disaster Situation: Framework and Cases. *International Journal of Information Systems for Crisis Response and Management, 2*(1), 11–23. doi:10.4018/jiscrm.2010120402

Lee, J., & Bui, T. (2000). A Template-based Methodology for Disaster Management Information Systems. In *Proceedings of the 33rd Hawaii International Conference on System Sciences.* Washington, DC: IEEE Computer Society.

Murphy, T., & Jennex, M. E. (2006). Knowledge Management, Emergency Response, and Hurricane Katrina. *International Journal of Intelligent Control and Systems*, *11*(4), 199–208.

NSTISSC. (1994). *National Training Standard for Information Systems Security (INFOSEC) Professionals, NSTISSI No. 4011*. Washington, DC: National Security Telecommunications and Information Systems Security Committee. Retrieved from http://niatec.info/pdf/4011.pdf

Patton, D., & Flin, R. (1999). Disaster Stress: An Emergency Management Perspective. *Disaster Prevention and Management*, *8*(4), 261–267. doi:10.1108/09653569910283897

Plotnick, C., & White, L. (2010). A Social Media Tsunami: the Approaching Wave. *International Journal of Information Systems for Crisis Response and Management*, *2*(1), i–iv.

Raman, M., Ryan, T., Jennex, M. E., & Olfman, L. (2010). Wiki Technology and Emergency Response: An Action Research Study. *International Journal of Information Systems for Crisis Response and Management*, *2*(1), 49–69. doi:10.4018/jiscrm.2010120405

Renaud, R., & Phillips, S. (2003). Developing an Integrated Emergency Response Programme for Facilities: The Experience of Public Works and Government Services Canada. *Journal of Facilities Management*, *1*(4), 347–364. doi:10.1108/14725960310808051

Sage, A. P., & Rouse, W. B. (1999). Information Systems Frontiers in Knowledge Management. *Information Systems Frontiers*, *1*(3), 205–219. doi:10.1023/A:1010046210832

Toomey, T., Frost, E., & Jennex, M. E. (2009). Strategies to Prepare Emergency Management Personnel to Integrate Geospatial Tools into Emergency Management. *International Journal of Information Systems for Crisis Response and Management*, *1*(4), 33–49. doi:10.4018/jiscrm.2009071003

Turoff, M. (2002). Past and Future Emergency Response Information Systems. *Communications of the ACM*, *45*(4), 29–32. doi:10.1145/505248.505265

Westfall, A., Jennex, M. E., Dickinson, S., & Frost, E. (2009). Event Report: Golden Phoenix 2008. *International Journal of Information Systems for Crisis Response and Management*, *1*(2), 72–79. doi:10.4018/jiscrm.2009040106

Wikipedia. (2010a). *Cloud Computing*. Retrieved November 25, 2010, from http://en.wikipedia.org/wiki/Cloud_computing

Wikipedia. (2010b). *Iranian presidential election, 2009*. Retrieved November 25, 2010, from http://en.wikipedia.org/wiki/Iranian_presidential_election,_2009#cite_note-gulfnews_Facebookblock-87

Wikipedia. (2010c). *2009–2010 Iranian election protests*. Retrieved November 25, 2010, from http://en.wikipedia.org/wiki/2009%E2%80%932010_Iranian_election_protests

Yu, S.-H., Kim, Y.-G., & Kim, M.-Y. (2004). Linking Organizational Knowledge Management Drivers to Knowledge Management Performance: An Exploratory Study. In *Proceedings of the 37th Hawaii International Conference on System Sciences (HICSS36)*. Washington, DC: IEEE Computer Society.

This work was previously published in International Journal of Information Systems for Crisis Response Management, Volume 2, Issue 4, edited by Murray E. Jennex, pp. 20-32, copyright 2010 by IGI Publishing (an imprint of IGI Global).

Chapter 16
Managing Crises in the Healthcare Service Chain:
Lessons from the Past and Future Directions

Panos Constantinides
Frederick University, Cyprus

ABSTRACT

This paper explores the strategic importance of information systems for managing such crises as the H1N1 outbreak and the Haiti earthquake in the healthcare service chain. The paper synthesizes the literature on crisis management and information systems for emergency response and draws some key lessons for healthcare service chains. The paper illustrates these lessons by using data from an empirical case study in the region of Crete in Greece. The author concludes by discussing some future directions in managing crises in the healthcare service chain, including the importance of distributive, adaptive crisis management through new technologies like mashups.

INTRODUCTION

Recent events from the SARS and H1N1 outbreaks in 2003 and 2009 respectively, to natural disasters such as hurricane Katrina in 2005 and the Haiti earthquake in 2010, have exposed the global healthcare service chain to high alerts of threat and disaster. Before these events, service chain management has been largely overlooked in healthcare even though the potential for direct risk reduction and improved quality of service

delivery is significant. For example, after the outbreak of H1N1 it became evident that flu vaccines were in short supply in parts of the world (Belluck, 2009). Evidence shows that, among the few firms that are presently involved in the production and delivery of flu vaccines, there was a switching from the production of seasonal flu vaccines between 2009-2010 to the production of the H1N1 vaccine, with increased shortages of the former and delayed deliveries of the latter (Dooren, 2009; McNeil, 2009). In turn, in February 2010,

DOI: 10.4018/978-1-4666-0167-3.ch016

it was estimated that 57 million people in the US alone had contracted H1N1 from which 257,000 were hospitalized and 17,000 died (Falco, 2010).

As evident from this example, the lack of attention on healthcare *service* chain management is largely due to a strong emphasis on healthcare *supply* chain management. The key difference between the two is that the latter places sole attention on the production, storage, distribution, and ultimate delivery of healthcare-related *products* such as flu vaccines, whereas the former places attention on healthcare *services* such as the management of flu vaccinations, communication about the behaviour of the H1N1 virus, and provision of related emergency services to affected and vulnerable parts of a population.

The recent focus on healthcare services rather than products (Corbin et al., 2001; Scotti et al., 2007), is part of a broader shift in management logic, from a product-dominant one, in which the outputs and discrete transactions of tangible (manufactured) goods was central, to a service-dominant one, in which intangibility, exchange processes and relationships are central (Vargo & Lusch, 2004, 2008). In this new service-dominant logic, services are defined as "the application of specialized competences (knowledge and skills) through deeds, processes, and performances for the benefit of another entity or the entity itself" (Vargo & Lusch, 2004, p. 2).

The importance of relational performances is particularly evident in healthcare service chains where the continuity of operations is vital to human welfare and the span and quality-of-life of patients. This is even more so in the case of crises such as natural and environmental disasters (e.g. floods, earthquakes), technical or mechanical disasters (e.g. gas leak), and human-induced threats or activities (e.g. epidemics, terrorist acts), where specialized competences, as performed by emergency personnel, could have significant consequences on the human welfare of both directly affected individuals, as well as the larger population of vulnerable geographical areas.

Such crises have been extensively examined and analysed within the field of crisis management. Crisis management is defined as a systematic attempt by organizational members to identify and detect possible crises, take actions and measures to prevent them, contain their effects or disruption, and finally recover (Pearson & Mitroff, 1993; Preble, 1997; Smits & Ally, 2003). However, crisis management (and disaster research more generally) is by nature a multidisciplinary field, with researchers coming from different research areas (e.g. environmental science, economics, sociology), and with each field attaching its own perspective (Quantarelli, Lagadec, & Boin, 2007). As a consequence, there are few if any comprehensive crisis management or disaster relief process models that would encompass all possible definitions of a crisis (Quantarelli & Perry, 2005; Boin et al., 2005).

In addition, despite an increasing interest in the role that information systems can play in the management of crises (Turoff, 2002; Turoff et al., 2004; Jennex, 2004; Chen et al., 2010), there have been few studies that integrate systems and network approaches to assist in the understanding of processes in the healthcare service chain (Keen et al., 2006). As Chen et al. (2010, p. 150) have noted "the existing emergency information systems are still constrained with respect to technology design, implementation, and management."

This paper takes the first step in addressing this research gap, by providing a synthesis of the literature on crisis management and emergency information systems. The paper achieves this by answering the following key research questions:

- How can new and emerging crises be better understood?
- How can information systems help in the management of new and emerging crises in the healthcare service chain?

While drawing on the key lessons learned from the literature, the paper then illustrates the strategic role of information systems in managing crises through an empirical case study in the region of Crete in Greece. The paper concludes by discussing some future directions in managing new and emerging crises in the healthcare service chain, including the importance of distributive, adaptive crisis management through new technologies such as mashups.

MANAGING CRISES IN THE HEALTHCARE SERVICE CHAIN: A SYNTHESIS OF THE LITERATURE

New and Emerging Crises in the Healthcare Service Chain

As mentioned in the introduction, service chain management differs from supply chain management in that the latter focuses on the transactional logistics involved in the ordering, movement, and payment of products from suppliers to providers, whereas the latter focuses on service-process flows and quality of care from providers to customers or patients. Thus, although the analysis could be informed by looking at how the literature on supply chain management has approached disruptions in the supply chain as a form of crisis management (Whyback et al., 2010), the interest is primarily on service chain crises that vary both in the ways in which they manifest and in their implications.

Certainly, both supply and service chains suffer from new and emerging crises, which are the product of several "endemic features of modern society" such as, globalization, access to an abundance of transportation types, as well as advances in information and communication technologies, all of which make it difficult to pinpoint the source or origin of a crisis (Boin & Hart, 2003; Quantarelli, Lagadec, & Boin, 2007). These endemic features promote a world that is more accessible both locally and remotely (access to more resources) but which is also more vulnerable to infestation by a single crisis. As a consequence, slight accidents within the intricate infrastructures responsible for the sustainability of both supply and service chains can rapidly escalate and create serious problems even to the most remote sites (Perrow, 1999). However, these new and emerging crises have more immediate and threatening implications for healthcare service chains.

A prime example is the SARS outbreak in 2003. On 12 March, 2003, the World Health Organization (WHO) issued a global alert for severe acute respiratory syndrome (SARS), a deadly new infectious disease with the potential for rapid spread from person to person and via international air travel (WHO, 2003). SARS emerged in the southern Chinese province of Guangdong in November 2002, but the worldwide epidemic was triggered in late February 2003 when an ill physician from Guangdong infected several other guests at a hotel in Hong Kong (Tsang et al., 2003). After this initial outbreak, the virus was able to infest a number of travellers, who then caused further outbreaks of the virus to Hong Kong, Vietnam, Singapore, and Canada (WHO, 2003). Although WHO and its partners had promptly initiated a coordinated investigation that gradually led to the identification of the etiologic agent, SARS-associated coronavirus (SARS-CoV), by the time SARS-CoV transmission was brought to an end in July 2003, more than 8,000 cases and 780 deaths had been reported from 29 countries (CDCP, 2004). The emergence of SARS-CoV provides a very good example of how modern crises can appear and spread abruptly, are difficult to be confined to their site of origin, and can lead to widespread health, social, and economic consequences. A more recent example is the H1N1 influenza virus outbreak of 2009 even though the impact was less severe (Trifonov et al., 2009).

Human-induced crises, such as the SARS and H1N1 outbreaks, but also natural disasters such as hurricane Katrina and the Haiti earthquake, have been shown to produce substantial shocks to both the demand and supply of healthcare services through increases in injuries, disease outbreaks, psychological trauma, diminished staff levels and capacity because of damaged buildings and supplies, transportation difficulties for both health providers and patients, and the presence of temporary substitute services (Tierney, 2005). As a consequence, crises may lead to substantial blows to the healthcare service chain over both short-term increases in emergency care and hospital-based outpatient care and extensive long-term consequences, such as increased expenditures, and prescription drugs use (Domino et al., 2003). Alternatively, cumulative crises, that is, crises arising from the cumulative choices and actions of stakeholders in the service chain, may also have great implications for the healthcare service chain. For example, the US Institute of Medicine's 2001 report characterised the then US health system as "plagued" by a number of medical errors, including poor preventive care, misdiagnoses and mistreatments, which have produced a number of health, social and economic problems to both the mass population and the US government (IOM, 2001). These medical errors can be defined as crises arising from the individual and cumulative misjudgements of healthcare professionals, as well as lack of necessary resources within the US national healthcare chain.

In summary, evidence shows that even initially modest incidents within the increasingly complex nature of the healthcare service chain can rapidly escalate and create serious problems even to the most remote sites. Consequently, the diverse range of effects triggered by such escalations can lead to misdiagnoses of underlying weaknesses if they are considered in isolation and not as part of the wider service chain. In effect, although awareness exists, there is lack of a clear strategic approach to the application of healthcare service chain management.

The attention is next turned to the field of crisis management to identify the key perspectives proposed by various researchers in understanding crises and developing an integrated strategy for crisis management.

Crisis Management Perspectives: Toward a Multidisciplinary Approach

As mentioned earlier, the cross-disciplinary nature of crises has contributed to "many different disciplinary voices, talking in different languages to different issues and audiences" (Shrivastava, 1993, p. 33). In an effort to make sense of the multidisciplinarity of the field, Pearson and Clair (1998) categorized crisis management according to three perspectives, namely, psychological, social-political, and technological-structural. Based on this categorization, Pearson and Clair (1998) examined the effect of each perspective on the "4Cs" for crisis studies, after Shrivastava's (1993) framework: the *causes* attributed for crises within each discipline; the *consequences* of crises; the *cautionary* measures advocated to prevent crises or minimize impact; and the *coping* techniques suggested in response to crisis occurrences. In brief, the psychological perspective attributes cognitive or behavioural causes to crises, with consequences on the assumptions held by individual members about their organization, and with cautionary measures focused in understanding vulnerabilities and potential harms, and coping techniques putting great emphasis on readjusting beliefs and assumptions (Janoff-Bulman, 1992; Pauchant & Mitroff, 1992). The social-political perspective attributes the breakdown in social-political institutions as the key causes to crises, with consequences on the shared values, beliefs and roles of organizations, and with cautionary measures focused on policies for guiding norms and behaviours, and coping techniques emphasizing reconstruction of collective action and adaptation (Hurst, 1995; Weick, 1993). Finally, the technological-structural perspective attributes the tight coupling of technological-managerial structures as the key causes of crises, with consequences for widespread disasters, and cautionary measures focused on avoidance of high-risk technologies, and coping techniques putting emphasis on triage efforts associated with treatment and recovery (Perrow, 1999). After having presented these three perspectives, Pearson and Clair (1998) concluded that crisis management has suffered from a fragmented paradigm and recommended that academics and practitioners attempt to synthesize the three perspectives into a single, multidisciplinary perspective.

More recently, Gilpin and Murphy (2008) took on the challenge toward synthesizing the three perspectives by drawing on complexity theory. Their key argument is that crisis management research needs to break free from models that focus on the crisis life cycle – which breaks the crisis down into discrete stages that follow a linear sequence, with most models agreeing on three general stages of *pre-crisis*, *crisis*, and *post-crisis* (Coombs, 2007) toward non-linear models that focus on changing, dynamic interactions between multiple causes, consequences, cautionary measures and coping techniques. In particular, Gilpin and Murphy (2008) offer a fresh approach to crisis management by placing great emphasis on complex systems principles, which are more readily applicable to new and emerging crises (Gilpin & Murphy, 2008, pp. 23-32).

First, *complex systems are composed of individual elements, or agents*. In crisis management terms, these may be individuals (e.g. members of a crisis response team; reporters; academics), organizations (e.g. a government agency; a disaster relief organization), or an entire city or nation (e.g. New Orleans, Haiti). In pooling their diverse vantage points, these agents may generate novel ways to cope with a crisis so that the final approach may be quite different from what the agents expected at the beginning of the process (cf. Weick, 1993).

Second, *agents in a complex system interact in ways that alter the system itself over time*. These interactions need not be physical; they may also relate to sharing information. Members of a crisis response team apply this principle when they do environmental surveillance in their effort to look for patterns built up from local interactions

– reports from the field, media coverage, etc. These local interactions often do not follow fixed guidelines and regulation by a higher authority (such as national emergency authorities), but are dynamically developed by the agents themselves in the course of their interaction based on their decision-making autonomy and the underlying culture of communication (Mara, 2004). In addition, the effects of these local interactions are "looped," meaning they can feed back at any point in the system, either positively (to encourage change) or negatively (to encourage stability) (Mitleton-Kelly, 2003). Through this, looping local interactions can produce adaptability by generating new patterns of behaviour that enable an organization to respond and operate more effectively than it would have by maintaining invariable behaviours. Finally, these interactions are nonlinear in that, the results of individual interactions are unpredictable: small causes can have a profound impact on the system, and large events may have minimal effect (Perrow, 1999).

Third, *complex systems are self-organizing*. Agents learn from their interactions, adapting to each other based on the feedback received, in an ongoing process known as "coevolution" or "emergence" – that is, unpredictable patterns of order that appear through a process of self-organization (Varela, 1995). That is the reason why a complex system does not allow any certain predictions as to how or in what direction the system as a whole will develop. Crisis management theorists have, in fact, argued that "for any one effect there may be five causes, and for any one cause there may be five effects" (Lagadec, 1993, p. 64). In turn, environmental scanning should not be carried as a rational analysis of linearly connected variables, but rather through "peripheral awareness" and "selective attention" to patterns and correspondences that emerge from background events while "tuning in" to salient information (Blandford & Wong, 2004).

Fourth, *complex systems are unstable*. As mentioned above, a complex system is constantly evolving. Indeed, stability is not a desired state. Thus, any attempt to comprehend a crisis that does not include the dimension of time can be considered only an incomplete understanding of the crisis' complex system or, at best, a snapshot of a specific point in time. This moment-to-moment instability also expresses the most challenging characteristics of the crisis' complex system: the need to act in an atmosphere of uncertainty and "feeling of powerlessness and extreme danger" that result from "intervening in any way . . . [in] a sensitive system in which everything is interrelated, [and] can have drastic and unexpected results" (Lagadec, 1993, p. 178).

Fifth, *complex systems are dynamic*. Because the evolution of the system is the result of iterative interaction between its agents, past history helps to produce present behavior. The memory of a complex system is present in the experiences and personal opinions of individual agents, as well as in the rituals and other features of a shared culture (Richardson, Mathieson, & Cilliers, 2000). This is why many scholars have argued that improvisational responses to possible crisis simulations are superior to overly specified crisis plans because they allow for variations to build up around the basic core of crisis management processes, resulting in a range of adaptive responses (Finch & Welker, 2004; Weick, 1993).

Sixth, *complex systems have permeable and ill-defined boundaries*. Here complexity-based thinking departs from other approaches that assume the existence of distinct borders between a system and its environment, even though systems are constantly adapting to their changing environments. Complex systems theory revises this perspective by integrating the environment as part of the system itself. That is why complexity science is understood as the study of parts of complex systems with an emphasis on interactive relationships rather than autonomous entities (van Uden et al., 2001).

Seventh, *complex systems are irreducible*. If a system is truly complex, it is more than the sum of its parts and, in order to understand a complex system, it is necessary to trace out the entire history of the system (van Uden et al., 2001). However, the irreducibility of a complex system raises serious problems for mainstream crisis planning that schematizes and simplifies potential crisis situations into their generic components – a practice that runs counter to the need to situate complex systems in terms of history, context, and relationship networks.

As Gilpin and Murphy (2008) stress, the seven principles outlined above do not operate in isolation rather they are interdependent. The H1N1 outbreak provides an example of these interdependencies by showing how events unfolded in a system of many interacting agents. Boundaries between sites of infection, treatment facilities, and geographical areas across countries became insignificant, because the virus affected populations across the global healthcare service chain. In fact, with increased transportation within and across national boundaries, and the airborne nature of the virus, it became irrelevant to talk about local or even national healthcare service chains and to focus instead on traces of the virus across the irreducible parts of the global healthcare service chain and the dynamic impact on both demand and supply of healthcare services (WHO, 2009; Baker et al., 2009). Most importantly, since the initial outbreak, the H1N1 virus has coevolved in unpredictable patterns: it "has generated scientific surprises and policy controversies, tested [crisis] plans and preparations made in expectation of such global health events, and raised concerns and fears about what might be over the horizon concerning influenza and other emerging infectious diseases" (Fidler, 2009, p. 767). In particular, the WHO's pandemic alert system – and more broadly global public-health decision-making – was put under severe criticism by many member states and independent experts due to the (later evident) H1N1 virus' moderate impact (Fidler, 2009; Wilson et al., 2010). That is, the H1N1 outbreak – like other recent crises such as hurricane Katrina and the

Haiti earthquake – have revealed weaknesses in the surveillance and response capabilities of many countries that remain unaddressed by a global, integrated strategy.

The next section explores some recent advances in information and communication technologies to understand the role that such technologies can play in surveillance and response to crises in the healthcare service chain.

The Strategic Role of Information Systems for Emergency Response & Crisis Management

Since 9/11, there have been considerable efforts to propose improvements in the development and implementation of information systems to aid in the surveillance and response of different crises (Mork, 2002). The key lesson learned from the 9/11 event is the strategic and technical fallacy of making the integration of communications between incompatible systems (fire, police, medical, etc.) dependent upon a single physical command and control center (Turoff et al., 2004). Instead, it is argued that efforts should focus on developing an integrated communications capability that can react as a distributed virtual system with no required need for the individuals involved to be in a single physical location (Turoff et al., 2004).

The need for more flexible and adaptable information systems has grown out of the realization that many of the failures of the past were due to the incorrect models adopted. Mendonça et al. (2007) argue that many emergency information systems of the past were built on the fallacy of the hierarchical, military model managing complex crises as individual "incidents"; the fallacy of developing all-inclusive doctrines and procedures to guide complex crisis management efforts; and the fallacy of achieving a universally common operating picture and situational awareness. Instead, the successful implementation of emergency information systems in crisis management efforts depends on the recognition that there is a wide range of tasks undertaken by emergency personnel with varying skills and abilities since they are coming from both established organizations and from adhocracies; and that, as a consequence, various information systems will need to be mixed and matched to support these personnel in accomplishing their tasks in crisis management (Mendonça et al., 2007).

This argument has more recently been supported in field studies (Durbin et al., 2010; Mils et al., 2009). For example, drawing on data from the 2007 Southern California wildfire events, Durbin et al. (2010) argued that rather than depending on traditional network infrastructures – which are often destroyed or malfunctioning during the disaster – for coordinating crisis management, emergency personnel are better off using alternative, mix-and-match tools such as cell phones, laptops, and spreadsheets. Similarly, many researchers in the fields of crisis management and emergency information systems have recognized the opportunities afforded by such technologies as blogs and wikis, cloud computing, and digital dashboards (Palen et al., 2009; Turoff, 2002), which when implemented together, can create a virtual information infrastructure that behaves very much like a complex system and which is more flexible and adaptable to new and emerging crises. Experts on disaster management and homeland security have argued that such a virtual infrastructure "generates the creativity, flexibility, and public involvement needed to respond to rapidly changing, unforeseeable circumstances" (Mils et al., 2009, pp. 8-9).

In summary, new and emerging crises have generated a new set of conditions requiring a more adaptive management strategy within and across healthcare service chains. It has been argued that complexity theory offers an insightful approach to synthesizing the multidisciplinarity of the field of crisis management and that, in fact, the use of new information and communication technologies reflect many of the principles of complex systems.

In the next section, the key lessons derived from the literature review are illustrated in the context of an empirical case study in the region of Crete in Greece. The key objective of this empirical illustration is to point at the limitations of traditional technologies and the need to explore alternative tools for crisis management and response.

MANAGING CRISES IN THE HEALTHCARE SERVICE CHAIN OF CRETE: TWO ILLUSTRATIVE EXAMPLES

Background to the Case Study

Crete is one of the 13 healthcare regions of Greece. Crete covers a geographical area of over 8,336 square kilometers and services a resident population of more than 500,000 people. During the summer period, tourists and other visitors raise the population to more than 1,000,000 people. Crete has 8 hospitals, 17 primary healthcare centres, and 6 community doctors. In addition, the regional emergency services of Crete are run through a central coordination centre in Heraklion (the capital) with three more units distributed in the region's remaining districts: Rethymno, Chania, and Lassithi.

Through a series of research projects run by CreteTech (a pseudonym), a semi-governmental research and development (R&D) institute, Crete became one of the first regions of Greece to develop and implement innovative information systems for managing crises. In the next subsections, two such information systems are briefly discussed, namely, (1) a pre-hospital emergency management system run by the regional emergency services, (2) and a telecardiology system supporting teleconsultations between a hospital and a group of primary healthcare centres.

The Pre-Hospital Emergency Management System

Based on computerized triage protocols, the Pre-hospital Emergency Management System (PhEMS) has a number of tasks which are considered vital for the effective management of critical medical emergencies: determine level of case severity; initiate appropriate response priorities; provide appropriate information and guidelines to emergency personnel; and provide first-aid directions to the general public. Figure 1 provides a graphic representation of the PhEMS.

In brief, the PhEMS works as follows. The operators at the pre-hospital emergency management centre have three screens in front of them: one screen shows the patient/incident record, which the operators fill with the patient's information at the time they receive the call; the second screen shows the triage protocols which change instantly as the operators select the condition of the patient in the patient/incident screen; and the third screen shows the geographical location of the ambulance unit via GPS. As soon as the operators receive a call they ask a set of questions that appear on the protocols screen. The four key questions asked refer to the medical category of the case, the patient's age, the level of consciousness, and the respiratory condition. Following this standardised procedure they reach the point when they have to classify the incident under one of the predefined categories such as cardiac arrest, allergy attack etc. As soon as they define the category, the protocols screen instantly presents a series of questions and medical procedures to further categorize the condition of the patient. These questions lead to a final scaled score, which indicate whether a condition is critical, less critical and no critical at all. These conditions are indicated with the colours red, orange, yellow and green. A green or yellow colour indicates that a basic life support ambulance unit needs to be dispatched with the yellow colour being more urgent, an orange colour requiring an advanced

Figure 1. The Pre-hospital emergency management system in the region of Crete

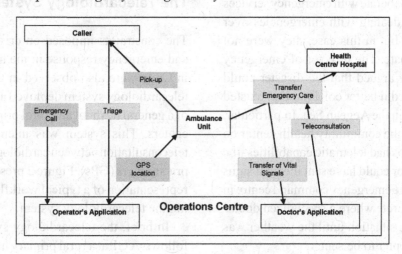

life support unit, and a red colour requiring immediate response by a mobile intensive care unit, equipped with more specialized medical devices, specialised doctors, and with access to telemedicine applications. Furthermore, the doctors at the pre-hospital emergency care centre or remote units have a separate screen in front of them, which gives them access to patient/incident files. On those screens they can monitor the vital signs of the patient in real-time as they are being sent over a telemedicine application from the ambulance unit at the site of the incident and provide teleconsultation. They can also access all these data at a later time, to further examine the medical procedures followed, and to acquire research and statistics of all the incidents handled by the emergency centre.

Ever since the initial installation of the system in 1998, which was followed by three more improvement/upgrade stages, the PhEMS has had 70% success rate in correctly identifying the nature of emerging crises and helping the regional healthcare service chain to generate an effective first response to critical health emergencies (see Constantinides et al 2008, for more details).

However, the reliance on a single physical command and control center based on a traditional

network infrastructure (despite employing GPS and telematics) created a number of constraints already mentioned in the literature. These included not being able to coordinate an effective first response to areas cut off from the range of command of the control centre and losing emergency response capabilities altogether in the event that the infrastructure supporting the control centre malfunctioned (e.g. poor radio communications).

A very striking example of the constraints of the centralized command model (and fatal in this case) is a helicopter accident over an island in the Aegean Sea during a rescue mission. As the director of emergency services in Crete explained in an interview in 2003, ten people, including the patient in emergency and the whole emergency crew died in that accident. In brief, the centralized command centre in Athens received a call for a patient in critical condition who was at the time at the island of Paros in the Aegean Sea. Unfortunately, due to poor communication between the community doctor in Paros and the dispatch operator in Athens, the latter dispatched a helicopter with two doctors and a crew to the island while ignoring the bad weather forecasts of strong winds and stormy sea with a result that the helicopter crashed in the sea and all died. Emergency services in Crete often collaborate with emergency services in Athens when dealing with emergencies over the Aegean Sea, but in this case, they were not asked to participate. The director of emergency services in Crete argued that the disaster could have been avoided if better collaboration existed between islands in the Aegean Sea. In particular, he argued that if the community health center on the island of Paros had telematic capabilities, the community doctor could have sent the vital signs of the patient to the emergency command centre in Athens or even Crete where a specialized doctor could consult the situation until the weather was clear for a helicopter to be sent.

The director of emergency services in Crete added that emergency personnel in Crete often found themselves in similar situations as those described above while responding to emergency calls in remote, mountainous, rural areas in Crete where telematic and radio communications were poor. He recognized the need for new technologies in supporting emergency response beyond the traditional infrastructure usually employed by emergency services including ones that could be used by the public.

The Telecardiology System

The constraints imposed on crisis management and emergency response in the healthcare chain in Crete were also observed in the context of a telecardiology system deployed across a network of a general hospital and rural primary healthcare centers. This system was intended to support teleconsultation between cardiologists and general practitioners (GPs). Figure 2 presents a graphical representation of a typical workflow scenario using the telecardiology system.

In brief, the telecardiology system works as follows. A GP at a rural primary healthcare center admits a patient suffering severe chest pain. After examining the patient, the clinical findings raise the suspicion of a possible heart attack. At this point, before the introduction of the telecardiology system, the GP would have either called a specialized cardiologist on the phone to ask for a second opinion or get assistance from the pre-hospital emergency services to transfer the patient to the general hospital where a specialized cardiologist would take full responsibility of the patient. The first option is very limiting, as the cardiologist would have to depend on the GP's judgment

Figure 2. The telecardiology system

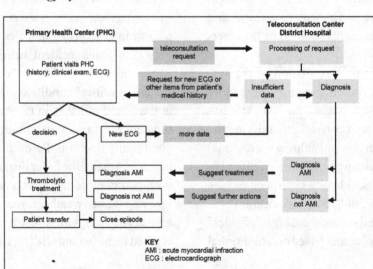

and evaluation of the patient's condition without having any of the clinical tests at hand. These would have to be sent by mail or with an ambulance if the patient was transferred. The second option would start to create a problem if all patients with suspected heart problems were transferred to the hospital. This would cause a work overload to the hospital staff, increasing waiting times and delaying the provision of healthcare services to, perhaps, more acute medical cases. Instead, the telecardiology system enabled the GP to request assistance from a general hospital by means of teleconsultation. In this option, the GP submits a consultation request that includes his/her evaluation of the clinical findings, the patient's medical history, including a digital electrocardiograph (ECG) and any other laboratory data, to the telecardiology system. The submission of the request triggers an alert, which is observable by participating cardiologists. A teleconsultation session between a GP and a cardiologist would take the form of asynchronous data transfer, or synchronous, real-time monitoring of the patient's vital signs and ECG, as well as video/audio conferencing. Finally, the cardiologist would advise the GP on the type of treatment to provide the patient or alternatively the cardiologist would request that the patient be transferred to the hospital. The teleconsultation session remains active until the GP files an outcome report, at which time the episode becomes part of the archive. That is, all teleconsultation sessions become part of the patient's electronic healthcare record.

The main group of users who got involved in the use of the telecardiology system comprised of a GP in a remote primary healthcare center and two cardiologists at the coronary care unit/intensive care unit at a general hospital. After an initial period of use, the system was found to be easily used by all involved doctors; it provided a short response time appropriate for emergencies; teleconsultation provided GPs with confidence in

their decision making, being at the same time an education tool; unnecessary transfers to the district hospital were avoided; and finally, there was an *a priori* knowledge of a pending emergency hospital admission.

After this initial evaluation, the system was supposed to be scaled up to six more primary healthcare centres in the district of Heraklion. However, the system was subjected to a number of inhibiting factors that eventually caused its collapse. These included issues of technology adoption including the relatively limited IT knowledge base of the new group of users compared to that of the initial group of users, as well as the limited amount of technical support provided by CreteTech due to insufficient funds (Constantinides & Barrett, 2006).

Most importantly, for the purposes of this paper, the system was constrained by its very dependence on traditional network infrastructures, which often malfunctioned and (due to a lack of funds) were not adequately supported. A participating cardiologist explained:

In the first stages of installation, CreteTech installed a system that would send me a message on my mobile saying that a request was sent to me via the teleconsultation system. But because of network problems and because the requests weren't as many at the time, this service was cancelled... So, the system, as it is now, is not very practical. ...I can't sit in front of the computer all the time.

Thus, as in the example of the PhEMS, even though that the telecardiology system provided a useful tool for detecting signs and symptoms of an emerging crisis (e.g. a cardiac disease), preventing a patient's condition from reaching a fatal state (e.g. heart attack), and also supporting an effective response and containment of a possible critical health emergency, it was constrained by its dependence on traditional network infrastructures.

DISCUSSION AND CONCLUSION

In both the PhEMS and the telecardiology system the importance of information systems in helping healthcare professionals manage crises in the healthcare service chain was evident and significant. At the same time, however, in both cases there was an evident need to break free from traditional models of crisis management (cf. Mendonça et al., 2007), such as centralized command centres (cf. Turoff et al., 2004) toward alternative mix-and-match tools such as mobile phone notification (cf. Durbin et al., 2010). This is not to say that traditional models are no longer needed – e.g. the centralized command centre at the emergency services in Crete has, in fact, saved a lot of lives since its implementation (Constantinides et al., 2008). Rather, such traditional models need to be complemented by new and emerging technologies such as mashups.

Mashups refer to web-based services that weave data from different sources into a new data source or service. Mashups are becoming increasingly widespread, especially in the context of combining geographic data and displaying such integrated data on maps. For example, HealthMap was developed by the Children's Hospital Informatics Program in Boston to integrate disparate data sources within Google Maps toward a unified and comprehensive view of the current global state of infectious diseases and their effect on human and animal health. This freely available web service integrates outbreak data of varying reliability, ranging from media sources (e.g. Google News) to personal accounts (e.g. ProMED), and more valid alerts (e.g. World Health Organization) (Boulos et al., 2008).

Such Web 2.0 technologies can support public health monitoring and research, including infectious disease surveillance and molecular epidemiology, while reducing the burden of decision-making of emergency experts by distributing data gathering and analysis activities across a network of participants. By promoting data sharing and community collaboration among diverse users, these Web 2.0 technologies can help in analyzing historical trends of emergency-related data over time or detecting emergent crisis in real-time. For example, in both the PhEMS and telecardiology systems, if individuals with information about an emerging crisis were allowed to send messages or tweets via web-based or mobile applications to each other and to experts leading the crisis management efforts, they would create greater possibilities of achieving a more efficient and coordinated emergency response.

In conclusion, this paper contributes to recent research exploring the strategic importance of information systems for managing new and emerging crises in the healthcare service chain. After conducting a review of the literature on crisis management and information systems for emergency response, the paper argues that complexity theory offers an insightful approach to synthesizing the multidisciplinarity of the field of crisis management. This argument is supported in the observation that the use of new information and communication technologies such as, Web 2.0 services, reflect many of the principles of complex systems. Through an empirical illustration of how traditional crisis management models and infrastructure networks – although partly successful – fail to address the complexities of new and emerging crisis, the paper then argues that a virtual information infrastructure comprised of flexible and adaptive mix-and-match tools can generate more creative and efficient responses to rapidly changing and unforeseeable circumstances.

REFERENCES

Baker, M. G., Kelly, H., & Wilson, N. (2009). Editorial: Pandemic H1N1 influenza lessons from the southern hemisphere. *Euro Surveillance : European Communicable Disease Bulletin*, *14*(42), 1–5.

Belluck, P. (2009, November 13). W.H.O. rushes drugs to nations hit by swine flu. *New York Times*.

Blandford, A., & Wong, W. (2004). Situation Awareness in Emergency Medical Dispatch. *International Journal of Human-Computer Studies*, *61*, 421–452. doi:10.1016/j.ijhcs.2003.12.012

Boin, A., & Hart, P. (2003). Public leadership in times of crisis: mission impossible? *Public Administration Review*, *63*(5), 544–553. doi:10.1111/1540-6210.00318

Boin, R. A., Hart, P., Stern, E., & Sundelius, B. (2005). *The politics of crisis management: Public leadership under pressure*. Cambridge, UK: Cambridge University Press. doi:10.1017/CBO9780511490880

Boulos, M. N. K., Scotch, M., Cheung, K. H., & Burden, D. (2008). Web GIS in practice VI: a demo playlist of geo-mashups for public health neogeographers. *International Journal of Health Geographics*, *7*(38).

Centers for Disease Control and Prevention (CDCP). (2004). *Public Health Guidance for Community-Level Preparedness and Response to Severe Acute Respiratory Syndrome (SARS)*. Washington, DC: Department of Health and Human Services.

Chen, R., Rao, H. R., Sharma, R., Upadhyaya, S., & Kim, J. (2010). An Empirical Examination of IT-Enabled Emergency Response: The Cases of Hurricane Katrina and Hurricane Rita. *Communications of the Association for Information Systems*, *26*(8), 141–156.

Constantinides, P., & Barrett, M. (2006). Negotiating ICT development & use: the case of a regional telemedicine system in Crete. *Information and Organization*, *16*(1), 27–55. doi:10.1016/j.infoandorg.2005.07.001

Constantinides, P., Kouroubali, A., & Barrett, M. (2008). Transacting Expertise in Emergency Management and Response. In *Proceedings of ICIS 2008*. Retrieved from http://aisel.aisnet.org/icis2008/15

Coombs, W. T. (2007). *Ongoing crisis communication: Planning, managing and responding* (2nd ed.). Thousand Oaks, CA: Sage.

Corbin, C. L., Kelley, S. W., & Schwartz, R. W. (2001). Concepts in service marketing for healthcare professionals. *American Journal of Surgery*, *181*(1), 1–7. doi:10.1016/S0002-9610(00)00535-3

Domino, M. E., Fried, B., Moon, Y., Olinick, J., & Yoon, J. (2003). Disasters and the public health safety net: hurricane Floyd hits the North Carolina Medicaid program. *American Journal of Public Health*, *93*(7), 1122–1127. doi:10.2105/AJPH.93.7.1122

Dooren, J.C. (2009, November 10). FDA approves GlaxoSmithKline's H1N1 vaccine. *Dow Jones Newswire*.

Durbin, T., Jennex, M. E., Frost, E., & Judge, R. (2010). Achieving Electric Restoration Logistical Efficiencies during Critical Infrastructure Crisis Response: A Knowledge Management Analysis. *International Journal of Information Systems for Crisis Response and Management*, *2*(3), 36–50. doi:10.4018/jiscrm.2010070103

Falco, M. (2010, February 12). H1N1 virus' death toll as high as 17,000, CDC estimates. *CNN Medical News*.

Fidler, D. (2009). H1N1 after action review: learning from the unexpected, the success and the fear. *Future Microbiology*, *4*, 767–769. doi:10.2217/fmb.09.54

Finch, M. R., & Welker, L. S. (2004). Informed organizational improvisation: A metaphor and method for understanding, anticipating, and performatively constructing the organization's precrisis environment . In Millar, D. P., & Heath, R. L. (Eds.), *Responding to crisis: A rhetorical approach to crisis communication* (pp. 189–200). Mahwah, NJ: Erlbaum.

Gilpin, D. R., & Murphy, P. J. (2008). *Crisis Management in a Complex World*. New York, NY: Oxford University Press. doi:10.1093/acprof:oso/9780195328721.001.0001

Hurst, D. K. (1995). *Crisis and renewal*. Boston, MA: Harvard Business School Press.

Institute of Medicine (IOM). (2001). *Crossing the Quality Chasm: A New Health System for the 21st Century*. Washington, DC: National Academy Press.

Janoff-Bulman, R. (1992). *Shattered assumptions*. New York, NY: Free Press.

Jennex, M. E. (2004). Emergency Response Systems: The Utility Y2K Experience. *Journal of Information Technology Theory and Application, 6*(3), 85–102.

Keen, J., Moore, J., & West, R. (2006). Pathways, networks and choice in health care. *International Journal of Health Care Quality Assurance, 19*, 316–327. doi:10.1108/09526860610671373

Lagadec, P. (1993). *Preventing chaos in a crisis: Strategies for prevention, control, and damage limitation* (Phelps, J. M., Trans.). New York, NY: McGraw-Hill.

Marra, F. J. (2004). Excellent crisis communication: Beyond crisis plans . In Millar, D. P., & Heath, R. L. (Eds.), *Responding to crisis: A rhetorical approach to crisis communication* (pp. 311–325). Mahwah, NJ: Erlbaum.

McNeil, D. G., Jr. (2009, November 24). Shifting vaccine for flu to elderly. *New York Times*.

Mendonça, D., Jefferson, T., & Harrald, J. (2007). Collaborative adhocracies and mix-and-match technologies in emergency management. *Communications of the ACM, 50*(3), 44–49. doi:10.1145/1226736.1226764

Mills, A., Chen, R., Lee, J. K., & Rao, H. R. (2009). Web 2.0 Emergency Applications: How Useful Can Twitter be for Emergency Response. *Journal of Information Privacy & Security, 5*(3), 3–26.

Mitleton-Kelly, E. (2003). Ten principles of complexity and enabling infrastructures . In Mitleton-Kelly, E. (Ed.), *Complex systems and evolutionary perspectives on organisations: The application of complexity theory to organisations* (pp. 23–50). New York, NY: Pergamon Press.

Mork, L. (2002). Technology Tools for Crisis response. *Risk Management, 49*(10), 44–50.

Palen, L., Vieweg, S., Liu, S., & Hughes, A. L. (2009). Crisis in a Networked World: Features of Computer-Mediated Communication in the April 16, 2007 Virginia Tech Event. *Social Science Computer Review*, 467–480. doi:10.1177/0894439309332302

Pauchant, T. C., & Mitroff, I. I. (1992). *Transforming the crisis-prone organization*. San Francisco, CA: Jossey-Bass.

Pearson, C., & Mitroff, I. I. (1993). From crisis prone to crisis prepared: a framework for crisis management. *The Academy of Management Executive, 7*(1), 48–59.

Pearson, C. M., & Clair, J. A. (1998). Reframing crisis management. *Academy of Management Review, 23*(1), 59–76. doi:10.2307/259099

Perrow, C. (1999). *Normal accidents: living with high-risk technologies* (2nd ed.). Princeton, NJ: Princeton University Press.

Perry, R. W., & Quarantelli, E. L. (Eds.). (2005). *What is a disaster? New answers to old questions*. Philadelphia, PA: Xlibris.

Preble, J. F. (1997). Integrating the crisis management perspective into the strategic management process. *Journal of Management Studies, 34*(5), 769–791. doi:10.1111/1467-6486.00071

Quantarelli, E. L., Lagadec, P., & Boin, A. (2007). A heuristic approach to future disasters and crises . In Rodriguez, H., Quantarelli, E. L., & Dynes, R. (Eds.), *Handbook of Disaster Research* (pp. 16–41). Berlin, Germany: Springer. doi:10.1007/978-0-387-32353-4_2

Richardson, K. A., Mathieson, G., & Cilliers, P. (2000). The theory and practice of complexity science: Epistemological considerations for military operational analysis. *SysteMexico, 1*(2), 25–66.

Scotti, D. J., Harmon, J., & Behson, S. J. (2007). Links among high-performance work environment, service quality, and customer satisfaction: an extension to the healthcare sector. *Journal of Healthcare Management, 52*(2), 109–124.

Shrivastava, P. (1993). Crisis theory/practice: Towards a sustainable future. *Industrial and Environmental Crisis Quarterly, 7,* 23–42.

Smits, S. J., & Ally, N. E. (2003). Thinking the unthinkable – leadership's role in creating behavioural readiness for crisis management. *Communication Review, 13*(1), 1–23.

Tierney, K. J. (2005). The 9/11 Commission and disaster management: Little depth, less context, not much guidance. *Contemporary Sociology, 34,* 115–121. doi:10.1177/009430610503400204

Trifonov, V., Khiabanian, H., & Rabadan, R. (2009). Geographic Dependence, Surveillance, and Origins of the 2009 Influenza A (H1N1) Virus. *The New England Journal of Medicine, 61*(2), 115–119. doi:10.1056/NEJMp0904572

Tsang, K. W., Ho, P. L., Ooi, G. C., & Yee, W. K. (2003). A cluster of cases of severe acute respiratory syndrome in Hong Kong. *The New England Journal of Medicine, 348,* 1977–1985. doi:10.1056/NEJMoa030666

Turoff, M. (2002). Past and Future Emergency Response Information Systems. *Communications of the ACM, 45*(4), 29–32. doi:10.1145/505248.505265

Turoff, M. (2004). The Design of a Dynamic Emergency Response Management Information System (DERMIS). *Journal of Information Technology Theory and Application, 5*(4).

van Uden, J., Richardson, K. A., & Cilliers, P. (2001). Postmodernism revisited? Complexity science and the study of organizations. *Journal of Critical Postmodern Organization Science, 1*(3), 53–67.

Varela, F. J. (1995). The re-enchantment of the concrete . In Steels, L., & Brooks, R. (Eds.), *The artificial life route to artificial intelligence: Building embodied, situated agents* (pp. 11–20). Mahwah, NJ: Erlbaum.

Vargo, S. L., & Lusch, R. E. (2004). Evolving to a New Dominant Logic for Marketing. *Journal of Marketing, 68,* 1–17. doi:10.1509/jmkg.68.1.1.24036

Vargo, S. L., & Lusch, R. E. (2008). Service-Dominant Logic: Continuing the Evolution. *Journal of the Academy of Marketing Science, 36*(1), 1–10. doi:10.1007/s11747-007-0069-6

Weick, K. E. (1993). The collapse of sensemaking in organizations: the Mann Gulch disaster. *Administrative Science Quarterly, 38,* 628–652. doi:10.2307/2393339

WHO. (2003). *WHO issues a global alert about cases of atypical pneumonia*. Geneva, Switzerland: Author.

WHO. (2009). *Influenza A (H1N1) – Update 54*. Geneva, Switzerland: Author. Retrieved from http://www.who.int/csr/don/2009_06_26/en/index.html

Whybark, D.C., Melnyk, S.A., Day, J., & Davis, E. (2010). Disaster Relief Supply Chain Management: New Realities, Management Challenges, Emerging Opportunities. *Decision Line*, 4-7.

Wilson, K., Brownstein, J., & Fidler, D. (2010). Strengthening the International Health Regulations: lessons from the H1N1 pandemic. *Health Policy and Planning, 25*, 505–509. doi:10.1093/heapol/czq026

This work was previously published in International Journal of Information Systems for Crisis Response Management, Volume 2, Issue 4, edited by Murray E. Jennex, pp. 33-47, copyright 2010 by IGI Publishing (an imprint of IGI Global).

Chapter 17
The Role of Social Networks in Emergency Management:
A Research Agenda

Linna Li
University of California at Santa Barbara, USA

Michael F. Goodchild
University of California at Santa Barbara, USA

ABSTRACT

Lack of relevant information, particularly geospatial information, is one of the major challenges in emergency management. In the past few years, geospatial information created by volunteers and facilitated by social networks has become a promising data source in time-critical situations. This paper discusses the roles that social networks can play in the crowdsourcing of geospatial information for emergency management, data generation and dissemination through social networks, and investigates the relationships and interactions in social networks. Research issues arise in the areas of data access, data quality, information synthesis, emerging patterns of human behaviors in emergencies, analysis and visualization of nested social networks, implementation of information systems for emergency management, privacy, and equity.

INTRODUCTION

The increasing complexity of society and the intensity of the interactions between humans and their environment make us more vulnerable than ever to unexpected events. Recent disasters (e.g., Hurricane Katrina in 2005, the Wenchuan Earthquake in 2008, the Haiti and Chile Earthquakes in 2010) remind us again of the fact that we are far from being prepared for emergencies. In these disasters,

the direct damage to society has been enormous in terms of death, injury, and property loss. The long-term economic impact, both domestically and internationally, is more difficult to estimate. Modern technologies, especially remote sensing and GIS, have been used to monitor the situation, to locate damaged areas, and to assess severity.

Yet despite this, the full potential of geospatial data generation and dissemination mediated by information technology has not been fully realized

DOI: 10.4018/978-1-4666-0167-3.ch017

in crisis situations (NRC, 2007). Geospatial information provided by governments is inadequate in emergencies because of cost and long production cycles, while massive volumes of imagery from satellites and aircraft may be more timely but are limited to phenomena that can be seen from above. In the past few years, an alternative source of data has emerged, created by citizen journalists who collect, report, and disseminate information. Such volunteered geographic information (VGI) (Goodchild, 2007) is created by amateurs using online mapping services over the Internet, such as OpenStreetMap (OSM) or Ushahidi. VGI has been proved useful in rapidly developing emergencies such as the recent Santa Barbara fires (Goodchild & Glennon, 2010), where the need for timeliness often outweighs concerns about accuracy. During the 2010 Haitian Earthquake, a mapping community was formed immediately by people all over the world, and geospatial data about Port-au-Prince were quickly generated using OSM, and used in the rescue effort.

Social networks have proven critical in such situations, because they are able to mobilize the necessary volunteers; to provide the means to share tools; and to facilitate the loose kinds of dispersed organization that are needed to make the efforts of volunteers run smoothly. In this paper we outline some of the open questions that have arisen in this context and that together might form the basis for a research agenda aimed at improving our understanding of the role social networks can play in time-critical community mapping. The paper is based on discussions that occurred in December, 2010, at a specialist meeting organized by the Center for Spatial Studies of the University of California, Santa Barbara, on the topic of Spatio-Temporal Constraints on Social Networks. At the meeting over 40 specialists from around the world discussed the state of the art in this area, the topics that needed to be researched and appropriate priorities for each topic. Although the meeting covered much broader ground, this paper focuses on the specific domain of emer-

gency management, and summarizes the relevant discussion. Full details of the meeting, including the position papers prepared by the participants, the presentations made during the meeting, and reports of the various discussion groups, can be found at http://www.ncgia.ucsb.edu/projects/spatio-temporal/.

The rest of this paper is organized as follows. The next section discusses pressing issues in the use of geospatial data and tools for emergency management. The following section then discusses the potential benefits of integrating studies on social networks into this context, followed by a series of research questions raised by this integration. The paper ends with some concluding remarks.

EMERGENCY MANAGEMENT

In emergencies, there is a critical time constraint on evacuating affected people, locating and delivering available resources, as well as generating relevant information and distributing it to appropriate parties in a timely manner. Relevant data are crucial to making informed decisions about where to focus attention and where to distribute limited resources; however, how to obtain reliable, accurate, and timely geospatial data is always a challenge, especially in situations where disasters develop rapidly. It is extremely difficult for government agencies to send a sufficient number of trained people to the affected area for mapping and data collection. When a disaster happens, professional emergency workers are rapidly overwhelmed and scarce emergency services may be quickly depleted. In the report to the US Congress on Hurricane Katrina, Secretary of Homeland Security Michael Chertoff emphasized "the importance of having accurate, timely and reliable information about true conditions on the ground" and pointed out that the response efforts during Katrina "were significantly hampered by a lack of information from the ground" (Chertoff, 2005).

Another primary challenge in handling emergencies is information sharing and communication in order to facilitate coordination. Information needs to be appropriately shared and promptly exchanged between involved parties at the appropriate place and time. Professional emergency workers may have a special emergency management system to communicate with each other and between departments at federal, regional, and local levels. Effective communication is also vital between emergency managers and local residents for execution of evacuation plans, and between residents to help each other to avoid risks in a self-organized manner. In addition, information updates are also important for local residents for emotional reasons. Lack of up-to-date information about the disaster and the status of family, pets, and friends may aggravate negative emotions such as fear, stress, and anxiety, which may lead to mass panic. However, existing communication channels established by various levels of government are neither sufficient nor adequately utilized to respond to major disasters. For example, the lack of an adequate and effective communication system to inform and guide the public was identified as one of the failures in the response and recovery efforts during Hurricane Katrina (White House, 2006); and in the Santa Barbara fires of 2007–2009 the capacity of the official Web sites was often insufficient to meet the demand.

BENEFITS OF USING SOCIAL NETWORKS

As discussed above, there are limited resources from government agencies to gather geospatial information rapidly, and effective communication mechanisms are lacking for information sharing and collaboration between professional emergency managers and citizens during emergencies. Social networks can play two major roles in effective emergency management. First, information generated and disseminated over social networks is incredibly valuable for disaster response. Second, the study of the relationships, behaviors, and interactions in social networks may provide important insights for gathering information, planning evacuations and sheltering, and other rescue efforts.

On the one hand, during emergencies, official sources for covering a localized disaster may be insufficient or inaccurate due to the lack of capability and resources or due to more severe disasters taking place in other places that require more attention. On the other hand, human sensors that can observe and monitor the disaster process are often densely distributed and information generated by them can be rapidly shared. The time to acquire the official geospatial information regarding a disaster can be long, while the information generated and distributed by users of online social networks can be instantaneous. In some other situations where information is strictly censored by government, social networks enable people to obtain relevant information, challenge conventional official information sources, and circumvent news blackouts. During the SARS outbreak in China in 2003, for example, text-message usage in Guangdong province had tripled between February 8th and 10th compared to the same period in the previous year, indicating high levels of social networking activity. These citizens knew this information before the Chinese government reported it to the World Health Organization on February 11th and they shared the locations of outbreaks, symptoms, and possible remedies (Gordon, 2007).

VGI is one particular type of information with a location component which is generated by social networks and is vital for emergency management. This alternative source of geospatial information over the Internet often has comparable accuracy to authoritative sources and appears to be superior to official sources in terms of currency. The importance of locations in emergencies can never be over-emphasized. Timely identification of affected people may make a difference between life and death, and timely allocation of

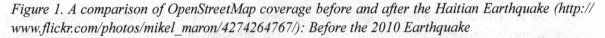

Figure 1. A comparison of OpenStreetMap coverage before and after the Haitian Earthquake (http://www.flickr.com/photos/mikel_maron/4274264767/): Before the 2010 Earthquake

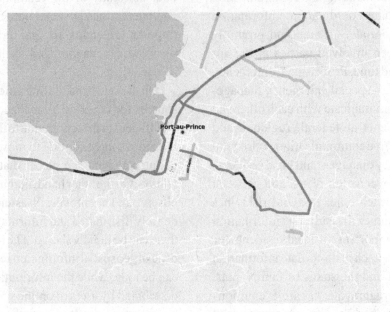

resources to locations of greatest need is crucial for disaster relief. Several examples have shown the importance of VGI in disaster response. During the 2010 Haitian Earthquake, a group of OSM users from all over the world rapidly produced a detailed street map of Port-au-Prince which was used by crisis responders on the ground in Haiti, based on digitization of satellite imagery facilitated by social networks such as Crisis Mappers Net. The Humanitarian OpenStreetMap Team (H.O.T), through the CrisisCamp events of volunteers linked through the Crisis Mappers network, formed an open community to connect everyone involved and to integrate the work of thousands of networked volunteers world-wide in the production and maintenance of a digital map of Haiti. After an original call to action for Haiti at 7:08pm EST on January 12, the CrisisMappers Google Group had 706 members and a history of 2364 messages, and over 574 individuals were sharing profiles through Crisis Mappers Net as of March 1, 2010 (Meier & Ziemke, 2010). Before the earthquake, the OSM map of Port-au-Prince

had very limited coverage (Figure 1), but within only 48 hours, the dataset became possibly the most complete and accurate data source for that area (Figure 2). In the 2009 Jesusita Fire in Santa Barbara, several individuals established a website, with the Google Map API, to collect relevant information from both official sources and data contributed by local residents using online social network sites such as Twitter, Flickr, and blogs. In these cases, VGI is particularly crucial for disaster response in areas with insufficient data, such as Haiti. Furthermore, maps of potential risks and social vulnerability (Cutter, 2003) may be generated to describe the various probabilities of hazards in different locations and the ability of different individuals and groups to cope with disasters, which can guide disaster mitigation and preparedness.

In addition to data generated from social networks, studies of relationships, interactions, and patterns in social networks are also useful in all stages of disasters. Identification of abnormal patterns in social networks within a spatio-temporal context may automatically discover locations that need more attention. For example, geo-tagged tweets were used to detect unusual social events in Japan (e.g., local festivals) by comparing tweet patterns to the usual behavior patterns of twitter users (Lee & Sumiya, 2010). Similarly, analysis of social networks may recognize the outbreak of a disease before it is noticed and confirmed by official sources. Furthermore, analysis of leaders and groups in a disaster-response effort is critical for performing tasks better.

There are three major types of social groups in emergency response. First, affected communities may be immediately involved in activities (e.g., engaging in conversations using social networking services) to report relevant information motivated by self-interest. They report what they see, take pictures and videos, and transmit rapidly to others information about what is happening at their locations. Some individuals may also establish local community sites to gather information for a particular disaster from various sources, including both official and volunteered information. Second,

professional emergency workers equipped with capabilities to perform large-scale rescue efforts are assigned to disaster relief after it is reported to the government. These trained professionals are capable of coping with different disaster scenarios and have access to essential emergency assets and services; however, they may be very unfamiliar with the local situation. Third, a large number of highly motivated volunteers contribute for humanitarian reasons. They are not directly related to affected people as relatives or friends and they may not be close to the affected community geographically, but they have access to necessary computational resources to generate appropriate geospatial data. As one major contributor in the Haitian earthquake mapping effort from the Netherlands said: "Given any disaster, together with good satellite imagery, I would go at it again in a heartbeat, no matter where a disaster would take place!" In disasters, these three groups of people work together towards a common goal to reduce the impacts of disasters; however, this may be the first time that they collaborate with

Figure 2. A comparison of OpenStreetMap coverage before and after the Haitian Earthquake (http:// www.flickr.com/photos/mikel_maron/4274264767/): January 14, 2010

each other, and coordination is required when a large number of people are involved in an activity. Social network analysis may offer useful insights into this problem.

CHALLENGES IN USING SOCIAL NETWORKS

Although social networks have a great potential to benefit the acquisition and use of geospatial data and tools in emergency management, this application also raises a number of research questions across a wide range of disciplines, including emergency management, geography, sociology, computer science, geographic information science, and ethics.

First, data access and data quality are two important issues to consider before information generated in social networks can benefit emergency management. Is there an automatic way to discover relevant information for a particular disaster over the Web when a range of tools and websites are used by different groups of people? In addition, there is always a trust issue in accepting information generated by volunteers. An individual may be faced with a choice between available but potentially unreliable information synthesized by volunteers, and authoritative yet possibly unavailable information from government agencies (Goodchild & Glennon, 2010). Should he or she wait for the official information from government which may be slower, or should he or she trust VGI that is asserted without validation? Although an average citizen may choose the risk of false positives over the risk of false negatives because the consequences of the latter are more devastating, the answers to the following questions may help them make better decisions. How can we validate the information generated by volunteers on the Web? How can we quantify the uncertainty in a piece of information? Are there any metrics to evaluate the data quality of a particular contributor, e.g., from knowledge of his

or her personal background, or from an evaluation of data previously generated by the same person? Is it possible to produce automatically a probability distribution of data values from multiple sources? A more perplexing situation would be a conflict between information sources, especially a contradiction between an official source and a volunteer. As discussed above, information from official sources may be validated when it is received but the delay may make it obsolete when a citizen reads it. It is also useful to compare the value and appropriateness of various data types among maps, text, images, and videos through different Web services including OSM, Twitter, Flickr, Youtube, etc. Is data quality related to data format or medium? For example, are pictures and videos more objective and accurate than text messages?

Faced with information from various sources with different levels of uncertainty, another crucial question is how to synthesize geospatial information effectively from sensors (e.g., remote sensing imagery) and human observations (e.g., text, pictures, and videos), ideally in real time. Provenance and uncertainty of different sources should be maintained in synthesis, which is still a challenging issue in the database and GIScience communities. How to conflate geospatial data with various accuracies, different levels of detail, and in different formats is still an open question. Semantic interoperability is also critical in integration of data from different social groups who use different concepts to think and different languages to communicate. In addition, what data type would be the most appropriate form for integration and synthesis of various sources to facilitate reasoning and decision making? For instance, should all information be linked by geographic locations and conflated into a base map to provide a holistic view of relevant knowledge? What type of information is needed in different stages of disaster management? What type of information is needed to support evacuation by different modes, from private vehicles to pedestrians?

Besides the use of alternative data sources, it is also very important to understand the emerging pattern of volunteers who join social networks to generate and share geospatial data during emergencies. A more general research issue concerns how a social network forms, is maintained, and evolves as an emergency develops. Can social network theories in sociology be used to explain human behaviors in emergencies? How does the number of volunteers increase as the disaster develops? What factors determine the geographic distribution of information generators dynamically? What are the socioeconomic characteristics of habitual volunteers in generating and disseminating information in emergencies? When a number of highly motivated volunteers are available to generate useful information in response to a disaster, is there an effective way to assign tasks and to organize the community? Are they currently self-organized during crisis mapping efforts? Should the mapping tasks be systematically partitioned? For example, to produce geospatial information for an area, should we partition the task horizontally, which means one volunteer is assigned to work on a subarea, or should we partition the task hierarchically, which means one volunteer is assigned to work on a particular theme of the whole area? Is there a mechanism to prioritize data production in terms of areas and themes? Is there a relationship between the type of contributed information and the distance from the volunteer to the contributed area? For instance, it may be easier for a distant volunteer to generate geometries of streets using remote sensing images as opposed to street names. How can we use this relationship to assign tasks according to the distance between a volunteer and a target area? In addition, how can we identify qualified individuals with required expertise and skills and encourage them to contribute to information generation? For example, how can we identify trained GIS professionals (e.g., GIS practitioners, teachers, or students) and people with local knowledge (e.g., geographers or social scientists) when geospatial information is needed

or the cultural background of affected people is crucial for evacuation? Studying behavior patterns of volunteers, such as contributors of VGI, may offer insights in these areas.

Another research issue directly related to emergency data and volunteer behaviors discussed above is social network support to facilitate information generation and dissemination, particularly VGI. Social networks allow people to access hundreds of friends, to get acquainted with like-minded people, and to coordinate millions of hours of human work. How can we utilize existing social networks to grow the VGI contributor community? How can we promote participation through socio-psychological incentives? Some social networks are not originally designed for collaborative mapping in time-critical situations. In emergencies, how can we harness different social networks to build a crowd dedicated to crisis mapping? When multiple social networks are involved, how should we define clear roles for volunteers, in order to eliminate overlap in work and facilitate coordination? Besides, social networks can be very useful for monitoring VGI quality. Similar to the self-reporting system on many user-generated-content websites, users can flag a piece of VGI as accurate or inaccurate. Social networks may also build up a moderation system where people gradually gain reputation by overall veracity and reliability. How should we give people privileges as moderators and editors in quality control? People tend to trust people in their social networks. How can we establish trust networks within existing social networks in emergencies by integrating various social networks through common nodes? As discussed above, there are three major social groups in disaster response. How can we achieve effective networking among affected communities, the emergency management agencies, and VGI contributor communities? To what extent do people involved in traditional mapping constitute a social network, and what can be learned from its structure and operation? How can the dynamic embedded networks of volunteers be represented, and what new metrics are needed to monitor them? How can we maintain a social network of volunteers propelled by a previous disaster response effort and adapt it to another VGI project? For example, mapping communities have been formed after the Haitian Earthquake. How can we utilize social networks to motivate people to continue contributing to collaborative mapping in their leisure time, even when there is no major disaster? In this way, many of the tasks performed by OSM volunteers in the aftermath of the Haiti earthquake may be moved from emergency response to the earlier phases of risk assessment, mitigation, and preparedness. When a disaster happens, only some modifications of existing data are needed to reflect the landscape change caused by the disaster.

Social networks are embedded in geographic space and time and nested with other networks, such as transportation networks and information networks. Correlation may exist between movements in one network and activities in another network. For example, movements of cars between two locations on the road network may reflect a connection of people at the same two locations in a social network. We need to keep in mind that people rarely act independently in emergencies, but rather evacuate within groups. Parents may go to school to pick up their children before leaving town. Therefore, understanding social networks is critical for developing an optimal rescue plan such as an evacuation route. Another example is that the activities in online social networks (e.g., comments on an event) may reflect activities in the physical world (an event that people are currently experiencing, such as a football game or a fire). The study of the interactions is made possible with the development of location-based services and the large volumes of geospatial data generated by them. However, novel methods and new techniques need to be developed to capture the correlation between networks, to represent and analyze spatio-temporal dynamics of social networks, and to help emergency managers make

decisions at different scales. When different social networks are combined to perform a task towards a common goal (e.g., emergency response), how can information technology be used to reorganize social networks based on geographic proximity, expertise, skills, etc., to perform tasks better? How can we facilitate interaction and collaboration among major social groups involved in emergencies using information systems?

Social network analysis is promising for understanding the current situations of people involved in emergencies, but we do not have adequate methods to conduct analysis. First, it is helpful to distinguish between real social networks and implied social networks. Real social networks are the complex relationships of people at various levels, and implied social networks are inferred from human activities. Any data we collect using either online social-network services or cell phone records are only an approximation of real social networks with simplification or even misrepresentation. Therefore, it would be useful to investigate the uncertainty of collected social-network data. What is the percentage of relationships that are represented in a particular social-network data source? How can we collect social-network data about affected people from available sources? How can we identify useful social networks from masses of disparate data? Furthermore, how can we combine data from different social-networking services, e.g., Twitter, Facebook, or phone records? Besides, representation of complex multi-level social networks is also a big challenge. Is there an effective way to generalize large complex social networks? How can cartography and geovisual analytics contribute to representations of social networks? When large volumes of data are available, what would be an effective mechanism to use to sample? How should we identify different roles of people in social networks, e.g., leaders and followers? How do we identify emerging and abnormal patterns in spatio-temporal social networks? What models can be developed to simulate social networks embedded in spatially and temporally bounded environments, and to evaluate the impacts of possible decisions? How to measure and improve the efficiency of a social-network process for effective organization and spreading of information? How to enable a social network spatially, temporally, and culturally to accelerate rates of information diffusion? Is it possible to develop a theory for multi-level networks? How can we integrate existing social-network graphs with location-based services to analyze the geographic distribution of participants of a social network at a particular time-space point in order to make an optimal evacuation route taking into account social factors? When we want to send a message to a particular person who is in danger, is there a way to identify connections from this person to notify him or her?

In addition to conceptual understanding of social networks and use of valuable data, another big challenge is implementation of information systems to facilitate emergency response and to improve decision-making. During emergencies, it is very important to have effective communication between emergency managers and affected people. While social-networking tools have been used by local residents to share relevant information (Goodchild & Glennon, 2010; Longueville *et al.*, 2009; Vieweg, 2010), not much research has been done to investigate the effectiveness of using social-networking tools to disseminate information or to coordinate tasks by emergency managers during the response and recovery phases. Studies are needed on information diffusion over social networks and on the effectiveness of possible channels for distributing relevant information in emergencies so that emergency managers can wisely choose platforms for giving evacuation orders. If we want to build an information system to perform tasks better in emergencies, what are the key features of this system? Can we use or adapt existing social-network services to collect and disseminate relevant information? Are currently available social-networking tools (e.g., Twitter, Flickr, Facebook) an effective service for disaster

response? What kind of social-networking tools can be used to facilitate coordination between volunteers, and what features need to be added to enhance collaboration during emergencies? Is it possible to incorporate online social-networking tools into current emergency-management systems? What are the computational barriers? In addition, how can these tools be improved to address the needs of special groups including disabled individuals and people with language barriers?

Finally, there are two ethical issues: privacy and equity. When locations of residents are revealed to the public during emergencies, this information may invite future crimes, especially for disadvantaged people. Is there a way to get the required help for people and protect their privacy at the same time? Another issue concerns the various degrees of information accessibility between different groups of people. How can we reach people without access to mobile phones, computers, and the Internet? How can we disseminate relevant information to people who don't use online social-networking services? Online social networks are only a small portion of the representation of real social networks. How can we collect data on social networks that are not represented in the digital world? What would be the requirements for disseminating information to different user types, such as disabled groups and people speaking different languages or from different cultures?

CONCLUSION

Information technologies are evolving at a rapid speed and enabling people to take advantage of new opportunities and capabilities, and through them to create new information and valuable knowledge in an easily shareable format. Volunteer-created data in social networks are becoming increasingly influential, such as the geospatial data created by the OSM community. An intelligent socio-computational system for emergency management requires synthesis of data from various sources; collaboration among local residents, government agencies and volunteers; and a deep understanding of the social networks embedded in a spatio-temporal context. Methodological investigation and empirical studies in these areas may provide the foundation for establishing theories of multi-level social networks at different scales in emergency response. It is our hope that interdisciplinary research and development in social networks and emergency management will shed light on the appropriate technologies, infrastructures, and policies and in turn increase the community's resilience and effective response to disasters.

REFERENCES

Chertoff, M. (2005). *Statement by Homeland Security Secretary Michael Chertoff before the United States House Select Committee on Hurricane Katrina.* Retrieved from http://www.dhs.gov/xnews/testimony/testimony_0042.shtm

Cutter, S. L. (2003). GI Science, disasters, and emergency management. *Transactions in GIS, 7,* 439–445. doi:10.1111/1467-9671.00157

De Longueville, B., Smith, R. S., & Luraschi, G. (2009). "OMG, from here, I can see the flames!": a use case of mining location based social networks to acquire spatio-temporal data on forest fires. In *Proceedings of the 2009 International Workshop on Location Based Social Networks* (pp. 73–80).

Goodchild, M. F. (2007). Citizens as sensors: the world of volunteered geography. *GeoJournal, 69*(4), 211–221. doi:10.1007/s10708-007-9111-y

Goodchild, M. F., & Glennon, J. A. (2010). Crowdsourcing geographic information for disaster response: a research frontier. *International Journal of Digital Earth, 3*(3), 231–241. doi:10.1080/17538941003759255

Gordon, J. (2007). The mobile phone and the public sphere: mobile phone usage in three critical situations. *Convergence: The International Journal of Research into New Media Technologies, 13*(3), 307–319. doi:10.1177/1354856507079181

Lee, R., & Sumiya, K. (2010). Measuring geographical regularities of crowd behaviors for Twitter-based geo-social event detection. In *Proceedings of the 2nd ACM SIGSPATIAL International Workshop on Location Based Social Networks)* (pp. 1–10).

Meier, P., & Ziemke, J. (2010). *Growth, communications and response, uniting practitioners, scholars & developers at the cutting edge of crisis mapping—measuring our response: an executive summary.* International Network of Crisis Mappers (CM*Net).

National Research Council. (2007). *Successful response starts with a map: improving geospatial support for disaster management.* Washington, DC: National Academies Press.

Vieweg, S., Hughes, A., Starbird, K., & Palen, L. (2010, April). Microblogging during two natural hazards events: what twitter may contribute to situational awareness. In *Proceedings of the ACM Conference on Computer Human Interaction (CHI),* Atlanta, GA (pp. 1079–1088).

White House. (2006). *The federal response to Hurricane Katrina: lessons learned.* Washington, DC: Author.

This work was previously published in International Journal of Information Systems for Crisis Response Management, Volume 2, Issue 4, edited by Murray E. Jennex, pp. 48-58, copyright 2010 by IGI Publishing (an imprint of IGI Global).

Compilation of References

Abelson, J., Forest, P., Eyles, J., Smith, P., Martin, E., & Gauvin, F. (2003). Deliberations about deliberative methods: issues in the design and evaluation of public participation processes. *Social Science & Medicine, 57,* 239–251. doi:10.1016/S0277-9536(02)00343-X

Adams, R. J., & Ericsson, A. E. (2000). Introduction to the cognitive processes of expert pilots. *Journal of Human Performance in Extreme Environments, 5*(1), 44–62.

Agarwal, R., & Sambamurthy, V. (2002). Principles and models for organizing the IT function. *MIS Quarterly Executive, 1*(1), 1–16.

Agor, W. H. (1986). *The Logic of Intuitive Decision Making.* New York: Quorom Books.

Alavi, M., & Leidner, D. E. (1999). Knowledge Management Systems: Emerging Views and Practices from the Field. In *Proceedings of the 32nd Hawaii International Conference on System Sciences.* Washington, DC: IEEE Computer Society.

Alavi, M., & Leidner, D. E. (2001). Review: Knowledge Management and Knowledge Management Systems: Conceptual Foundations and Research Issues. *MIS Quarterly, 25*(1), 107–136. doi:10.2307/3250961

Alcantara-Ayala, I. (2002). Geomorphology, natural hazards, vulnerability and prevention of natural disasters in developing countries. *Geomorphology, 47*(2-4), 107–124. doi:10.1016/S0169-555X(02)00083-1

Alexander, D. (2000). Scenario methodology for teaching principles of emergency management. *Disaster Prevention and Management, 9*(2), 89–97. doi:10.1108/09653560010326969

Altay, N., & Green, W. G. (2006). OR/MS Research in Disaster Operations Management. *European Journal of Operational Research, 175*(1), 475–493. doi:10.1016/j.ejor.2005.05.016

Andersen, H. B., Garde, H., & Andersen, V. (1998). MMS: An Electronic Message Management System for Emergency Response. *IEEE Transactions on Engineering Management, 45*(2), 132–140. doi:10.1109/17.669758

Anderson, J. (2008). New trends in backup: Is your disaster recovery plan keeping up? *The eSecurity Advisor, 8*(2), 58.

Arnstein, S. R. (1969). A ladder of citizen participation. *Journal of the American Institute of Planners, 35*(4), 216–224.

Ashton, H. (2008). How prepared is your business for a calamity? *Japan Inc, 12*(1), 15–17.

Bajgoric, N. (2008). *Continuous computing technologies for enhancing business continuity.* Hershey, PA: Information Science Reference.

Baker, M. G., Kelly, H., & Wilson, N. (2009). Editorial: Pandemic H1N1 influenza lessons from the southern hemisphere. *Euro Surveillance : European Communicable Disease Bulletin, 14*(42), 1–5.

Baltzan, P., & Philips, A. (2008). *Business driven information systems.* Boston: McGraw-Hill/Irwin.

Bandura, A. (1982). Self-efficacy mechanism in human agency. *The American Psychologist, 37*(2), 122–147. doi:10.1037/0003-066X.37.2.122

Barabesi, A. L. (2003). *Linked: How Everything is Connected to Everything Else and What It Means for Business, Science and Everyday Life.* New York: Penguin Group.

Barnes, M. (2008). *HTTP Enabled Location Delivery (HELD) (IETF draft-ietf-geopriv-http-location-delivery-07). Internet Engineering Task Force*. IETF.

Basden, A., & Wood-Harper, A. T. (2006). A Philosophical Discussion of the Root Definition in Soft Systems Thinking: An Enrichment of CATWOE. *Systems Research and Behavioral Science*, *23*, 61–87. doi:10.1002/sres.689

Baskerville, R., & Wood-Harper, A. T. (1998). Diversity in Information Systems Action Research Methods. *European Journal of Information Systems*, *7*(2), 90–107. doi:10.1057/palgrave.ejis.3000298

Battle Command. (1994). *Leadership and Decision Making for War and Operations Other than War*. Fort Leavenworth, KS: Battle Command Battle Laboratory.

Baumgart, L., Bass, E., Philips, B., & Kloesel, K. (2008). Emergency Management Decision-Making During Severe Weather. *Weather and Forecasting*, *23*(6), 1268–1279. doi:doi:10.1175/2008WAF2007092.1

Beaumont, C. (2008, November 27). Mumbai attacks: Twitter and Flickr used to break news. *The Telegraph*. Retrieved December 2, 2010, from http://www.telegraph.co.uk/news/worldnews/asia/india/3530640/Mumbai-attacks-Twitter-and-Flickr-used-to-break-news-Bombay-India.html

Belblidia, M. S. (2010). Building Community Resilience through Social Networking Sites: Using Online Social Networks for Emergency Management. *International Journal of Information Systems for Crisis Response and Management*, *2*(1), 24–36. doi:10.4018/jiscrm.2010120403

Bellardo, S., Karwan, K. R., & Wallace, W. A. (1984). Managing the Response to Disasters Using Microcomputers. *Interfaces*, *14*(2), 29–39. doi:10.1287/inte.14.2.29

Belluck, P. (2009, November 13). W.H.O. rushes drugs to nations hit by swine flu. *New York Times*.

Benkler, Y. (2006). *The Wealth of Networks: How Social Production Transforms Markets and Freedom*. New Haven, CT: Yale University Press.

Bergvall-Kåreborn, B. (2002). Qualifying Function in SSM Modeling–A Case Study. *Systemic Practice and Action Research*, *15*(4), 309–330. doi:10.1023/A:1016396304746

Bergvall-Kåreborn, B., Mirijamdotter, A., & Basden, A. (2004). Basic Principles of SSM Modeling: An Examination of CATWOE from a Soft Perspective. *Systemic Practice and Action Research*, *17*(2), 55–73. doi:10.1023/B:SPAA.0000018903.18767.18

Berner, E. S. (Ed.). (2006). *Clinical decision support systems: Theory and practice* (2nd ed.). New York: Springer.

Bhimaraya, A. M. (2006). Disaster mitigation framework for India using quality circle approach. *Disaster Prevention and Management*, *15*(4), 621–635. doi:10.1108/09653560610686577

Bimber, B. (2003). *Information and American Democracy: Technology in the Evolution of Political Power*. Cambridge, UK: Cambridge University Press.

Blandford, A., & Wong, W. (2004). Situation Awareness in Emergency Medical Dispatch. *International Journal of Human-Computer Studies*, *61*, 421–452. doi:10.1016/j.ijhcs.2003.12.012

Boin, A., & Hart, P. (2003). Public leadership in times of crisis: mission impossible? *Public Administration Review*, *63*(5), 544–553. doi:10.1111/1540-6210.00318

Boin, R. A., Hart, P., Stern, E., & Sundelius, B. (2005). *The politics of crisis management: Public leadership under pressure*. Cambridge, UK: Cambridge University Press. doi:10.1017/CBO9780511490880

Boodhoo, N. (2010, January 18). Earthquake confirms value of social media. *Miami Herald*. Retrieved November 28, 2010, from http://www.miamiherald.com/2010/01/18/1432022/earthquake-confirms-value-of-social.html

Borodzicz, E. P. (2005). *Risks, Crisis & Security Management*. Chichester, UK: John Wiley & Sons.

Borrell, B. (2007, February 15). Type 911.gov. *Technology Review*. Retrieved February 1, 2009, from http://www.technologyreview.com/communications/18196/page1/

Botterell, A., & Addams-Moring, R. (2007). Public Warning in the Networked Age: Open Standards to the Rescue? *Communications of the ACM*, *50*(3), 59–60. doi:10.1145/1226736.1226767

Boudourides, M. A. (2003). Participation Under Uncertainty. In *Proceedings of VALDOR 2003: Values in Decisions on Risk*, Stockholm, Sweden.

Boulos, M. N. K., Scotch, M., Cheung, K. H., & Burden, D. (2008). Web GIS in practice VI: a demo playlist of geo-mashups for public health neogeographers. *International Journal of Health Geographics, 7*(38).

Bradbury, C. (2008). Disaster! *Manager: British Journal of Administrative Management, 62*, 14–16.

Brooke, J. (1996). *Systems Usability Scale: A 'quick and dirty' usability scale*. Retrieved March 24, 2004 from http://www.hcirn.com/ref/refb/broo96.php

Bryson, K.-M., Millar, H., Joseph, A., & Mobolurin, A. (2002). Using Formal MS/OR Modeling to Support Disaster Recovery Planning. *European Journal of Operational Research, 141*(3), 679–688. doi:10.1016/S0377-2217(01)00275-2

Buchanan, J. M., & Tullock, G. (1962). *The Calculus of Consent: Logical Foundations of Constitutional Democracy*. Ann Arbor, MI: University of Michigan Press.

Burnell, L., Priest, J., & Durrett, J. (2004). Developing and Maintaining Knowledge Management System for Dynamic, Complex Domains. In J. Gupta & S. Sharma (Eds.), *Creating Knowledge Based Organizations*. London: IGP.

Burton-Jones, A., Storey, V. C., Sugumaran, V., & Ahluwalia, P. (2005). A Semiotic Metrics Suite for Assessing the Quality of Ontologies. *Data & Knowledge Engineering, 55*, 84–102. doi:10.1016/j.datak.2004.11.010

Busher, M., Mogensen, P. H., & Kristensen, M. (2009). When and How (Not) to Trust it? Supporting Virtual Emergency Teamwork. *International Journal of Information Systems for Crisis Response Management, 1*(2), 1–15.

BusinessWeek. (2003). *Finance research forum*. Retrieved January 18, 2010, from http://investing.businessweek.com/research/common/symbollookup/symbollookup.asp?textIn=METG

Butler, B. S., & Gray, P. H. (2006). Reliability, Mindfulness, and Information Systems. *Management Information Systems Quarterly, 30*(2), 211–224.

Butler, T., & Murphy, C. (2007). Understanding the Design of Information Technologies for Knowledge Management in Organizations: A Pragmatic Perspective. *Information Systems Journal, 17*(2), 143–163. doi:10.1111/j.1365-2575.2007.00237.x

Campbell, C. L., DeWalle, B. V., Turoff, M., & Deek, F. P. (2004). *A Research Design for Asynchronous Negotiation of Software Requirements for an Emergency Response Information System*. Paper presented at the Americas Conference on Information Systems, New York.

Campbell, R. (1999). Controlling Crisis Chaos. *Journal of Emergency Management Australia, 14*(3), 51–54.

Canton, L. G. (2007). *Emergency Management: Concepts and strategies for effective programs*. Hoboken, NJ: John Wiley & Sons.

Capaldo, A. (2007). Network structure and innovation: The leveraging of a dual network as a distinctive relational capability. *Strategic Management Journal, 28*(6), 585–608. doi:10.1002/smj.621

Carley, K. M., & Harrald, J. R. (1997). Organizational Learning under Fire: Theory and Practice. *The American Behavioral Scientist, 40*(3), 310–332. doi:10.1177/0002764297040003007

Carnevale, D. (2003). Preparing for computer disasters. *The Chronicle of Higher Education*, 2–28.

Carver, S. (2003). The Future of Participatory Approaches Using Geographic Information: Developing a research agenda for the Ritchey, 2006st century. *URISA Journal, 15*(APA 1), 61-71.

Carver, L., & Turoff, M. (2007). Human-Computer Interactions: The Human and the computer as a team in emergency management information systems. *Communications of the ACM, 50*(3), 33–38. doi:10.1145/1226736.1226761

Carvin, A. (2008). *Hurricane Gustav Digital Support Brigade*. Retrieved July 27, 2009, from http://www.facebook.com/group.php?gid=25689101658

Caulfield, B., & Karmali, N. (2008). Mumbai: Twitter's Moment. *Forbes Magazine*. Retrieved April 20, 2009, from http://www.forbes.com/2008/11/28/mumbai-twitter-sms-tech-internet-cx_bc_kn_1128mumbai.html

Caulkins, J. P., Morrison, E. L., & Weidemann, T. (2005). Spreadsheet errors: Are they undermining decision making in your organization? *Public Management, 34*(1), 22–27.

CDC. (2009). *Novel H1N1 Situation Update*. Retrieved July 22, 2009, from http://www.cdc.gov/h1n1flu/update.htm

Centers for Disease Control and Prevention (CDCP). (2004). *Public Health Guidance for Community-Level Preparedness and Response to Severe Acute Respiratory Syndrome (SARS)*. Washington, DC: Department of Health and Human Services.

Centers for Disease Control and Prevention. (2009). *Social Media at the CDC*. Retrieved July 27, 2009, from http://www.cdc.gov/socialmedia/

Cerullo, V., & Cerullo, M. J. (2004). Business Continuity Planning: A Comprehensive Approach. *Information Systems Management, 21*(3), 70–78. doi:10.1201/1078/44432.21.3.20040601/82480.11

Checkland, P. (1999). *Systems Thinking, Systems Practice. Includes a 30-year retrospective*. Chichester, UK: John Wiley & Sons.

Checkland, P. (2000). Soft Systems Methodology: A Thirty Year Retrospective. *Systems Research and Behavioral Science, 17*, 11–58. doi:10.1002/1099-1743(200011)17:1+<::AID-SRES374>3.0.CO;2-O

Checkland, P., Challender, S., Clarke, S., Haynes, M., Hoebeke, L., & Leemhuis, J. (2000). The Emergent Properties of SSM in Use: A Symposium by Reflective Practitioners. *Systemic Practice and Action Research, 13*(6), 799–823. doi:10.1023/A:1026431613200

Checkland, P., & Poulter, J. (2006). *Learning for action: a short definitive account of soft systems methodology and its use, for practitioners, teachers and students*. Chichester, UK: John Wiley & Sons.

Checkland, P., & Scholes, J. (1990). *Soft Systems Methodology in Action*. Chichester, UK: John Wiley & Sons.

Checkland, P., & Scholes, J. (1999). *Soft Systems Methodology in Action. Includes a 30 year retrospective*. Chichester, UK: John Wiley & Sons.

Checkland, P., & Winter, M. (2006). Process and content: two ways of using SSM. *The Journal of the Operational Research Society, 57*, 1435–1441. doi:10.1057/palgrave.jors.2602118

Chen, R., Rao, H. R., Sharma, R., Upadhyaya, S., & Kim, J. (2010). An Empirical Examination of IT-Enabled Emergency Response: The Cases of Hurricane Katrina and Hurricane Rita. *Communications of the Association for Information Systems, 26*(8), 141–156.

Chertoff, M. (2005). *Statement by Homeland Security Secretary Michael Chertoff before the United States House Select Committee on Hurricane Katrina*. Retrieved from http://www.dhs.gov/xnews/testimony/testimony_0042.shtm

Chintapatla, B., Goulart, A., & Magnussen, W. (2010). Testbed Experiments on the Location to Service Translation (LoST) Protocol for Mobile Users. In *Proceedings of the IEEE Consumer Communications and Networking Conference (CCNC)*.

Chin, W. (1998). The Partial Least Squares Approach to Structural Equation Modeling . In Marcoulides, G. A. (Ed.), *Modern Methods for Business Research* (pp. 295–336). Mahwah, NJ: Lawrence Erlbaum Associates.

Chin, W., & Todd, P. (1995). One the use, usefulness and ease of use of structural equation modeling in MIS research: A note of caution. *Management Information Systems Quarterly, 19*(2), 237–246. doi:10.2307/249690

Christians, G., Ferre, J. P., & Fackler, P. M. (1993). *Good News: Social Ethics and the Press*. New York: Oxford University Press.

Chun, M., & Moody, J. (2009). CIO roles and responsibilities: Twenty-five years of evolution and change. *Information & Management, 46*(6), 323–334. doi:10.1016/j.im.2009.05.005

Churchman, C. W. (1979). The Systems Approach (revised and updated) New York: Dell Publishing.

Cirillo, A. (2002). *Disaster recovery plans are more important than ever*. AIS News.

Clausewitz, C. V. (1984). *On War*. Princeton, NJ: Princeton University Press.

Cohill, A. M. (2000). *Building e-communities: Getting everyone connected.* Address to the Governor's Commission on Information Technology, Richmond, VA.

Collins, H. (2009). Emergency Managers and First Responders Use Twitter and Facebook to Update Communities. *Emergency Management Magazine.* Retrieved July 27, 2009, from http://www.emergencymgmt.com/safety/Emergency-Managers-and-First.html

Comfort, L. K. (1999). *Shared risk: Complex systems in seismic response.* Pittsburg, PA: Pergamon.

Comfort, L. K. (2005). Risk, Security, and Disaster management. *Annual Review of Political Science, 8,* 335–356. doi:10.1146/annurev.polisci.8.081404.075608

Comfort, L. K. (2007). Crisis Management in Hindsight: Cognition, Communication, Coordination, and Control. *Public Administration Review,* 189–197. doi:10.1111/j.1540-6210.2007.00827.x

Comfort, L. K., Birkland, T. A., Cigler, B. A., & Nance, E. (2010). Retrospectives and Prospectives on Hurricane Katrina: Five Years and Counting. *Public Administration Review,* 669–678. doi:10.1111/j.1540-6210.2010.02194.x

Comfort, L., Ko, K., & Zagorecki, A. (2004). Coordinating in Rapidly Evolving Disaster Response Systems: The role of information. *The American Behavioral Scientist, 48,* 295–313. doi:10.1177/0002764204268987

Constantinides, P., Kouroubali, A., & Barrett, M. (2008). Transacting Expertise in Emergency Management and Response. In *Proceedings of ICIS 2008.* Retrieved from http://aisel.aisnet.org/icis2008/15

Constantinides, P., & Barrett, M. (2006). Negotiating ICT development & use: the case of a regional telemedicine system in Crete. *Information and Organization, 16*(1), 27–55. doi:10.1016/j.infoandorg.2005.07.001

Coombs, W. T. (2007). *Ongoing crisis communication: Planning, managing and responding* (2nd ed.). Thousand Oaks, CA: Sage.

Corbin, C. L., Kelley, S. W., & Schwartz, R. W. (2001). Concepts in service marketing for healthcare professionals. *American Journal of Surgery, 181*(1), 1–7. doi:10.1016/S0002-9610(00)00535-3

Cox, J. (2007). The case of the great hot-swap site. *New World (New Orleans, La.), 24*(30), 42–45.

Cross, R., & Baird, L. (2000). Technology Is Not Enough: Improving Performance by Building Organizational Memory. *Sloan Management Review, 41*(3), 41–54.

CRS. (2005). *Hurricanes Katrina & Rita: Damage and recovery* (CRS Report-3, Order code RS-22241).

Cummings, T. G. (1984). Transorganizational development . In Staw, B. M., & Cummings, L. L. (Eds.), *Research in organizational behavior* (*Vol. 6,* pp. 367–422). Greenwich, CT: JAI Press.

Cunningham, W. (2005). *Wiki History.* Retrieved October 29, 2005, from http://c2.com/cgi/wiki?WikiHistory

Cutter, S., Barnes, L., & Berry, M. Burton, C., Evans, E., Tate, E., et al. (2008). *Community and regional resilience: Perspectives from hazards, disasters, and emergency management* (CARRI Research Rep. No. 1). Oak Ridge, TN: Community and Regional Resilience Initiative, Oak Ridge National Laboratory.

Cutter, S. L. (2003). GI Science, disasters, and emergency management. *Transactions in GIS, 7,* 439–445. doi:10.1111/1467-9671.00157

Danielsson, M., & Ohlsson, K. (1999). Decision Making in Emergency Management: A Survey Study. *International Journal of Cognitive Ergonomics, 3*(2), 91–99. doi:doi:10.1207/s15327566ijce0302_2

Davenport, T. H., & Prusak, L. (1998). *Working Knowledge.* Cambridge, MA: Harvard Business School Press.

Davenport, T. H., DeLong, D. W., & Beers, M. C. (1998). Successful Knowledge Management Projects. *Sloan Management Review, 39*(2), 43–57.

Davies, P.(199). What is Evidence-Based Education? *British Journal of Educational Studies, 47*(2), 108–121. doi:10.1111/1467-8527.00106

Davis, C. (2001). Planning for the unthinkable: IT contingencies. *International Education Journal, 21*(4), 4–5.

Davis, F. (1989). Perceived usefulness, perceived ease of use, and user acceptance of information technology. *Management Information Systems Quarterly, 13*(3), 319–340. doi:10.2307/249008

Davison, R. M., & Martinsons, M.vG., & Kock, N. (2004). Principles of canonical action research. *Information Systems Journal, 14*, 65–86. doi:10.1111/j.1365-2575.2004.00162.x

Dawes, S., Cresswell, A., & Cahan, B. (2004). Learning from crisis: Lessons in human and information infrastructure from the world trade center response. *Social Science Computer Review, 22*(1), 52–66. doi:10.1177/0894439303259887

De Longueville, B., Smith, R. S., & Luraschi, G. (2009). "OMG, from here, I can see the flames!": a use case of mining location based social networks to acquire spatio-temporal data on forest fires. In *Proceedings of the 2009 International Workshop on Location Based Social Networks* (pp. 73–80).

Defelice, A. (2008). Preparing for the worst. *Accounting Technology, 20*(4), 14–19.

Diamantopoulos, A., & Siguaw, L. (n.d.). Formative versus Reflective Indicators in Organizational Measure Development: A Comparison and Empirical Illustration. *British Journal of Management, 17*, 263–282. doi:10.1111/j.1467-8551.2006.00500.x

Diamantopoulos, A., & Winklhofer, H. M. (2001). Index Construction with Formative Indicators: An Alternative to Scale Development. *JMR, Journal of Marketing Research, 38*(2), 269–277. doi:10.1509/jmkr.38.2.269.18845

Domino, M. E., Fried, B., Moon, Y., Olinick, J., & Yoon, J. (2003). Disasters and the public health safety net: hurricane Floyd hits the North Carolina Medicaid program. *American Journal of Public Health, 93*(7), 1122–1127. doi:10.2105/AJPH.93.7.1122

Dooren, J.C. (2009, November 10). FDA approves GlaxoSmithKline's H1N1 vaccine. *Dow Jones Newswire*.

Doughty, K. (2001). *Business Continuity Planning*. Boca Raton, FL: Auerbach/CRC Press.

Douglas, D., & Peucker, T. (1973). Algorithms for the reduction of the number of points required to represent a digitized line or its caricature. *The Canadian Cartographer, 10*(2), 112–122.

Drabek, T. E. (2006). Community Processes: Coordination. In H. Rodriguez, E. L. Quarantelli, & R. R. Dynes (Eds.), *Handbook of Disaster Research*. New York, NY: Springer Science + Business Media.

Drake, D., Steckler, N., & Koch, M. (2004). Information sharing in and across government agencies. *Social Science Computer Review, 22*(1), 67–84. doi:10.1177/0894439303259889

Drury, J., Klein, G. L., More, L., & Pfaff, M. (2009). A principled method of scenario design for testing emergency response decision-making. In J. Landgren & S. Jul, (Eds.), *Proceedings of the 6th International ISCRAM Conference*, Gothenburg, Sweden.

Dulgeroff, A. (2009). *Application of San Diego Gas & Electric Company (U 902 M) for authorization to recover costs related to the 2007 Southern California wildfires recorded in the Catastrophic Event Memorandum Account (CEMA)*. Retrieved from http://www.sdge.com/regulatory/documents/a-09-03-011/testimony-dulgeroff.pdf

Durbin, T., Jennex, M. E., Frost, E., & Judge, R. (2010). Achieving Electric Restoration Logistical Efficiencies during Critical Infrastructure Crisis Response: A Knowledge Management Analysis. *International Journal of Information Systems for Crisis Response and Management, 2*(3), 36–50. doi:10.4018/jiscrm.2010070103

Dwarkanath, S., & Daconta, M. (2006). Emergency services enterprise framework: A service-oriented approach. In B. Van de Walle & M. Turoff (Eds.), *Proceedings of the 3rd International Conference on Information Systems for Crisis Response and Management*.

Dynes, R. R. (1990). *Community emergency planning: False assumptions and inappropriate analogies*. Newark, DE: University of Delaware Disaster Research Center.

Dynes, R. R. (2000). *Governmental systems for disaster management*. Newark, DE: University of Delaware Disaster Research Center.

Ecker, K. (2008). Data disaster. *Inside Counsel, 18*(202), 42-45.

Ehrenberg, L. A., & Hirsch, S. E. (1996). *The war in American culture: Society and consciousness during World War II*. Chicago: University of Chicago Press.

Ernst & Young. (2002). *Global Information Security Survey 2002*. New York, NY: Author.

Eryilmaz, E., Cochran, M., & Kasemvilas, S. (2009). Establishing Trust Management in an Open Source Collaborative Information Repository: An Emergency Response Information System Case Study. In *Proceedings of the 42nd Hawaii International Conference on System Sciences*. Washington, DC: IEEE Computer Society.

Facebook. (2009). *Help Save the Philadelphia Fire Department*. Retrieved July 27, 2009, from http://apps.facebook.com/causes/242755

Falco, M. (2010, February 12). H1N1 virus' death toll as high as 17,000, CDC estimates. *CNN Medical News*.

Fallara, P. (2003). Disaster recovery planning. *IEEE Potentials, 22*(5).

Faulkner, B. (2001). Towards a framework for tourism disaster management. *Tourism Management, 22*, 135–147. doi:10.1016/S0261-5177(00)00048-0

Federal News Radio. (2009). *DHS Listens and Learns from Ogma*. Retrieved July 25, 2009, from www.federalnewsradio.com

FEMA. (2008). *Building a disaster-resistant university*. Retrieved June 30, 2010, from http://www.fema.gov/institution/dru.shtm

FEMA. (2009, April 8). *Acting Administrator Ward Speaks At The National Hurricane Conference*. Retrieved July 27, 2009, from http://www.fema.gov/news/newsrelease.fema?id=47933

Feng, S., & Law, C. (2002). Assisted GPS and its Impact on Navigation in Intelligent Transportation Systems. In *Proceedings of the 5th IEEE International Conference on Intelligent Transportation Systems* (pp. 926-993).

Fidler, D. (2009). H1N1 after action review: learning from the unexpected, the success and the fear. *Future Microbiology, 4*, 767–769. doi:10.2217/fmb.09.54

Finch, M. R., & Welker, L. S. (2004). Informed organizational improvisation: A metaphor and method for understanding, anticipating, and performatively constructing the organization's precrisis environment . In Millar, D. P., & Heath, R. L. (Eds.), *Responding to crisis: A rhetorical approach to crisis communication* (pp. 189–200). Mahwah, NJ: Erlbaum.

Fink, S. (1986). *Crisis Management. Planning for the Inevitable*. New York: American Management Association, AMACOM.

Fischer, H. W. (1998). The Role of the New Information Technologies in Emergency Mitigation, Planning, Response, and Recovery. *Disaster Prevention and Management, 7*(1), 28–37. doi:10.1108/09653569810206262

Fishbein, M., & Ajzen, I. (1975). *Belief, Attitude, Intention, and Behavior: An Introduction to Theory and Research*. Reading, MA: Addison-Wesley.

FitzGerald, J., & Dennis, A. (2005). *Business data communications and networking* (9th ed.). New York: Wiley.

Fonseca, B. (2004). NY IT prepares for IT disaster recovery. *eWeek, 7*(32), 9-10.

Forum. (2006). Retrieved December 2, 2009, from http://www.sun.com/events/forum2006/speakers.jsp#jtoigo

Foster, V., & Irusta, O. (2003). Does infrastructure reform work for the poor? *World Bank Policy, 3*.

Foster, H. D. (1980). *Disaster Planning: The Preservation of Life and Property*. New York, NY: Springer-Verlag.

Fox, M. S., Barbuceanu, M., Gruninger, M., & Lin, J. (1998). An Organization Ontology for Enterprise Modeling . In Prietula, M., Carley, K., & Gasser, L. (Eds.), *Simulating Organizations: Computational Models of Institutions and Groups* (pp. 131–152). Menlo Park, CA: AAAI/MIT Press.

Fox, M. S., & Gruninger, M. (1998). Enterprise Modeling. *AI Magazine, 19*(3), 109–121.

French, S., & Turoff, M. (2007). Decision support systems. *Communications of the ACM, 50*(3), 39–40. doi:10.1145/1226736.1226762

Fritz, C. E., & Mathewson, J. H. (1957). Convergence Behavior in Disasters: A Problem in Social Control. Washington, DC: Committee on Disaster Studies, National Academy of Sciences, National Research Council.

Fugate, C. (2009). *Post-Katrina: What it Takes to Cut the Bureaucracy and Assure a More Rapid Response After a Catastrophic Disaster*. Washington, DC: FEMA.

Gadomski, A. M., Bologna, S., Costanzo, G. D., Perini, A., & Schaerf, M. (2001). Towards Intelligent Decision Support Systems for Emergency Managers: the IDS Approach. *International Journal of Risk Assessment and Management, 2*(3/4), 224–242. doi:10.1504/IJRAM.2001.001507

Ganapati, N. E., & Ganapati, S. (2009). Enabling Participatory Planning After Disasters: A Case Study of the World Bank's Housing Reconstruction in Turkey. *Journal of the American Planning Association. American Planning Association, 75*(1), 41–59. doi:10.1080/01944360802546254

Gangemi, A. (2005). *Ontology Design Patterns for Semantic Web Content*. Paper presented at the 4th International Semantic Web Conference (ISWC 2005), Galway, Ireland.

Garton, L., Haythornthwaite, C., & Wellman, B. (1997). Studying Online Social Networks. *Journal of Computer-Mediated Communication, 3*(1).

Gaynor, M., Brander, S., Pearce, A., & Post, K. (2009). Open infrastructure for a nationwide emergency service network. *International Journal of Information Systems for Crisis Response and Management, 1*(2), 31–46. doi:10.4018/jiscrm.2009040103

Gefen, D., Straub, D., & Boudreau, M. (2000). Structural Equation Modeling Techniques and Regression: Guidelines for Research Practice. *Communications of AIS, 7*(7), 1–78.

Geier, D. L. (2009). Investigation on the Commission's own motion into the operations and practices of Cox Communications and San Diego Gas & Electric Company regarding the utility facilities linked to the Guejito Fire of October 2007.

Gertz, E. (2005, September 5). KatrinaWiki, Katrina PeopleFinder: Distributed Technology Responses to Disaster. *World Changing*. Retrieved April 15, 2009, from http://www.worldchanging.com/archives/003437.html

Gheidary, L. K. (2010, May). Social media and Iran's post-election crisis. In *Proceedings of the 7th International ISCRAM Conference*, Seattle, WA.

Gheorghe, A. V., & Vamanu, D. V. (2001). Adapting to New Challenges: IDSS for Emergency Preparedness and Management. *International Journal of Risk Assessment and Management, 2*(3/4), 211–223. doi:10.1504/IJRAM.2001.001506

Gilpin, D. R., & Murphy, P. J. (2008). *Crisis Management in a Complex World*. New York, NY: Oxford University Press. doi:10.1093/acprof:oso/9780195328721.001.0001

Ginsberg, M., & Kambil, A. (1999). Annotate: A Web-based Knowledge Management Support System for Document Collections. In *Proceedings of the 32nd Hawaii International Conference on System Sciences*. Washington, DC: IEEE Computer Society.

Gladwell, M. (2002). *Tipping Point: How Little Things Can Make a Big Difference*. New York: Little, Brown and Company.

Glass, J. (1979). Citizen Participation in Planning: The Relationship Between Objectives and Techniques. *American Planning Association Journal, 99*(2), 180–189. doi:10.1080/01944367908976956

Glick, M., & Kupiec, J. (2001). Strategic technology. *EDUCAUSE Review*, 11–12.

Golbeck, J. (2008a, December). *The Dynamics of Web-based Social Networks: Membership, Relationships, and Change*. Retrieved July 27, 2009, from http://www.cs.umd.edu/localphp/hcil/tech-reports-search.php?number=2008-36

Golbeck, J. (2008b, December). *Trust and Nuanced Profile Similarity in Online Social Networks*. Retrieved July 27, 2009, from http://www.cs.umd.edu/localphp/hcil/tech-reports-search.php?number=2008-39

Gold, L. (2007). Disaster recovery planning: How do you measure up? *Accounting Today, 21*(7), 31–35.

Goodchild, M. F. (2007). Citizens as sensors: the world of volunteered geography. *GeoJournal, 69*(4), 211–221. doi:10.1007/s10708-007-9111-y

Goodchild, M. F., & Glennon, J. A. (2010). Crowdsourcing geographic information for disaster response: a research frontier. *International Journal of Digital Earth*, *3*(3), 231–241. doi:10.1080/17538941003759255

Goode, B. (2002). Voice over Internet Protocol (VoIP). *Proceedings of the IEEE*, *90*(9), 1495–1517. doi:doi:10.1109/JPROC.2002.802005

Goodman, R. M., Speers, M. A., Mcleroy, K., & Fawcett, S. (1998). Identifying and Defining Dimensions of Community Capacity to Provide a Basis for Measurement. *Health Education & Behavior*, *25*, 258–277. doi:10.1177/109019819802500303

Gordon, J. (2007). The mobile phone and the public sphere: mobile phone usage in three critical situations. *Convergence: The International Journal of Research into New Media Technologies*, *13*(3), 307–319. doi:10.1177/1354856507079181

Government Computer News. (2009). *Security issues may lead DOD to ban use of social media*. Retrieved August 13, 2009, from http://www.gcn.com/Articles/2009/07/31/DOD-ban-social-media-security-issues.aspx

Gregory, W. J., & Midgley, G. (2000). Planning for disaster: developing a multi-agency counseling service. *The Journal of the Operational Research Society*, *51*, 278–290.

Gruber, T. R. (1993). A Translation Approach to Portable Ontology Specifications. *Knowledge Acquisition*, *5*, 199–220. doi:10.1006/knac.1993.1008

Gruber, T. R. (1995). Toward Principles for the Design of Ontologies Used for Knowledge Sharing. *International Journal of Human-Computer Studies*, *43*(5-6), 907–928. doi:10.1006/ijhc.1995.1081

Gruninger, M., & Fox, M. S. (1994). *The Role of Competency Questions in Enterprise Engineering*. Paper presented at the IFIP WG5.7 Workshop on Benchmarking - Theory and Practice, Trondheim, Norway.

Guarino, N. (1998, June 6-8). *Formal Ontology and Information Systems*. Paper presented at the First International Conference on Formal Ontologies in Information Systems, Trento, Italy.

Gupta, J. D., & Sharma, S. K. (2004). *Creating Knowledge Based Organizations*. Hershey, PA: IDEA Group Publishing.

Guth, D. (2008). *Untapped Potential: Evaluating State Emergency Management Web Sites 2008*. Lawrence, KS: University of Kansas.

Habermas, J. (1992). *The Structural Transformation of the Public Sphere: An Inquiry into a Category of Bourgeis Society*. Cambridge, MA: MIT Press.

Hackbarth, G. (1998, August). *The Impact of Organizational Memory on IT Systems*. Paper presented at the Fourth Americas Conference on Information Systems.

Haddow, G., Bullock, J., & Coppola, D. (2007). *Introduction to Emergency Management* (3rd ed.). Oxford, UK: Butterworth-Heinemann.

Hale, J. (1997). A layered communication architecture for the support of crisis response. *Journal of Management Information Systems*, *14*(1), 235–255.

Hardie, T., Newton, A., Schulzrinne, H., & Tschofenig, H. (2008). *LoST: A Location-to-Service Translation Protocol (IETF RFC 5222). Internet Engineering Task Force*. IETF.

Harrald, J. (2006). Agilitly and Discipline: Critical Success Factors for Disaster Response. *AAPSS Annals*, *604*(1), 256–272.

Harrald, J. (2009). Achieving Agility in Disaster Management. *International Journal of Information Systems and Crisis Management*, *1*(1).

Harrald, J. R. (2006). Agility and Discipline: Critical Success Factors for Disaster Response. *The Annals of the American Academy of Political and Social Science*, *604*(1), 256–272. doi:10.1177/0002716205285404

Hart, R. (2006). *Hurricanes: A primer on formation, structure, intensify change and frequency* (p. 13). Arlington, VA: The George C. Marshall Institute.

Harvard Research Group. (2004). *The total cost of downtime*. Retrieved September 10, 2009, from http://www.hrgresearch.com/pdf/paper4.pdf

Hayes, J. (2005). Reaping the whirlwind. *IEEE Review*, *13*(3), 29. doi:10.1049/ir:20051009

Hein, T. (2008). Minimize cost with preparation. *Multi-Housing News*, *43*(7), 27–28.

Herrmann, S. (2009). Social Media in Iran. *BBC UK News*. Retrieved August 14, 2009, from http://www.bbc.co.uk

Hiles, A. (Ed.). (2007). *The definitive handbook of business continuity management* (2nd ed.). Chichester, UK: John Wiley & Sons.

Hixson, R., Cobb, B., & Halley, P. (2007). 9-1-1: The Next Generation. *9-1-1 Magazine*, 18-21.

Hocevar, S. P., Thomas, G. F., & Jansen, E. (2006). Building collaborative capacity: an innovative strategy for homeland security preparedness . In Beyerlein, M. M., Beyerlein, S. T., & Kennedy, F. A. (Eds.), *Innovation through collaboration: Advances in Interdisciplinary Studies of Work Teams* (*Vol. 12*, pp. 255–274). Oxford, UK: JAI Press.

Hoey, S. (2008). How to stop document disasters. *For Buyers of Products. Systems & Services*, *45*(7), 68–69.

Hoftsede, G. (1991). *Cultures and Organizations: Software of the mind*. Berkshire, UK: McGraw-Hill.

Hoge, J. (2005). Business continuity planning must extend to vendors. *Bank Technology News*, *11*(3), 21.

Holliday, K. (2008). Planning for the worst. *Community Banker*, *17*(8), 32–35.

Holliday, K. (2008). Planning for the worst. *Community Banker*, *22*(8), 32–35.

Holsapple, C. W., & Joshi, K. D. (2000). An Investigation of Factors that Influence the Management of Knowledge in Organizations. *The Journal of Strategic Information Systems*, *9*, 235–261. doi:10.1016/S0963-8687(00)00046-9

Horan, T., & Schooley, B. (2007). Time critical information services. *Communications of the ACM*, *50*(3), 73–78. doi:10.1145/1226736.1226738

Housel, T., El Sawy, O., & Donovan, P. (1986). Information systems for crisis management. *Management Information Systems Quarterly*, *10*(4), 389–400. doi:10.2307/249195

Hovav, A., & D'Arcy, J. (2005). Capital market reaction to defective IT products: the case of computer viruses. *Computers & Security*, *24*(5), 409–424. doi:10.1016/j.cose.2005.02.003

Howe, J. (2008). *Crowdsourcing: Why the Power of Crowd is Driving the Future of Business*. New York: Crown Business.

Huber, G. P., Davenport, T. H., & King, D. (1998). Some Perspectives on Organizational Memory. In F. Burstein, G. Huber, M. Mandviwalla, J. Morrison, & L. Olfman (Eds.), *Proceedings of the 31st Annual Hawaii International Conference on System Sciences*, Hawaii.

Hughes, A. L., Palen, L., Sutton, J., Liu, S. B., & Vieweg, S. (2008). "Site-Seeing" in Disaster: An Examination of On-Line Social Convergence. In F. Fiedrich & B. Van De Walle (Eds.), *Proceedings of the 5th International ISCRAM Conference*, Washington, DC.

Humphrey, B. (2009). *Prepare and Protect Your Pets from Fireworks*. Retrieved July 25, 2009, from http://lafd.blogspot.com/

Hurst, D. K. (1995). *Crisis and renewal*. Boston, MA: Harvard Business School Press.

Hutchinson, J., Kotonya, G., Walkerdine, J., Sawyer, P., Dobson, G., & Onditi, V. (2008). Migrating to SOAs by way of hybrid systems. *IT Professional*, *10*(1). doi:10.1109/MITP.2008.15

IAEM. (2007). *Principles of Emergency Management*. Retrieved August 10, 2010, from http://www.iaem.com/EMPrinciples/documents/PrinciplesofEmergencyManagement.pdf

IAGS. (2004). *How much did the 9/11 terrorist attack cost America?* Retrieved March 2010, from http://www.iags.org/costof911.html

IDNDR. (1992). *Glossary: Internationally Agreed Glossary of Basic Terms Related to Disaster Management* (p. 83). Geneva, Switzerland: DHA.

Info-Tech. (2005). DRP in the education. *Benchmarking Report*. Retrieved November 2009, from http://www.infotech.com/search/?searchterm=Benchmarking+Report&page=6

Institute of Medicine (IOM). (2001). *Crossing the Quality Chasm: A New Health System for the 21st Century*. Washington, DC: National Academy Press.

Janoff-Bulman, R. (1992). *Shattered assumptions*. New York, NY: Free Press.

Jaques, M. (2006). Securing your IT continuity. *Financial Director*, *28*(7), 42.

Jarke, M., Jeusfeld, M., Quix, C., & Vassiliadis, P. (1999). Architecture and Quality in Data Warehouses: An Extended Repository Approach. *Information Systems, 24*(3), 229–253. doi:10.1016/S0306-4379(99)00017-4

Jarvis, C., Mackenzie, S., & Podsakoff, P. (2003). A Critical Review of Construct Indicators and Measurement Model Misspecification in Marketing and Consumer Research. *The Journal of Consumer Research, 30*(2), 199–218. doi:10.1086/376806

Jennex, M. E. (2007). Reflections on strong angel III: some lessons learned. In *Proceedings of the Fourth International Conference on Information Systems for Crisis Response and Management* (p.5).

Jennex, M. E. (2007, August 25). *Knowledge Management in Support of Crisis Response.* Paper presented at the ISCRAM China Workshop.

Jennex, M. E. (2007, January). Modeling Emergency Response Systems. In *Proceedings of the 40ᵗʰ Hawaii International Conference on System Sciences, HICSS40.* Washington, DC: IEEE Computer Society.

Jennex, M. E. (2008). A Model For Emergency Response Systems. In L. Janczewski & A. Colarik (Eds.), *Cyber Warfare and Cyber Terrorism* (pp. 383-391). Hershey, PA: Information Science Reference.

Jennex, M. E. (2009). Why Knowledge Management. In M. E. Jennex (Ed.), *Ubiquitous Developments in Knowledge Management: Integrations and Trends.* Hershey, PA: Information Science Reference.

Jennex, M. E., & Olfman, L. (2000). *Development Recommendations for Knowledge Management/ Organizational Memory Systems.* Paper presented at the Information Systems Development Conference.

Jennex, M. E., & Olfman, L. (2001). Development Recommendations for Knowledge Management/Organizational Memory Systems. In M. K. Sein, B. E. Munkvold, T. U. Orvik, W. Wojtkowski, W. G. Wojtkowski, S. Wrycza et al. (Eds.), *Contemporary Trends in IS Development* (pp. 209-222). Norwell, MA: Kluwer Academic.

Jennex, M. E., Olfman, L., & Addo, T. B. A. (2003). The Need for an Organizational Knowledge Management Strategy. In *Proceedings of the 36th Hawaii International Conference on System Sciences (HICSS36).* Washington, DC: IEEE Computer Society.

Jennex, M.E., & Zyngier, S. (2007). Security as a Contributor to Knowledge Management Success. *Information Systems Frontiers: A Journal of Research and Innovation, 9*(5), 493-504.

Jennex, M. E. (2004a). Emergency Response Systems: The Utility Y2K Experience. *Journal of Information Technology Theory and Application, 6*(3), 85–102.

Jennex, M. E. (2004b). Knowledge Management Strategy: Critical Issues. *Global Journal of E-Business and Knowledge Management, 1*(1), 35–44.

Jennex, M. E. (2005a). Knowledge Management Systems. *International Journal of Knowledge Management, 1*(2), i–iv.

Jennex, M. E. (2005b). What is Knowledge Management? *International Journal of Knowledge Management, 1*(4), i–iv.

Jennex, M. E. (2006). Open Source Knowledge Management. *International Journal of Knowledge Management, 2*(4), i–iv.

Jennex, M. E. (2010). Preface: Why Knowledge Management? In Jennex, M. E. (Ed.), *Ubiquitous Developments in Knowledge Management: Integrations and Trends* (pp. xviii–xxix). Hershey, PA: Information Science Reference.

Jennex, M. E., & Olfman, L. (2005). Assessing Knowledge Management Success. *International Journal of Knowledge Management, 1*(2), 33–49.

Jennex, M. E., & Olfman, L. (2006). A Model of Knowledge Management Success. *International Journal of Knowledge Management, 2*(3), 51–68. doi:10.4018/jkm.2006070104

Jennex, M. E., & Raman, M. (2009). Knowledge Management is Support of Crisis Response. *International Journal of Information Systems for Crisis Response Management, 1*(3), 69–82.

Jennex, M. E., Smolnik, S., & Croasdell, D. T. (2009). Towards a Consensus Knowledge Management Success Definition. *VINE: The Journal of Information and Knowledge Management Systems, 39*(2), 174–188.

Jennex, M., & Raman, M. (2009). Knowledge Management in Support of Crisis Response. [IJISCRAM]. *International Journal of Information Systems for Crisis Response Management, 1*(3), 69–83.

Jepson, K. (2008). How 1 small CU perfected its own recipe for disaster recovery. *Credit Union Journal, 23*(9), 20.

Joshi, H., Seker, R., Bayrak, C., Ramaswamy, S., & Connelly, J. (2007, July 15-18). *Ontology for Disaster Mitigation and Planning.* Paper presented at the Summer Computer Simulation Conference, San Diego, CA.

Kadlec, C., & Shropshire, J. (in press). Establishing the IT disaster recovery construct. *Journal of IT Management.*

Kaneiwa, K., & Mizoguchi, R. (2004, June 2-5). *Ontological Knowledge Base Reasoning with Sort-Hierarchy and Rigidity.* Paper presented at the Ninth International Conference on the Principles of Knowledge Representation and Reasoning (KR2004), Whistler, Canada.

Kash, T. J., & Darling, J. R. (1998). Crisis management: prevention, diagnosis and intervention. *Leadership and Organization Development Journal, 19*(4), 179–186. doi:10.1108/01437739810217151

Kaufmann, F. X. (1991). Introduction: issues and context. In Kaufmann, F. X. (Ed.), *The public Sector: Challenge for coordination and learning* (pp. 3–28). Berlin, Germany: Walter de Gruyter.

Keen, J., Moore, J., & West, R. (2006). Pathways, networks and choice in health care. *International Journal of Health Care Quality Assurance, 19*, 316–327. doi:10.1108/09526860610671373

Keinan, G., Friedland, N., & Ben-Porath, Y. (1987). Decision-making under stress: Scanning of alternatives under physical threat. *Acta Psychologica, 64*, 219–228. doi:doi:10.1016/0001-6918(87)90008-4

Kentouris, C. (2008). Strengthening data continuity, euro-clear adds backup site. *Securities Industry News, 20*(8), 8–10.

Kerstholt, J. (1996). *Dynamic Decision Making.* Soesterberg, The Netherlands: TNO Human Factors.

Kiefer, J. J., Mancini, J. A., Morrow, B. H., Gladwin, H., & Stewart, T. A. (2008). *Providing access to resilience-enhancing technologies for disadvantaged communities and vulnerable populations* (CARRI: PARET Rep.). Oak Ridge, TN: Community & Regional Resilience Initiative, Institute for Advanced Biometrics and Social Systems Studies, Oak Ridge National Laboratory.

Kille, A. (2006). *Wikis in the Workplace: How Wikis Can Help Manage Knowledge in Library Reference Services.* Retrieved April 24, 2006, from http://libres.curtin.edu.au/libres16n1/Kille_essayopinion.htm

Killian, L. (2002). An Introduction to Methodological Problems of Field Studies in Disasters. In R. Stallings (Ed.), *Methods of Disaster Researched.* Newark, DE: International Research Committee on Disasters.

Kim, J. Y., Song, W., & Schulzrinne, H. (2006). *An Enhanced VoIP Emergency Services Prototype.* Paper presented at the 3rd International Information Systems for Crisis Response and Management (ISCRAM) Conference.

Kontogiannis, T., & Kossiavelou, Z. (1999). *Stress and team performance: principles and challenges for intelligent decision aids,* Safety Science, December, Vol.33, Issue 3, pp. 103 -128,.

Koskinen, K. U. (2001). Tacit Knowledge as a Promoter of Success in Technology Firms. In *Proceedings of the 34th Hawaii International Conference on System Sciences.* Washington, DC: IEEE Computer Society.

Kostman, J. T. (2004). 20 Rules for Effective Communication in a Crisis. *Disaster Recovery Journal, 17*(2), 20.

Kouzmin, A., Jarman, A. M. G., & Rosenthal, U. (1995). Inter-organizational policy processes in disaster management. *Disaster Prevention and Management, 4*(2), 20–37. doi:10.1108/09653569510082669

Kowalski-Trakofler, K., & Vaught, T. (2003). Judgment and decision making under stress: an overview for emergency managers. *International Journal of Emergency Management, 1*(3), 278–289. doi:doi:10.1504/IJEM.2003.003297

Kumar, N., & Vragov, R. (2009). Active Citizen Participation Using ICT Tools. *Communications of the ACM, 52*(1), 118–121. doi:10.1145/1435417.1435444

Kushma, J. (2007). Role Abandonment: Should we leave this myth behind. *Natural Hazards Observer, XXXI*(5).

Lagadec, P. (1993). *Preventing chaos in a crisis: Strategies for prevention, control, and damage limitation* (Phelps, J. M., Trans.). New York, NY: McGraw-Hill.

Laliberte, B. (2007). How disaster-tolerant is your company? *Business Communications Review, 32*(4), 44–49.

Lamoreaux, L. (2009). Twitter.com and coordinated Mayhem, Counter Terrorism. *Journal of Counterterrorism and Homeland Security International, 15*(2).

Lam, W. (2002). Ensuring Business Continuity. *IT Professional, 4*(3), 19–25. doi:10.1109/MITP.2002.1008533

Lang, G., & Benbunan-Fich, R. (2010). The Use of Social Media in Disaster Situation: Framework and Cases. *International Journal of Information Systems for Crisis Response and Management, 2*(1), 11–23. doi:10.4018/jiscrm.2010120402

Lang, T., & Allen, L. (2008). Reflecting on Scenario Practice: The Contribution of a Soft Systems Perspective . In Ramírz, R., Selsky, J. W., & van der Heijden, K. (Eds.), *Business Planning for Turbulent Times, New Methods for Applying Scenarios* (pp. 47–63). London, UK: Earthscan.

Laura, L. (2006). Lesson learned from Katrina. In *Proceedings of the ACUC Disaster Recovery Planning Conference*. Retrieved February 2, 2010, from http://grants.nih.gov/grants/OLAW/IACUCConf2006_Levy.pdf

Law Office Management & Administration Report. (2008). *Emergence Preparedness Resources, 8*(9), 1-2.

Lawrence, P., & Lorsch, J. (1967). Differentiation and Integration in Complex Organizations. *Administrative Science Quarterly, 12*, 1–30. doi:10.2307/2391211

Lee, J., & Bui, T. (2000). A Template-based Methodology for Disaster Management Information Systems. In *Proceedings of the 33rd Hawaii International Conference on System Sciences*. Washington, DC: IEEE Computer Society.

Lee, R., & Sumiya, K. (2010). Measuring geographical regularities of crowd behaviors for Twitter-based geo-social event detection. In *Proceedings of the 2nd ACM SIGSPATIAL International Workshop on Location Based Social Networks)* (pp. 1–10).

Lee, A. (1989). A scientific methodology for MIS case studies. *Management Information Systems Quarterly, 13*(1), 33–50. doi:10.2307/248698

Lee, L., Choi, B., Kim, J., & Hong, S. (2007). Culture-technology: Effects of cultural characteristics on the post-adoption beliefs of mobile internet users. *International Journal of Electronic Commerce, 11*(4), 1–51. doi:10.2753/JEC1086-4415110401

Legislature, W. S. (n.d.). *Definitions*. Retrieved August 13, 2009, from http://apps.leg.wa.gov/rcw/default.aspx?cite=38.52.010

Leuf, B., & Cunningham, W. (2001). *The WIKI WAY. Quick Collaboration of the Web*. Reading, MA: Addison-Wesley.

Lewin, K. (1947a). Frontiers in Group Dynamics. *Human Relations, 1*(1), 5–41. doi:10.1177/001872674700100103

Lewin, K. (1947b). Frontiers in Group Dynamics II. *Human Relations, 1*(2), 143–153. doi:10.1177/001872674700100201

Lindgren, R., Henfridsson, O., & Schultze, U. (2004). Design principles for competence management systems: A synthesis of an action research study. *MIS Quarterly, 28*(3), 435–472.

Lindström, J. (2009). *Models, methodology and challenges within strategic information security for senior managements. Unpublished doctoral disseration*. Sweden: Luleå University of Technology.

Lindström, J., Samuelsson, S., & Hägerfors, A. (2010). Business Continuity Planning Methodology. *Disaster Prevention and Management, 19*(2), 243–255. doi:10.1108/09653561011038039

LIS. (1997). *The case study as a research method*. Retrieved December 2009, from http://www.ischool.utexas.edu/~ssoy/usesusers/l391d1b.htm

Little, E. (2003, September 16). *A Proposed Methodology for the Development of Application-Based Formal Ontologies.* Paper presented at the KI2003 Workshop on Reference Ontologies and Application Ontologies, Hamburg, Germany.

Liu, S. B., Palen, L., Sutton, J., Hughes, A. L., & Vieweg, S. (2008). In Search of the Bigger Picture: The Emergent Role of On-Line Photo Sharing in Times of Disaster. In F. Fiedrich & B. Van De Walle (Eds.), *Proceedings of the 5th International ISCRAM Conference,* Washington, DC (pp. 140-149).

Lohrman, D. (2007). Disaster Recovery: A process – not a destination. *Public CIO, 8*(2), 54.

Louisiana Office of Homeland Security & Emergency Preparedness. (2005). *Lessons learned.* Retrieved March 10, 2010, from http://emergency.louisiana.gov/

Luftman, J., & Kempaiah, R. (2008). Key issues for IT executives 2007. *Management Information Systems Quarterly Executive, 7*(2), 99–112.

Lyons, B. (2007). *Preparing for a disaster: Determining the essential functions that should be up first. (Tec. Rep. No. 14).* Bethesda, MD: SANS Institute.

Macintosh, A. (2006). eParticipation in Policy-making: The Research and the Challenges. In P. Cunningham & M. Cunninghal (Eds.), *Exploiting the Knowledge Economy: Issues, Applications, Case Studies.* Amsterdam, The Netherlands: IOS Press.

Mackenzie, S., Podsakoff, P., & Jarvis, C. (2005). The problem of Measurement Model Misspecification in Behavioral and Organizational Research and Some Recommended Solutions. *The Journal of Applied Psychology, 90*(4), 710–730. PubMed doi:10.1037/0021-9010.90.4.710

Maier, R. (2002). *Knowledge Management Systems: Information and Communication Technologies for Knowledge Management.* Berlin, Germany: Springer-Verlag.

Mancini, J. A., Bowen, G. L., Martin, J. A., & Ware, W. B. (2003). *The community connections index.* Paper presented at the Hawaii International Conference on Social Sciences, Honolulu, HI.

Mancini, J. A., Bowen, G. L., Ware, W. B., & Martin, J. A. (2007). *Engagement, participation, and community efficacy: Insights into social organization.* Paper presented at Hawaii International Meeting on Social Sciences, Honolulu HI.

Manjoo, F. (2009, April, 10). The reluctant Twitterer's dilemma. *Slate Magazine.* Retrieved April 10, 2009, from http://www.slate.com/id/2215829/

Manoj, B. S., & Hubenko Baker, A. (2007). Communication Challenges in Emergency Response. *Communications of the ACM, 50*(3), 51–53. doi:10.1145/1226736.1226765

Marich, M., Horan, T., & Schooley, B. (2008). Understanding IT governance within the San Mateo County emergency medical service agency. In F. Fiedrich & B. Van de Walle (Eds.), *Proceedings of the 5th International Conference on Information Systems for Crisis Response and Management (ISCRAM2008)* (pp. 451-461).

Marich, M. (2008). *Toward a high performance architecture for time-critical information services: Sequential case studies and action research of regional EMS systems.* Claremont, CA: Claremont Graduate University, School of Information Systems and Technology.

Marra, F. J. (2004). Excellent crisis communication: Beyond crisis plans . In Millar, D. P., & Heath, R. L. (Eds.), *Responding to crisis: A rhetorical approach to crisis communication* (pp. 311–325). Mahwah, NJ: Erlbaum.

Mathiassen, L., & Nielsen, P. A. (2000). Interaction and Transformation in SSM. *Systems Research and Behavioral Science, 17,* 243–253. doi:10.1002/(SICI)1099-1743(200005/06)17:3<243::AID-SRES316>3.0.CO;2-9

Mattison, D. (2003). Quickwiki, Swiki, Twiki, Zwiki and the Plone Wars – Wiki as PIM and Collaborative Content Tool. *Searcher: The Magazine for Database Professionals, 11*(4), 32.

McLaughlin, L. (2008). Rethinking disaster recovery. *CIO, 21*(6), 23–26.

McLennan, J., Holgate, A., & Wearing, A. (2003, September). *Human Information Processing aspects of Effective Emergency Incident Management Decision Making.* Paper presented at the Human Factors of Decision Making in Complex Systems Conference, Dunblane, Scotland.

McNeil, D. G., Jr. (2009, November 24). Shifting vaccine for flu to elderly. *New York Times*.

Mearian, L. (2004). Key financial firms compare notes on disaster recovery. *Computerworld, 38*(31), 43.

Mecella, M., Angelaccio, M., Krek, A., Catarci, T., Buttarazzi, B., & Dustdar, S. (2006, May 14-17). *WORKPAD: An Adaptive Peer-to-Peer Software Infrastructure for Supporting Collaborative Work of Human Operators in Emergency/Disaster Scenarios.* Paper presented at the International Symposium on Collaborative Technologies and Systems (CTS'06), Las Vegas, NV.

Meier, P., & Ziemke, J. (2010). *Growth, communications and response, uniting practitioners, scholars & developers at the cutting edge of crisis mapping—measuring our response: an executive summary*. International Network of Crisis Mappers (CM*Net).

Mendonça, D., Jefferson, T., & Harrald, J. (2007). Collaborative adhocracies and mix-and-match technologies in emergency management. *Communications of the ACM, 50*(3), 44–49. doi:10.1145/1226736.1226764

Michigan State University Disaster Recovery Planning. (2003). Retrieved March 5, 2010, from http://www.drp.msu.edu/WhyPlan.htm

Mileti, D. S. (1999). *Disasters by Design*. Washington, DC: Joseph Henry Press.

Miller, G. A. (1956). The magical number seven, plus or minus two: Some limits on our capacity for processing information. [Retrieved from http://www.well.com/user/smalin/miller.html]. *Psychological Review, 63*, 81–97. doi:10.1037/h0043158

Mills, A., Chen, R., Lee, J. K., & Rao, H. R. (2009). Web 2.0 Emergency Applications: How Useful Can Twitter be for Emergency Response. *Journal of Information Privacy & Security, 5*(3), 3–26.

Mingers, J. (1992). Questions and suggestions in using soft systems methodology. *Systemist, 14*, 54–61.

Mingers, J., & White, L. (in press). A review of the recent contribution of systems thinking to operational research and management science. *European Journal of Operational Research*.

Mitchell, J. K. (1999). *Crucibles of Hazard: Mega-Cities and Disasters in Transition*. Tokyo: United Nations University Press.

Mitleton-Kelly, E. (2003). Ten principles of complexity and enabling infrastructures . In Mitleton-Kelly, E. (Ed.), *Complex systems and evolutionary perspectives on organisations: The application of complexity theory to organisations* (pp. 23–50). New York, NY: Pergamon Press.

Moe, T. L., & Pathranarakul, P. (2006). An integrated approach to natural disaster management. *Disaster Prevention and Management, 15*(3), 396–413. doi:10.1108/09653560610669882

Monaco, F. (2001). *IT disaster recovery near the world trade center*. Retrieved March 12, 2010, from http://net.educause.edu/ir/library/pdf/eqm0144.pdf

Mork, L. (2002). Technology Tools for Crisis response. *Risk Management, 49*(10), 44–50.

Mowshowitz, A. (1997). Virtual organization. *Communications of the ACM, 40*(9), 30–37. doi:10.1145/260750.260759

Murphy, T., & Jennex, M. E. (2006). Knowledge Management, Emergency Response, and Hurricane Katrina. *International Journal of Intelligent Control and Systems, 11*(4), 199–208.

Myers, N. (1999). *Manager's guide to contingency planning for disasters: Protecting vital facilities and critical operations*. New York: Wiley.

National Research Council. (2007). *Successful response starts with a map: improving geospatial support for disaster management*. Washington, DC: National Academies Press.

NENA. (2006). *NENA recommended method(s) for location determination to support IP-based emergency services* (No. 08-505 v1). Retrieved from http://www.nena.org/standards/technical/voip/location-determination-ip-based-emergency-services

NENA. (2007a). *NENA Functional and Interface Standards for Next Generation 9-1-1 Version 1.0 (i3)* (No. 08-002). Retrieved from http://www.nena.org/standards/technical/voip/functional-interface-NG911-i3

NENA. (2007b). *IP-capable PSAP Minimum Operational Requirements Standard* (No. 58-001). Retrieved from http://www.nena.org/standards/operations/IP-PSAP-minimum-requirements

NENA. (2010). *NENA 9-1-1 Deployment Reports & Maps.* Retrieved from http://nena.ddti.net

Neuman, W. L. (2003). *Social research methods* (5th ed.). Boston: Pearson Education.

Newlon, C. M., Pfaff, M., Patel, H., de Vreede, G., & MacDorman, K. F. (2009). Mega-Collaboration: The Inspiration and Development of an Interface for Large-Scale Disaster Response. In J. Landgren, U. Nulden, & B. Van De Walle (Eds.), *Proceedings of the 6th International ISCRAM Conference*, Gothenburg, Sweden.

News, B. B. C. (2000). *Yahoo attack exposes web weakness.* Retrieved March 3, 2010, from http://news.bbc.co.uk/2/hi/science/nature/635444.stm

Nisha de Silva, F. (2001). Providing Spatial Decision Support for Evacuation Planning: A Challenge in Integrating Technologies. *Disaster Prevention and Management, 10*(1), 11–20. doi:10.1108/09653560110381787

Norris, F. H., Stevens, S. P., Pfefferbaum, B., Wyche, K. F., & Pfefferbaum, R. L. (2007). Community Resilience as a Metaphor, Theory, Set of Capacities, and Strategy for Disaster Readiness. *American Journal of Community Psychology, 41*, 127–150. doi:10.1007/s10464-007-9156-6

Noy, N., & McGuinness, D. (2001). *Ontology Development 101: A Guide to Creating Your First Ontology* (No. KSL-01-05 and SMI-2001-0880).

Noy, N. (2004). Semantic Integration: A Survey of Ontology Based Approaches. *SIGMOD Record, 33*(4), 65–69. doi:10.1145/1041410.1041421

Noy, N., & Hafner, C. (1997). The State of the Art in Ontology Design. *AI Magazine, 18*(3), 53–74.

NSTISSC. (1994). *National Training Standard for Information Systems Security (INFOSEC) Professionals, NSTISSI No. 4011.* Washington, DC: National Security Telecommunications and Information Systems Security Committee. Retrieved from http://niatec.info/pdf/4011.pdf

Obama, B. H. (2009, March 28). Weekly Address: Crisis and service. *White House Blog.* Retrieved March 28, 2009, from http://www.whitehouse.gov/blog/09/03/27/Weekly-Address-Crisis-and-Service/

OECD. (2007). *Participative Web: User-Created Content. Report presented to the Working Party on the Information Economy.* Retrieved August 1, 2009, from http://www.oecd.org/dataoecd/57/14/38393115.pdf

Organization, G. B. R. (2003). *The cost of lost data.* Retrieved March 8th, 2009, from http://gbr.pepperdine.edu/033/dataloss.html

Pabrai, U. (2004). Contingency planning and disaster recovery. *Certification Magazine, 5*(8), 38–39.

Palen, L., & Liu, S. B. (2007). Citizen Communications in Crisis: Anticipating a Future of ICT-Supported Public Participation. In *Proceedings of CHI 2007,* San Jose, CA (pp. 727-736).

Palen, L., Vieweg, S., Sutton, J., Liu, S. B., & Hughes, A. (2007). Crisis Informatics: Studying Crisis in a Networked World. In *Proceedings of the 3rd International Conference on e-Social Science*, Ann Arbor, MI.

Palen, L. (2008). Online Social Media in Crisis Events. *EDUCAUSE Quarterly*, (3): 76–78.

Palen, L., Hiltz, S. R., & Liu, S. B. (2007). Online Forums Supporting Grassroots Participation in Emergency Preparedness and Response. *Communications of the ACM, 50*(3), 54–58. doi:10.1145/1226736.1226766

Palen, L., Vieweg, S., Liu, S., & Hughes, A. L. (2009). Crisis in a Networked World: Features of Computer-Mediated Communication in the April 16, 2007 Virginia Tech Event. *Social Science Computer Review*, 467–480. doi:10.1177/0894439309332302

Panko, R. (2003). *Corporate computer and network security* (*Vol. 3*, pp. 223–225). Upper Saddle River, NJ: Prentice Hall.

Panko, R. P. (2007). Two experiments in reducing overconfidence in spreadsheet development. *Journal of Organizational and End User Computing, 19*(1), 1–23.

Parliament of Victoria. (2005). *Victorian Electronic Democracy - Final Report*. Retrieved October 29, 2005, from http://www.parliament.vic.gov.au/sarc/E-Democracy/Final_Report/Glossary.htm

Patton, D., & Flin, R. (1999). Disaster Stress: An Emergency Management Perspective. *Disaster Prevention and Management*, *8*(4), 261–267. doi:10.1108/09653569910283897

Pauchant, T. C., & Mitroff, I. I. (1992). *Transforming the crisis-prone organization*. San Francisco, CA: Jossey-Bass.

Pearson, C. M., & Clair, J. A. (1998). Reframing crisis management. *Academy of Management Review*, *23*(1), 59–76. doi:10.2307/259099

Pearson, C., & Mitroff, I. I. (1993). From crisis prone to crisis prepared: a framework for crisis management. *The Academy of Management Executive*, *7*(1), 48–59.

Perrow, C. (1999). *Normal accidents: living with high-risk technologies* (2nd ed.). Princeton, NJ: Princeton University Press.

Perry, R. W., & Quarantelli, E. L. (Eds.). (2005). *What is a disaster? New answers to old questions*. Philadelphia, PA: Xlibris.

Peterson, J. (2005). *A Presence-based GEOPRIV Location Object Format (IETF RFC 4119). Internet Engineering Task Force*. IETF.

Peterson, R. (2003). Lighting a dark corner of disaster recovery. *Journal of Academy of Business and Economics*, *253*, 15–17.

Petfinder. (2005). Retrieved January 23, 2010, from http://www.petfinder.com/forums/viewtopic.php?p=861990&sid=2c51d1d64870febd87acbcb4d22c3c05

Petter, S., Straub, D., & Rai, A. (2007). Specifying formative constructs in information systems research. *Management Information Systems Quarterly*, *31*(4), 623–656.

Phang, C. W., & Kankanhalli, A. (2008). A Framework of ICT Exploitation for E-Participation Initiatives. *Communications of the ACM*, *51*(12), 128–132. doi:10.1145/1409360.1409385

Pidgeon, N., Kasperson, R., & Slovick, P. (Eds.). (2003). *The social amplification of risk*. Cambridge, UK: Cambridge University Press.

Pinto, H. S., & Martins, J. P. (2004). Ontologies: How Can They Be Built? *Knowledge and Information Systems*, *6*(4), 441–464. doi:10.1007/s10115-003-0138-1

Plotnick, L., White, C., & Plummer, M. (2009). Design Issues. In *Proceedings of America's Conference on Information Systems (AMCIS)*, San Francisco. Retrieved July 28, 2009, from http://www.plano.gov

Plotnick, L., White, C., & Plummer, M. (2009). The Design of an Online Social Network Site for Emergency Management: A One-Stop Shop. In *Proceedings of the 15th Americas Conference on Information Systems*, San Francisco.

Plotnick, C., & White, L. (2010). A Social Media Tsunami: the Approaching Wave. *International Journal of Information Systems for Crisis Response and Management*, *2*(1), i–iv.

Plotnick, L., & White, C. (2010). A Framework to identify best practices: Social media and web 2.0 technologies in the emergency domain. *International Journal of Information Systems for Crisis Response and Management*, *2*(1), 37–48. doi:10.4018/jiscrm.2010120404

Plotnick, N. (1999). When disaster plans fall short. *PC Week*, *28*(2), 58.

Polk, J., & Rosen, B. (2009). *Location conveyance for the session initiation protocol (IETF draft-ietf-sip-location-conveyance-13). Internet Engineering Task Force*. IETF.

Polk, J., Schnizlein, J., & Linsner, M. (2004). *Dynamic host configuration protocol option for coordinate-based location configuration information (IETF RFC 3825). Internet Engineering Task Force*. IETF.

Preble, J. F. (1997). Integrating the crisis management perspective into the strategic management process. *Journal of Management Studies*, *34*(5), 769–791. doi:10.1111/1467-6486.00071

Pregmon, M. (2007). IT disaster recovery: Are you up and ready? Part 1: Analysis. *Journal of the Quality Assurance Institute*, *27*(2), 23–24.

Pregmon, M. (2007). IT disaster recovery: Are you up and ready? Part 2: Internal Control. *Journal of the Quality Assurance Institute, 27*(3), 25–28.

Pregmon, M. (2007). IT disaster recovery: Are you up and ready? Part 3: The recovery planning process. *Journal of the Quality Assurance Institute, 27*(4), 10–12.

Pregmon, M. (2008). IT disaster recovery: Are you up and ready? Part 4: IT virtualization. *Journal of the Quality Assurance Institute, 28*(1), 26–27.

Preparata, F., & Shamos, M. (1985). *Computational Geometry – An Introduction*. New York: Springer.

Putnam, R. (2000). *Bowling Alone: The Collapse and Revival of American Community*. New York: Simon and Schuster.

Quantarelli, E. L., Lagadec, P., & Boin, A. (2007). A heuristic approach to future disasters and crises . In Rodriguez, H., Quantarelli, E. L., & Dynes, R. (Eds.), *Handbook of Disaster Research* (pp. 16–41). Berlin, Germany: Springer. doi:10.1007/978-0-387-32353-4_2

Ragin, C. C. (1987). *The Comparative Method: Moving Beyond Qualitative and Quantitative Strategies*. Berkeley, CA: University of California Press.

Raman, M., & Ryan, T. (2004). *Designing Online Discussion Support Systems for Academic Setting-"The Wiki Way"*. Paper presented at the Americas Conferences on Information Systems (AMCIS), New York.

Raman, M., Ryan, T., Jennex, M. E., & Olfman, L. (2010). Wiki Technology and Emergency Response: An Action Research Study. *International Journal of Information Systems for Crisis Response and Management, 2*(1), 49–69. doi:10.4018/jiscrm.2010120405

Raman, M., Ryan, T., & Olfman, L. (2006). Knowledge management systems for emergency preparedness. *International Journal of Knowledge Management, 2*(3), 33–50. doi:10.4018/jkm.2006070103

Ramsaran, C. (2005). Running ahead of the pack. *Bank Systems & Technology, 1*(4), 1–3.

Rao, L., McNaughton, M., Osei-Bryson, K.-M., & Haye, M. (2009). *The Role of Ontologies in Disaster Recovery Planning*. Paper presented at the 15th Americas Conference on Information Systems (AMCIS), San Francisco, CA.

Rao, L., & Osei-Bryson, K.-M. (2007). Towards Defining Dimensions of Knowledge Systems Quality. *Expert Systems with Applications, 33*(2), 368–378. doi:10.1016/j.eswa.2006.05.003

Rao, L., Reichgelt, H., & Osei-Bryson, K.-M. (2009). An Approach for Ontology Development and Assessment Using a Quality Framework. *Knowledge Management Research and Practice, 7*, 260–276. doi:10.1057/kmrp.2009.12

Reed, J., Krizman, K., Woerner, B., & Rappaport, T. (1998). An overview of the challenges and progress in meeting the E-911 requirements for location service. *IEEE Communications Magazine*, 30–37. doi:10.1109/35.667410

Reeder, S. (2002). *Improve higher education information security*. Retrieved July 23, 2009, from http://www.giac.org/certified_professionals/practicals/gsec/1982.php

Reisinger, D. (2008). Disaster recovery goes virtual. *InformationWeek, 11*(88), 23–23.

Renaud, R., & Phillips, S. (2003). Developing an Integrated Emergency Response Programme for Facilities: The Experience of Public Works and Government Services Canada. *Journal of Facilities Management, 1*(4), 347–364. doi:10.1108/14725960310808051

Repositories, I. (2006). *An opportunity for CIO: Campus impact*. Retrieved January 27, 2010, from http://net.educause.edu/ir/library/pdf/erm0626.pdf

Retelle, M. (2008). Plan for disaster. *Credit Union Magazine, 21*(9), 80.

Richardson, K. A., Mathieson, G., & Cilliers, P. (2000). The theory and practice of complexity science: Epistemological considerations for military operational analysis. *SysteMexico, 1*(2), 25–66.

Rihoux, B. (2006). Qualitative comparative analysis (qca) and related systematic comparative methods: Recent advances and remaining challenges for social science research. *International Sociology, 21*(5), 679–706. doi:10.1177/0268580906067836

Ringland, G. (1998). *Scenario Planning: Managing for the Future*. New York, NY: John Wiley & Sons.

Ritchey, T. (2006). Problem structuring using computer-aided morphological analysis. *The Journal of the Operational Research Society*, 57, 792–801. doi:10.1057/palgrave.jors.2602177

Ritchie, B. W. (2004). Chaos, crises and disasters: a strategic approach to crisis management in the tourism industry. *Tourism Management*, 25, 669–683. doi:10.1016/j.tourman.2003.09.004

Roberts, W. (2006, October). Business Continuity Planning for disasters is just good planning. In *Proceedings of the Military Communications Conference (MILCOM 2006)*, Washington DC.

Rodriguez, D. M. (1997). *Dominating Time in the Operational Decision Making Process*. Newport, RI: U.S. Naval War College.

Rolich, P. (2008). Setting priorities: Business continuity from an IT perspective – is it better to be right or liked? *Tech Decisions*, 9(2), 11–14.

Rosen, B., & Polk, J. (2009). *Best current practices for communication services in support of emergency calling (IETF draft-ietf-ecrit-phonebcp-08). Internet Engineering Task Force*. IETF.

Rosenberg, J., Schulzrinne, H., Camarillo, G., Johnston, A., Peterson, J., & Sparks, R. (2002). *SIP: Session Initiation Protocol (IETF RFC 3261). Internet Engineering Task Force*. IETF.

Ross, J. W. (2003). Creating a sustainable IT architecture competency: Learning in stages. *Management Information Systems Quarterly Executive*, 2(1), 31–43.

Ross, J. W., & Beath, C. (2006). Sustainable IT outsourcing success: Let enterprise architecture be your guide. *Management Information Systems Quarterly Executive*, 5(4), 181–192.

Rowe, G. (2005). A Typology of Public Engagement Mechanisms. *Science, Technology & Human Values*, 30(2), 251–290. doi:10.1177/0162243904271724

Rowe, G., & Frewer, L. J. (2000). Public Participation Methods: A Framework for Evaluation. *Science, Technology & Human Values*, 25(1), 3–29. doi:10.1177/016224390002500101

Sage, A. P., & Rouse, W. B. (1999). Information Systems Frontiers in Knowledge Management. *Information Systems Frontiers*, 1(3), 205–219. doi:10.1023/A:1010046210832

Salas, E., Driskell, E., & Hughs, S. (1996). The study of stress and human performance. In Driskell, J. E., & Salas, E. (Eds.), *Stress and Human Performance* (pp. 1–45). Mahwah, NJ: Lawrence Erlbaum Associates.

Sawyer, S., Reagor, S., Tyworth, M., & Thomas, J. (2005, March 17-19). From response to foresight: Managing knowledge and integrated criminal justice. In S. Newell & R. Galliers (Eds.), *Proceedings of the 2005 Organizational Learning and Knowledge Capabilities Conference*. Cambridge, MA: Bentley College.

Sayed, A., Tarighat, A., & Khajehnour, N. (2005). Network-based wireless location. *IEEE Signal Processing Magazine*, 22(4), 24–40. doi:doi:10.1109/MSP.2005.1458275

Schaffhauser, D. (2005). Disaster recovery: The time is now. *Campus Technology*. Retrieved February 18, 2010, from http://campustechnology.com/Articles/2005/10/Disaster-Recovery-The-Time-Is-Now.aspx

Scheeres, J. (2001). *Attack can't erase stored data*. Retrieved January 21, 2010, from http://www.wired.com/techbiz/media/news/2001/09/47004

Schekkerman, J. (2004). *How to survive in the jungle of enterprise architecture frameworks*. Victoria, Canada: Trafford Publishing.

Scholl, J. (2005). Interoperability in e-Government: More than just smart middleware. In *Proceedings of the 38th Hawaii International Conference on System Sciences (HICSS38)*.

Schooley, B., Horan, T., & Marich, M. (2010). User Perspectives on the Minnesota Interorganizational Mayday Information System. In B. Van de Walle, M. Turoff, & R, Hiltz (Eds.), *Information Systems for Emergency Management* (Vol. 16, pp. 193-225). Armonk, NY: M.E. Sharpe.

Schooley, B., Horan, T., & Naomani, A. (2008). *A report of the symposium: Improving emergency medical response with inter-organizational information systems symposium summary.*

Schooley, B., & Horan, T. (2007). End-to-end enterprise performance management in the public sector through inter-organizational information integration. *Government Information Quarterly, 24*(4), 755–784. doi:10.1016/j.giq.2007.04.001

Schulzrinne, H., Tschofenig, H., Hardie, T., & Newton, A. (2007). LoST: A Protocol for Mapping Geographic Locations to Public Safety Answering Points. In *Proceedings of the IEEE International Performance, Computing, and Communications Conference (IPCCC)* (pp. 606-611).

Schulzrinne, H. (2008). *Synchronizing Location to Service Translation (LoST) Servers (IETF draft-ietf-ecrit-lost-sync-00). Internet Engineering Task Force.* IETF.

Schulzrinne, H., & Arabshian, K. (2002). Providing emergency services in Internet telephony. *IEEE Internet Computing, 6*(3), 39–47. doi:doi:10.1109/MIC.2002.1003130

Schulzrinne, H., & Marshall, R. (2008). *Requirements for emergency context resolution with Internet technologies (IETF RFC 5012). Internet Engineering Task Force.* IETF.

Scotti, D. J., Harmon, J., & Behson, S. J. (2007). Links among high-performance work environment, service quality, and customer satisfaction: an extension to the healthcare sector. *Journal of Healthcare Management, 52*(2), 109–124.

Seeger, M. W., Sellnow, T. L., & Ulmer, R. R. (2003). *Communication and Organizational Crisis.* Westport, CT: Praeger Publishers.

Segev, A. (2009). Adaptive Ontology Use for Crisis Knowledge Representation. [IJISCRAM]. *International Journal of Information Systems for Crisis Response Management, 1*(2), 16–30.

Senge, P. M., Smith, B., Schley, S., Laur, J., & Kruschwitz, N. (2008). *The Necessary Revolution: How Individuals and Organizations are Working Together to Create a Sustainable World.* New York: Doubleday.

Shachtman, N. (2009). Marines Ban Twitter, MySpace, Facebook. *Wired.com.* Retrieved August 28, 2009, from http://www.wired.com/dangerroom/2009/08/marines-ban-twitter-myspace-facebook/

Sharma, S., & Osei-Bryson, K.-M. (2008, January 7-10). *Organization-Ontology Based Framework for Implementing the Business Understanding Phase of Data Mining Projects.* Paper presented at the 41st Annual Hawaii International Conference on System Sciences, Big Island, HI.

Shepherd, A. (2009). Disaster recovery — lessons from Tulane's response to Katrina. *Record, 21*(3), 10.

Sheth, S., McHugh, J., & Jones, F. (2008). A dashboard for measuring capability when designing, implementing and validating business continuity and disaster recovery projects. *Journal of Business Continuity & Emergency Planning, 2*(3), 221–239.

Shimrat, M. (1962). Algorithm 112: Position of point relative to polygon. *Communications of the ACM Archive, 5*(8), 434. doi:doi:10.1145/368637.368653

Shirkey, C. (2008). *Here Comes Everybody: The Power of Organizing with Organizations.* New York: Penguin Press.

Shklovski, I., Palen, L., & Sutton, J. (2008). Finding Community Through Information and Communication Technology During Disaster Events. In *Proceedings of the Conference on Computer Supported Cooperative Work (CSCW '08),* San Diego, CA (pp. 1-10).

Shneiderman, B., & Preece, J. (2007, February 16). 911.gov. *Science, 315,* 944. doi:10.1126/science.1139088

Shrivastava, P. (1993). Crisis theory/practice: Towards a sustainable future. *Industrial and Environmental Crisis Quarterly, 7,* 23–42.

Sicilia, M.-A., Lytras, M., Rodriguez, E., & Garcia-Barriocanal, E. (2006). Integrating Descriptions of Knowledge Management Learning Activities into Large Ontological Structures: A Case Study. *Data & Knowledge Engineering, 57*(2), 111–121. doi:10.1016/j.datak.2005.04.001

Skertchly, A., & Skertchly, K. (2001). Catastrophe management: Coping with totally unexpected extreme disasters. *Australian Journal of Emergency Management, Autumn 2001.*

Skertchly, A., & Skertcly, K. (2001). Catastrophe management: coping with totally unexpected extreme disasters. *The Australian Journal of Emergency Management, 16*(1).

Sliwa, C. (2005). Retailers unsure about the status of stores, systems. *Computerworld, 39*(3), 5.

Smith, C. A. P., & Hayne, S. (1991). A Distributed System for Crisis Management. In *Proceedings of the 24th Hawaii International Conference on System Sciences, HICSS* (Vol. 3, pp. 72-81).

Smith, D. (2004). For whom the bell tolls: Imagining accidents and the development of crisis simulation in organizations. *Simulation & Gaming, 35*(3), 347–362. doi:10.1177/1046878104266295

Smits, S. J., & Ally, N. E. (2003). Thinking the unthinkable – leadership's role in creating behavioural readiness for crisis management. *Communication Review, 13*(1), 1–23.

Smyth, E. (2001). *Would the Internet Widen Public Participation?* Unpublished master's thesis, University of Leeds.

Sobol, M., & Klein, G. (2009). Relation of CIO background, IT infrastructure, and economic performance. *Information & Management, 46*(5), 271–278. doi:10.1016/j.im.2009.05.001

Song, W., et al. (2008). *Next Generation 9-1-1 Proof-of-Concept System.* Paper presented at SIGCOMM '08.

Sriraj, P. S., & Khisty, C. J. (1999). Crisis Management and Planning Using Systems Methodologies. *Journal of Urban Planning and Development, 125*(3), 121–133. doi:10.1061/(ASCE)0733-9488(1999)125:3(121)

Staab, S., Schnurr, H.-P., Studer, R., & Sure, Y. (2001). Knowledge Processes and Ontologies. *IEEE Intelligent Systems, 16*(1), 26–34. doi:10.1109/5254.912382

Stein, E. W., & Zwass, V. (1995). Actualizing Organizational Memory with Information Systems. *Information Systems Research, 6*(2), 85–117. doi:10.1287/isre.6.2.85

Stewardson, K. (2009). *San Francisco Residents Can Tweet 311, Government Technology: Solutions for state and local government for the information age.* Retrieved July 25, 2009, from http://www.sfgov.org/site/mayor_index.asp?id=105288

Straub, D. (1994). The effect of culture on IT diffusion: E-mail and FAX in Japan and US. *Information Systems Research, 5*(1), 23–47. doi:10.1287/isre.5.1.23

Sure, Y., Erdmann, M., Angele, J., Staab, S., Studer, R., & Wenke, D. (2002). *OntoEdit: Collaborative Ontology Development for the Semantic Web.* Paper presented at the First International Semantic Web Conference (ISWC 2002), Sardinia, Italy.

Susman, G. I., & Evered, R. D. (1978). An Assessment of the Scientific Merits of Action Research. *Administrative Science Quarterly, 23*, 582–603. doi:10.2307/2392581

Sutton, J., Palen, L., & Shklovski, I. (2008). Backchannels on the Front Lines: Emergent Uses of Social Media During in the 2007 Southern California Wildfires. In *Proceedings of the 5th International ISCRAM Conference,* Washington, DC.

Sutton, J., Palen, L., & Shklovski, I. (2008). Backchannels on the Front Lines: Emergent Uses of Social Media in the 2007 Southern California Wildfires. In F. Fiedrich & B. Van De Walle (Eds.), *Proceedings of the 5th International ISCRAM Conference*, Washington, DC.

Symposium, L. P. (2009). *Past lessons informing future action.* Retrieved February 10, 2010, from http://peer.berkeley.edu/events/pdf/10-2009/Topping_PEER%2010-17-09.pdf

Telecommunications Industry Association. (2006). *Link layer discovery protocol for media endpoint devices (LLDP-MED) (ANSI-TIA-1057).* Arlington, VA: Author.

Thacker, S. (2009). *Working with Partners to Achieve Success.* Retrieved July 25, 2009, from http://www2a.cdc.gov/podcasts/index.asp

Thaler, R. H., & Sunstein, C. R. (2008). *Nudge: Improving Decisions about Health, Wealth and Happiness.* Ann Arbor, MI: Caravan Book.

Thibodeau, P., & Mearian, L. (2005). Users start to weigh long-term IT issues. *Computerworld, 39*(37), 61–67.

Tierney, K. J. (2006). Businesses and Disasters: Vulnerability, Impacts, and Recovery. In H. Rodriguez, E. L. Quarantelli, & R. R. Dynes (Eds.), *Handbook of Disaster Research*, New York, NY: Springer Science + Business Media.

Tierney, K. J. (2005). The 9/11 Commission and disaster management: Little depth, less context, not much guidance. *Contemporary Sociology, 34*, 115–121. doi:10.1177/009430610503400204

Toomey, T., Frost, E., & Jennex, M. E. (2009). Strategies to prepare emergency management personnel to integrate geospatial tools into emergency management. *International Journal of Information Systems for Crisis Response and Management, 1*(4), 33–49. doi:10.4018/jiscrm.2009071003

Toomey, T., Frost, E., & Jennex, M. E. (2009). Strategies to Prepare Emergency Management Personnel to Integrate Geospatial Tools into Emergency Management. *International Journal of Information Systems for Crisis Response and Management, 1*(4), 33–49. doi:10.4018/jiscrm.2009071003

Townsend, F. F. (2006). *The Federal Response to Hurricane Katrina, Lessons Learned.* Washington, DC: U.S. Department of Homeland Security.

Trifonov, V., Khiabanian, H., & Rabadan, R. (2009). Geographic Dependence, Surveillance, and Origins of the 2009 Influenza A (H1N1) Virus. *The New England Journal of Medicine, 61*(2), 115–119. doi:10.1056/NEJMp0904572

Trist, E., & Bamforth, K. (1951). Some social and psychological consequences of the longwall method of coal getting. *Human Relations, 4*, 3–38. doi:10.1177/001872675100400101

Tsang, K. W., Ho, P. L., Ooi, G. C., & Yee, W. K. (2003). A cluster of cases of severe acute respiratory syndrome in Hong Kong. *The New England Journal of Medicine, 348*, 1977–1985. doi:10.1056/NEJMoa030666

Tschofenig, H., Schulzrinne, H., Shanmugan, M., & Newton, A. (2007). Protecting First-Level Responder Resources in an IP-based Emergency Services Architecture. In *Proceedings of the IEEE International Performance, Computing, and Communications Conference (IPCCC)* (pp. 626-631).

Turban, E., Aronson, J. E., Liang, T., & Sharda, R. (2006). *Decision support and business intelligence systems* (8th ed.). Upper Saddle River, NJ: Prentice Hall.

Turoff, M., & Hiltz, S. R. (1995). Computer Based Delphi Processes. In M. Adler & E. Ziglio (Eds.), *Gazing Into the Oracle: The Delphi Method and its Applications to Social Policy and Public Health* (pp. 56-88). London: Kingsley Publishers

Turoff, M., Chumer, M., Van de Walle, B., & Yao, X. (2004). The Design of a Dynamic Emergency Response Management Information System. *Journal of Information Technology Theory and Application.*

Turoff, M., Chumer, M., Yao, X., Konopka, J., & Van de Walle, B. (2005, April). Crisis Planning via Scenario Development Gaming. In *Proceedings of the 2nd International ISCRAM Conference*, Brussels, Belgium.

Turoff, M., Plotnick, L., White, C., & Hiltz, S. R. (2008). Dynamic Emergency Response Management for Large Scale Decision Making in Extreme Events. In F. Fiedrich & B. Van De Walle (Eds.), *Proceedings of the 5th International ISCRAM Conference,* Washington, DC (pp. 462-470).

Turoff, M., White, C., & Plotnick, L. (2009). *Dynamic Emergency Response Management For Large Scale Extreme Events.* International Journal for Information Systems and Crisis Response Management.

Turoff, M. (2002). Past and future emergency response information systems. *Communications of the ACM, 45*(4), 29–32. doi:10.1145/505248.505265

Turoff, M., Chumer, M., Hiltz, S. R., Klashner, R., Alles, M., Vasarhelyi, M., & Kogan, A. (2004). Assuring Homeland Security: Continuous monitoring, control & assurance of emergency preparedness. *Journal of Information Technology Theory and Application, 6*(3), 1–24.

Turoff, M., Chumer, M., Van de Walle, B., & Yao, X. (2004). The design of a dynamic emergency response management information system (DERMIS). *Journal of Information Theory, Technology, and Applications, 5*(4), 1–36.

Turoff, M., & Hiltz, S. R. (1982). Computer Support for Group versus Individual Decision Support. *IEEE Transactions on Communications, 30*(1), 82–91. doi:doi:10.1109/TCOM.1982.1095370

Twitter. (2009). *Salvation Army.* Retrieved, July 24, 2009, from http://twitter.com/salvationarmy/

U.C. Berkeley & Stanford University Press. (2002). *Recovery-Orientated Computing Press, 3.*

U.S. Naval War College. (1996). *Operational Decision Making. Instructional P Per NWC 4108.* Newport, RI: Joint Military Operations Department, U.S. Naval War College.

US EPA. (2009). Development document for final effluent guidance and standards. *National Service Center for Environmental Publications*, 20-26.

Van De Walle, B., & Turoff, M. (2007). Emergency Response Information Systems: Emerging Trends and technologies. *Communications of the ACM, 50*(3), 29–32. doi:10.1145/1226736.1226760

Van Kirk, M. (2004). Collaboration in BCP Skill Development. *Disaster Recovery Journal, 17*(2), 40.

van Uden, J., Richardson, K. A., & Cilliers, P. (2001). Postmodernism revisited? Complexity science and the study of organizations. *Journal of Critical Postmodern Organization Science, 1*(3), 53–67.

Vanmechelen, K., Stuer, G., & Broeckhove, J. (2006). *Pricing substitutable grid resources using commodity market models.* Retrieved from http://www.coms.ua.ac.be/publications/files/KVM_GECON_2006.pdf

Varela, F. J. (1995). The re-enchantment of the concrete . In Steels, L., & Brooks, R. (Eds.), *The artificial life route to artificial intelligence: Building embodied, situated agents* (pp. 11–20). Mahwah, NJ: Erlbaum.

Vargo, S. L., & Lusch, R. E. (2004). Evolving to a New Dominant Logic for Marketing. *Journal of Marketing, 68*, 1–17. doi:10.1509/jmkg.68.1.1.24036

Vargo, S. L., & Lusch, R. E. (2008). Service-Dominant Logic: Continuing the Evolution. *Journal of the Academy of Marketing Science, 36*(1), 1–10. doi:10.1007/s11747-007-0069-6

Vazey, M., & Richards, D. (2006). A Case-Classification-Conclusion 3Cs Approach o Knowledge Acquisition: Applying a Classification Logic Wiki to the Problem Solving Process. *International Journal of Knowledge Management, 2*(1), 72-88. Wikipedia. (2006). *Wiki.* Retrieved March 30, 2006, from http://en.wikipedia.org/wiki/Wiki

Vellliquette, D. (2005) Computer security considerations in disaster recovery planning (Tech. Rep. No. 11). Bethesda, MD: SANS Institute.

Venkatesh, V. (2000). Determinants of Perceived Ease of Use: Integrating Control, Intrinsic Motivation, and Emotion into the Technology Acceptance Model. *Information Systems Research, 11*(4), 342–365. doi:10.1287/isre.11.4.342.11872

Venkatesh, V., Morris, M. G., Davis, G. B., & Davis, F. D. (2003). User acceptance of information technology: Toward a unified view. *MIS Quarterly, 27*(3), 425–478.

Venkatesh, V., Morris, M., Davis, G., & Davis, F. (2003). User acceptance of information technology: Toward a unified view. *Management Information Systems Quarterly, 27*(3), 425–478.

Verstraete, C. (2004). Planning for the unexpected. *IEE Manufacturing Engineer, 83*(3), 18–21. doi:10.1049/me:20040304

Vieweg, S., Hughes, A., Starbird, K., & Palen, L. (2010, April). Microblogging during two natural hazards events: what twitter may contribute to situational awareness. In *Proceedings of the ACM Conference on Computer Human Interaction (CHI)*, Atlanta, GA (pp. 1079–1088).

Vieweg, S., Palen, L., Liu, S. B., Hughes, A. L., & Sutton, J. (2008). Collective Intelligence in Disaster: Examination of the Phenomenon in the Aftermath of the 2007 Virginia Tech Shooting. In F. Fiedrich & B. Van De Walle (Eds.), *Proceedings of the 5th International ISCRAM Conference*, Washington, DC (pp. 44-54).

Vijayan, J. (2005). Data security risks missing from disaster recovery plans. *Computerworld, 39*(41), 16–18.

Von Krogh, G. (1998). Care in Knowledge Creation. *California Management Review, 40*(3), 133–153.

Wagner, C. (2004). WIKI: A Technology for Conversational Knowledge Management and Group Collaboration. *Communications of the Association for Information Systems, 13*, 265–289.

Wand, Y., & Wang, R. Y. (1996). Anchoring Data Quality Dimensions in Ontological Foundations. *Communications of the ACM, 39*(11), 86–95. doi:10.1145/240455.240479

Wang, Z.-N., & Wu, Y.-Y. (2008, September). Coping Strategy on Non-structured Problems of Enterprise Crisis Management: Based on Seamless Integration of CMP and Checkland SSM. In *Proceedings of the 2008 International Conference on Wireless Communications, Networking and Mobile Computing (WiCOM'08)*, Dalian, China.

Wang, R. Y., Storey, V. C., & Firth, C. P. (1995). A Framework for Analysis of Data Quality Research. *IEEE Transactions on Knowledge and Data Engineering, 7*(4), 623–640. doi:10.1109/69.404034

Waugh, W. L., & Tierney, K. (Eds.). (2007). *Emergency management: Principles and practice for local government*. Washington, DC: ICMA Press.

Weick, K. E. (1993). The collapse of sensemaking in organizations: the Mann Gulch disaster. *Administrative Science Quarterly, 38*, 628–652. doi:10.2307/2393339

Weick, K. E. (1998). Improvisation as a mindset for organizational analysis. *Organization Science, 9*(5), 543–555. doi:10.1287/orsc.9.5.543

Weinberger, D. (2007). *Everything is Miscellaneous: The Power of New Digital Disorder*. New York: Times Books.

Weissenberger, S., Lo, H., & Hickman, M. (1995, July 30-August 2). A methodology for evaluating systems architectures. In *Proceedings of the Vehicle Navigation and Information Systems Conference* (pp. 397-403).

Wenger, E., McDermott, R., & Snyder, W. (2002). *Cultivating Communities of Practice*. Boston: Harvard Business School Press.

Westfall, A., Jennex, M. E., Dickinson, S., & Frost, E. (2009). Event Report: Golden Phoenix 2008. *International Journal of Information Systems for Crisis Response and Management, 1*(2), 72–79. doi:10.4018/jiscrm.2009040106

Whelton, P. (2005). *Rebuilding Tulane after hurricane Katrina*. Retrieved December 3, 2009, from http://www.thelancet.com/journals/lancet/article/PIIS0140-6736(06)68248-2/fulltext

White House. (2006). *The federal response to Hurricane Katrina: lessons learned*. Washington, DC: Author.

White, C., Hiltz, S. R., & Turoff, M. (2008). *United We Respond: One Community, One Voice*. Paper presented at the Information Systems for Crisis Response and Management Conference 2008, Washington, DC.

White, C., Plotnick, L., Addams-Moring, R., Turoff, M., & Hiltz, S. R. (2008). Leveraging A Wiki To Enhance Virtual Collaboration In The Emergency Domain. In *Proceedings of the 41st Hawaii International Conference on System Sciences*, Hawaii. Washington, DC: IEEE Computer Society.

White, C., Plotnick, L., Kushma, J., Hiltz, S. R., & Turoff, M. (2009). An Online Social Network for Emergency Management. In J. Landgren, U. Nulden, & B. Van de Walle (Eds.), *Proceedings of the 6th International IS-CRAM Conference*.

White, C., Turoff, M., & de Walle, B. V. (2007). *A Dynamic Delphi Process Utilizing a Modified Thurstone Scaling Method: Collaborative Judgment in Emergency Response*. Paper presented at the 4th Annual Information Systems on Crisis and Response Management, Delft, The Netherlands.

WHO. (2003). *WHO issues a global alert about cases of atypical pneumonia*. Geneva, Switzerland: Author.

WHO. (2009). *Influenza A (H1N1) – Update 54*. Geneva, Switzerland: Author. Retrieved from http://www.who.int/csr/don/2009_06_26/en/index.html

Whybark, D.C., Melnyk, S.A., Day, J., & Davis, E. (2010). Disaster Relief Supply Chain Management: New Realities, Management Challenges, Emerging Opportunities. *Decision Line*, 4-7.

Wiedemann, P. M., & Femers, S. (1993). Public participation in waste management decision making: Analysis and management of conflicts. *Journal of Hazardous Materials, 33*, 355–368. doi:10.1016/0304-3894(93)85085-S

Wiencko, J. A. (1993/1994).The Blacksburg electronic village. *Bulletin of the American Society for Information Science*.

Wikipedia. (2008). *Facebook*. Retrieved July 24, 2009, from http://en.wikipedia.org/wiki/Facebook

Wikipedia. (2010a). *Cloud Computing*. Retrieved November 25, 2010, from http://en.wikipedia.org/wiki/Cloud_computing

Wikipedia. (2010b). *Iranian presidential election, 2009.* Retrieved November 25, 2010, from http://en.wikipedia. org/wiki/Iranian_presidential_election,_2009#cite_note-gulfnews_Facebookblock-87

Wikipedia. (2010c). *2009–2010 Iranian election protests.* Retrieved November 25, 2010, from http://en.wikipedia. org/wiki/2009%E2%80%932010_Iranian_election_protests

Wilson, S. (2010). *Next generation disaster communications technology now a reality with LifeNet.* Retrieved September 25, 2010, from http://www.scs.gatech.edu/ news/next-generation-disaster-communications-technology-now-reality-lifenet

Wilson, B. (2001). *Soft Systems Methodology. Conceptual Model Building and Its Contribution.* Chichester, UK: John Wiley & Sons.

Wilson, J., & Oyola-Yemaiel, A. (2001). The evolution of emergency management and the advancement towards a profession in the United States and Florida. *Safety Science, 39*, 117–131. doi:10.1016/S0925-7535(01)00031-5

Wilson, K., Brownstein, J., & Fidler, D. (2010). Strengthening the International Health Regulations: lessons from the H1N1 pandemic. *Health Policy and Planning, 25*, 505–509. doi:10.1093/heapol/czq026

Winstead, D., & Legeai, C. (2007*). Lessons learned from Katrina.* Retrieved June 4, 2009, from http:// ap.psychiatryonline.org/cgi/content/full/31/3/190

Wold, G. H. (2002). Disaster Recover Planning Process. *Disaster Recovery Journal, 5*(1), 29–34.

Wu, P., Preece, J., Shneiderman, B., Jaeger, P., & Qu, Y. (2007). *Community Response Grids for Older Adults: Motivations, Usability, and Sociability.* Retrieved March 28, 2009, from http://www.cs.umd.edu/localphp/hcil/ tech-reports-search.php?number=2007-07

Wu, X., & Schulzrinne, H. (2004). SIPc, a multi-function SIP user agent. In *Proceedings of the IFIP/IEEE International Conference, Management of Multimedia Networks and Services (MMNS'04)* (pp. 269-281).

Wylder, J. (2004). *Strategic Information Security.* Boca Raton, FL: Auerbach/CRC Press.

Yao, X., Turoff, M., & Chumar, M. (2009). *Designing a Group Support System to Review and Practice Emergency Plans in Virtual Teams.* Paper presented at the 6th Annual Information Systems on Crisis and Response Management, Washington, DC.

Yasin, R. (2008). Enhanced SOA. *Government Computer News*. Retrieved January 24, 2009, from http://gcn.com/ Articles/2008/09/10/Enhanced-SOA.aspx

Yin, K. (1984). *Case study research: Design and methods* (p. 12). Newbury Park, CA: Sage.

Yoo, B., & Donthu, N. (2002). The effects of marketing education and cultural values on marketing ethics of students. *Journal of Marketing Education, 24*(2), 92–103.

Yu, S.-H., Kim, Y.-G., & Kim, M.-Y. (2004). Linking Organizational Knowledge Management Drivers to Knowledge Management Performance: An Exploratory Study. In *Proceedings of the 37th Hawaii International Conference on System Sciences (HICSS36).* Washington, DC: IEEE Computer Society.

Zalud, B. (2008). Carrying on after disaster. *For Buyers of Products. Systems & Services, 45*(7), 12–14.

Zhang, D., Zhou, L. Jr, & Nunamaker, J. F. (2002). A Knowledge Management Framework for the Support of Decision Making in Humanitarian Assistance/Disaster Relief. *Knowledge and Information Systems, 4*, 370–385. doi:10.1007/s101150200012

Zhan, W., & Goulart, A. (2009). Statistical Analysis of Broadband Wireless Links in Rural Areas. *The Journal of Communication, 4*(5), 320–328.

Zigurs, I., & Buckland, B. (1998). A theory of task/technology fit and group support systems effectiveness. *MIS Quarterly, 22*(3), 313–334. doi:10.2307/249668

Zuber-Skerrit, O., & Fletcher, M. (2007). The quality of an action research thesis in the social sciences. *Quality Assurance in Education, 15*(4), 413.

Zwass, V. (2010). Series Editor Introduction. In B. Van de Walle, M. Turoff, & R. Hiltz (Eds.), *Information Systems for Emergency Management* (Vol. 16, pp. ix-xii). Armonk, NY: M.E. Sharpe.

About the Contributors

Murray E. Jennex is an associate professor at San Diego State University, editor in chief of the *International Journal of Knowledge Management*, editor in chief of Idea Group Publishing's Knowledge Management book series, and president of the Foundation for Knowledge Management (LLC). Dr. Jennex specializes in knowledge management, system analysis and design, IS security, e-commerce, and organizational effectiveness. Jennex serves as the Knowledge Management Systems Track co-chair at the Hawaii International Conference on System Sciences. He is the author of over 80 journal articles, book chapters, and conference proceedings on knowledge management, end user computing, international information systems, organizational memory systems, ecommerce, security, and software outsourcing. He holds a BA in chemistry and physics from William Jewell College, an MBA and an MS in software engineering from National University, an M.S. in telecommunications management and a PhD in information systems from the Claremont Graduate University. Dr. Jennex is also a registered professional mechanical engineer in the state of California and a Certified Information Systems Security Professional (CISSP).

* * *

Miriam Belblidia received her MPA degree in urban and regional affairs from the University of Pittsburgh's Graduate School of Public & International Affairs, focusing on civil security and disaster management. She worked as a member of the Interactive, Intelligent, Spatial Information Systems (IISIS) team at the University of Pittsburgh's Center for Disaster Management, researching response networks for communities at risk of flooding in the Pittsburgh region. She currently resides in New Orleans and works in the City's Hazard Mitigation Office.

Raquel Benbunan-Fich is an associate professor of information systems at the Zicklin School of Business, Baruch College, City University of New York. She received her PhD in management information systems from Rutgers University, Graduate School of Management. Her research interests include virtual teams and virtual collaboration, IT usage, user behavior and social computing applications, evaluation of Web-based systems, and research productivity of IS faculty. Her research has been published in *Communications of the ACM, Decision Support Systems, European Journal of Information Systems, IEEE Transactions on Professional Communication, Information & Management, International Journal of Electronic Commerce, Journal of Strategic Information Systems* and other journals.

Bharath Chintapatla is a masters student in Computer Science at Texas A&M University. He received his BTech in Computer Science & Engineering from Indian Institute of Technology, Guwahati in August 2008. His research interests include network protocols, wireless technologies, and network security.

Keith Clement is an Assistant Professor in the Department of Criminology at California State University, Fresno and Director of the Graduate Homeland Security Program. Professor Clement teaches undergraduate courses in Comparative (International) Criminal Justice and graduate courses in Psychology of Terrorism and Crisis Response and Essentials of Homeland Security. His research interests include risk perception of border security, transnational crimes, and its effect on security, and interoperability/communications issues. He also serves as Planning Director for the CSU Council for Emergency Management and Homeland Security (CEMHS), a 525+ member organization linking universities and colleges with key stakeholders to build EM-HS education and training programs and curriculum. He is a recipient of a United States Department of Homeland Security (DHS) Early Career Faculty Award under the Scientific Leadership Award for MSI Program.

Panos Constantinides is an Assistant Professor of Management Information Systems at Frederick University's Business School. Before joining Frederick University, Panos held positions at Lancaster University's Management School, and the Judge Business School at the University of Cambridge, where he also earned his PhD. Panos has looked at IS development and implementation issues in different healthcare settings in association with different organizations, from BT Health (UK), Synbiotix (UK & Cyprus), and the Institute of Computer Science at the Foundation for Research and Technology Hellas (Greece). Some of Panos' work has appeared in the journals *MIS Quarterly*, *Information & Organization*, and the *Journal of Applied Behavioral Science*. His more recent research focuses on problems of collective action around the development of information infrastructures, and the coordination of multidisciplinary teams.

Teresa Durbin holds a Bachelor of Applied Arts & Sciences degree in Public Administration with an Emphasis in City Planning, and a Master of Science degree in Homeland Security with a Specialization in Communications and Information Systems. She has over 10 years of management experience in utility accounting and regulatory work, supply chain systems administration, and help desk supervision for a large investor-owned utility. She has experience in responding to the logistics effort supporting gas and electric service restoration after large scale service interruptions resulting from regional emergencies or catastrophes. Ms. Durbin has an understanding of intergovernmental relations and specifically private-to-public interactions and requirements. She has participated in policy analysis and Rule-making filings at the State level related to merger-related filing and compliance requirements. Ms. Durbin coordinates the Business Resumption and Continuity Plan as well as the Pandemic Plan and Response training in a division-wide effort. Her Masters thesis and research analyzed the benefits and potential results of different information systems and decision support methodologies in the logistical effort related to utility service restoration, post-emergency.

Gideon F. For-mukwai is a certified emergency manager with over 10 years of experience working in Southern Africa, South East Asia and the United States. He is currently a graduate fellow at the Reynolds School of Journalism, University of Nevada, Reno, where he is in the last semester of a master's degree program focusing on new and traditional media. Prior to coming to the US, he owned and managed

XtraMile Emergency Solutions, an emergency training outfit that he founded in 2004 in Singapore. In his former employment as a senior officer in the Singapore Civil Defense Force, he managed training programs for public safety officials from several uniform groups from beyond Singapore. Today, Gideon trains and speaks internationally on how emergency management community can build and strengthen public engagement through the use of new media.

Eric Frost directs the SDSU Viz Center and co-directs the Homeland Security Master's Program, which includes about 130 Homeland Security practioners from many Federal agencies, state and local government, NGOs, industry, and governments. Much of the program is based on actual interaction with real operational training in the US-Mexico border region, as well as many other international Homeland Security groups such as in Mexico, Central Asia, India, Africa, and Indonesia. Frost and his colleagues use many new technologies and protocols that are enhanced during exercises such as Strong Angel III (http://www.strongangel3.net/) for situational awareness for many challenges including H1N1 using tools such as http://www.geoplayer.com/gateways for Banda Aceh, Katrina, Indonesia, and Haiti disasters (http://hypercube.telascience.org/haiti). Frost and co-workers work with sensor networks, wireless and optical communication, data fusion, visualization, and decision support for first responders and humanitarian groups, especially crossing the civilian-military boundary, especially in unusual coalition areas such as Somalia, Afghanistan, India. Haiti, and Mexico including using Cloud Computing (http://www.inrelief.org) with Navy to impact Humanitarian assistance like Haiti and Mexico earthquakes.

Michael F. Goodchild is Professor of Geography at the University of California, Santa Barbara, and Director of UCSB's Center for Spatial Studies. He received his B.A. degree from Cambridge University in Physics in 1965 and his Ph.D. in geography from McMaster University in 1969, and has received four honorary doctorates. He was elected member of the National Academy of Sciences and Foreign Member of the Royal Society of Canada (2002), member of the American Academy of Arts and Sciences (2006), and Foreign Member of the Royal Society and Corresponding Fellow of the British Academy (2010); and in 2007 he received the Prix Vautrin Lud. He was editor of *Geographical Analysis* between 1987 and 1990 and editor of the Methods, Models, and Geographic Information Sciences section of the *Annals of the Association of American Geographers* from 2000 to 2006. He serves on the editorial boards of ten other journals and book series, and has published more than 15 books and 400 articles. He was Chair of the National Research Council's Mapping Science Committee from 1997 to 1999, and currently chairs the Advisory Committee on Social, Behavioral, and Economic Sciences of the National Science Foundation. His current research interests center on geographic information science, spatial analysis, and uncertainty in geographic data.

Ana Goulart received a bachelor's degree in electrical engineering from the Federal School of Engineering of Itajuba (EFEI), in Brazil. While working in the industry, she received a M. Sc. degree in Information Systems Management from the Pontifical Catholic University of Campinas, in 1997. She moved to the United States in 1997 where she earned a M. Sc. in Computer Engineering at North Carolina State University, Raleigh, NC; followed by a Ph.D. in Electrical and Computer Engineering at Georgia Tech, Atlanta, GA, in 2005. She is currently an Assistant Professor in the Electronics and Tele-communications Engineering Technology program at Texas A&M University, in College Station, TX. Her research interests include wireless communications, protocols for real-time voice and video communications, IP-based emergency communications, networked robotics, and rural telecommunications.

Dan Harnesk, Ph.D is an Assistant Professor at the division of Information System Science, Lulea University of Technology, Sweden where his main research efforts focus on crisis and emergency management, and information security. Dan is also the research manager of the Information Security Group, InfoSec@LTU. He has particular interest in socio-technical aspects of information systems/security design. He obtained his doctoral degree in computer and systems science at LTU, introducing a concept for social, transaction and IT alignment in SME interfirm relationships. Dan's teaching duties at the LTU currently consist of Master level courses in Strategic development of IS and Scientific Methods.

Manley Haye is Manager of Technical Operational Systems at Jamaica Public Service Company. He graduated from the University of the West Indies (UWI) in 1980 with a Bachelors degree in Electrical Engineering and earned the MBA from the Mona School of Business/UWI in 2000. Since joining JPS in 1980, Mr. Haye has served the company in several capacities in Power Plant maintenance, System Planning and Information. In his current role, he leads a team of Engineers and Analysts, which provides IT services to the core business units in Generation and Customer Operations. His current focus is on the implementation of an Enterprise GIS which will provide the basis for dramatic improvements in critical business processes such as Loss analysis and loss reduction, T&D Asset Management and Maintenance, Outage Management and Trouble call resolution and Emergency Response coordination and System Restoration.

Thomas A. Horan, Ph.D. is the founding Director of the Kay Center for E-Health Research and Associate Professor of Information Systems at Claremont Graduate University, Claremont, California. Dr. Horan has 25 years of research experience, specializing in the design and assessment of electronic health systems at the federal, state and local level. He has served as Principal Investigator for over $3 million in research and evaluation grants, including funding from the National Science Foundation, California HealthCare Foundation, Blue Shield Foundation, Kay Family Foundation, and Social Security Administration. In addition, Dr. Horan has served in several policy capacities, including as a Senior Analyst for the US General Accounting Office and as a member of American Health Information Community (AHIC) Consumer Empowerment Workgroup. Dr. Horan has over published over 70 technical articles and conference proceedings and two books on information systems. He is a member of the American Medical Informatics Association (AMIA) and Association of Information Systems (AIS). He has both his Masters and Doctoral degrees from Claremont Graduate University.

Robert Judge holds undergraduate degrees in Biology and Botany, an MBA, and a PhD in the Management of Information Systems and Technology from Claremont Graduate University. His career spans the semiconductor, aerospace, consumer electronics, and Internet Service industries at mid-management and executive levels. He has held functional responsibilities that include Materiel, Manufacturing, Information Systems, Marketing, Project Management and Customer Support. Throughout the last 20+ years of his career, he has served both San Diego State University and the University of San Diego as an adjunct professor teaching graduate and undergraduate courses in Operations, Supply Chain Management, Manufacturing Planning and Control Systems, Project Management and Information Systems. His current research interests lie in understanding how barriers to knowledge flow arise as small organizations grow, and also in how Knowledge Management Systems in Supply Chains can influence innovation and the flow of non-logistical knowledge.

Christopher Kadlec, PhD, is Assistant Professor of Information Technology, College of Information Technology, at Georgia Southern University. He holds a BS in Management from the School of Business at the University of Mississippi. He held positions in IT support for 12 years before he received a PhD. from the University of Georgia in Management Information Systems. His experience in IT support drives his research interests: IT disaster recovery planning, power users, self-regulated learning, data center design, and server room heat management. He has been consulting for 16 years in the areas of network design, network implementation, systems design, systems deployment, pedagogical design, and corporate/military education.

Elina Laaksonen is a senior master programme student at Luleå University of Technology focusing on information security. Elina has previously consulted within network security on an international basis. Elina holds a Bachelor of Engineering degree from Turku University of Applied Sciences.

Guido Lang is a doctoral student in information systems at the Zicklin School of Business, Baruch College, City University of New York. He holds a MS in business from the University of Bern (Switzerland). Prior to joining Zicklin, he was the managing director of the TEWI Center for Information Systems Technology, a joint research center of Swiss universities. His research interests include virtual communities, group decision-support systems, and social computing applications.

Linna Li is a postdoc at the Center for Spatial Studies at the University of California, Santa Barbara, interested in geographic information science theories and applications. Li received a B.S. in Earth and Space Sciences from Peking University in China in 2004, an M.S. in Geography from the University of South Carolina in 2006, and a Ph.D. in Geography from the University of California, Santa Barbara in 2010. She has a wide range of research interests, from geographical knowledge representation and communication to geovisualization, spatial analysis and modeling. Currently she is working on two projects: conflation of heterogeneous geospatial data from different sources and volunteered geographic information (VGI).

John Lindström, Ph.D is a member of the Information Security Group at Lulea University of Technology. John has previously worked for about 15 years with product and service development, and technical and management consulting in the information security business. John's main research interests are within information security, crisis and emergency management. John holds a doctoral degree within computer and systems science on strategic information security. John teaches Master level courses in management of information security and e-services.

Walt Magnussen is the Director for the Texas A&M University Telecommunications Office, and the Director for the Texas A&M Internet2 Evaluation Center. As Telecommunications Director, Dr. Magnussen manages all aspects of telecommunications for the third largest university in the United States. As the Director of the ITEC, he leads the Voice-over-Internet Protocol (VoIP) and Internet Protocol Television (IPTV) initiatives for Internet2, a consortium of the 209 leading research universities in the United States. Dr. Magnussen has been the lead for many other projects completed within the ITEC, including lead in the development of the Next Generation 9-1-1 (NG9-1-1) Proof of Concept projects for the United States' Departments of Commerce and Transportation. Dr. Magnussen acquired his bachelor's and master's degrees from the University of Minnesota, and his doctoral degree from Texas A&M University.

Michael J. Marich, Ph.D. has over 30 years experience in the development of aerospace and defense systems. Dr. Marich is also a Research Associate at Claremont Graduate University, where his research involving the application of information technology to Emergency Medical Services systems has led to numerous peer-reviewed publications and national and international presentations. He received his Ph.D. from Claremont Graduate University. He holds a Master of Science degree in Computer Science and Technology and a Bachelor of Technology degree in Electrical Engineering.

Maurice McNaughton has engaged in the management of enterprise-level IT Projects and Operations at several large Organizations, and held the position of Chief Information Officer at the national electric utility (JPS) between 1993 and 2006. He pursued his PhD studies in Decision Sciences at Georgia State University, Atlanta, USA where he completed his Dissertation Thesis on the topic: Deregulation, Uncertainty, and Information Technology In the Electric Utility Industry: A Transaction Cost Interpretation of the Drivers and Consequences of Vertical Disintegration. Dr. McNaughton is currently Director of the Centre of Excellence at the Mona School of Business, where he is developing an Application-oriented Research Agenda around the use of ICTs to enable Business Innovation in the Small Medium Enterprise sector.

Marko Niemimaa is a senior master programme student at Luleå University of Technology focusing on information security. Marko has previously worked with internet security providers, managed teams and consulted within network security on an international basis. Marko holds a Bachelor of Information Technology degree from Helsinki University of Applied Sciences.

Lorne Olfman is dean of the School of Information Systems and Technology and professor of Information Science at Claremont Graduate University (CGU) and Fletcher Jones Chair in Technology Management. He came to Claremont in 1987 after graduating with a PhD in Business (Management Information Systems) from Indiana University. Olfman's research interests include: how software can be learned and used in organizations, the impact of computer-based systems on knowledge management, and the design and adoption of systems used for group work. Along with Terry Ryan, Olfman co-directs the Social Learning Software Lab (SL²). A key component of Olfman's teaching is his involvement with doctoral students; he has supervised 38 students to completion. Lorne is an active member of the information systems community.

Kweku-Muata Osei-Bryson is Professor of Information Systems at Virginia Commonwealth University since 1998, where he also served as the Coordinator of the IS PhD program during 2001-2003. He has also worked as an Information Systems practitioner in industry and government. He holds a Ph.D. in Applied Mathematics (Management Science & Information Systems) from the University of Maryland at College Park, a MS in Systems Engineering from Howard University, and a BS in Natural Sciences from the University of the West Indies at Mona. His research areas include: Data Mining, Knowledge Management, IS Security, e-Commerce, Database Systems, IT & Productivity, Multi-Criteria Decision Analysis, IS Outsourcing. He serves as an Associate Editor of the *INFORMS Journal on Computing*, on the Editorial Board of the Computers & Operations Research journal and the International Advisory Board of the Journal of the Operational Research Society.

Linda Plotnick is an assistant professor of computer science in the mathematical, computing, and Information Sciences Department at Jacksonville State University. Her research interests include leadership and trust issues in partially distributed teams, social media in emergency management, the effects of the threat rigidity thesis in the emergency domain and public warning for extreme events. She has published and presented papers at AMCIS, ISCRAM, HICSS, and ICIS conferences.

Murali Raman obtained his PhD in MIS from the School of Information Systems and Technology and professor of information science at Claremont Graduate University (CGU). He is a Fulbright and Rhodes Scholar. Raman is a lecturer with the Faculty of Management, Multimedia University Malaysia (MMU). His research interests include: design and evaluation of information systems to support knowledge management within academia and corporations alike. Raman prior experience includes design and implementation of a knowledge management system using wiki technology to support emergency preparedness for the Claremont Colleges.

Lila Rao is the Academic Director and a Lecturer at the Mona School of Business at The University of the West Indies. She holds a Ph.D. in Information Systems from The University of the West Indies and a MSc. in Computer Science from the University of Waterloo, Canada, and a BSc. Degree in Computer Science from the University of the West Indies, Mona. She is the co-academic director for the MIS graduate programme and has taught a number of courses at the graduate and undergraduate level. She has some experience in industry working as a programmer and system analyst. Her research interests include data warehousing, information and knowledge quality dimensions, ontologies and technology adoption. She has published in the Data and Knowledge Engineering, Expert Systems with Applications, Knowledge Management Research & Practice and Information Systems Frontiers journal. She also has papers published in the proceedings of FLAIRS Research Symposium, e-business workshop, IRMA, AMCIS and ICEIS.

Terry Ryan is associate professor of information systems and technology at Claremont Graduate University. He earned a PhD from Indiana University in 1989 and came to Claremont in 2001. Ryan's research concerns how IS can be used to support: teaching and learning in university and organizational settings, online discussions and dialogues, and preparing for and responding to emergencies. His current projects are aimed at advancing both IS theory and IS artifacts. With Lorne Olfman, Terry is co-director of the CGU Social Learning Software Lab.

Benjamin L. Schooley, MBA, Ph.D. has over 12 years experience planning, researching, assessing, designing, implementing, and managing IT systems. He is currently a Research Faculty member at the School of Information Systems and Technology, Claremont Graduate University in Claremont, CA. As a Research Fellow at the Kay Center for e-Health Research, he leads applied research projects supported by grants from such organizations as the National Science Foundation (NSF), Department of Transportation, Social Security Administration (SSA), and Special Hope Foundation. His multi-year research on end-to-end performance management information systems for Emergency Medical Services (EMS), funded by NSF, has involved in-depth analyses for the Mayo Clinic EMS system, (Rochester, MN) and for Santa Clara County, CA and San Mateo County, CA EMS Systems. He is currently leading a system assessment and development project for SSA's Ticket-to-Work program. He has published over 20 technical and research articles on these topics. He is a member of the American Medical Informatics Association (AMIA), IEEE Computer Society, and the Association of Computing Machinery. He earned his Bachelor's degree from Brigham Young University and both his MBA and Ph.D. from Claremont Graduate University.

Jordan Shropshire, PhD, is Assistant Professor of Information Technology, College of Information Technology, at Georgia Southern University. Dr. Shropshire completed his Bachelor degree at the Warrington College of Business, University of Florida. He recently completed his PhD in MIS at the College of Business, Mississippi State University. His dissertation concerned employee compliance with organizational information security protocols at banks and hospitals. His research interests include information security, IT disaster recovery planning, networking, and IT management. He has published or served as reviewer for a number of journals, such as MIS Quarterly, Journal of Computer Information Systems, European Journal of Information Systems, and Information & Organization. He has served as a presenter, track chair, or reviewer for conferences such as International Conference on Information Systems (ICIS), American Conference on Information Systems (AMCIS), and the Decision Science Institute (DSI).

Murray Turoff is a Distinguished Professor Emeritus at the New Jersey Institute of Technology. He is a co editor of a recent book on *Emergency Management Information Systems* (M.E. Sharp 2010). Besides his early and continuing work with the Delphi Method, he spent most of academic research career in the design and evaluation of Computer Mediated Communication systems. After 9/11 he turned his attention back to his early work in Emergency Management and related work in Planning and Foresight and Delphi Design. In 2004 he was a cofounder of the international organization ISCRAM (Information Systems for Crisis Response and Management).

Zhongxian Wang is a professor at Montclair State University, New Jersey, USA. Professor Wang teaches Operations Analysis, Production/Operations Management, Decision Support & Expert Systems, Business Statistics, Operations Research, and Management Sciences. He is a member of Institute for Operations Research and the Management Sciences (INFORMS), Information Resources Management Association (IRMA), The Decision Sciences Institute (DSI), The Production and Operations Management Society (POMS).

Connie White is a doctoral candidate in information systems at the New Jersey Institute of Technology. She presently holds a position with emergency management at Jacksonville State University. Her current work explores how Web 2.0 technologies can be leveraged in the emergency domain. Her dissertation, *A Dynamic Delphi System to Support Decision Making by Large Groups of Crisis Management Experts*, focuses on the creation of a crisis management system that is used by large groups dispersed geographically where decisions must be made under uncertainty and among domain driven subgroups. Her research interests include social networking, decision making, Thurstone's Law of Comparative Judgment, artificial intelligence and emergency management. Homepage:http://sites.google.com/site/conniemwhite/

Ruben Xing is an Associate Professor at Management & Information Systems, Montclair State University. He received his doctoral degree from Columbia University, New York. Having worked for more than 15 years in the IT industry, he has held senior IT management positions at several large financial conglomerates in metropolitan New York. His current research interests include Broadband and Wireless Communications, the Internet security, Disaster Recover/Business Continuity Planning, and Supply Chain Management.

James Yao is a professor in the Management and Information Systems dept at Montclair State University. He received his Ph D of Technology in 1997 from Mississippi State University.

Anna Zacchi received a Laurea cum laude in Information Science from the Universita' degli Studi di Milano, Italy, and her M. Sc. in Computer Science from Texas A&M University. She is currently a Ph.D. student in the department of Computer Science and Engineering at Texas A&M University. From 2007 to 2009 she collaborated in the Next Generation 911 (NG-911), project sponsored by US Department of Transportation (DoT); the purpose of the project was to develop a proof-of-concept for NG911. In 2009-10 she participated in the NSF funded research project about NG-911 security. She is now working on a research project in the field of Human Computer Interaction.

Yanli Zhang is currently Assistant Professor in the Management and Information Systems Department at Montclair State University. She graduated with a Ph.D. in Management from Rutgers University in May 2007, concentrating on strategy and international business. Her research interests focus on topics of knowledge, networks, and innovation.

Index